British Social Attitudes
Attitudes
the
13th report

Social and Community Planning Research (SCPR) is an independent, non-profit social research institute. It has a large professional staff together with its own interviewing and coding resources. Some of SCPR's work - such as the survey reported in this book - is initiated by the institute itself and grant-funded by research councils or foundations. Other work is initiated by government departments, local authorities or quasi-government organisations to provide information on aspects of social or economic policy. SCPR also works frequently with other institutes and academics. Founded in 1969 and now Britain's largest social research institute, SCPR has a high reputation for the standard of its work in both qualitative and quantitative research. SCPR has a Survey Methods Centre and, with Nuffield College Oxford, houses the Centre for Research into Elections and Social Trends (CREST), which is an ESRC Research Centre. It also houses, with Southampton University, the Centre for Applied Social Surveys (CASS), an ESRC Resource Centre, the two main functions of which are to run courses in survey methods and to establish and administer an electronic social survey question bank.

The contributors

Daphne Ahrendt
Associate Project Director, International Survey Research Limited

Steven Barnett
Senior Lecturer at the Centre for Communication and Information Studies, University of Westminster

Lindsay Brook
Research Director at SCPR and Co-director of the *British Social Attitudes* survey series

Caroline Bryson
Senior Researcher at SCPR and Co-director of the *British Social Attitudes* survey series

John Curtice
Senior Lecturer in Politics and Director of the Social Statistics Laboratory, University of Strathclyde

David Donnison
Professor Emeritus, University of Glasgow

Lizanne Dowds
Research Fellow, Centre for Social Research, Queen's University, Belfast

Geoffrey Evans
Fellow in the Centre for European Studies, Nuffield College, Oxford

Arthur Gould
Senior Lecturer in the Department of Social Sciences, Loughborough University

John Hall
Senior Research Officer in the Public Finances Sector of the Institute for Fiscal Studies

Roger Jowell
Director of SCPR and Co-director of the British Social Attitudes survey series; Visiting Professor at the London School of Economics and Political Science

Francis McGlone
Senior Research Officer at the Family Policy Studies Centre

Alison Park
Research Director at SCPR and Co-director of the *British Social Attitudes* survey series

Ian Preston
Research Fellow at the Institute for Fiscal Studies; Lecturer in Economics at University College, London

Ceridwen Roberts
Director of the Family Policy Studies Centre

Andrew Shaw
Senior Researcher at SCPR

Peter Spencer
Professor of Economics at Birkbeck College, University of London

Katarina Thomson
Research Director at SCPR and Co-director of the *British Social Attitudes* survey series

Ken Young
Professor of Politics and Vice-Principal, Queen Mary and Westfield College, University of London

British Social Attitudes
the
13th report

Edited by
Roger Jowell
John Curtice
Alison Park
Lindsay Brook
& Katarina Thomson

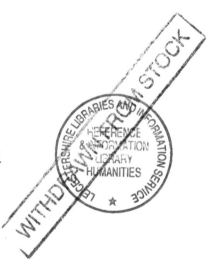

Dartmouth

Published by
Dartmouth Publishing Company Limited
Gower House
Croft Road
Aldershot
Hants GU11 3HR
England

Dartmouth Publishing Company
Old Post Road
Brookfield
Vermont 05036
USA

ISSN 0267 6869
ISBN 1 85521 607 8

Printed in Great Britain at the University Press, Cambridge

Contents

Introduction

This report, like its twelve predecessors, focuses on the latest *British Social Attitudes* survey, drawing where necessary on earlier surveys in the series in order to explain trends. A further volume also published by Dartmouth, *Understanding Change in Social Attitudes* (Taylor and Thomson, 1996 forthcoming), which integrates accumulated findings from the series with an examination of methods of measuring attitude change, is appearing at about the same time as this Report.

The continued existence of the *British Social Attitudes* survey series is due to its many generous funders, in particular the Sainsbury Family Charitable Trusts who remain the core funders, providing around a quarter of the series' annual costs. But we are also indebted to numerous other funders for their long-term commitment which provides earmarked support for particular modules or topics within the survey. Regular support of this kind continues to come from the Department for Education and Employment, the Home Office, the Department of Health, the Department of Social Security, the Countryside Commission, the Economic and Social Research Council (ESRC), the Charities Aid Foundation and the Nuffield Foundation. The ESRC also finances the project's participation in the *International Social Survey Programme* (ISSP), bringing a welcome cross-national perspective to the series.

For the first time this year we include a chapter on public attitudes towards matters of taste and decency in the mass media, based on a module funded by a consortium consisting of the British Board of Film Classification (BBFC), the Broadcasting Standards Council (BSC) and ICSTIS (the Independent Committee for the Supervision of Standards of Telephone Information

Services). This year's chapter (Chapter 2) focuses on the portrayal of sex in the media. Next year's will concentrate on the portrayal of violence.

We are appreciative not only of the generous and loyal support from such a diverse range of sources, but also for the manner in which it is given. The 'rules of engagement' place control over all matters of content and first dissemination in the annual Report firmly in the hands of the project team rather than of the funders, thus ensuring that the series remains (and is seen to remain) an independent and authoritative source of information and comment.

Each annual *British Social Attitudes* survey consists of an hour-long face to face interview with a probability sample of around 3,500 British adults, followed by a much shorter self-completion supplement. There are *three* versions of the questionnaire, each administered to one-third of the sample. Some modules of questions are asked of all respondents, some of two-thirds, and some of one third. The face to face interview is carried out by SCPR interviewers using lap-top computers.

In addition to the main British survey, there is also an annual *Northern Ireland Social Attitudes* (NISA) survey, funded by all the Northern Ireland Departments. Now in its seventh year, the fieldwork is carried out by our colleagues at the Central Survey Unit of the Northern Ireland Statistics and Research Agency (NISRA), using substantially the same questionnaire as in Britain, but with certain additions of local interest.

We regularly report some of these findings in our annual volumes (see, for instance, Chapters 6 and 7), but more comprehensive accounts are to be found in NISA's own series of reports, the latest being Breen *et al* (1996).

Further afield, the *British Social Attitudes* series remains closely involved in the *International Social Survey Programme* which now comprises 27 member nations spanning four continents. For 11 successive years now, ISSP member nations have administered a mutually-designed questionnaire module on a rotating set of topics to at least 1,000 random adults in their respective countries. Chapter 7 draws on the recent module on 'national identity', a subject that will be dealt with in more detail in BSA's next 'special international report' in 1998.

New developments within the *British Social Attitudes* series include:

- A module of questions on the public's understanding of science, to be reported on next year. Funded jointly by the Nuffield Foundation and the Office of Science and Technology, it contains questions in conjunction with colleagues at the Science Museum, some of which replicate items contained in an earlier SCPR survey conducted in 1988.

- A specially-devised module of questions, funded by the Office of the National Lottery, tapping public attitudes (and behaviour) in relation to the Lottery in general and scratchcards in particular.

- A repeat airing for our module of questions on political trust, funded by the Leverhulme Trust, which will also be reported upon in next year's volume.

- A module of questions on housing, with new questions alongside ones asked in earlier years, funded by the Department of the Environment and covering a range of questions about people's attitudes towards their homes and neighbourhoods.

- An expanded module of questions on transport. Funded for some time by the Countryside Commission as part of a set of questions on the countryside and the environment, new financial support from the Department of Transport has enabled a range of new questions to be included, giving a better balance to the module.

The *British Social Attitudes* series has long had close links with the *British Election Studies* and the *British Election Panel Study*. Not only have all three surveys been conducted by SCPR for some time, but they are also integral to the work of the Centre for Research into Elections and Social Trends (CREST) - an ESRC Research Centre which links SCPR and Nuffield College, Oxford. Although each of the three time-series focuses on a distinct aspect of the terrain of social and political attitude measurement in Britain, they have been fortunate in being able to feed off one another by replicating questions, developing standardised scales and jointly introducing methodological innovations. These links have been recognised and extended by the ESRC in its recent award to CREST of the 1996/97 *British Election Study*, whose campaign panel survey will, in fact, be recruited from among 1996 *British Social Attitudes* survey respondents, allowing the effects of the 'long campaign' to be monitored and interpreted. In 1997, as in 1992, the *British Election Study* will replace the *British Social Attitudes* survey.

The number of our colleagues who contribute critically to the success of the *British Social Attitudes* survey gets larger each year. We were fortunate this year in welcoming Caroline Bryson to the team. Within SCPR we are also particularly indebted to our interviewers and area managers for their skills, endurance and persistence in coping with an ever-growing and ever more complicated survey, and to our colleagues in other parts of the institute who supervise the fieldwork, data preparation and data processing. As we go to press we reiterate our appreciation to Lis Box for having produced the camera-ready copy from our messy and numerous drafts. Outside SCPR we owe huge debts to Ann Mair of the Social Statistics Laboratory at the University of Strathclyde for her annual efforts to produce a meticulous SPSS system file, and to the staff of Dartmouth Publishing - especially Sonia Hubbard and Ann Newell - for their endurance in getting this Report and its companion volume, *Understanding Change in Social Attitudes,* to press within ever-shrinking deadlines.

Our sincere thanks are as always also due to the 3,500 or so anonymous respondents in England, Scotland and Wales and a further 1,500 or so in Northern Ireland who gave their time without reward save for making their voices heard. We hope that this volume justifies their efforts.

The Editors

References

Breen, R., Devine, P. and Dowds, L. (eds.) (1996), *Social Attitudes in Northern Ireland: the Fifth Report,* Belfast: Appletree Press.

Taylor, B. and Thomson, K. (eds.) (1996, forthcoming), *Understanding Change in Social Attitudes,* Aldershot: Dartmouth.

1 One nation again?

*John Curtice**

During the 1980s it became increasingly fashionable to talk of Britain being divided, economically and politically, between North and South. The recession of the early 1980s had hit manufacturing industry in Scotland and the North of England hard. Then the subsequent boom of the mid-1980s centred on the financial and service industries of London and the South East. As a result, differences in economic indicators such as house prices and unemployment rates widened considerably throughout Britain (Smith, 1989). Meanwhile, although they were comfortably re-elected in both 1983 and 1987, support for the Conservative Party became increasingly concentrated in the economically successful rural and suburban shires of the southern half of England (Curtice and Steed, 1986; Curtice and Steed, 1988).

Eight years ago, we examined the impact that Britain's 'North-South' divide appeared to be having on the country's social and political attitudes (Curtice, 1988). We discovered then that people living in the northern half of Britain were noticeably more pessimistic about the economy than those in the southern half.[1] This pessimism remained even after geographic variations in people's social characteristics and the character of their immediate neighbourhood were taken into account. We also found a difference in attitudes towards the way in which the economy should be run, with those in the North being keener than those in the South on government intervention and on measures to reduce economic inequalities. It seemed that differences

* John Curtice is Senior Lecturer in Politics, Director of the Social Statistics Laboratory at the University of Strathclyde and Deputy Director of the ESRC Centre for Research into Elections and Social Trends.

in economic experience were being reflected in people's attitudes towards the market economy - and that this, in part, explained why the Conservatives' enthusiasm for the free market received a more whole-hearted welcome in the southern half of the country than it did in the North.

Since then, however, Britain's economic geography has been transformed. The recession of the late 1980s hit the southern half of the country much harder than it did the North, with the North then enjoying the full fruits of the subsequent recovery. Certainly, differences between regional unemployment rates have narrowed significantly. In 1986, for instance, the unemployment rate in the Northern region was nearly eight points higher than in the South East.[2] By 1994 it was just three and a half points higher. Meanwhile, unemployment in Scotland had fallen below the United Kingdom average for the first time since the Great Depression of the 1930s. By contrast, the level of unemployment in London was second only to that in the Northern region of England. Differences in house prices have narrowed as well. If we draw a line from the Mersey to the Humber, house prices south of this line were still below their 1990 values in 1994. Northwards, however, and in Wales, the average house has either retained or increased its 1990 value.

True, much of Britain's economic wealth is still concentrated in London and the South East of England where Gross Domestic Product (GDP) per head and average earnings remain well ahead of those in the country as a whole. But Britain's experience in the 1990s would appear to question the assumption that its northern half is necessarily destined to remain economically disadvantaged and peripheral (Griffin, 1992; Church, 1995).

Meanwhile, by the early 1990s, there was already some evidence that social attitudes were responding to these changing economic circumstances (Curtice, 1992). Differences in levels of economic pessimism had narrowed considerably. And, although the North was still less willing than the South to embrace a free-market philosophy, the ideological gap between them had narrowed somewhat. Intriguingly, the Conservatives also regained some of their lost northern support in the 1992 general election (Curtice and Steed, 1992).

Our principal objective in this chapter is to examine whether the continued relative economic prosperity of the North has had any further impact on social attitudes. Has the northern half of Britain shaken off its economic pessimism? Does the ideological divide between North and South over a best way of running the economy show any sign of disappearing? In short, does Britain show signs of becoming one nation again?

Of course, the issue is not this simple. Even if we were to find that social attitudes were becoming more homogenous, Britain's political and economic experiences during the 1980s have left an additional political legacy - a desire for autonomy. Indeed, demands for separate parliaments for Scotland and Wales (and even regional assemblies within England) have now been incorporated into Labour party policy. So, we will also consider what geographic differences exist in attitudes towards the sorts of issues that might

become the responsibility of such bodies. Might, for instance, any future regional parliaments or assemblies be likely to come under pressure from public opinion to follow sharply different policies from one another? Or could the impetus for their creation in fact be assuaged by Britain's new economic geography?

Data and definitions

The *British Social Attitudes* survey interviews approximately 3,600 people each year. However, many questions are only asked of one-third of the sample (that is, around 1,200 people). This gives us a reasonable estimate of the views of the country as a whole, but can rarely help us look at how attitudes vary between different parts of the country. For example, such a sample will contain only around 110 people from Scotland and 60 from Wales - too few cases to be sure that any differences we find between them are statistically significant. However, because we repeat many questions every year, we can combine the results from more than one year in order to secure an adequate sample size within each area.

In this chapter we have brought together the results from the last three *British Social Attitudes* surveys, conducted between 1993 and 1995. When combined, they comprise over 10,000 people. And, for many of the questions we examine, we are able to compare this group with those from two earlier periods: 1983-87 (when the economic divide between North and South was at its height) and 1989-91 (by which time it showed signs of narrowing). Consequently, we are not only able to examine the magnitude of any differences between particular areas of Britain, but also whether these differences have widened or narrowed since the 1980s.

Of course, attitudes towards economic and social issues vary according to people's individual social backgrounds. And different parts of Britain clearly vary in their social composition. Owner-occupation is, for instance, noticeably lower in Scotland and in London than elsewhere. London and the South East of England contain more people in professional and managerial occupations than does the rest of the country (Church, 1995). Consequently, we might expect some differences in attitudes between particular areas simply to reflect variations in the kinds of people contained within those areas. In order to overcome this problem, we have also undertaken some multivariate analysis to ascertain the strength of association between particular social attitudes and area - independently of the respondent's social background.

As in previous reports, we will consider six separate areas of Britain. Apart from Scotland and Wales, we identify four different regions within England. These are the North of England (consisting of the Northern, North West, and Yorkshire and Humberside standard regions), the Midlands (the East and West Midlands), the South of England (the South East outside London, South

West and East Anglia) and London. These groupings respect the principal economic and political dividing lines of the 1980s, while ensuring that there are adequate respondents within each category to be able to pursue analysis fruitfully.

Perceptions of the North-South divide

Is the British public aware of the extent to which Britain's economic geography has changed? In our most recent survey we repeated a set of questions first asked in 1987 (at the height of the North-South divide). The first asked:

> *People in Britain often talk about the differences between the North and the South. How about employment prospects generally - are they better in the North, better in the South, or is there no real difference?*[3]

The same question was then also asked about opportunities to set up a business, the chances of young people being able to buy their first home, standards in education, and the National Health Service. In 1987, a clear majority believed that both employment prospects and business opportunities were better in the South than in the North. But, as the next table shows, the picture is rather muddier now. True, there are still relatively few people who believe that either employment prospects or business opportunities are *better* in the North than they are in the South. But the proportion of people who think that employment prospects are better in the South has dropped substantially, from a close to unanimous 84 per cent in 1987 to 58 per cent in 1995 (a drop of 26 percentage points). And the proportion believing that business opportunities are better in the South than in the North has also fallen, from 54 per cent to 41 per cent. However, what was once the 'upside' of the northern economy - the belief that it was easier for a young couple to buy a house there - shows signs of falling off, with the proportion who think that there is 'no real difference' between North and South in this respect rising from 27 per cent to 40 per cent.

Perceptions of differences between North and South

| | | 1987 | | | | 1995 | |
| | | Better in ... | | No real | | Better in ... | No real |
		North	South	difference		North	South	difference
Employment prospects	%	1	84	14	%	6	58	32
Opportunities to set up business	%	5	54	39	%	8	41	47
National Health Service	%	5	17	75	%	7	12	77
Education standards	%	9	21	70	%	9	21	67
Chance of buying first home	%	51	20	27	%	43	14	40
Base				*1281*				*1054*

These data suggest that the public certainly seem to have taken some notice of Britain's changing economic geography. And a similar picture emerges when examining people's perceptions of their area's economic well-being, compared to the well-being of Britain as a whole. We asked:

> *Compared with other parts of Britain over the last ten years, would you say that this part of Britain has been getting more prosperous than average, stayed about average, or been getting less prosperous?*

As the next table shows, the perception that the economy in the North is weaker than that in the South remains. In 1995, 59 per cent of those living in the North of England, Scotland and Wales said that the economy in their part of Britain had become 'less prosperous than average', compared with only 34 per cent of those in the South of England, London and the Midlands. But if we compare this with data from 1992, we find that the proportion of northerners who believe that their part of Britain has become less prosperous has declined - and the proportion of southerners thinking the same has increased.

Perceptions of relative area prosperity

	1992		1995	
	North/ Scotland/ Wales	**South/ Midlands/ London**	**North/ Scotland/ Wales**	**South/ Midlands/ London**
% saying their area has become ...	%	%	%	%
... less prosperous than average	59	34	52	37
... stayed about average	28	34	33	43
... more prosperous than average	17	27	12	16
Base	*1846*	*1688*	*485*	*749*

Source: 1992, *British Election Study*

Economic evaluations

Has this recognition of Britain's changing economic geography had any effect on differences in the levels of economic optimism and pessimism expressed by those in different areas? Here it is useful to distinguish between 'sociotropic' and 'egocentric' economic evaluations (Kiewet, 1983). Sociotropic evaluations are what the public thinks about the state of the economy as a whole. Egocentric evaluations refer to what people think about their *own* personal economic circumstances. Our expectation is that egocentric evaluations are more likely to be sensitive to changes in economic geography than are sociotropic evaluations. The reasoning behind this is simple. If an area's economy is doing better than it was, we would expect the economic circumstances of many individuals within that area to have

improved. As a result, we would expect them to be more optimistic about their personal circumstances than those living in an area whose economy is doing worse than it was. In contrast, the impact of an improved local economy on people's evaluations of the *national* economy is likely to be more indirect. True, they may take their cue from what they see around them in their particular area and be influenced accordingly. But, equally, people may base their judgements on what they hear and read about the economy in the national media whose message is the same anywhere.

We look first at three questions which tap sociotropic economic expectations about the year ahead. As the next table shows, these do vary by area, but do not reveal evidence of a strong North-South divide. Only when it comes to inflation are those living in Scotland, Wales and the North of England all more pessimistic than those living elsewhere. Nor do responses to these questions show any clear relationship between local economic experiences and attitudes. For instance, despite their recent experiences, those living in the South of England are consistently a little more optimistic about the performance of the British economy than the rest of the country. This finding holds true even once differences in the social composition of particular areas of Britain are taken into account in a multivariate analysis. This details of this can be found in the Appendix to this chapter.

Sociotropic economic evaluations, by area (1993-95)

	Scotland	North of England	Wales	Midlands	London	South of England
% of respondents saying:						
Expect prices to go up a lot in next year	38	37	41	31	33	29
Expect unemployment to go up a lot in next year	27	25	22	20	24	17
Britain's industrial performance will decline over next year	26	25	16	21	24	19
Base	*367*	*989*	*208*	*670*	*419*	*1209*

It would appear that, as we anticipated, sociotropic economic evaluations are somewhat resistant to changes in the fortunes of a particular area. This is underlined if we compare our 1993-95 data to those from the period 1989-91. Consider, for example, evaluations of Britain's economic performance. True, optimism among the Scots as to Britain's industrial performance has risen. But, so too has optimism risen in the South of England. Meanwhile, in the North of England there was actually a rise in the proportion taking a pessimistic view. And on neither of the two other items in the table does the pattern of increasing optimism or pessimism reflect the actual changes in the relative economic strength of different areas.

Sociotropic economic evaluations, by area (1993-95 *vs* 1989-91)

	Scotland	North of England	Wales	Midlands	London	South of England
% point difference between the two periods						
Expect prices to go up a lot in next year	-7	-12	-12	-12	-8	-12
Expect unemployment to go up a lot in next year	+3	+5	-2	+2	+6	0
Britain's industrial performance will decline over next year	-3	+1	-6	0	-2	-4

Note: A minus sign indicates a decline in the level of pessimism, a plus sign a rise in the level of pessimism.

What, then, of egocentric evaluations - people's perceptions of their own economic situation? Firstly, let us consider four measures of pessimism from the 1993-1995 period. As the next table shows, there is no evidence here of any geographic pattern at all. Rather, what is most remarkable is the degree of uniformity in the answers from each area. In so far as there is any exception to this rule, it is that Londoners find it more difficult to live on their existing household income and are more concerned than average about unemployment rather than inflation (see the Appendix to this chapter for more details).

Egocentric economic evaluations, by area (1993-95)

	Scotland	North of England	Wales	Midlands	London	South of England
% of respondents saying:						
Income has fallen behind prices in last year	51	52	49	49	51	49
Unemployment of greater concern to me and my family than inflation	47	42	43	49	52	47
Expect income to fall behind prices in next year	45	47	46	47	44	42
Living on household income difficult	22	22	23	23	32	22
Base	*367*	*989*	*208*	*670*	*419*	*1209*

Such findings are further underlined when we look at evaluations of the state of the local labour market. For example, we asked employees how long they thought it would take them to find to find an acceptable job if they were to lose their existing one. On average, it was Londoners who thought it would take longest (an estimated 5.7 months), while those living in the North of

England and the South of England both said it would take 4.5 months. Similarly, it was Londoners who were most concerned about their job security. Around a third thought that the number of people employed at their workplace was likely to fall in the next twelve months, compared with about a quarter in the North of England.

This is an utterly different picture from that obtained in the mid-1980s. Then, those living in Scotland, the North of England and Wales were consistently more pessimistic in their evaluation of their personal economic circumstances than those living elsewhere. Subsequently, however, the northern half of the country has gradually and consistently become more optimistic, and the southern half more pessimistic. This is shown quite clearly in the following table. Most dramatic of all the changes is that, while the proportion for whom unemployment is a greater concern than inflation has fallen in Scotland and the North of England, it has risen by over twenty percentage points in London and the South of England.

Egocentric economic evaluations, by area (1993-95 *vs* 1983-87)

	Scotland	North of England	Wales	Midlands	London	South of England
% point difference between the two periods						
Income has fallen behind prices in last year	+1	-3	-5	+2	+9	+6
Unemployment of greater concern to me and my family than inflation	-3	-8	+2	+8	+23	+22
Expect income to fall behind prices in next year	-4	-2	-5	+3	+8	+5
Living on household income difficult	-6	-7	-7	-4	+5	+2

Note: A minus sign indicates a decline in the level of pessimism, a plus sign a rise in the level of pessimism.

It thus seems that egocentric evaluations have changed in a way which clearly reflects the varying economic fortunes of different parts of Britain over the last decade. Conversely, trends in sociotropic evaluations (those relating to the national economy as a whole), appear less strongly related to changes in local economic realities.

Economic ideology

We now turn from people's evaluations of how well the economy is doing, to their attitudes on the way in which it should be *run*. As noted at the beginning of this chapter, in the mid-1980s those living in the North were

less willing to embrace a free market philosophy than those in the South. But perhaps their attitudes have changed, now that the market economy seems to be treating their area more favourably?

To answer this we can look at a number of questions designed to tap attitudes towards the proper role of government in the economy and the desirability (or otherwise) of greater economic equality. All were questions which, in the 1980s, exhibited some of the largest differences in attitudes between the North and the South.

As the next table shows, the remnants of a North-South divide are still apparent. In general, those living in the South of England are the most likely to adopt a more pro-free market/right-wing position, and those living in Scotland the most likely to take a more anti-free market/left-wing position. For instance, less than half of those in the South agree that "unemployment benefit is too low and causes hardship", while as many as seven in ten Scots take this view. But, for the most part, the differences between the remaining areas are small. For example, only on one question is there more than a four percentage point difference between the North of England and the Midlands. Multivariate analysis confirms that this is no more than we would expect given the differences in their social composition (see the Appendix to this chapter).

Economic ideology, by area (1993-95)

% agreeing that:	Scotland	North of England	Wales	Midlands	London	South of England
Unemployment should be a higher priority than inflation[a]	77	70	63	72	72	65
There is one law for the rich and one for the poor[b]	75	73	73	74	68	66
Ordinary people do not get their fair share of the nation's wealth[b]	70	71	65	67	62	59
Unemployment benefit is too low and causes hardship[c]	69	57	50	55	55	47
Big business benefits owners at the expense of workers[d]	66	61	58	63	59	56
Government should re-distribute income from the better off to the less well off[d]	60	61	48	48	51	43
Base:						
(Item marked a)	*367*	*989*	*208*	*670*	*419*	*1209*
(Items marked b)	*406*	*1098*	*268*	*743*	*451*	*1475*
(Item marked c)	*731*	*1949*	*407*	*1319*	*843*	*2399*
(Items marked d)	*661*	*1848*	*420*	*1249*	*759*	*2433*

Moreover, there is some evidence that geographic differences in attitudes towards the economy have been narrowing. As the following table shows, in Scotland and the North of England there has been little change in attitudes towards the level of unemployment benefit since 1989-91, while in the three southern regions of England there has been a modest increase in the proportion believing unemployment benefit is "too low". Equally, there has been a sharper increase in the South than in the North in the proportion of people who believe that "big business benefits owners at the expense of workers". However, on the other items in the table there is no systematic difference between the trends shown by North and South. Indeed, when it comes to whether people get their "fair share of the nation's wealth", the distribution of attitudes now is almost exactly the same as it was at the turn of the decade.

Economic ideology, by area (1993-95 vs 1989-91)

	Scotland	North of England	Wales	Midlands	London	South of England
% agreeing that:						
Unemployment should be a higher priority than inflation	+19	+14	+5	+19	+17	+19
There is one law for the rich and one for the poor	+10	+2	+2	+7	+5	+3
Ordinary people do not get their fair share of the nation's wealth	+1	0	0	0	-4	0
Unemployment benefit is too low and causes hardship	+2	0	-12	+5	+4	+6
Big business benefits owners at the expense of workers	0	+5	-3	+10	+6	+9
Government should redistribute income from the better off to the less well off	+2	+7	-7	+1	0	0

Note: A plus sign indicates that more responses have become more left-wing/anti-free market; a minus sign that they have become less so.

So it appears that the narrowing of Britain's North-South economic divide has had some influence on attitudes towards how the economy should be run. But, equally, such attitudes are evidently more resistant to change than are evaluations of one's own economic circumstances. They certainly do not simply change after a few years of good economic fortune. The ideological polarisation of Britain may have abated, but there remains considerable disagreement between the extremes (in this case, the South of England and Scotland) over how the country's economy might best be run.

Prospects for regional parliaments

There then remain some notable differences between particular areas in their attitudes towards the effectiveness of the market, and the desirable level of economic equality. But these are not areas of public policy intended to become the responsibility of either a Scottish or Welsh parliament, or of regional assemblies in England. True, such bodies might be given responsibility for economic development measures designed to try and attract industry to their area. But there has been no suggestion that such parliaments or regional assemblies might have the ability directly to influence, say, levels of economic inequality.

There are, however, a number of *other* areas of public policy over which regional parliaments or assemblies might be given some responsibility. And there is evidence that the demands that might be faced by these bodies could vary from one part of the country to another. One possible example is education. This is a field where, traditionally, policy can already vary somewhat from one local authority to another. Moreover, such policy variations cover key issues, such as whether secondary education is organised on selective or comprehensive lines. Meanwhile, Scotland already has its own separate educational system, quite different to that south of the border.

And there are indeed some striking differences throughout Britain in attitudes towards secondary education. In Scotland, for instance, only one in three believe that "children should go to a different kind of secondary school, according to how well they do at primary school". Support for selective schooling is also lower than average in Wales, with four in ten adopting this stance. By contrast, in the North of England and the Midlands, a little under half favour selection - and in London and the South of England just over half do so. Regional parliaments and assemblies could then play a key role in adapting educational policy to local opinion.

A second possible role for regional parliaments or assemblies might be in influencing local levels of taxation and public spending. Both the Labour Party and the Scottish Constitutional Convention have suggested that any future Scottish parliament should be given limited powers to increase (or reduce) taxation in Scotland in order to increase (or reduce) spending. The premise behind this proposal appears to be that Scots have different attitudes towards public spending than do those in England or Wales.

Yet, as the next table shows, this is not actually the case. The proportion of Scots who say they would like to see taxes rise in order to spend more on health, education and social benefits is around three in five - a similar proportion to that found in Wales and the English regions. Equally, there are relatively few differences throughout Britain in priorities for public spending, although Londoners are particularly keen (and Scots less keen) to see more spending in education.

Attitudes towards tax and spending, by area (1993-95)

	Scotland	North of England	Wales	Midlands	London	South of England
% favouring:						
Increase taxes and spend more on health, education and social benefits	62	62	62	58	63	60
Base	*927*	*2538*	*558*	*1722*	*1104*	*3198*
% naming as first priority for extra government spending:						
Health	49	44	49	46	43	45
Education	22	29	27	28	36	29
Housing	8	6	7	7	8	7
Base	*513*	*1363*	*286*	*924*	*594*	*1666*

It is, then, not entirely clear that the areas over which regional parliaments or assemblies might be given some responsibility necessarily match those in which there are real geographic differences in public preferences. On the one hand, this suggests that devolution may not satisfy public opinion as much as its proponents claim it would. But, on the other hand, it also suggests that public pressure for regional parliaments and assemblies to pursue policies that might be in conflict with those of other parliaments or assemblies (including Westminster) may not be as great as opponents fear it could be.

Symbols and institutions

Demands for greater autonomy for particular parts of the United Kingdom do not, however, necessarily rest only on differences in economic well-being or a wish to pursue different public policies. After all, the United Kingdom is a multinational state, consisting of three separate nations, England, Scotland and Wales, together with Northern Ireland whose status as a separate entity is disputed. We might find, therefore, that demands for the creation of Scottish and Welsh parliaments arise from a wish to assert a separate national identity or reflect lower levels of adherence to common symbols of 'Britishness'.

  Our surveys do not enable us to consider this topic in detail, but they do provide us with some clues. Perhaps the most important symbol of Britishness, and one that might be expected to bind the component nations of the United Kingdom together, is the monarchy. So, if support for the monarchy is lower in Scotland or Wales, this might be indicative of a weaker sense of attachment to the United Kingdom as a whole.

  We do indeed find that, when asked "how important or unimportant do you think it is for Britain to continue to have a monarch", only around a half of Scots thought it was important - compared with around two-thirds of those in

each of the English regions. However, in Wales, support for the monarchy is just as high as it is in the North of England, and somewhat higher than it is in London. This may provide some clues as to why the campaign for a separate parliament has been rather stronger in Scotland than in Wales.

Attitudes towards the Monarchy, by area (1993-95)

% agreeing that:	Scotland	North of England	Wales	Midlands	London	South of England
Important for Britain to continue to have a monarchy	50	64	64	71	59	70
Base	*216*	*579*	*144*	*139*	*408*	*763*

A second clue available to us concerns attitudes towards Britain's membership of the European Community. We might anticipate that those with a strong sense of attachment to the United Kingdom may be more opposed to closer British involvement in the European Union. Indeed, previous research has indicated that opposition to the European Union is associated with a strong sense of Britishness (Heath and Taylor, 1995). Moreover, the nationalist parties in both Scotland and Wales embrace the idea of 'Independence in Europe', suggesting that continued access to the large economic market of the European Union means that separation from the United Kingdom is economically viable.

As the next table shows, Scotland does indeed prove to be marginally keener than average on closer relations with the European Union. But, even so, it is not so keen as London. Indeed, when it comes to the possibility of replacing the pound with a single European currency, Scots (who have their own bank notes) are rather more Euro-sceptic than anyone else. Wales, meanwhile, does not demonstrate any particular enthusiasm for Europe at all. Indeed, once differences in the social composition of these areas are taken into account, it is the low level of support for Europe in the South of England which is the most distinctive difference between the constituent parts of Britain (see the Appendix to this chapter).

Attitudes towards the European Union, by area (1993-95)

% agreeing that:	Scotland	North of England	Wales	Midlands	London	South of England
Britain's relationship with the EU should be closer	36	30	30	32	39	29
Britain should do all it can to unite fully with the EU	41	33	37	40	48	33
Britain's policy should be to increase EU powers/form a single EU government	41	31	36	33	43	33
Keep pound as only currency for Britain	69	67	62	62	55	63
Base	*360*	*964*	*214*	*670*	*412*	*1233*

Conclusion

The narrowing of the economic divide between the North and South of Britain does appear to have influenced the nation's social attitudes. True, there remains a perception that, in some respects, the economy of the southern half of the country is still stronger than that of the North. But the economic expectations of those living in the North are now no more pessimistic than the expectations of those living in South - at least so far as their own personal economic situation is concerned. Equally, although there are still differences in attitudes towards economic inequality and in beliefs about the way in which the economy should be run (most especially between Scotland and the South of England), these differences are generally a little weaker than they were in the 1980s.

As we noted at the beginning of this chapter, the 1992 general election marked a slight reversal of the geographic concentration of Conservative support in the southern half of the country. Our evidence suggests that the conditions are ripe for this trend to continue, as indeed proved the case in the 1994 European Elections (Curtice and Steed, 1995). As the incumbent government, the Conservatives might expect to benefit from the relative improvement in economic evaluation in the North. Moreover, this area now appears a little more receptive to the party's economic philosophy. Britain's changed economic geography may then help to reduce the strength of some of its political divisions as well.

It would seem that, economically, Britain does appear to be coming closer to being one nation again. But whether this will be sufficient to end the impetus for the creation of regional parliaments or assemblies is not so clear. At least in some parts of Britain, the impetus may well arise out of a weaker sense of attachment to a sense of Britishness than because of any lack of economic well-being. And there are at least some areas of public policy where, if given the necessary powers, such bodies might be able to respond to differing local climates of public opinion. However, perhaps it is precisely because different parts of Britain are no longer so economically divided that such a system of government could be made to work.

Notes

1. We include in 'the North' those living in Scotland, Northern England and Wales. 'The South' includes people living in the Midlands, East Anglia, London and Southern England.
2. The Northern region comprises Cleveland, Cumbria, Durham, Northumberland, Tyne and Wear; the South East comprises Bedfordshire, Berkshire, Buckingham, Essex, Hampshire, Hertfordshire, Isle of Wight, Kent, Oxfordshire, Surrey and Sussex (East and West).
3. Respondents in Scotland were asked about 'Scotland' rather than 'this part of Britain'. Similarly, those in Wales were asked about 'Wales'.

References

Church, J. (1995), *Regional Trends 1995*, **30**, London: HMSO.

Curtice, J, (1988), 'One nation?' in Jowell, R., Witherspoon, S. and Brook, L. (eds.), *British Social Attitudes: the 5th Report*, Aldershot: Gower.

Curtice, J. (1992), 'The North-South divide', in Jowell, J., Brook, L., Prior, G. and Taylor, B. (eds.), *British Social Attitudes: the 9th Report*, Aldershot: Dartmouth.

Curtice, J. and Steed, M. (1986), 'Proportionality and exaggeration in the British Electoral System', *Electoral Studies,* **5**, 209-28.

Curtice, J. and Steed, M. (1988), 'Analysis', in Butler, D. and Kavanagh, D. (eds.), *The British General Election of 1987*, London: Macmillan.

Curtice, J. and Steed, M. (1992), 'The results analysed', in Butler, D. and Kavanagh, D. (eds.), *The British General Election of 1992*, London: Macmillan.

Curtice, J. and Steed, M. (1995), 'An analysis of the results', in Butler, D. and Westlake, M. (eds.), *The 1994 European Election in Britain*, London: Macmillan.

Evans, G. (1995), 'The State of the Union: attitudes towards Europe', in Jowell, R., Curtice, J., Park, A., Brook, L. and Ahrendt, D. (eds.), *British Social Attitudes: the 12th Report*, Aldershot: Dartmouth.

Griffin, T. (ed.) (1992), *Regional Trends 1992,.*27, London: HMSO.

Heath, A. and Taylor, B. (1995), 'British national sentiment', paper presented to the Annual Conference of the Political Studies Association, University of Glasgow.

Kiewet, D. (1983), *Macro-economics and Micro-politics: The Electoral Effects of Economic Issues*, Chicago: University of Chicago Press.

Smith, D. (1989), *North and South: Britain's Economic, Social and Political Divide*, Harmondsworth: Penguin.

Appendix

Multivariate analysis

The following tables show the logistic regression coefficients for each region. The coefficients presented are deviation coefficients measuring the difference between attitudes in each region and in Britain as a whole. Unless otherwise specified, the models control for class, housing tenure and unemployment (of either the respondent or his/her spouse/partner).

In each case, the 'dependent variable' of the model is shown in the left-hand side of the table. The analyses exclude those who did not answer the question or responded "don't know".

In the following tables, all coefficients statistically significant at a five per cent significance level are marked with an asterisk. Regression techniques and statistical significance are explained in Appendix I to this Report.

The impact of region on sociotropic evaluations, 1993-1995

A plus sign indicates that the level of economic pessimism is higher in the region than in Britain as a whole, a minus sign that it is lower.

As the table shows, the coefficients for the South of England are statistically significant for all three items and are all negative (indicating that those in this region are less pessimistic than those in Britain as a whole).

	Scotland	North of England	Wales	Midlands	London	South of England
Expect prices to go up a lot in next year	+0.04	+0.07	+0.23	-0.18*	+0.02	-0.19*
Expect unemployment to go up a lot in next year	+0.15	+0.11	-0.04	-0.11	+0.17	-0.28*
Britain's industrial performance will decline over next year	+0.21	+0.17*	-0.29	-0.07	+0.16	-0.18*

Base: 3660, 3634 and 3535 respectively.

The impact of region on egocentric evaluations, 1993-1995

Here, as above, a plus sign indicates that the level of economic pessimism is higher in the region than in Britain as a whole, a minus sign that it is lower.

Note that on two of the items shown below *none* of the regional coefficients are significant. On the two remaining items, the coefficient for London is statistically significant and positive (indicating that Londoners are more pessimistic than those in the country as a whole).

	Scotland	North of England	Wales	Midlands	London	South of England
Income has fallen behind prices in last year	-0.10	+0.10	-0.07	-0.01	+0.06	+0.01
Unemployment of greater concern to me and my family	+0.00	-0.20*	-0.08	+0.07	+0.19*	+0.01
Expect income to fall behind prices in next year	-0.04	+0.07	+0.01	+0.09	-0.02	-0.11
Living on household income difficult	-0.34*	-0.10	-0.08	+0.02	+0.46*	+0.03

Base: 3661, 3655, 3594 and 3693 respectively.

The impact of region on economic ideology, 1993-1995

Here a plus sign indicates that the region is more right-wing or pro-free market than Britain as a whole, a minus sign that it is more left-wing or anti-free market.

Note that the coefficients for the South of England are statistically significant and negative for all six items. For four of the items, the coefficients for Scotland are significant and positive. Among the other four regions there are just two significant coefficients.

% agreeing that:	Scotland	North of England	Wales	Midlands	London	South of England
Unemployment should be a higher priority than inflation	+0.33*	+0.01	-0.32*	+0.06	+0.11	-0.19*
There is one law for the rich and one for the poor	+0.13	+0.02	+0.11	+0.09	-0.14	-0.21*
Ordinary people do not get their fair share of the nation's wealth	+0.15	+0.23*	-0.02	+0.04	-0.16	-0.23*
Unemployment benefit is too low and causes hardship	+0.53*	+0.01	-0.18	-0.02	-0.02	-0.31*
Big business benefits owners at the expense of workers	+0.19*	+0.00	-0.09	+0.09	-0.03	-0.15*
Government should redistribute income from the better off to the less well off	+0.35*	+0.01	-0.06	-0.08	+0.04	-0.26*

Base: 3626, 4185, 4182, 7014, 6969 and 6993 respectively.

The impact of region on attitudes towards the European Union, 1993-1995

In these models we also controlled for educational qualifications, as those with higher qualifications tend to be more favourably disposed than average towards Europe (Evans, 1995). A plus sign indicates that the region is more pro-European Union than Britain as a whole, a minus sign that it is less pro-European Union. The exception to this concerns the item on monetary union. Here a positive coefficient indicates *opposition* to a single currency.

Note that support for the European Union in the South of England is *lower* than that in Britain as a whole once class, housing tenure, unemployment and education are taken into account. On the first three items, the coefficients for the South are statistically significant and negative. In contrast, the significant coefficients for London show that its population is more favourably disposed towards the European Union than average. None of the coefficients for Scotland or Wales is significant.

	Scotland	North of England	Wales	Midlands	London	South of England
Britain's relationship with the EU should be closer	+0.09	-0.08	+0.03	-0.03	+0.20*	-0.21*
Britain should do all it can to unite fully with the EU	+0.04	-0.12	+0.02	-0.07	+0.32*	-0.32*
Britain's policy should be to increase EU powers/form a single EU government	+0.20	-0.17*	+0.11	-0.09	+0.15	-0.21*
Keep pound as only currency for Britain	+0.18	+0.08	+0.06	-0.11	-0.25*	+0.05

Base: 3350, 3340, 3372, and 3536 respectively.

2 Portraying sex: the limits of tolerance

Steven Barnett and Katarina Thomson[*]

This chapter examines public reactions to the portrayal of sex in the media and, in particular, views on whether certain age groups should be protected from such images. We try to find out not only whether reactions differ according to the form of media in which the sex scene appears - television, cinema, videos, radio, magazines, adult premium-rate telephone services - but also according to the context of the sex scene itself - whether it is part of a developing plot or seemingly 'gratuitous'. To the extent that people vary in their attitudes, we investigate the main sources of variation.

The debate about the absolute freedom to publish *versus* the need to protect individuals or society from 'harmful' images or words goes back to the first days of the printing press. Whether the content at issue happens to be blasphemy, violence, sex, profanity, racial and other forms of abuse, or politics, it is a moral dilemma which turns on the question of whether unfettered freedom of speech is compatible with the collective well-being of society and its citizens.

The philosophical roots of this dilemma have been most famously articulated by John Stuart Mill in his "one very simple principle" to govern the relationship between individual freedom and the limits of any coercive role for society: "that the sole end for which mankind are warranted, individually or collectively, in interfering with the liberty of action of any of

[*] Steven Barnett is Senior Lecturer at the Centre for Communication and Information Studies, University of Westminster. Katarina Thomson is a Research Director at SCPR and a Co-director of the *British Social Attitudes* survey series.

their number, is self-protection. That the only purpose for which power can be rightfully exercised over any member of a civilised community, against his will, is to prevent harm to others" (1989: 13). It is this notion of preventing harm to others which has underpinned approaches to regulation in most contemporary Western societies.

Interpretations of the notion of 'harm'

What might constitute harm in this context? Most contemporary debates tend to focus on two different potential manifestations of harm: behavioural and attitudinal. The former model is based on the notion that exposure to certain words or images is likely to have a material impact on the behaviour of individuals, leading perhaps to anti-social behaviour which is manifestly harmful to the collective good. Most cultural forms, from music hall to rock and roll, have been accused in their time of directly inciting unruly, violent or otherwise unsavoury behaviour (Pearson, 1983). In particular, however, film and television - with their mass appeal and their ability to combine the power of sound and visual image - have attracted special attention. It is now not uncommon, for instance, in trials for murder or violence for the offence to be linked in some way (either within the court or in subsequent newspaper reports) to the influence of films, television or videos.

Yet research evidence remains ambivalent about the existence of any direct effect of prior exposure to representations of sex, violence or drug-taking on subsequent real-life behaviour (see Cumberbatch and Howitt, 1989). It is therefore ironic that the only *criminal* offence in this area, based on the 1959 Obscene Publications Act, defines a publication to be obscene "if its effect.... is, if taken as a whole, such as to tend to deprave and corrupt persons who are likely, in all the circumstances, to read, see, or hear the matter contained or embodied in it". True, the test is not necessarily a behavioural one, since the definition of depravity and corruption has been left to jurors in individual cases to decide, but some kind of causal link between seeing a publication and a change in mental or behavioural orientation is certainly implied (Robertson, 1993). To infringe the Act, it is not enough merely to have offended people, even in large numbers.

The criminal law, however, is rarely invoked nowadays in this area in Britain. Much more important in terms of controlling mass media content in Britain today are the various regulatory bodies which have been established over the years in the different media (and which take account of the law within their own codes). Broadcasting is covered by statutory regulation, but films, advertising (other than on radio or television), the press, and premium-rate telephone services, are all covered by voluntary self-regulation or independent regulation through industry codes. And, with the exception of the British Board of Film Classification (BBFC, 1996: 3-4), the decisions of these bodies on whether to censure or disallow publication tends to be based

on attitudinal rather than behavioural considerations. In other words, the implicit or explicit notion of 'harm' they employ is based on the offence the material is likely to cause rather than on whether it is likely to stimulate actual anti-social behaviour.

Control over broadcast material is exercised by a combination of statutory and regulatory guidelines. What is transmitted on television or radio and, often more important, *when* it goes on air, tends to be governed by elusive concepts such as 'taste', 'decency' or the avoidance of 'offence'.

In this respect, the Independent Television Commission (ITC) (which regulates all non-BBC television) is governed in general terms by section 6(1)(a) of the 1990 Broadcasting Act, which it then interprets in a detailed programme code.[1] On sex and nudity, for example, the code says:

> Much of the world's great drama and fiction has been concerned with love and passion, and it would be wrong to require writers to renounce all intention to shock or disturb; but the aim should not be to offend (1995: 4).

In respect of explicit sex, the code continues: "The portrayal of sexual behaviour, and of nudity, needs to be defensible in context and presented with tact and discretion". In practice, the Code does not permit representations of sexual intercourse until after nine o'clock in the evening, except in special circumstances. That nine o'clock 'watershed' has become a crucial threshold for terrestrial television, after which parents are expected to take greater responsibility for what their children may be exposed to.

The BBC is governed in the same general terms as the Broadcasting Act by Section 5.1(d) of the Agreement which accompanies its Royal Charter. The BBC Producers' Guidelines attempt to flesh out these generalisations with rules that acknowledge the tension between free speech and causing harm: "As a general rule we will have failed if any instance causes widespread offence. But the right to run contrary to general expectations when circumstances justify it must also be safeguarded" (1993: 86). Like the ITC, the BBC stresses the importance of context - both in terms of timing and content.

The Broadcasting Standards Council (BSC), set up as a statutory body specifically to monitor taste and decency issues, has also developed a code of practice which covers violence, sex, and taste and decency. The section covering the portrayal of sex deals separately and in detail with five different programme categories, but its overall approach is that "the role of [general] channels is to observe sensitively how and why offence may be given in their treatment of sexual matters so that they can avoid offending in ignorance or gratuitously" (1994: 36). In broadcasting, then, the notion of harm has been explicitly defined as giving offence.

In cinema, the British Board of Film Classification (BBFC) - which has no legal status, but whose rating decisions are rarely challenged by local

authorities - works more explicitly on the basis of what is likely to be acceptable and appropriate to different age-groups. Thus, in '15' rated films, "impressionistic sex is acceptable, as is heavier violence and bad language.... The '18' category allows adult themes to be presented in more explicit detail: the viewer is assumed to be morally mature and able to judge for him or her self the material being shown" (1992: 2). But the BBFC also has a special duty to classify almost every video available for sale or rent - a role it was given under the 1984 Video Recordings Act, amended in 1994. It is required to have "special regard to the likelihood of (certified) video works being viewed in the home", and "to any harm that may be caused to potential viewers or, through their behaviour, to society...." (BBFC, 1995: 3) - a requirement which was, in fact, included in the BBFC guidelines before the Act. So, different standards apply to cinema films and videos apparently because of their different viewing contexts. The result is that the BBFC will on occasions make more cuts or impose stricter classifications on the video than on the film version.

In advertising and in the new breed of 'adult' premium rate telephone lines, the relevant industry bodies invoke public taste and offensiveness as the guiding principle for defining acceptable material. Thus, the Advertising Standards Authority's Code states that "Advertisements should contain nothing that is likely to cause serious or widespread offence..... Compliance with the Codes will be judged on the context, medium, audience, product and prevailing standards of decency" (ASA 1995: 8), while the Independent Committee for the Supervision of Standards of Telephone Information Services (ICSTIS) Code advises that "services and promotional material must not be of a kind that are likely to... cause grave or widespread offence" (ICSTIS, 1995: 1.3.3). Notably, the only mass medium in which there is no codified statement of the need to take account of offending *taste and decency* is the press. The Press Complaints Commission does have a Code of Practice, but it deals with matters other than taste (PCC, 1995).

Crucial, then, to the modern approach to regulation, is the concept of what sort of material is acceptable or offensive to whom and under what circumstances. The notion of harm therefore tends to be 'defined' as transgressing some unwritten, uncodified contemporary societal norms. Only rarely, however, and by no means by all regulators and interpreters, are these societal norms rigorously measured. For the most part they are imputed.

Previous research evidence

Over the years, a number of studies have been conducted, mostly by broadcasting bodies, in an attempt to guide decisions. For instance, the ITC and its predecessor the Independent Broadcasting Authority have carried out an annual study since 1973 which monitors the extent to which and the reasons why viewers are offended by television programmes. According to

their most recent report (ITC, 1996), 44 per cent found at least some material offensive.   This overall proportion has not varied much over the years, although offence caused by ITV and BBC1 have declined somewhat, and offence caused by BBC2 and Channel Four have risen. The causes of offence have also remained static with three main identifiable categories, in order: bad language, violence and sex. This rank order is maintained on each of the four channels, with around 14 per cent of viewers citing bad language, around 11 per cent violence, and around 10 per cent sexual content, the remainder mentioning a range of other factors.

This research also provides clues as to the social groups most likely to be offended.   For instance, women are much more likely to be offended by television programmes than are men (50 per cent *versus* 36 per cent), and there is the expected direct correlation with age: the older the viewer, the more likely they are to have been offended (a quarter of 16-24 year-olds compared to nearly 60 per cent of the over 65s).

While the ITC research is a useful indicator of trends, it does not explore in any detail the concept of 'offence', nor the effect of different *contexts* in which offence might be caused. Nor does it deal with more policy relevant issues on which public opinion may have a role to play, such as the conflict between the right to publish and the protection of individual sensibilities, or the rights of different minority groups in society to see (or not see) different sorts of programme. Some of these issues have been explored in the past by the Broadcasting Standards Council.

In their first piece of research (conducted in 1988), the BSC substituted the word "disgusted" for "offended" in an attempt to gauge depth of feeling, but the stronger word seemed to elicit more rather than fewer objectors (BSC, 1989). Moreover, this change of emphasis produced a different rank order in the sources of concern. The generic 'bad taste' was the most cited cause of disgust, relating as it might to a multitude of material from scenes of famine in the news to satirical sketches on Spitting Image. But sexual content, violence and bad language, which closely followed bad taste, were now in the opposite order from that in the ITC research.

The inference then is that bad language is particularly likely to cause *offence*, but not necessarily the moral outrage or deep embarrassment that sexual content may provoke, both of which may be better connoted by the word *disgust*. In both cases the numbers affected are, however, a minority of the population. In any event, these two studies demonstrate the importance of question wording in this area where subtle changes can produce significant differences, a point we shall return to in connection with our own research. The BSC study also addressed the trade-off between censorship and freedom of expression, asking respondents to choose between two conflicting statements. The first statement was: "I would give up the chance to watch some TV programmes rather than risk someone being deeply offended by the programme". The second was: "I should have the right to choose whether or not to watch a TV programme even if someone is deeply offended by it".

The population as a whole were divided roughly down the middle (though when the word 'harmed' was substituted for the word 'offended', the proportion who would sacrifice their rights for the protection of others rose to over two in three). In general, older people are more willing to accept censorship rather than offend others - either because older people are themselves more likely to be offended by certain programmes, or because age confers a greater willingness to defer to other people's feelings.

A study by the Broadcasting Research Unit (Docherty *et al*, 1988) of Channel 4 programmes investigated the extent to which viewers' attitudes on taste, decency and offence were influenced by the context of a scene with sexual content within a programme. Respondents were asked, for instance, how acceptable it was to show a topless model or a full frontal male nude in different types of programme. The findings show that responses varied significantly according to context. What was deemed to be acceptable for most people in a relevant documentary was acceptable to only a minority in a situation comedy or (more surprisingly) in a serious play. However, fewer than one in five people (rising to over two in five for the full-frontal male scene), would find nudity of this sort unacceptable in *any* programme.

The importance of both programme and viewing context was confirmed in a large-scale BSC study of attitudes to sex on television in 1992. The study asked about "sex....shown in quite explicit detail" in different sorts of programmes. Nearly 75 per cent of respondents said they would find it to be acceptable in a documentary about sex and around 60 per cent in a film or a television programme in which it was an important part of the story. The length of the sex scene was, however, important, with most people saying "a few seconds" were acceptable. By contrast, only around 20 per cent would find such a scene acceptable in a soap opera or sitcom, and only seven per cent in a programme shown before nine o'clock in the evening. The study's conclusion was that context mattered in two different respects. First, sex scenes were widely acceptable only when they were "seen to have a role to play in the unfolding of the plot, to be relevant to the storyline" (Millwood Hargrave, 1992: 72). Secondly, their acceptability depended on the viewing context. Sex scenes viewed in the presence of children, in particular, were likely to elicit more embarrassment and to be regarded with less tolerance than those scheduled when children were less likely to be present. A related area of study has been the issue of exploitation of women, in particular in advertising. Research by the Advertising Standards Authority (ASA) confirmed the importance of context. They found that the most offensive advertisements are those "which exploit nudity, semi-nudity or sex in a manner which is irrelevant to the product being advertised" (ASA, 1990: 17).

The *British Social Attitudes* module

Whereas research to date has demonstrated how sensitive public opinion can be to questions of context and wording, what it has not so far addressed is how attitudes might differ between different media. As new media forms proliferate, these issues become increasingly important.

The 1995 *British Social Attitudes* survey included a module of questions on attitudes to the portrayal of sex in the media, and the intention is that a 'taste and decency' module should be included regularly in the survey series, dealing with different aspects in different years and repeating each module periodically. In fact, the module in the 1996 survey - to be reported in *the 14th Report* in 1997 - deals with violence in the media.

One of the aims of the module was to identify those features of different media which might contribute to different views of what is or is not acceptable. For instance, how much does private *versus* public viewing matter? Do judgements of acceptability differ when a film is being viewed in one's home on video as opposed to in a public cinema? By the same token, how much does restricted *versus* mass access affect judgements of these issues; for instance, do views about subscription television differ from those about terrestrial TV, and should radio broadcasts have different rules from those of pre-recorded telephone services? We examine each of these issues.

Differences between the media

We asked respondents for their attitudes towards the portrayal of two sexual scenes. The first question was posed as follows:

> *I am now going to ask what you think should be allowed or not allowed to be shown on the television or at the cinema. Thinking first about a frank scene in a film showing a man and a woman character having sex.*

Later we asked:

> *Now I want to ask you about a different kind of scene that may appear in a film. This, instead of a male and a female character, there is a frank scene of two adult male characters having sex.*

The intention was to present two scenarios on which there would be a range of opinions, including a proportion who would want to see them banned altogether. The wording was chosen to get across subtly that the scene was being simulated by actors rather than being 'real' sex. Further questions asked about attitudes towards the same scenes appearing on a range of different media. In all, the seven different media we covered were:

(i)   a film at the cinema;
(ii)   a film on one of the regular television channels;
(iii)   a film on a paid satellite or cable channel;
(iv)   a film on video for sale or rent;
(v)   still photograph of the same sex scene in an adult magazine;
(vi)   a radio drama in which you could hear a man and a woman character (two male characters) having sex; and
(vii)   premium-rate pre-recorded adult telephone services.

For each medium, respondents were asked how accessible the scene should be, with the choice of categories defined separately for each medium, but designed to be made roughly equivalent to one another. For instance, we posited age limits of 18, 15 or 12 for the cinema, video and the photograph in an adult magazine (in the latter case referring to the age at which someone might buy the magazine in an ordinary shop), and time limits of midnight, ten o'clock, nine o'clock and eight o'clock for regular television, satellite/cable television and radio. In every case, these answer options were supplemented by 'not allowing it at all' and, at the other extreme, allowing it to be shown to anyone at any time. For telephone services we gave three options of banning them altogether, making them "available but only to adults who have chosen to have the service", and making them available on all private telephone lines. For the cinema we also had an option of "only at special adult cinemas", just as for satellite/cable television we had an option of "only on a special adult channel" and for videos and photographs in adult magazines an option of "only in special adult shops".[2]

In analysing the data, we have operated on the assumption that a ten o'clock time limit may be considered roughly equivalent to an 18 age limit, nine o'clock to a 15 age limit, and eight o'clock to a 12 age limit. These are the equivalences applied by the ITC in their Programme Code (ITC, 1995: 6).

The data thus allow us to look at the distinctions people make between the different media. The framing of the questions enabled us to find out, among other things, whether people become progressively less worried about the portrayal of explicit sex as the restrictions on viewing get tighter and when the viewing of it is in private rather than in public.

Frank heterosexual sex scenes

As the next table shows, people *do* make distinctions between different media, but perhaps not to the extent we might have expected. They are more restrictive about regular television channels and radio than about satellite/cable television, videos or the cinema. In the absence of any clue in the questions as to the context of the frank heterosexual sex, around one in four would like to see such scenes banned altogether from regular television and radio, and around one in five would like to see them banned from

satellite and cable television, videos and the cinema. Still photographs in adult magazines generate a little less censoriousness. A further sizeable proportion (from a sixth to a third, depending on the medium) adopt the next most restrictive option of "only on a special adult channel"/"only at special cinemas"/"only in special shops"/"only after midnight".

So people do indeed seem most likely to reserve their most restrictive views for the most accessible of the media - regular television channels and radio. This may have something to do with intrusion into the home of embarrassing or offensive scenes which the viewer has not really chosen to watch (beyond switching the television on). Or it may be to do with the greater likelihood of exposure of the scene to children when it is on television. Views on the availability of videos for private viewing are more similar to those on the cinema than they are to those on television or radio - perhaps because video viewing is more a matter of deliberate choice or because the age limits, like those at the cinema, are enforceable by 'outsiders', albeit not as effectively as at the cinema.

However, the distinctions between the media should not be overstated. Given the fact that the television and radio questions had answer options with *time* limits and the cinema and video questions had answer options with *age* limits, it is surprising how similar the answers actually were. In broad terms, around 40 to 50 per cent of the population would prefer either to ban frank heterosexual sex scenes or at least to place severe restrictions on their availability. For most of the media, another 40 to 50 per cent would be content with an age 18 or a ten o'clock watershed. However, as we shall show later, these findings become more complicated when we introduce the notion of the context of the sex scene as the figures then change considerably.

Film with frank scene of man and woman having sex

Should be:	Regular TV	Satellite/ Cable	Video for sale or rent	Cinema	Radio	Still photo in adult magazine
	%	%	%	%	%	%
Not allowed at all	27	21	20	19	24	17
Special adult channel/ cinema/shop	na	17	22	19	na	31
After midnight	18	14	na	na	14	na
After 10pm/18+	40	31	45	47	36	41
After 9pm/15+	13	11	10	12	15	8
After 8pm/12+	2	5	1	3	9	2

Base: 1172

na = not asked

Frank homosexual sex scenes

Turning now to the frank homosexual sex scene, we find the same *relative* differences between the media, with the regular television channels once again attracting the most restrictive views and the photograph in the adult magazine the least restrictive ones. Again, videos and cinema attract very similar views. However, the *absolute* level of restrictiveness is much higher for the homosexual scene, amounting to a majority (54 per cent) who want an outright ban on the regular television channels and 37 per cent or more who would ban such a scene from each of the other media (even in still photographic form). Around a fifth to a third would like to see such scenes restricted to special cinemas, special adult channels, special shops or shown only after midnight, while most of the remainder would favour an age 18 or ten o'clock watershed.

Film with frank scene of two adult men having sex

	Regular TV	Satellite/ Cable	Video for sale or rent	Cinema	Radio	Still photo in adult magazine
Should be:	%	%	%	%	%	%
Not allowed at all	54	47	42	45	48	37
Special adult channel/ cinema/shop	na	19	27	25	na	35
After midnight	19	12	na	na	18	na
After 10pm/18+	19	15	26	25	20	24
After 9pm/15+	6	5	3	4	7	2
After 8pm/12+	1	2	1	1	5	1

Base: 1172

na = not asked

An interesting feature about both of the previous tables is the tiny minority of people (in single figure percentages) who could be classified as outright libertarians, believing that the claims of free expression always outweigh the claims of restricted access. Again, however, we shall show that, when the notion of context is introduced, attitudes do shift.

Premium-rate adult telephone services

Given that people's censoriousness about the portrayal of sex is greater with respect to universally available regular television channels than to more restricted outlets, we would have expected relatively uncensorious attitudes towards adult telephone services - which are available only to the person who seeks them out. But this was not the case. We asked:

> *There are certain telephone numbers which people can ring to hear*
> *sexual recorded messages. Please use this card to say how widely*
> *you think these telephone numbers should be available. Imagine a*
> *telephone number where a woman describes sexual acts with a man*
> *and uses explicit language.*

In the equivalent question about homosexual sex read:

> *Imagine a telephone number where a man describes sexual acts with*
> *another man and uses explicit language.*

The availability of sexually explicit telephone services generated much greater disapproval even than sex on the regular television channels. More than twice the proportion that had favoured a ban on heterosexual sex in films on television approved of a ban on telephone sexual services.[3] Moreover, those who thought that such services should be available "only to adults who had chosen to have the service" overwhelmingly favoured an opt-in (applying for a special code) over an opt-out. Interestingly, however, the extent of disapproval in the case of telephone services was not noticeably different according to whether the telephone service related to heterosexual or homosexual sex (56 and 60 per cent respectively wanting such a ban).

Nor were people keen on allowing advertisements for such adult telephone services, with much the same proportions (55 per cent and 60 per cent respectively) wanting advertisements for heterosexual and homosexual telephone services banned altogether, even from adult magazines.

So the privacy of the sexual portrayal does not, in itself, seem to be the dominant factor in people's judgements, as telephone services certainly provide private encounters. The nature of the encounter seems to matter too. There are a number of possible reasons for this: the almost universal availability of telephones, the easy access for children, the intimacy of the telephone, the 'pay-as-you-go' nature of the transaction, and the possible assumption by some respondents that the portrayal might be 'real life' as opposed to the implicit fictional representations given in the other media.

Interim conclusions

So far we have found rather restrictive views on the portrayal of sex in the media. As always, there is no *consensus* among the public, but there is certainly a tendency towards restrictiveness rather than permissiveness about when and to whom frank sex scenes should be available in the mass media. There are indeed differences between the media, with the outlets that are the most accessible (regular television and radio) attracting the most restrictive attitudes (apart from telephone services, which are perhaps a special case).

But the differences between the media are generally relatively small. Nonetheless, before we conclude that there is a public clamour for a more restrictive approach to the portrayal of sex in the media, we need to distinguish between different sorts of portrayal. In short, we need to find out whether a scene's sexual content *per se* is the primary issue of concern, regardless of what sort of film or programme it appears in, or whether context matters too.

The impact of context

In framing the questions discussed so far on the portrayal of sex scenes, we were, of course, aware that we were asking them in a vacuum. In effect, respondents had to make judgements about scenes in the absence of what may have been highly relevant information for them relating to the gratuitousness or otherwise of the portrayal. We therefore followed this up with a separate set of questions. First we asked:

> *We have been talking about films and videos in general, but there are, of course, different types of film. Some contain sex scenes which are part of a developing relationship between the main characters. Others show sex scenes which don't seem to be essential to the plot. Think first of films in which a frank sex scene between a man and a woman character does **not** seem to be essential to the plot. Should they **ever**, in your view, be ...*
>
> *... allowed to be seen by 12 year olds?*
> *... allowed to be seen by 15 year olds?*
> *... allowed to be seen by 18 year olds?*
> *... allowed to be seen by anyone at all?*

We then asked:

> *And how about films in which a frank sex scene between a man and a woman character **is** part of a developing relationship between the main characters.*

And finally, we asked:

> *Now how about **educational videos** containing a frank sex scene of a man and a woman character having sex.*

As predicted by the Broadcasting Research Unit findings, reported earlier, it turns out that the context of the sex scene does makes a very substantial difference to people's judgements. The proportion wanting a film with a

frank sex scene banned altogether, not very high even when the sex scene is 'gratuitous' - at around 20 per cent - falls to only 12 per cent when the sex scene is 'relevant', and to eight per cent when it is part of an educational video. By the same token, the proportion who think that even 12 year olds should be allowed to see it rises from a derisory four per cent in the case of the 'gratuitous' sex scene, to 13 per cent for the 'relevant' scene and to 39 per cent for the educational video.

The impact of context

	Gratuitous sex scene	Plot-based sex scene	Educational video
	%	%	%
Not allowed to anyone at all	19	12	8
Not allowed to 18+ except in certain circumstances	3	2	1
Allowed for aged 18+	52	38	17
Allowed for aged 15+	21	33	34
Allowed for aged 12+	4	13	39

Base: 1172

When we compare these results with those we obtained from our 'context-free' questions about a cinema film given earlier, it seems that the respondents must have had a 'gratuitous' sex scene in mind. Certainly the earlier answers bear a much closer resemblance to the answers here in the first column than to those in either the second or third columns. This should be borne in mind when interpreting the earlier levels of censoriousness among the British public discussed earlier.

Sexual swearwords

As noted, there is evidence that bad language on television causes even more offence than sexual content (ITC, 1996). We asked:

> *And finally on this subject, some say that sexual swearwords have no place in films or in television; others say that they are so much part of modern life that they are acceptable nowadays. ... [at] what times, if any, would you say a film containing lots of sexual swearwords should be allowed to be shown on the regular television channels?*

The question was then repeated for films at the cinema and videos for sale and rent. Once again, the most restrictive views relate to the regular television channels. There is strong minority support for banning sexual swearwords altogether - greater indeed than for banning the heterosexual sex

scene - and the most popular category is again an 18 age limit or a ten o'clock watershed.   But there is less support for restricting films with sexual swearwords to special adult cinemas or shops or for showing then only after midnight. And more people seem to feel that a 15 age limit or a nine o'clock watershed is appropriate for films with many sexual swearwords.   So attitudes to sexual swearwords are slightly more polarised than are attitudes to sex scenes, producing even less consensus on an appropriate policy.

Film with lots of sexual swearwords

	Regular TV	**Video for sale or rent**	**Cinema**
Should be:	%	%	%
Not allowed at all	29	25	23
Special adult channel/cinema/shop	na	13	10
After midnight	15	na	na
After 10pm/18+	36	40	42
After 9pm/15+	16	17	20
After 8pm/12+	4	3	3

Base: 1172

na = not asked

Variations in attitudes across the population

So far we have seen that there is widespread public disapproval of the explicit and gratuitous portrayal of sex by the media, but there is also widespread disapproval of outright bans on such material. We now dig a little deeper into the data to find out not only what proportions of the total population fall into these different camps, but also which groups take which views. After all, different media are popular with different kinds of people; and most media consumption takes place in different contexts and at different times of the day. Is this related to people's views? This analysis might also give us some clues about likely future trends in attitudes.

  So we shall investigate briefly here the extent to which views on sex in the media are related to four main sets of factors: the socio-demographic characteristics of respondents; their level of media exposure; their general beliefs and value systems; and their attitudes towards questions of sexual morality in general, rather than to the portrayal of sex *per se*.

  A useful way of summarising the results of a series of questions is to construct an additive index (or scale) of attitudes. The assumption behind such an index is that a person's answers to each question reflect his or her general underlying beliefs or attitudes rather than being just a top-of-the-head response to that question. In other words, this approach is justified if a

person's response to one question is a reasonably reliable predictor of their answers to a series of related questions.

This does indeed turn out to be the case. Respondents tend to give similar answers to each of our questions about the sex scenes irrespective of the medium to which the question referred.[4] We have therefore been able to construct three indices of censoriousness or permissiveness - one relating to the heterosexual sex scene, one to the homosexual sex scene and one relating to swearwords, each *combining* the responses to the different media questions.[5] (The construction of the indices is described in greater detail in the Appendix to this chapter).

Scores on the indices range from one to six. A score of one indicates that the respondent wanted the scene banned in all circumstances and a score of six that the respondent would allow it to be shown to anyone or at any time. So, for simplicity, the whole spectrum of public opinion from 'ban everything' to 'allow everything' is encompassed in an index of only six points. This means that seemingly quite small differences in index scores can turn out to be significant, in both the statistical and colloquial sense of the word.

Given the generally rather restrictive views of the British population that we have already reported, it is hardly surprising that the scores on the indices are fairly skewed towards the lower end (especially the one relating to the portrayal of homosexual sex).

Distributions of the permissiveness indices scores
(low scores = restrictive attitudes; high scores = permissive attitudes)

Score:	Heterosexual sex	Homosexual sex	Swearwords
	%	%	%
1 - 1.99	25	54	28
2 - 2.99	38	29	22
3 - 3.99	32	15	37
4 - 4.99	5	2	11
5 - 6	1	*	2
Base:	*1125*	*1136*	*1153*

With the aid of these relatively crude but generally robust 'permissiveness indices', we can now examine just which subgroups score relatively high or low on permissiveness and restrictiveness.

Socio-demographic factors

We looked first at socio-demographic factors, which we knew would be related to attitudes on these issues. Not only was there evidence from earlier research on broadcasting that age and gender were discriminators of attitudes, but earlier findings from the *British Social Attitudes* series itself (see, for instance, Airey and Brook, 1986), show that attitudes to moral issues in general are closely related to factors such as age, gender and religion.

  Naturally, we are looking here for relationships rather than causes. The fact that attitudes and other variables are correlated says nothing for the moment about the direction of causation. We try to tease out likely causes and effects later by means of multivariate statistical techniques.

Permissiveness indices scores by socio-demographic factors

(low scores = restrictive attitudes; high scores = permissive attitudes)

	Heterosexual sex		Homosexual sex		Swearwords	
		Base		*Base*		*Base*
All	2.55	*1125*	1.91	*1136*	2.60	*1153*
Age						
18-24	3.13	*91*	2.39	*91*	3.52	*92*
25-44	2.90	*444*	2.25	*442*	2.98	*447*
45-64	2.41	*328*	1.71	*332*	2.42	*335*
65+	1.76	*260*	1.29	*268*	1.70	*275*
Gender						
Men	2.66	*516*	1.94	*523*	2.74	*531*
Women	2.45	*609*	1.87	*613*	2.48	*622*
Religious attendance						
Once a week	1.99	*101*	1.50	*101*	1.87	*102*
Once a month	2.44	*123*	1.98	*122*	2.39	*127*
Less often	2.59	*84*	1.92	*83*	2.65	*86*
No religion	2.95	*817*	2.21	*830*	3.21	*838*
Highest educational qualification						
Degree	3.00	*98*	2.71	*101*	3.13	*104*
Higher education below degree	2.65	*141*	2.02	*140*	2.67	*143*
A-level (or equivalent)	2.85	*167*	2.15	*168*	3.01	*167*
O-level (or equivalent)	2.71	*218*	1.99	*218*	2.73	*222*
CSE (or equivalent)	2.42	*92*	1.74	*94*	2.37	*97*
None/foreign	2.19	*409*	1.53	*415*	2.22	*420*

Age, as expected, makes a substantial difference to attitudes in all three columns. In respect of heterosexual sex, for instance, the 18-24 age group

(albeit a fairly small group) has an average score of 3.13, comfortably the most permissive score to appear anywhere in the column, while those aged 65 and over have an average score of 1.76, approaching the lowest score available on any of the three indices. This contrast is just as stark in relation to sexual swearwords, but not in relation to homosexual sex. Not only are the absolute levels of index scores here more restrictive, but the age difference, although still apparent, is not quite as large. Indeed, the differences based on educational qualifications are actually larger.

We cannot, of course, draw inferences from a cross-sectional study about why this age difference has arisen. It could be because people become more restrictive in these matters as they get older (whether through the process of ageing *per se* or through life-cycle milestones such as parenting), or that people carry their attitudes with them into older age - a so-called 'cohort effect' - in which case society's attitudes are likely to become more permissive as younger cohorts replace the older ones.[6]

Gender differences are much smaller than age differences and, in the case of homosexual sex, not statistically significant. But, as we shall see, such gender differences as there are do not disappear when we control for the effect of age.

Religiosity is certainly important to attitudes, particularly so in relation to sexual swearwords: regular 'church' attenders have an average score of 1.87, compared to a score of 3.21 for those with no religion - the most permissive score in the table other than in the 18-24 age group. Because religious attendance tends to vary with age, the size of this difference is somewhat exaggerated, but as we shall see, it does not disappear altogether when we control for the effect of age.

We have not included socio-economic group differences in the table because they are too small to show interesting patterns. Educational qualifications do, however, discriminate. Broadly, the higher one's education, the more permissive one is, particularly in relation to the homosexual sex scene.

We also looked at the possible effects of parenthood on attitudes, but found no consistent patterns. Our hypothesis was that people with current parental responsibilities, particularly perhaps those with children in the age groups (secondary school age) where sex becomes an issue, would be more restrictive than those without children, thus displaying a typical 'life-cycle effect'. But the effects are small and are not included in the table. While parental responsibility does appear to have some effect - for example those with children aged five or over are a little more restrictive than their counterparts who do not have children - it does not seem to have a major impact, and it has almost no impact on attitudes towards swearwords. Ruling out this 'life-cycle effect' as a major determinant of attitude change does suggest that the observed relationship between age and attitudes identified above is to a substantial degree a 'cohort effect'.

Combining the socio-demographic factors

We have shown that age, for instance, is strongly related to attitudes towards the portrayal of sex in the media. But, as noted, age is also related to several other socio-demographic variables, such as education and religious attendance, so we need to disentangle the individual effects if we are to be able to assess the importance of each factor relative to the others. To do this, we have to create a multivariate statistical model which allows us to look at each factor in turn, taking the others into account, so that its particular influence can be identified (see the Appendix to this chapter - Model 1 - for details).

The statistical model identified the following factors, in order of importance, as having a significant impact on the permissiveness indices scores:

Heterosexual sex	**Homosexual sex**	**Swearwords**
Age	Age	Age
Church attendance	Education	Church attendance
Education	Church attendance	Education
Gender	Parental responsibility	Gender
Parental responsibility	Non-manual occupation	

Age then turns out to be by far the most important factor in all three cases in its own right. Religious attendance and education also retain a strong relationship to attitudes, even when the effect of other factors such as age are taken into account. The modelling confirms the lower importance of parental responsibility and class on attitudes. Gender too is of less importance than age, religion or education, but men do tend to be significantly more permissive than women even when all the other factors are taken into account.

These socio-demographic factors account for around a third of the variance in attitudes towards the heterosexual sex scene and swearwords and for around two fifths of the variance in attitudes towards the homosexual sex scene. By any standards of statistical modelling in the social sciences, this is a substantial amount to have been accounted for. Even so, there must be other factors not included in the models above.

Media exposure

We had anticipated that exposure to media would be related to attitudes to the portrayal of sex in the media. Our hypothesis was that greater exposure to television viewing, satellite or cable channels, video watching and cinema going would be related to more permissive attitudes towards the portrayal of sex in the media.

A close look at the data shows, however, that our hypothesis was far too simple.   True, there are some relationships between media exposure and attitudes to the portrayal of sex, but they are rather weak ones, and not necessarily in the expected direction.

Permissiveness indices scores by media exposure
(low scores = restrictive attitudes; high scores = permissive attitudes)

	Heterosexual sex		Homosexual sex		Swearwords	
Television viewing: hours per week		*Base*		*Base*		*Base*
0 - 14	2.63	*300*	2.00	*302*	2.64	*307*
15 -20	2.70	*170*	2.10	*172*	2.82	*175*
21 -30	2.53	*328*	1.82	*330*	2.60	*335*
31+	2.41	*322*	1.79	*327*	2.44	*332*
Whether respondent has satellite/cable TV						
Has satellite/cable TV	2.71	*226*	2.03	*229*	2.83	*230*
Does not	2.51	*899*	1.87	*907*	2.54	*923*
How often respondent watches rented or bought videos						
Once a week or more	2.71	*104*	1.99	*104*	2.89	*103*
Once a month or more	2.86	*182*	2.16	*185*	3.02	*187*
Once a year or more	2.74	*314*	2.04	*314*	2.79	*318*
Less often	2.34	*310*	1.77	*314*	2.27	*319*
No video recorder	2.17	*215*	1.60	*219*	2.26	*226*
How often respondent goes to the cinema						
Once a month or more	3.21	*90*	2.50	*89*	3.34	*90*
Once a year or more	2.86	*345*	2.18	*346*	3.02	*349*
Less often	2.28	*690*	1.67	*701*	2.27	*714*

As for television viewing, the figures suggest that the relationship is quite contrary to the one we had anticipated.   In general, those who watch most television tend to be more restrictive in their attitudes towards the portrayal of sex.   But this turns out to be largely because the volume of television viewing is also tied up with age.   When we control for the effect of age, the amount of television viewing largely ceases to have a significant relationship with attitudes.   The availability of satellite or cable television also seems to have a relationship with attitudes, this time in the expected direction.   But again, when we control for age, the relationship disappears.

The frequency of watching videos and of going to the cinema do have stronger relationships with attitudes and, although they become weaker when we control for age, they remain significant.   In general, those with greater exposure to videos and the cinema are more likely to be permissive in their

attitudes towards the portrayal of sex. But, curiously, the pattern does not hold for the group that watches the most videos, and this oddity remains after controlling for age. We wondered whether this group might include a disproportionately large number of parents who watched videos with their young children but this appears not to be the case. When we combine all four media exposure factors with age into one model (see Model 2 in the appendix to this chapter for details), age remains by far the most dominant factor. The only media exposure factor to retain a reasonable amount of importance is cinema attendance. The most frequent cinema-goers, regardless of age, are the least censorious about the portrayal of sex.

In summary, then, the relationship between media exposure and attitudes appears to be weak, somewhat inconsistent and dwarfed by comparison with the impact of age.

The role of underlying belief and value systems

The factors we have investigated so far (socio-demographic characteristics and media exposure) account for some but by no means all of the variation in people's attitudes towards the portrayal of sex in the media. We turn now to the possible role of underlying belief and value systems (see Jowell and Park, 1996) as a source of variation.

The *British Social Attitudes* dataset contains among its standard scales of questions one designed to measure underlying values on a 'libertarian-authoritarian' dimension (see Appendix I of this Report). When we divide sample members according to their scores on this scale we find that the most libertarian group scored, for instance, an average of 3.13 on the permissiveness index for the heterosexual sex scene compared with 2.45 for the most authoritarian group.[7] Here then is another strong relationship, which retains statistical significance after controlling for the effect of age.

Permissiveness indices scores by underlying libertarian-authoritarian values

(low scores = restrictive attitudes; high scores = permissive attitudes)

	Heterosexual sex		Homosexual sex		Swearwords	
		Base		*Base*		*Base*
Most libertarian quintile	3.13	*139*	2.67	*143*	3.38	*145*
2nd quintile	2.82	*181*	2.12	*181*	2.83	*182*
3rd quintile	2.57	*230*	1.87	*231*	2.59	*233*
4th quintile	2.33	*205*	1.73	*208*	2.29	*214*
Most authoritarian quintile	2.45	*217*	1.56	*217*	2.28	*217*

But all of the above models fail to take account of one further source of variation in people's attitudes towards the portrayal of sex in the media - moral attitudes towards sex itself: perceptions of 'right' and 'wrong' in sexual relations.

The *British Social Attitudes* series includes three long-running questions about pre-marital, extra-marital and homosexual sex that we can use as a proxy for this dimension. These 'sexual morality' questions are:

> *Now I would like to ask you some questions about sexual relationships. If a man and a woman have sexual relations before marriage, what would your general opinion be?*

> *What about a married person having sexual relations with someone other than his or her partner?*

> *What about sexual relations between two adults of the same sex?*

In each case, respondents are asked to make judgements on a five-point scale running from "always wrong" to "not at all wrong". In general, there is widespread agreement that pre-marital sex is acceptable and that extra-marital sex is not. Views are divided on homosexual sex (55 per cent say it is always wrong, but 29 per cent say that it is rarely or not at all wrong). Earlier research has shown that a moral disapproval of homosexuality does not necessarily feed through into approval for discrimination against homosexuals (Snape *et al*, 1995), but we were interested to see whether it did feed through into a desire to have the portrayal of homosexual sex scenes restricted in the media.

As shown in the next table, people's answers to the sexual morality questions are indeed closely related to their attitudes towards the portrayal of sex in the media. Attitudes to *pre-marital* sex, for instance, are related strongly and straightforwardly to all three permissiveness indices and in the expected direction. Indeed, those who say that pre-marital sex is "always wrong" tend to have the most restrictive scores we have seen anywhere - more restrictive even than those in the 65 and over group.

A relationship also exists between views on *extra-marital* sex and the portrayal of sex in the media. In general, the more disapproving of extra-marital sex one is, the more restrictive are one's attitudes towards the portrayal of sex in the media. The group who think extra-marital sex is rarely wrong or not wrong at all seem to hold inconsistent views, but this group is so small that not much reliance can be placed on this finding.

In the case of attitudes to *homosexual* sex, we see again the expected relationship in a straightforward way: those who think homosexual sex is wrong are more likely to hold restrictive views about the portrayal of sex in the media - and particularly about the portrayal of homosexual sex.

Permissiveness indices scores by moral values about sex

(low scores = restrictive attitudes; high scores = permissive attitudes)

	Heterosexual sex		Homosexual sex		Swearwords	
Pre-marital sex		*Base*		*Base*		*Base*
Always wrong	1.62	*104*	1.22	*106*	1.59	*109*
Mostly wrong	1.99	*101*	1.33	*101*	1.78	*105*
Sometimes wrong	2.30	*178*	1.63	*181*	2.22	*180*
Rarely wrong	2.66	*107*	2.04	*106*	2.85	*108*
Not wrong at all	2.89	*574*	2.21	*579*	3.01	*586*
Extra-marital sex						
Always wrong	2.31	*615*	1.66	*621*	2.33	*630*
Mostly wrong	2.81	*316*	2.16	*316*	2.92	*320*
Sometimes wrong	2.99	*128*	2.37	*128*	2.96	*130*
Rarely wrong	2.73	*15*	1.89	*16*	2.96	*17*
Not wrong at all	2.80	*19*	2.19	*19*	2.42	*19*
Homosexual sex						
Always wrong	2.22	*517*	1.41	*525*	2.18	*532*
Mostly wrong	2.49	*123*	1.79	*124*	2.56	*124*
Sometimes wrong	2.84	*105*	2.23	*108*	2.96	*108*
Rarely wrong	3.04	*75*	2.57	*74*	3.11	*76*
Not wrong at all	3.04	*243*	2.64	*244*	3.19	*247*

Notably, each of the three sexual morality questions retained their significance when the scores on the other two questions *and* the effect of age were taken into account (see Model 4 in the appendix to this chapter). Indeed, the relationship between attitudes towards the *practice* of homosexual sex and attitudes towards the *portrayal* of homosexual sex is actually stronger than that between age and the portrayal of homosexual sex. This could signal a possible future liberalisation of attitudes towards the portrayal of homosexual sex in the media, since the *British Social Attitudes* surveys also find that disapproval of homosexuality has fallen from a high point of 75 per cent in 1987 (at the height of the AIDS scare and its almost exclusive association at that time with gay men) to its present level of 55 per cent.

A combined model

When we take the logical final step in our analysis and combine all those factors that we have been found to be significant into one model (Model 5 in the appendix to this chapter), we find that the following factors, in order of importance, have the most significant relationships with our permissiveness indices scores:

Heterosexual sex	Homosexual sex	Swearwords
Age	Attitude to homosexual sex	Age
Attitude to pre-marital sex	Age	Attitude to pre-marital sex
Gender	Education	Libertarian-authoritarian
Libertarian-authoritarian	Libertarian-authoritarian	Cinema attendance
Cinema attendance	Church attendance	Gender
Attitude to homosexual sex	Attitude to extra-marital sex	Attitude to homosexual sex
Parental responsibility		Church attendance

This combined model explains over 45 per cent of the variance in attitudes towards the portrayal of sex in the media - none of the models without the sexual morality questions explained more than about a third. This confirms the importance of people's wider attitudes to sexual morality in predicting their attitudes to the portrayal of sex in the media. Indeed, while age is still in general the most important factor in explaining such attitudes, attitudes towards other aspects of sexual morality now appear as comfortably the second most important factor and, in the case of the portrayal of homosexuality, the most important one. We still cannot be sure whether this results from life-cycle changes or cohort effects - that is whether the relatively permissive young of today will become more restrictive as they get older, or whether they will carry their more permissive attitudes with them into older age. But, given the earlier discussion about the relative lack of importance of parental responsibility, the cohort explanation is tentatively the safer bet, with each generation likely to retain (at least to some extent) its earlier-formed attitudes to moral issues of this kind.

The importance of people's more general belief and value systems in determining attitudes towards the portrayal of sex in the media is also shown by the prominent appearance of the libertarian-authoritarian scale score in all three models. These underlying values are not simply a proxy for the specific items on sexual morality. In all three models, two of the three sexual morality questions retain significance even after controlling for the effect of the libertarian-authoritarian beliefs. This is, of course, particularly true of attitudes towards the portrayal of homosexual sex where the most relevant sexual morality question (attitudes towards the practice of homosexuality) is the most important factor in the model.

Even having controlled for the three major predictive variables - age, general value systems and attitudes to aspects of sexual morality - we find that religiosity still retains its importance, particularly in people's attitudes to swearwords. Gender too makes an appearance, with women being more restrictive than men on the heterosexual sex scene and on swearwords. (Could this be because so much of the media's traditional focus on sexuality has been designed largely for male consumption?) And education still matters with respect to attitudes to the homosexual sex scene, the more educated being the more permissive. The only media exposure variable to make it into the combined model - cinema attendance - is significantly

associated with permissiveness in relation to the heterosexual sex scene and swearwords.

A word of caution

We have implicitly treated the respondents' answers here as if they were based on robust and strongly-held attitudes, careful judgements, deep-seated values, long-standing prejudices, or a combination of all of these. And indeed the answers about the different media showed a high degree of stability. It would, however, be remiss if we did not report that a very different picture might have been painted if we had relied for our analysis instead on a set of agree-disagree items included in the self-completion supplement of the questionnaire.

% who agree or agree strongly that ...

... people over the age of 16 are old enough to decide for themselves what they want to see and read	48
... the easy availability of pornography will lead to more sex crimes	54
... we should be more worried about the amount of violence on TV than the amount of sex on TV	62
... adults should be allowed to see whatever films they like, even if some people think the films violent or pornographic	55

Base: 1023

If we had only had these questions to go by, we might have concluded that the British are, on the whole, a pretty permissive lot as far as the portrayal of sex was concerned. There is certainly a correlation between the answers people give to these questions and those they give to our other questions reported earlier. What is surprising, however, is that the correlation is not greater. For example, among those who would *ban* a frank heterosexual sex scene on regular television, even after midnight, over one in three also agree that adults should be allowed to see whatever films they want. Although it is possible to imagine arguments that would make these positions logically coherent, it seems more likely that respondents are somewhat inconsistent in their views - perhaps responding greatly to the context in which the question is put.[8] If so, answers will vary greatly according to the specific cue and context of the question asked. We have already seen, for instance, that our initial impression of the British as a prudish nation was greatly tempered when the context of the sex scene was taken into account. This makes surveys of public attitudes towards subjects like these particularly difficult. Many questions are needed, from all angles - and the more specific the better - if the ground is to be covered adequately, let alone if the aim is to dig

beneath the surface. This needs to be borne in mind when comparing results from different surveys.

Conclusions

One of our main aims was to compare attitudes towards the 'rules' that should govern the treatment of much the same material by different media. In the absence of any reference to context, we find that about one in five people take a hard line on censorship, wanting a complete ban on explicit heterosexual scenes, wherever they appear. (A slightly higher proportion would ban these scenes altogether from television and a slightly smaller proportion would ban all magazine photographs that portrayed them.) A further fifth or so of the population would like to see access to such films or programmes restricted to special adult cinemas, shops or channels, or to be shown only after midnight. Most of the remainder of the population, constituting comfortably the largest group, would like to see an 18 age limit or a ten o'clock watershed on such scenes - but again, only when the context is not specified. Attitudes are much more restrictive towards the portrayal of frank homosexual sex scenes and adult premium-rate telephone services.

Despite the overall similarity between attitudes to the portrayal of sex by different media, the data do shed some light on the particular properties of different media that cause concern. While reactions towards an explicit sex scene in a cinema or on a video were almost identical, there is some evidence that restricted or conditional access to a particular media outlet *does* incline people to become more permissive. The two freely available broadcast media, for instance - terrestrial television and radio - attracted the highest proportion of absolute censors, despite the fact that radio's absence of pictures might have made the portrayals less offensive to some. So the introduction of barriers to access, such as smartcards, which require a positive act of personal selection, as well as preventing certain age groups from having access to this sort of material, would probably allay many anxieties.

The exception to this rule appears to be the phenomenon of adult premium-rate telephone services. On the one hand, this is the one medium which combines several factors that might ameliorate the impact of offensive material: sound only, privacy, and restricted to those who exercise the choice to dial a particular number. Yet some 56 per cent of the population still feel that these services should be banned altogether, representing a higher proportion of unconditional censors than for any of the other scenarios. As noted, there are a number of possible reasons for this and further research would be required to disentangle various potential contributing factors.

Responses to questions about the *context* in which explicit sex scenes appear demonstrate conclusively that most people's attitudes to what is permissible are by no means absolute. To the extent that a frank sex scene is justified by plot or purpose, most people are much more permissive towards it.

Importantly, our data offer strong evidence that people's initial responses to questions about sex in the media are based on the assumption that their portrayal is gratuitous rather than otherwise, demonstrating one of the difficulties of generalising from research in this field.

The single most important factor that relates to people's attitudes towards the portrayal of sex in the media is their age. The older one is, the more restrictive one's attitudes are likely to be. This seems to be caused at least partly by a so-called 'cohort effect', the phenomenon of carrying one's prior attitudes from youth into old age. If so, the aggregate national attitude is likely to become more permissive over time. The link between permissiveness and education, which was particularly strong for the homosexual sex scene, would tend to act in the same direction. In any event, the only life-cycle effect that we were able to measure on this occasion - parental responsibility - had only a weak relationship with attitudes.

After age, the next most influential factors predicting attitudes to the portrayal of sex in the media are attitudes to sexual morality and underlying value systems in general. For each of the three scenarios we presented - a heterosexual sex scene, a homosexual sex scene, and a film containing many sexual swearwords - there was at least one attitudinal factor which counted for more than gender, educational background or even religiosity. This helps to explain to some extent the large difference in public attitudes to the portrayal of homosexual sex scenes as compared to heterosexual sex scenes. It appears to be not so much the *representation* of the act in the media that many people object to as the act itself, and therefore its portrayal. Indeed, the more censorious or restrictive people are about aspects of sexual morality in general, the more restrictive they will tend to be about the portrayal of sex in the media.

Media regulators and policy makers will doubtless wish to take note of this relationship, since as public attitudes towards homosexuality change (and there is evidence that they are already changing fairly rapidly), so the perceived offence from its portrayal is likely to diminish. They will also wish to take note of the confirmatory evidence we have presented of the critical importance of context in mitigating the potential offence of explicit sexual scenes.

Notes

1. For each licensed service, the ITC must ensure "that nothing is included in its programmes which offends against good taste or decency or is likely to ... be offensive to public feeling". Section 90(1)(a) places precisely the same obligation on the Radio Authority in respect of licensing all non-BBC radio stations.
2. Note that for satellite and cable television, *both* the answer options of "only on a special adult channel" and "only after midnight" were available. In the scales and the multivariate analysis used later in the chapter, these two categories have been combined.
3. This finding should, however, be interpreted with some caution, since the answers may be affected by the so-called 'format effects'. The telephone questions had much shorter

lists of answer categories than did the questions about the other media, and both the length and labelling of the answer scale can affect answers (see, for instance, Foddy, 1993).

4. This can be seen if we examine the correlations between the questions about each scene. The lowest correlation (Kendal's tau-b) between any pair of questions about the same scene was 0.49. All the correlations are statistically significant at the 0.1% level.

5. An exploratory factor analysis using an oblique rotation covering all fifteen questions from the three scenarios uncovered three factors corresponding to the three scenarios. The three factors had correlations between each other ranging from 0.59 to 0.70. Separate factor analyses of each of the three scenarios failed to uncover more than one factor in each.

6. A correlation between attitudes and age may arise in three different ways - 'ageing/life-cycle effects', 'cohort effects' and 'period effects'. The data from any one cross-sectional survey cannot fully disentangle these statistically, although the data can be used to give some pointers (see, for example, Heath and Martin, 1996 forthcoming).

7. There is one slight aberration in that the most authoritarian group are actually slightly more permissive on the heterosexual sex scene than the next most authoritarian group, but the general pattern is clear nonetheless.

8. In the case of two of the self-completion attitude statements - people deciding for themselves, and adults being allowed to see whatever films they want - there may well be some 'acquiescence bias': the tendency of some respondents to agree with any statement rather than disagree (see, for example, Schuman and Presser, 1981). In the 1996 *British Social Attitudes* survey, which deals with attitudes towards the portrayal of violence in the media, these questions have been replaced by 'forced choice' questions, where respondents have to choose between two diametrically opposed statements.

References

Advertising Standards Authority (1990), *Herself Reappraised,* London: ASA.

Advertising Standards Authority (1995), *British Codes of Advertising and Sales Promotion,* London: ASA.

Airey, C and Brook, L. (1986), 'Interim report: social and moral issues', in Jowell, R., Witherspoon, S. and Brook, L. (eds.), in *British Social Attitudes: the 1986 report,* Aldershot: Gower.

Andrews, F., Morgan, J. and Sonquist, J. (1967), *Multiple Classification Analysis: a report on a computer program for multiple regression using categorical predictors,* Ann Arbor, Michigan: Survey Research Centre, Institute for Social Research.

BBC (1993), *Producers' Guidelines,* London: BBC.

British Board of Film Classification (1992), *A Student's Guide to Film Classification and Censorship in Britain,* London: BBFC.

British Board of Film Classification (1995), *Annual Report 1994-5,* London: BBFC.

British Board of Film Classification (1996), *Annual Report 1995-6,* London: BBFC.

Broadcasting Act 1990, London: HMSO.

Broadcasting Standards Council (1989), *Annual Report 1988-9,* London: BSC.

Broadcasting Standards Council (1994), *A Code of Practice,* 2nd Edition, London: BSC.

Cumberbatch, G. and Howitt, D. (1989), *A Measure of Uncertainty,* London: John Libbey.

Docherty D., Morrison D. and Tracey M. (1988), *Keeping Faith? Channel 4 and its Audience,* London: John Libbey.

Foddy, W. (1993), *Constructing questions for interviews and questionnaires: theory and practice in social research,* Cambridge: Cambridge University Press.

Heath, A. and Martin, J. (1996, forthcoming), 'Changing attitudes towards abortion: life-cycle, period and cohort effects' in Taylor, B. and Thomson, K. (eds.), *Understanding Change in Social Attitudes,* Aldershot: Dartmouth.

Independent Committee for the Supervision of Standards of Telephone Information Services (1995), *Code of Practice, 7th Edition,* London: ICSTIS.

Independent Television Commission (1995), *The ITC Programme Code*, London: ITC.

Independent Television Commission (1996), *Television: The Public's View 1995*, London: ITC.

Jowell, R. and Park, A. (1996, forthcoming), 'Questioning British attitudes' in Taylor, B. and Thomson, K. (eds.), *Understanding Change in Social Attitudes,* Aldershot: Dartmouth.

Millwood Hargrave, A. (1992), *Sex and Sexuality in Broadcasting,* London, John Libbey.

Mill, J.S. (1989), *On Liberty and Other Writings*, Collini, S. (ed.), Cambridge: Cambridge University Press.

Pearson, G. (1983), *Hooligan: a history of respectable fears*, London: Macmillan.

Press Complaints Commission (1995), *Code of Practice*, London: PCC.

Robertson, G. (1993), *Freedom, The Individual and the Law (7th edition),* London: Penguin.

Schuman, H. and Presser, S. (1981), *Questions and Answers in Attitude Surveys: Experiments on Question Form, Wording, and Context*, San Diego: Academic Press, Inc.

Snape, D., Thomson, K. and Chetwynd, M. (1995), *Discrimination Against Gay Men and Lesbians: a Study of the Nature and Extent of Discrimination Against Homosexual Men and Women in Britain Today*, London: SCPR.

Acknowledgements

SCPR is grateful to the British Board of Film Classification, the Broadcasting Standards Council and the Independent Committee for the Supervision of Standards of Telephone Information Services for their financial support which enabled us to ask the questions reported in this chapter. We are also grateful to these bodies, and particularly to James Ferman of the BBFC who convened the group, for their ideas and guidance in devising and designing the questions.

Appendix

Permissiveness indices

To construct the indices, the scores on the six questions for the heterosexual and homosexual scenarios and three questions for the swearword scenario were summed and divided by six or three respectively, giving indices which run from 1 (= most restrictive) to 6 (= most permissive). The categories of "only on special adult channels" and "only after midnight" were combined for the satellite and cable television questions, giving all the questions the same number of answer categories, numbered one to six.

Cronbach's alpha for the indices are:

Heterosexual sex scene index	0.91
Homosexual sex scene index	0.94
Swearword index	0.94

Multivariate modelling

The multivariate modelling was done using Multivariate Classification Analysis (MCA). MCA is a technique for examining the interrelationships between several independent (explanatory) variables and an interval level (or above) dependent variable (here, the indices scores). The independent variables need be no more than nominal level measures. MCA shows the effect of each independent variable after taking into account the effects of all other independent variables that are entered into the model (Andrews *et al*, 1967).

MCA produces a partial beta for each independent variable roughly equivalent to a standardised partial regression coefficient. This is a measure of the ability of the variable to explain variation in the dependent variable after adjusting for the effects of all other independent variables. For the model as a whole, MCA produces a multiple correlation coefficient, which when squared (R^2) indicates the proportion of the variance in the dependent variable explained by all the independent variables together (after adjusting for degrees of freedom).

A major limitation of the this technique, however, is that it requires a large amount of computer power. The number of independent variables, and the number of levels within each variable, entered into the model therefore needs to be kept strictly limited. Some summarising of variables was therefore necessary before carrying out the modelling.

The models reported here are main effects models. In the larger models it was impossible to compute interaction effects owing to empty cells. The smaller models have therefore also been presented as main effects models in the interest of comparability.

Respondents for whom the heterosexual sex scene, homosexual sex scene or swearwords index score is unobtainable (due to "Don't know" answers, refusal or missing data) are excluded from the analysis for that scale.

A word of warning: the selection of the independent variables is, of course, done by the human being not by the computer program. Any model is only as good as the selection of independent variables.

Model 1 - Socio-demographic characteristics

Dependent variables:

- heterosexual sex scene index score
- homosexual sex scene index score
- swearwords index score

Independent variables:

RAGECAT - respondent's age
1   18-24
2   25-44
3   45-64
4   65+

Since age is such an important independent variable, cases where age was unavailable were excluded from the analysis.

RSEX - respondent's gender
1   male
2   female

CHATTEND - religious attendance
1   Once a week or more
2   Less often but at least once a month
3   Less often than that
4   No current religion and not brought up in any religion

RMANUAL - manual/non-manual in current or last job
1   Non-manual
2   Manual/no information

HEDQUAL - highest educational qualification
1   Degree
2   O-level or above, below degree
3   CSE/None/Foreign qualification

CHILDRE2 - children of the respondent in the household
0   No children
1   Child under 5, no child 5-19
2   Child under 5 and child 5-19
3   Child 5-19, no child under 5

	Heterosexual sex	Homosexual sex	Swearwords
	Beta	Beta	Beta
RAGECAT	0.44**	0.34**	0.44**
RSEX	0.10**	0.04	0.11**
CHATTEND	0.19**	0.15**	0.21**
RMANUAL	0.04	0.07**	0.03
HEDQUAL	0.15**	0.25**	0.12**
CHILDRE2	0.09**	0.08*	0.05
R^2	0.325	0.290	0.331
Base	*1123*	*1133*	*1149*

**   Significant at 1% level
*   Significant at 5% level

Model 2 - Media exposure plus age

Dependent variables:

- heterosexual sex scene index score
- homosexual sex scene index score
- swearwords index score

Independent variables not previously described:

TOTALTV - hours watched per week
1   0 - 14 hours
2   15 - 20 hours
3   21 - 30 hours/ Miscellaneous answers
4   31+ hours

SATELLI2 - whether has access to satellite/cable TV
1   Has satellite/cable TV
2   Does not have satellite/cable TV

VIDFILM - how often watches video films
1   once a week or more
2   less often than once a week, but at least once a month
3   less often than once a month, but at least once a year
4   less often than once a year
5   no video

CINEOFT - how often goes to the cinema
1   once a week or more
2   less often than once a week, but at least once a month
3   less often than once a month, but at least once a year
4   less often than once a year

	Heterosexual sex	Homosexual sex	Swearwords
	Beta	Beta	Beta
RAGECAT	0.40**	0.35**	0.40**
TOTALTV	0.03	0.07*	0.03
SATELLI2	0.01	0.00	0.04
VIDFILM	0.10*	0.08	0.09*
CINEOFT	0.15**	0.16**	0.16**
R^2	0.285	0.224	0.296
Base	*1123*	*1133*	*1149*

**   Significant at 1% level
*   Significant at 5% level

Model 3 - general belief systems scales plus age

Dependent variables:

*   heterosexual sex scene index score
*   homosexual sex scene index score
*   swearwords index score

Independent variables not previously described:

LEFTRIGQ - left-right scale in quintiles
1   Leftmost quintile
5   Rightmost quintile

LIBAUTHQ - libertarian-authoritarian scale in quintiles
1   Most libertarian quintile
5   Most authoritarian quintile

WELFAREQ - welfare scale in quintiles
1   Least welfarist quintile
5   Most welfarist quintile

Respondents for whom the left-right, libertarian-authoritarian or welfare scale score is unobtainable (due to "Don't know" answers, refusals or missing values) are excluded from the analysis.

	Heterosexual sex	Homosexual sex	Swearwords
	Beta	Beta	Beta
RAGECAT	0.47**	0.38**	0.47**
LEFTRIGQ	0.07	0.07	0.05
LIBAUTHQ	0.21**	0.28**	0.21**
WELFAREQ	0.07	0.07	0.09*
R^2	0.335	0.300	0.338
Base	*965*	*973*	*984*

**   Significant at 1% level
*   Significant at 5% level

Model 4 - sexual morality questions plus age

Dependent variables:

- heterosexual sex scene index score
- homosexual sex scene index score
- swearwords index score

Independent variables not previously described:

PMS - views on pre-marital sex
1   always wrong
2   mostly wrong
3   sometimes wrong
4   rarely wrong
5   not at all wrong

EXMS - views on extra-marital sex
1   always wrong
2   mostly wrong
3   sometimes wrong
4   rarely wrong
5   not at all wrong

HOMOSEX - views on homosexual sex
1   always wrong
2   mostly wrong
3   sometimes wrong
4   rarely wrong
5   not at all wrong

Cases of "don't know", refusal or "it depends" on PMS, EXMS, and HOMOSEX were excluded from the analysis.

	Heterosexual sex	Homosexual sex	Swearwords
	Beta	Beta	Beta
RAGECAT	0.34**	0.21**	0.35**
PMS	0.24**	0.09*	0.25**
EXMS	0.10**	0.10**	0.09*
HOMOSEX	0.15**	0.44**	0.14**
R^2	0.373	0.419	0.379
Base	*1004*	*1011*	*1021*

** Significant at 1% level
* Significant at 5% level

Model 5 - combined model

Owing to size restrictions imposed by the SPSS implementation of the MCA procedure, the combined model was restricted to those variables which had been found to be significant at the 1% level in the earlier models.

Dependent variables:

- heterosexual sex scene index score
- homosexual sex scene index score
- swearwords index score

	Heterosexual sex	Homosexual sex	Swearwords
	Beta	Beta	Beta
RAGECAT	0.31**	0.18**	0.30**
RSEX	0.13**	n.i.	0.13**
CHATTEND	0.07	0.09**	0.10**
RMANUAL	n.i.	0.01	n.i
HEDQUAL	0.07	0.13**	0.03
CHILDRE2	0.09*	n.i.	n.i.
CINEOFT	0.11**	0.05	0.14**
LIBAUTHQ	0.12**	0.13**	0.16**
PMS	0.19**	n.i.	0.21**
EXMS	0.08	0.09*	n.i.
HOMOSEX	0.11*	0.39**	0.11*
R^2	0.447	0.466	0.454
Base	*881*	*918*	*909*

**	Significant at 1% level
*	Significant at 5% level
n.i.	Not included

3 Relative values: kinship and friendship

Francis McGlone, Alison Park and Ceridwen Roberts[*]

Concern about the state of the modern family is now widespread - often cited in terms of increasingly high levels of marital breakdown, a growth in cohabitation, juvenile delinquency, and lone parenthood. A number of social and economic changes have been blamed, ranging from increased female participation in the workforce and growing levels of job insecurity to changing government welfare policies and the decline of 'traditional family values'.

Most debate focuses on the nuclear family (comprising parents and children only), rather than on the wider family such as grandparents, cousins and so on. This is perhaps because the 'extended family' is held to be a thing of the past and people are seen to be isolated from the comfort and support that wider kin can provide. At the same time, wider family networks may be becoming more important when it comes to providing care and support. With increasing pressure on welfare state budgets, public policy interest is turning to the informal sector to provide care which can be supported by the statutory sector. Wider kin have also been targeted as key players in overcoming many of the factors that contribute towards 'poor parenting' (Utting, 1996).

Unfortunately, many of the policy discussions involving the family are conducted in the absence of any solid data. Have kinship ties really

---

[*] Francis McGlone is a Senior Research Officer at the Family Policy Studies Centre; Alison Park is a Research Director at SCPR and Co-director of the *British Social Attitudes* survey series; Ceridwen Roberts is Director of the Family Policy Studies Centre.

weakened? Has increased female participation in paid work really had an impact on the extended family? Are people really less willing than they used to be to help their relatives? Alternatively, are families binding together more than in the recent past to offer mutual aid and support in the face of new job insecurities, gaps in health services and changing welfare provision?

This chapter addresses some of these issues by examining the extent of family networks in Britain in the 1990s. We try to establish, for instance, how closely people live to their relatives, how much contact they have with them, the importance they attach to these networks and whether or not they feel that they can be called into service as sources of help and advice. In an attempt to discover whether the situation is static or changing, we shall also refer back wherever possible to comparable data from the 1986 *British Social Attitudes* survey.

Keeping in touch - the extent of family networks

Living with relatives

People are, of course, most likely to have contact with those who share their household. But the proportion of people who live with relatives, aside from partners and spouses, has been declining and the proportion who live alone has been rising. In one sense, then, this can be interpreted as evidence of a decline in the importance of the family (see, for instance, Carlson, 1993). Certainly, compared with the 1950s, fewer people nowadays live with their relatives. At that time, many adult children would routinely remain in their parents' home until they married, and even newly-married couples could not often afford to set up home on their own for some time (Willmott, 1986).

Yet, when we first covered this subject in 1986, we found that substantial proportions of people did actually share their home with one or more adult family members other than their spouse or partner. For instance, nearly four in ten parents of grown-up children lived in the same household as one or more of them. Moreover, around a fifth of people with living parents, and seven per cent of those with adult siblings, shared their home with them.

As the table below shows, all these proportions have declined over the past nine years. One-third of those with adult children now live with one or more of them, but this represents a drop of six per cent in less than a decade, and the proportions living with their parents or a sibling have also dropped sharply in the same period.

% living with a particular relative

	1986	Base	1995	Base
Adult child	38	700	32	1047
Mother	20	801	14	1138
Father	21	602	13	896
Adult sibling	7	1187	4	1748

Note: bases exclude those without the relative in question.

The key factor behind this decline is that the group who have always been by far the most likely to live with a parent (the 18-24 year olds) seem to have changed their behaviour in the intervening period. For instance, while around two in three 18 to 24 year olds lived with a parent in 1986, less than one half did so in 1995. This drop has happened despite changes in social security benefits (such as lower rates of Income Support for the under-25s), increasing unemployment and a tighter housing market, all of which would have made it more difficult for the young to set up home on their own (Finch, 1989a; Ermisch *et al*, 1995). It would appear that these changes have been more than offset by the extremely rapid increase over the last decade in the number of young people who leave their parental home in order to go to college or university (Berrington and Murphy, 1994). In any event, among older age groups there has been no change in the proportions living with a parent.

Living near relatives

Changing patterns of geographical and social mobility since the 1950s have resulted in fewer people living in close proximity to family members (Willmott, 1986). Even so, family members tend not to be scattered far and wide. Our data suggest that most people (around 60 per cent) still live within an hour's journey time from at least one close relative, and between a quarter and a third live less than 15 minutes away. Most commonly, the family member in closest proximity is an adult child. As many as around two-thirds of parents with grown-up children live less than an hour's journey time away from at least one of their sons or daughters, and around half of these live less than 15 minutes away.

Journey time to relative's home

		Less than 15 minutes	15 minutes to 1 hour	1 to 3 hours	3 hours or more	Base
Mother	%	31	34	17	16	1026
Father	%	28	30	17	18	822
Adult sibling	%	23	37	19	20	1702
Adult child	%	30	37	14	10	812
Other relative	%	30	36	17	15	1796

Note: bases exclude those without the relative in question, as well as those who live with this relative.

However, although a high proportion of people remain geographically close to family members, there has once again been a small decline over the last decade. For instance, while in 1986 70 per cent of people lived within an hour's journey time from their mother, this figure had dropped five percentage points by 1995.

% with relative where relative lives within one hour's journey

	1986		1995	
		Base		Base
Mother	70	643	65	1026
Father	67	477	62	822
Adult sibling	63	1092	59	1702
Adult child	69	420	74	812
Other relative	69	1218	67	1796

Note: bases exclude those without the relative in question, as well as those living with this relative.

Contact with relatives

So the last decade has seen a slight decline in the proportion of people who either live with a relative or within an hour's journey of one. But, of course, physical proximity is by no means the whole story. More important is the extent to which people stay in touch with family members.

As the next table shows, most people do maintain regular contact with close relatives. Nearly half of those with a mother living elsewhere see her at least once a week, and a further fifth see her at least once a month. Contact with fathers is slightly less frequent: of those who do not live with their father, around 40 per cent see him every week. What is more striking about contact with fathers, however, is the proportion of respondents - one in ten - who *never* see their father. The comparable figure for mothers is one in thirty-three.

Parents in our sample were very likely to be in frequent and regular touch with one or more of their adult sons or daughters. Around six in ten parents whose adult child had left home see him or her at least once a week (including one in ten who see them every day). Only one per cent report 'never' seeing their son or daughter.

According to our data, parent/child relationships are by far the most dominant as far as contact is concerned. Brothers and sisters, for instance, are far less likely to keep in regular contact with one another. Indeed, although they are seen less often than parents or children, relatives by marriage (the most common being a mother-in-law) are more commonly visited than other direct blood relatives such as siblings. Not surprisingly, close friends are also seen more often than most relatives. Nearly six in ten of those with close friends see their best friend on a weekly basis.

Frequency of seeing non-resident relatives/friends

		Daily	At least once a week	At least once a month	Less often	Never	Base
Mother	%	8	40	21	27	3	1026
Father	%	6	33	20	29	9	822
Adult sibling	%	4	25	21	45	4	1702
Adult child	%	10	48	16	18	1	812
Other relative	%	3	31	26	37	1	1796
'Best friend'	%	10	48	22	17	*	1768

Note: bases exclude those without the relative/friend in question, as well as those living with this relative/friend.

People also maintain a high level of contact with relatives by telephone. For instance, nearly three in four parents speak to their son or daughter at least once a week.

Is contact with the family more limited today than it was in the past? Some research certainly suggests that it is. For instance, by comparing data from various local studies on married women's contacts with their mothers, Willmott (1986) found that the proportion of women seeing their mothers once a week had clearly fallen since the 1950s. And when we compare our own findings with those of 1986, we find that contact with all types of relatives appears to have fallen even in the last decade, and this is particularly true of contact with parents. Consequently, while in 1986 nearly 60 per cent of people with a non-resident mother saw her at least once a week, only around half did so in 1995. Contact with fathers, siblings and children has declined sharply too. Moreover, it is not the case that friends are supplanting relatives in this respect. On the contrary, the proportion of people who see their best friend on a weekly basis has also fallen sharply in the last decade.

So it appears that people have generally become less likely than they were to visit or be visited by anyone.

% of respondents seeing relative/friend at least once a week

	1986		1995	
		Base		*Base*
Mother	59	*643*	49	*1026*
Father	51	*477*	40	*822*
Sibling	33	*1092*	29	*1702*
Adult child	66	*420*	58	*812*
Other relative	42	*1218*	35	*1796*
'Best friend'	65	*1224*	59	*1768*

Note: bases exclude those without the relative in question, as well as those living with this relative.

As far as relatives are concerned, this could, of course, be a consequence of people living further away from them than they did in the past. Certainly, the data show that those who live closer to relatives tend to see them more often. But, since average journey times between relatives has increased only very slightly since 1986, this is unlikely on its own to account for the scale of decline in family contact that has taken place. In fact, as the next table shows, frequency of contact with mothers, for instance, has declined even once geographical proximity is taken into account.

**Frequency of contact with mother living one hour's journey
from respondent's home**

	1986	1995
	%	%
Daily	11	11
Weekly	67	61
Monthly	15	21
Less often	8	6
Base	*450*	*671*

An alternative explanation - that direct contact with relatives has fallen as a result of the new role of friends as 'families of choice' (see, for instance, Weeks *et al*, 1996) - is just as unlikely since, as we have noted, contact with 'best friends' seems to have dropped in tandem with contact with family.

A more plausible explanation for the change is the continuing transformation of the role of women in society. Studies in the 1950s and 1960s identified the strongest kinship tie as being between mothers and daughters, with women being more likely than men to keep in touch with

relatives in general (Willmot, 1986). Since then, not only has geographical mobility increased, but so of course has the proportion of women who work outside the home. Might this have affected their traditional kinship roles in particular, with inevitable implications for general levels of contact between family members?

According to our data, women are still considerably more likely than men to keep in frequent contact with relatives.

% of men and women seeing relative at least once a week

	Men		Women	
		Base		Base
Mother	42	450	53	576
Father	35	365	42	457
Adult sibling	24	748	32	954
Adult child	53	336	62	476
Other relative	34	779	35	1017

Note: bases exclude those without the relative in question, as well as those living with this relative.

But this is only part of the story. Looking at the trend between 1986 and 1995, we certainly see the expected decline in family contact among women, but we see a similar decline among men. However, the decline has been markedly sharper among women in full-time work. In 1986, around two-thirds of women in full-time work (compared to only one half of men in full-time work) saw their mother weekly. Now men and women who work full-time have become almost indistinguishable in this respect - 46 per cent and 45 per cent respectively seeing their mother weekly. This represents near-stasis for full-time working men, but the drop of nearly 20 percentage points in only nine years as far as full-time working women are concerned is indeed a precipitous one.

% seeing non-resident mother at least once a week

	1986		1995	
		Base		Base
Men				
All	50	308	42	450
In full-time work	49	266	46	314
Women				
All	65	335	53	576
In full-time work	64	97	45	177

So, since we are comparing here those in full-time work in each of the two years, it is not the fact that more women work full-time, but perhaps the

nature of the work they do that might be the culprit. It is entirely plausible that, over the last decade, the nature of women's full-time work has changed more than has men's, and that the sorts of women entering the full-time workforce in the 1990s differ from those in the 1980s.[1] In any event, male and female full-time workers are becoming more like one another in their kinship roles than they used to be, and this is not because the roles of men have changed. This can be seen in the light of increasing levels of work commitment among women over the last decade (indeed, on some measures, working women now display greater work commitment than men (Hedges, 1994)). And full-time working men and women report similar levels of stress in their jobs - substantially more than that reported by women working part-time (Curtice, 1993).

Contact with family - summary

If measured in terms of contact, the importance of the family has declined slightly over the last decade. People are less likely to live with kin than they were and they see them less often. However, the idea that this represents some sort of crisis for the family seems to be a gross exaggeration. After all, as many as around one half of adults whose mother is alive still see her at least weekly. Moreover, since contact with friends is also lower than it was a decade ago, our data argue that it is social contact rather than family contact alone that is suffering from the competition of other commitments such as work. Certainly, as far as women in full-time work are concerned, their reduced role in sustaining family contacts might well be related to the changing nature of and pressure from their jobs and to the rise in their commitment to work. It is not surprising, therefore, to find that full-time working women are nowadays little different from their full-time male counterparts in the amount of family networking in which they engage.

Naturally, frequency of contact tells us little about the *quality* of relationships (Allan, 1979). More revealing is the level of help and reliability of support that family members offer to one another. Indeed, it is the giving and receiving of help that constitutes "part of people's image of what constitutes 'a family'" (Finch and Mason, 1993). So we now turn to this element of family life.

Helping one another

To whom would you turn?

Who would be the first port of call in times of need? What role does the family play in providing support and help? We asked respondents about a

number of "problems that can happen to anyone", and - if they came up - to whom would they turn for help. The situations covered were as follows:

... *there are some household and garden jobs you really can't do alone - for example, you may need someone to hold a ladder, or to help you move some furniture;*

... *you had an illness and had to stay in bed for several weeks, and needed help around the home with shopping and so on;*

... *you needed to borrow a large sum of money;*

... *you were very upset about a problem with your husband, wife or partner, and haven't been able to sort it out with them;*

... *you felt just a bit down or depressed, and you wanted to talk about it.*

The next table identifies who was most commonly chosen as the first source of help in each case, showing the unsurprising dominance of spouses and partners when it comes to practical problems - and the bigger role for parents and friends when problems are emotional.

	Household job	Help while ill	Borrowing money	Marital problems	Depression
	%	%	%	%	%
No-one	1	1	7	8	3
Spouse/partner	58	61	21	9	47
Parent	8	13	20	15	8
Child	13	11	6	17	7
Sibling	4	3	4	12	6
Friend	7	5	2	27	21
Bank	n.a.	n.a.	32	n.a.	n.a.

Base: 2077

n.a. = not applicable

So, the majority of people would naturally rely on the help of a spouse or partner for the more routine domestic tasks we specified. More importantly, perhaps, around a half would also turn first to their spouse or partner if they were feeling depressed. As for other relatives, parents come more into their own for help with less routine problems for which a spouse or partner may well be inappropriate - such as borrowing money or marital problems - though in the latter case, friends outstrip parents, children and siblings as more likely sources of support. Friends are also the second most likely source of support for depression. Notably, around one in 12 people said they would not turn to anyone for help with marital problems, not even their spouse.

With one exception, few mentioned 'professionals' as a first source of help. For instance, only two per cent mentioned marital counselling as a source of help with marital problems, and a similarly small proportion mentioned the church. On the other hand, when the hypothetical problem was a financial one, the most common response was a Bank or Building Society.

Whom someone can turn to in times of need depends, of course, on who is *available*. So, given the importance of partners and spouses as sources of help, we need to establish how those without regular partners respond. Taking depression as an example, the next table shows how single people differ from married people in their responses. As the last three columns of the table show, parents, children and friends come much more into the picture for single people. Just whom they would turn to for help varies mainly - it seems - according to their own age and circumstances. Thus widows and widowers would be most inclined to talk to their children about it, divorcees would be more likely to turn to friends, and the never-married would be more likely to turn to their parents. Notably, siblings do not feature very strongly as sources of emotional support in these circumstances.

First source of help for depression, by marital status

	Married/living as married	Separated/ divorced	Widowed	Single
	%	%	%	%
No-one	3	3	9	2
Spouse/partner	65	7	1	18
Parent	4	12	1	24
Child	4	10	42	*
Sibling	5	10	6	10
Friend	13	44	22	40
Base	*1201*	*238*	*252*	*385*

Responses to all these questions also varied according to sex in a way that suggests that notions of traditional male and female roles remain widespread and far-reaching. Thus men were more likely than women to rely on their spouse or partner to nurse them through a sickness, while women were more likely than men to rely on friends or children in such circumstances. By the same token, women were more likely than men to turn first to their spouse or partner for help with a household job or for borrowing money. The next table shows the differences by gender with respect to help with marital problems. Of some interest perhaps is the higher proportion of men than women who would turn to *nobody* in these circumstances (around one in ten men and one in 20 women).

First source of help with marital problem, by gender

	Men	Women
	%	%
No-one	11	5
Spouse/partner	13	6
Parent	14	16
Child	14	19
Sibling	11	12
Friend	24	31
Base	*913*	*1164*

Responses to these questions have not changed markedly since they were first asked in 1986. The exception to this concerns the role of friends, who are now more likely than they were to be relied on for emotional support in marital problems or depression. This increase appears, however, to be at the expense of turning, as a first choice, to spouses or partners and not at the expense of other relatives. On the other hand, the non-married are also more likely now than they were to turn to friends rather than family members for emotional support.

Experience of help and helping

So, when presented with hypothetical situations, people tend to cite kin as their first port of call in times of need. To what extent, however, are we just tapping notions of *appropriateness* (Finch, 1989b) rather than a portrayal of what would actually happen if the situation arose?
  We therefore also asked:

> In the **past five years**, have you yourself **provided** regular help or care for an **adult** relative, friend, neighbour or colleague because of pregnancy, an illness, disability or other problem?

> And in the **past five years** have you **received** regular help or care from an **adult** relative, friend, neighbour or colleague because of pregnancy, an illness, disability or other problem?

Everyone who said they had provided help was also asked for details of the recipient, while those who had received help were asked to identify the provider.
  Around two in five people had provided regular care for an adult at some period during the past five years, and around one in five had received such care at some point.[2] Not unexpectedly, women are much more likely than men to have provided care (48 per cent as opposed to 34 per cent), but they

are also more likely than men to report having received care (26 per cent as opposed to 17 per cent). A large part of this latter difference stems from the above average tendency of *young* women (between 25 and 34) to have received care, presumably during pregnancy.

For whom do people provide care? As the next table shows, the most common person to whom care has been provided is a parent (this applies to one-third of all cases). Around one in five had provided care for a partner or spouse and a similar proportion for another family member. The main recipients of male care were spouses and parents, while the recipients of female care were more evenly distributed.

Recipient of care given by respondent

	All	Men	Women
	%	%	%
Spouse/partner	19	29	12
Parent/parent-in-law	34	31	36
Other family member	22	19	25
Friend	10	7	13
Neighbour	5	5	5
Base	*912*	*334*	*578*

When we look at the opposite side of the coin - those *receiving* care - the next table confirms that men are more likely than women to receive care from their spouse or partner, while women are more likely than men to receive care from a parent or another family member. Only around one in ten respondents (mainly men) had received care from a friend or neighbour, and other sources hardly featured at all.

Origin of care received by respondent

	All	Men	Women
	%	%	%
Spouse/partner	46	53	41
Parent/parent-in-law	16	9	18
Other family member	19	12	23
Friend	8	10	6
Neighbour	2	2	1
Base	*489*	*173*	*316*

We also asked:

> *Have you in the **past five years** helped out an **adult** relative, friend, neighbour or colleague with a loan or gift of money of, £100 or more, to help with some emergency or problem?*
>
> *And in the **past five years** have you personally **received** a loan or gift of money of, £100 or more from an **adult** relative, friend, neighbour or colleague to help with some emergency or problem?*

As many as a third (31 per cent) had lent or given money to a relative or friend, and around the same proportion had received such help. Men were slightly more likely than women to have helped out in this way (34 and 29 per cent respectively), with the beneficiary most likely to be another family member (usually a son or daughter). Sixteen per cent had lent or given money to a friend. Similarly, of those who had received help with money, the majority had received it from a parent or parent-in-law (59 per cent).

Recipient of money loaned or given

	All	Men	Women
	%	%	%
Spouse/partner	7	8	6
Parent/parent-in-law	10	10	11
Other family member	58	53	62
Friend	16	18	14
Base	*685*	*336*	*349*

Origin of money loaned or given

	All	Men	Women
	%	%	%
Spouse/partner	4	6	3
Parent/parent-in-law	59	60	58
Other family member	15	16	24
Friend	7	7	6
Base	*685*	*297*	*349*

Some kinship studies have suggested that working class people provide more help for their relatives than do middle class people, but Willmott challenges this view, arguing that "in certain respects it may now be true that, if anything, middle-class people give and receive rather more" (1986: 25). Our data suggest that class differences in the provision and receipt of care are largely insignificant - except when it comes to lending money. In this respect the middle classes (or non-manual workers) are indeed more likely than

manual workers to have provided help (35 per cent as opposed to 27 per cent).   But this may reflect no more than the greater access to financial resources among the middle-classes generally.

   In summary, our data on informal support and care suggest that the family remains a very important source of help.   But friends also matter when it comes to care or financial help.   As earlier research has found, friends are indeed an important source of practical, often long-term help in times of crisis, typically to people they have known for a long time (O'Connor, 1992). Friends in this respect become 'fictive kin': "She's like a sister to me. I can always turn to her" (Allan, 1989). Since the questions about actual examples of help given and received were asked for the first time on *British Social Attitudes* in 1995, we will have to wait for future rounds to look for evidence of change.

Attitudes towards relatives and friends

We have already seen that the family, far from being in decline, seems to be in enduringly good shape.   True, fewer people live with kin nowadays, and people are seeing slightly less of their family than they were a decade ago, perhaps on account of the changing demands of work.   Nonetheless, the family remains a key (perhaps *the* key) social network and the primary source of informal care and support for many.   Friends are probably becoming increasingly important too, but hardly at the expense of family networks.

Defining the role of the family

We turn now to people's attitudes towards the family, and the extent to which these attitudes substantiate our findings so far. How much do people believe that the family ought to have a role as a source of care and support? Are friends seen as having a less important role than relatives? To this end, we asked respondents how much they agreed or disagreed with a number of positive and negative statements about the family.   These statements are shown in the next table.

   According to these questions, most people are indeed family-centred, believing it to be important for contact to be maintained with both close relatives and the extended family, even those with whom they have little in common. That principle is, however, honoured to some degree in the breach. A smaller proportion (46 per cent as opposed to 55 per cent) actually claim that they themselves try to keep in touch with their extended family. Notably, the data clearly show that the family is seen as overwhelmingly more important than friends - by a margin of around eleven to one. Similarly, by a margin of around four to one, people would rather spend their time with their family than their friends. So much then for the death of the family.

Attitudes towards the family

		Agree	Neither agree nor disagree	Disagree
People should keep in touch with close family members even if they don't have much in common	%	70	18	10
People should keep in touch with relatives like aunts, uncles and cousins even if they don't have much in common	%	55	31	12
People should always turn to their family before asking the state for help	%	48	19	29
I try to stay in touch with all my relatives, not just my close family	%	46	22	27
I'd rather spend time with my friends than with my family	%	13	23	59
Once children have left home, they should no longer expect help from their parents	%	12	13	72
On the whole, my friends are more important to me than members of my family	%	7	12	76

Base: 2077

Our data confirm the fact that the most dominant family tie is that between parents and children, even after children have left the family home. Both in terms of contact and as a mechanism for family support, this is a critical relationship. This is also borne out by the high proportion of people (72 per cent) who disagree with the view that adult children should cease to call on their parents for help. In contrast, a much smaller proportion (48 per cent) supported the view that people should appeal for help from their family before going to the state for help. The implicit reference to financial help in that statement may well have had some effect on the response. Nonetheless, while many people believe that staying in touch with their family is important, they do not necessarily see the family as the most appropriate first port of call in times of need. Contact is one thing and asking for help is quite another.

What determines how family-centred we are?

To find out what sorts of people are most and least likely to be family-centred, we placed people on a continuum, based on their answers to the key questions on this subject. In essence, we calculated a single 'score' for each respondent from 1 to 5 on an index, where high scores indicate a more - and low scores a less - family-centred outlook.[3]

The next table shows the mean scores of various different groups on what we shall call our family orientation index.

Family orientation index

	Mean score	Base
All	3.51	1923
Age		
18 - 44	3.32	947
45 or over	3.70	973
Sex		
Men	3.45	848
Women	3.56	1075
Age and sex		
Men aged 18 - 44	3.30	408
Women aged 18 - 44	3.34	539
Men aged 45 or over	3.59	439
Women aged 45 or over	3.80	534

The extent to which one has a family-orientated (or family-centred) outlook then turns out to depend primarily on one's age: those aged 45 or older are substantially more family-centred than are their younger counterparts (with mean scores of 3.7 and 3.3 respectively). The strength of the relationship is illustrated by responses to the statement about the importance of the extended family. While 41 per cent of 18-34 year olds agree that "people should keep in touch with relatives like aunts, uncles and cousins, even if they don't have much in common", some 54 per cent of those aged 35-44 agree, and 68 per cent of those aged 55 or over agree.

At first sight women seem more family-centred than men, but this difference is partly a function of age. Women and men who are under 45 barely differ in their degree of family orientation. It is women *over* 45 who are substantially more family-centred than their male counterparts.

There are two ways of interpreting the dominant influence of age on people's attitudes towards the family. The first is that we are seeing a secular shift in attitudes, with younger generations becoming less family-centred than their predecessor generations. If so, as these younger generations replace older cohorts, society is likely to become less family-centred over time. If, on the other hand, one's sense of family responds more to the stage in the life cycle one happens to have reached, then we can expect no major overall change over time, merely a continuing generation gap as now. Thus, people would simply become more family conscious as they acquire families of their own through marriage and parenthood and, as a consequence, begin to value the help and support that an extended family network tends to provide. In the absence of trend data on these particular questions, we cannot rigorously evaluate these two alternative explanations. We can, however, go some way

by examining the relationship between certain life stages and family-centredness to see, for instance, whether *within* particular age groups, being married or having children does seem to make a difference to the people's sense of family orientation.

Our evidence on this point turns out to support the view that it is indeed age rather than life cycle that has the strongest influence on one's degree of family orientation, and that in consequence attitudes to the family are likely to change over time. Thus, while married people as a whole (or those living as married) are indeed significantly more family-centred than those who are either single or separated/divorced[4], this difference vanishes once age is taken into account. For those aged under 45, for instance, being married or single makes no difference to the degree of family orientation. Similarly, the apparent relationship between parenthood and family orientation vanishes once age is taken into account. So, younger generations are, it seems, less family-centred than their older counterparts and may well remain so as they get older. This process may indeed have been going on for many generations. Yet it has not so far made much of a dent in the still very high levels of contact and support that most families manage to sustain.

Does one's degree of family orientation vary too according to one's values, beliefs and convictions? Do religious people, for instance, differ from non-religious ones in this respect? Certainly it would be surprising if people with different world views did not have different attitudes towards such a central part of life when they vary so much in other respects (Jowell and Park, 1996 forthcoming).

Virtually all religions have something to say about family and community, and it appears that being associated with a religion (which particular religion does not matter) is indeed associated with being more family-centred. Moreover, even among those who profess a religion, regular attenders at church (or the equivalent) turn out to be more family-centred than occasional attenders. Notably, these associations hold true even after age has been taken into account.

Family-orientation and religion: mean scores

Belongs to a religion:	Mean score	Base
- all	3.64	1156
- attends church at least once a month	3.80	372
- attends church less often	3.63	331
- rarely attends church	3.51	449
Does not belong to a religion	3.31	765

In order to examine the association between attitudes towards family and other wider social values, we were also able to draw on an attitude scale that is included regularly in the *British Social Attitudes* survey, our 'libertarian-authoritarian' scale (described in detail in Appendix I of this Report). For

this chapter, we have divided our sample into five roughly equal quintiles from the most authoritarian (highest scores) to the most libertarian (lowest scores) on the scale.

As the next table shows, there is a strong positive relationship between high scores and on the scale and high scores on the family orientation index (a relationship which holds even after age and religion is taken into account). This is, perhaps, not surprising. After all, many debates about the family link its supposed decline and fall to a number of popular authoritarian concerns such as 'traditional values' and law and order. We might therefore expect those who share such concerns to score higher than average on a measure which endorses notions of familial duty.

Family orientation and the libertarian-authoritarian scale

	Mean score	Base
Most authoritarian/least libertarian quintile	3.74	390
Next quintile	3.60	390
Next quintile	3.44	447
Next quintile	3.47	379
Least authoritarian/most libertarian quintile	3.19	294

Conclusion

In spite of its many detractors, family life in Britain continues to thrive. Most people are in regular contact with their immediate family who remain of primary importance in their lives. The family is still the dominant source of support and care for most people. There has been a drop in contact over the last decade (from a very high base), alongside a small increase in people's reliance on friends for support. There is evidence that this is linked to changes in the nature of full-time women's work, with its greater demands and call for commitment. Could it be that the 'enterprise culture' has in this respect taken its toll on family life?

Moreover, people's attitudes towards family life correspond largely with their behaviour. Most people believe in principle and practice in keeping in contact with both immediate and extended family members. There is, however, a clear association between strong family-centred attitudes and age. The older one is the more one adheres to the virtue of contact with the wider family ("even if they don't have much in common"), suggesting that for the young the family is increasingly in competition with other aspects of both social life and work and that its dominance as a social force will indeed diminish over time.

But it is important to keep these secular trends in perspective. For the bulk of people their family continues to be a central and enduring part of their

lives - as secure as can reasonably be expected against the supposed threats from social, cultural and even occupational pressures.

Notes

1. There is some evidence that full-time working women in 1995 do differ from those in 1986. There were, for instance, fewer 18 to 24 year old women in the full-time workforce in 1995 than there were a decade before (corresponding to the rapid increase in higher education that has occurred since then), but this drop is compensated for by a rise in the proportion of women aged 25 to 34. In terms of marital status, the 1986 and 1995 groups do not differ and, although more women working full-time were mothers in 1995 than in 1986, this difference was not significant.
2. The discrepancy between the proportions of people providing care and the proportion receiving it might reflect a tendency for those who receive care to receive it from more than one person, or it may be that people are more likely to remember giving than receiving care, or some of those receiving care may well be less likely to respond to surveys on grounds of incapacity or institutionalisation.
3. The index is formed from the answers to the following three agree-disagree items:

   People should keep in touch with close family members even if they don't have much in common

   People should keep in touch with relatives like aunts, uncles and cousins even if they don't have much in common

   I try to stay in touch with all my relatives, not just my close family

   Answers are recorded on a five-point scale ranging from "agree strongly" (scored 1) to "disagree strongly" (scored 5). A respondent's score on the index is thus the sum of his or her scores on these three items, divided by three.
4. In fact the widowed as a group are the most family-centred of all, but primarily because they are substantially older than average and disproportionately female.

References

Allan, G. (1979), *A Sociology of Friendship and Kinship,* London: George Allan and Unwin.

Allan, G. (1989), *Friendship: Developing a Sociological Perspective,* Hemel Hempstead: Harvester Wheatsheaf.

Berrington, A. and Murphy, M. (1994), 'Changes in the living arrangements of young adults in Britain during the 1980s', *European Sociological Review,* **10:3**.

Carlson, A. (1993), 'Liberty, order and the family', in Davies, J. (ed.), *The Family: Is It Just Another Lifestyle Choice?, Choice in Welfare,* **15**, London: IEA Health and Welfare Unit.

Curtice, J. (1993), 'Satisfying work - if you can get it', in Jowell, R., Brook, L. and Dowds, L. (eds.), *International Social Attitudes: the 10th BSA Report,* Aldershot: Dartmouth.

Ermisch, J., DiSalvo, P. and Joshi, H. (1995), 'Household formation and housing tenure decisions of young people', *Occasional Paper* **95:1**, Colchester: ESRC Research Centre on Micro-social change, University of Essex.

Finch, J. (1989a), *Family Obligations and Social Change,* Cambridge: Polity Press.

Finch, J. (1989b), 'Kinship and friendship', in Jowell, R., Witherspoon, S. and Brook, L. (eds.), *British Social Attitudes: Special International Report,* Aldershot: Gower.

Finch, J. and Mason, J. (1993), *Negotiating Family Responsibilities,* London: Tavistock/ Routledge.

Hedges, B. (1994), 'Work in a changing climate', in Jowell, R., Curtice, J., Brook, L. and
    Ahrendt, D. (eds.), *British Social Attitudes: the 11th Report,* Aldershot: Dartmouth.
Jowell, R. and Park, A. (1996, forthcoming), 'Questioning British attitudes', in Taylor, B.
    and Thomson, K. (eds.), *Understanding Change in Social Attitudes,* Aldershot: Dartmouth.
O'Connor, P. (1992), *Friendships Between Women,* Hemel Hempstead: Harvester
    Wheatsheaf.
Utting, D. (1996), 'Families and parenting', *Occasional Paper* **22**, London: Family Policy
    Studies Centre.
Weeks, J., Donovan, C. and Heaphy, B. (1996), 'Families of choice: patterns of non-
    heterosexual relationships, a literature review', *Social Science Research Papers*, **2**,
    London: South Bank University.
Willmott, P. (1986), 'Social networks: informal care and public policy', *Policy Studies
    Institute Research Report,* **655**, London: Policy Studies Institute.

Acknowledgements

This work was carried out with funding from the ESRC under its Population
and Household Change programme (grant number L315253023). We are
grateful to the Council for its financial support. We also wish to thank Kate
Smith of the Family Policy Studies Centre for her computing support.

4 Reactions to a flexible labour market

Peter Spencer [*]

Introduction

In the Spring of 1995, as this round of the *British Social Attitudes* survey began, the British economy was experiencing a remarkable recovery. Unemployment had been falling for two years, and price and wage inflation remained very subdued, holding out the prospect of sustained non-inflationary economic expansion. It appeared that the government's economic reforms and, in particular, its attempts to encourage greater flexibility among the workforce, had dramatically improved the working of the economy. Yet government popularity, which usually responds favourably to such economic upturns, failed to improve as much as might have been expected. Ironically, one possible reason for this was the public's dislike for the very policies credited with improving Britain's economic position - especially those aimed at promoting a more flexible labour market.

This chapter looks at two possible reasons as to why policies aimed at promoting greater labour market flexibility might be unpopular - namely, the consequences of such policies for job security and for social inequality. We begin by reviewing the various forces which have influenced the employment market since 1979 focusing, in particular, on the ways in which these forces are thought to have affected the shape and flexibility of the labour market, people's feelings of job insecurity and public concern about the distribution of income. After considering some of the indications of a more flexible

[*] Peter Spencer is Professor of Economics at Birkbeck College, University of London.

labour market, we examine whether people's *attitudes* towards work have become more flexible over time. We then turn to the possible consequences of a liberalised labour market for security, wage differentials and income inequality.

Globalisation, technology and economic policy

Many of the economic forces affecting Britain in the 1980s and 1990s were global in nature. It has been argued that technological developments are affecting the demand for different types of workers (Katz and Murphy, 1992), notably automation (which has reduced the demand for unskilled labour), and information technology (which has undermined the managerial labour market). Another global factor might be competition from emerging economies (Wood, 1994), largely a consequence of the liberalisation of world capital and product markets, which has allowed workers in emerging economies to compete more effectively with those in developed countries. Britain was certainly not alone in experiencing these sorts of pressures - many analysts believe that they have held back employment prospects and real wages, particularly for unskilled workers, throughout the OECD. However, in Britain, their impact was combined with those of the results of various government reforms - producing a unique and distinctive outcome.

The impact of global forces on the labour market of any given country clearly depend upon its market structure. Generally speaking, most economists believe that countries with 'flexible' labour markets (like the United States) have experienced a fall in the relative wages of unskilled workers and growing income inequality as a result of these global developments, while those with 'inflexible' markets (like many European nations) have experienced increased unemployment of unskilled workers (Atkinson, 1997 forthcoming).[1]

In Britain, since the Conservative party came to power in 1979, a major government objective has been to liberalise the labour market, making it more like its American counterpart with the purpose of improving its underlying performance. Consequently, the recent experiences of the British labour market have been quite different to those of other European countries. There are other reasons as to why we might expect government policies to have made Britain's recent labour market experience distinctive. Simply allowing 'the market' to work in a labour market previously cushioned from many economic forces would be expected to have implications for job security and wage differentials. In particular, the government was keen to make the labour market more flexible by restoring incentives and changing workers' attitudes towards pay and jobs. It began its programme by abolishing its predecessor's incomes policy and went on gradually to reform the trades unions and reduce employment protection laws. This policy was buttressed by the programme of privatisation and contracting-out of

government services which evolved once the Conservative party came to power. At the same time, there was a significant shift towards contracting-out and 'demergers' in the private sector. Because the degree of competition in the labour market is closely bound up with that of the product market, these competition policies are likely to have affected conditions in the jobs market.

We have seen, then, that during the last two decades the British labour market has been subject to some quite unique forces, and that these might be expected to have had distinctive results. Two, in particular, emerge. Firstly, there was a sharp upward break in the trend towards self-employment in the early 1980s, which is not prominent elsewhere, and which is considered by the government to be a sign of success in improving the flexibility of the labour market. Second, and more importantly, Britain experienced a dramatic increase in income inequality. Although inequality has also increased in the United States and in a few other countries, the increase in Britain has been much more pronounced than elsewhere. The average pre-tax earnings of the top ten per cent of the working population rose from 2.8 times those of the bottom ten per cent in 1979 to 3.4 times in 1995 (OECD, 1996). Although this difference may not appear to be very significant - an increase of just 20 per cent - it means that those in the low income group have not seen any rise in their living standards despite the economic growth in the economy since 1979. This has been enough to shift Britain out of the European league into the American one. In fact, on some measures, the distribution of income in Britain is now as unequal as that in the United States (Atkinson, 1997 forthcoming).

The effect of these global, technical and legislative changes is, of course, a matter of great current debate, especially within Britain. So far, the literature has concentrated upon worries about *insecurity*, paying relatively little attention to public concern about *income inequality*. While the Labour Party's (Borrie) Commission on Social Justice (1993) reviewed both of these issues, its Report focused narrowly on the problem of insecurity alone. It concluded that economic developments and policies had destroyed the idea of a job for life - remarking that "employment insecurity affects us all". In a similar vein, Will Hutton (1994) argues that only 40 per cent of the workforce enjoy what can be termed 'secure' employment, the remainder either being in 'insecure' employment (such as casual labour or involuntary part-time work) or being utterly marginalised.[2]

It is generally thought that the climate of job insecurity has undermined consumer confidence and government popularity. Research in the early 1990s suggested that worries about job security and the pace of change were paramount for all social groups, leading to serious tensions and problems at home (Buck et al, 1994). Similarly, others have linked a 'workaholic' culture and growing job insecurity to ill-health and family breakdown (Cooper, 1996). Set against this, however, is the argument that job insecurity has always been a fact of life for the majority and that the notion of a 'job for life'

was always confined to (and, indeed, still applies to) a minority of workers (Robinson, 1995; Burgess and Rees, 1996). Certainly, official statistics show that turnover in the labour market was nearly as high in the halcyon days of the 1960s as it is at present (Gregg and Wadsworth, 1995). And official statistics certainly do not support the argument that those in work are working longer hours than they were in the past.[3]

Employment trends

We shall start by reviewing the way in which people describe their 'economic activity' to see whether this tells us anything about more flexible forms of employment. Of course, these data (like many discussed in this chapter) are strongly influenced by the economic cycle of recession and expansion, and we will try to distinguish these effects from longer run trends.

  The next table shows that there has been no upwards trend in the proportion of people in paid work during the 1990s. This contrasts with experience during the previous recovery, which began in the recession year of 1981 and lasted until the peak year of 1990. Then the proportion of people in paid work rose from a low of 52 per cent in 1984 to a high of 56 per cent during the 'Lawson boom' of 1989. This is broadly in line with data from the *Labour Force Survey*, which shows that the growth in employment in 1993 to 1995 has been limited because more people now move from unemployment into inactivity, rather than into paid work. For instance, of those leaving unemployment in 1993, only 60 per cent went into work, compared to 75 per cent in 1981, and 80-90 per cent in the late 1970s (Gregg and Wadsworth, 1995).

Current activity (1983 - 1995)

	1983	1984	1985	1986	1987	1989	1990	1991	1993	1994	1995
	%	%	%	%	%	%	%	%	%	%	%
In paid work	53	52	53	56	55	56	55	53	51	52	52
Unemployed	6	6	8	7	7	4	4	7	8	6	6
Sick or disabled	2	4	2	2	3	3	2	3	4	5	5
Wholly retired	15	17	14	15	16	18	19	17	17	17	18
Looking after home	20	19	19	17	17	16	16	16	16	13	14
Base	*1761*	*1675*	*1804*	*3100*	*2847*	*3029*	*2797*	*2918*	*2945*	*3469*	*3633*

What, however, of those who *are* in work? Does this group exhibit any evidence of more flexible employment patterns? Two key issues to consider in this context are self-employment and part-time working (with both commonly being seen as indications of increased labour market flexibility). And, on both these measures, flexibility has increased since the mid-1980s. Thus, while 16 per cent of employees worked part-time (less than 30 hours)

in 1985, 20 per cent did so a decade later, in 1995. Over the same period, the proportion of those in work who were self-employed increased from 12 per cent to 17 per cent. True, these figures partly reflect the changing composition of the workforce (and, in particular, the increasing participation of married women). But, even if we arrange the respondents into different sex and age groups, we still find the same trends - an increased tendency to work on a part time or self employed basis. Again, these data are broadly in line with the *Labour Force Survey.*

Attitudes towards employment

Employment trends do point, then, towards increasing liberalisation of the labour market. But what of people's *attitudes* towards employment? Do these show signs of adapting to the requirements of an increasingly flexible labour market? To examine this, we can consider people's responses to a number of questions asked regularly as part of the *British Social Attitudes* survey series.

Firstly, what would people do if they were to lose their job? Certainly, the majority of employees - nearly nine in every ten - say they would start looking for another job in these circumstances. There has been little change in the proportion giving this response since our survey began. However, estimates as to how long it would take to find another job vary considerably according to the state of the economic cycle at the time.

As the next table shows, economic expansion between 1983 and 1989 saw the percentage of people who thought they would find work within three months increase from 46 per cent to 70 per cent, a remarkable increase in such a short time. The recession then cut such optimism substantially, with this figure dropping back down to 44 per cent again by 1994. Since then, hand-in-hand with the economic recovery, optimism about being able to find new work in under three months has increased.

Employees' assessment of time needed to find 'acceptable replacement job' if own job lost

	1983	1984	1985	1986	1989	1993	1994	1995
	%	%	%	%	%	%	%	%
Less than 3 months	46	55	57	54	70	46	44	52
3 months or more	54	45	42	46	30	54	56	48
Base	*599*	*521*	*580*	*1080*	*1092*	*749*	*1099*	*1145*

Base: all employees who would start looking for work straight away if they lost their current job. Percentages are calculated after excluding those who responded "don't know" or who did not answer the question.

Do beliefs about the amount of time it would take to find work depend entirely on the economic cycle? It would seem not. Certainly a lower proportion of employees in 1994 and 1995 thought they could find work within three months than did so in 1984 and 1985, respectively (marking similar points in the employment cycle). This suggests that people now think it would take longer to find a job than they did previously.

   This change in attitudes is confined to those in work. We asked those who were unemployed and who thought it would take them three months or more before they found an acceptable job how willing they would then be to take on what they "now consider to be an *unacceptable job*". Responses to this question reveal that unemployed people seem to have become more choosy about the kind of jobs that they are prepared to take up. This suggests that government policies have failed, so far, to diminish the job expectations and reservations of the unemployed.

Willingness of the unemployed to take an 'unacceptable' job

	1983	1985	1989	1993	1994
	%	%	%	%	%
Very willing	24	18	10	11	9
Quite willing	31	26	25	28	29
Not very willing	41	51	58	61	61
Base	*63*	*48*	*56*	*86*	*122*

Base: all unemployed who thought it would take three months or more before they found
         an acceptable job.

Of course, a flexible job market is not just characterised by a propensity to accept any job that comes along. Another option is to retrain for a new job - and yet another is to move to an area with better job prospects. We asked all employees who thought it would take three months or more to find an acceptable replacement for their present job how willing they would be in these circumstances "to retrain for a different job". As shown in the next table, a majority *are* willing to retrain, but there has been no increase in this proportion over time. However, willingness to retrain does vary over the course of the economic cycle, in the opposite direction to the assessment of the time it would take to find a replacement job. Thus, the proportion who would be "very willing" to retrain falls during an expansion phase (as jobs become easier to find) from 54 per cent in 1983 to 44 per cent in 1989 (then rising again in line with the economic cycle, reaching 49 per cent by 1995).

Willingness of employees to retrain

	1983	1984	1985	1986	1989	1993	1995
	%	%	%	%	%	%	%
Very willing	54	50	50	49	44	51	49
Quite willing	25	32	30	29	34	31	33
Not very willing	11	15	16	17	17	16	16
Base	*350*	*253*	*262*	*516*	*340*	*433*	*569*

Base: all employees who thought that, if they lost their current job, it would take three months or more before they found an acceptable job.

Asking the same question of those who were unemployed and expected to remain so for a further three months produces a similar pattern. However, the proportion of unemployed who state that they are "not very willing" to retrain for a different line of work is higher than that among employees.

Willingness of unemployed to retrain

	1983	1985	1986	1989	1993	1994	1995
	%	%	%	%	%	%	%
Very willing	50	42	38	31	40	40	44
Quite willing	30	31	32	31	30	33	34
Not very willing	14	23	27	32	30	27	22
Base	*63*	*48*	*126*	*56*	*86*	*122*	*121*

Base: all unemployed who thought it would take three months or more before they found an acceptable job.

One of the oft-cited features of the American flexible labour market is its high degree of geographical mobility. However, as the next table shows, there is little evidence that this characteristic applies in Britain. We asked those who were unemployed and expected to remain so for at least three months how willing they would be "to move to a different area to find an acceptable job". Generally, between three and four in every ten say they would be willing to do this but, once again, the economic cycle affects their decisions. As we might expect, people see less need to move during peak times when unemployment is relatively low (as was the case in 1989) than they do in an early recovery year when local jobs are likely to be harder to find (like 1993).

Willingness of unemployed to move in search of a job

	1983	1985	1989	1993	1994
	%	%	%	%	%
Willing	37	42	24	31	35
Not very willing	57	52	69	69	64
Base	*63*	*48*	*56*	*86*	*103*

Base: all unemployed who thought it would take three months or more before they found an acceptable job.

We also asked the unemployed whether they had "ever *actually* considered moving to a different area to find work". The proportion saying that they have considered moving has crept up from around a third in the 1980s to around two-fifths in the mid-1990s, suggesting that there may have been some increase in people's willingness to contemplate geographical mobility.

Whether the unemployed have considered moving area in search of work

	1983	1987	1989	1993	1994	1995
	%	%	%	%	%	%
Yes	34	30	32	36	40	41
No	65	69	67	63	60	59
Base	*147*	*192*	*123*	*217*	*234*	*215*

So, to conclude our brief consideration of people's attitudes towards employment, there seems little evidence of any major change in line with the increasing flexibility of the labour market itself. True, attitudes and expectations do vary over time, but such changes by no means reflect an underlying shift in the values of the British workforce. Rather, like many data relating to the economy and employment, they appear to mirror more short-term fluctuations in the economic cycle (see Jowell and Park, 1996, forthcoming).

Increasing insecurity?

We turn now to one of the commonly-cited consequences of a more flexible labour market - increased job insecurity. We have already seen that there is some dispute about the extent to which this is actually a consequence, so the first question we address is whether or not job insecurity has actually increased over the last decade or so. And, if it has increased, has it hit all social groups equally or have some suffered more than others?

A job for life?

Firstly, we need to see whether the 'job for life' has vanished, as has been suggested by a variety of theorists (see, for example, Hutton, 1993). One way of examining this is to look at employer tenure - the length of time that an employee has been with their current employer. This is shown in the next table.

As the table shows, data relating to job tenure vary considerably according to the economic cycle. Thus, during the recession of 1991 (during which output fell sharply), 86 per cent of full-time employees had been with their current employer for a year or more, and 48 per cent for five years or more. Four years on, in 1995, job tenure had increased somewhat, with 88 per cent having been with their employer for a year or more, and 59 per cent for five years or more. Not surprisingly, the job tenure of part-time workers tends to be shorter than that of full-time workers.

The percentages for the full sample are very close to those reported for 1993 by Gregg and Wadsworth (1995).[4] They reveal a diverse labour market, with many jobs turning over quickly, but stability for some. For instance, nearly a third of full-time workers have been in their job for ten years or more, with no tendency for this to fall back in recent years. Currently, more than half of the workforce has been with the same employer for more than five years, and this fraction has been increasing during the recovery. Clearly, there does remain a privileged (and not insubstantial) group with considerable security of tenure.

Length of continuous employment with present employer

	1991	1993	1994	1995
Full-time employees				
1 year or more	86	86	87	88
2 years or more	75	77	79	77
5 years or more	48	54	59	59
10 years or more	33	33	35	33
20 years or more	11	13	15	13
Base	*974*	*903*	*1124*	*1129*

Job turnover

Clearly length of tenure tells only a partial story. It tells us nothing as to *why* people stay in, or leave, their jobs. After all, leaving one's employer can be either a voluntary or involuntary decision. It is likely that a decline in the number and quality of jobs available will make people less likely to leave their job voluntarily. Further, it may be the case that an increase in

involuntary job movement (such as that arising from redundancy) is offset by a fall in the proportion of people resigning voluntarily.

In order to examine this in more detail, we can examine employees' responses to a question regarding the likelihood of their leaving their current employer over the next year, and the reasons given as to why they might leave. As the next table shows, a surprisingly large proportion (about a quarter) of the workforce expect to leave - another sign of high turnover in many types of job. Over time, there is a tendency for these numbers to rise, and for those expecting to stay in their job to fall. However, these trends are distorted by the effect of the economic cycle. In particular, there is a rise in the percentage of workers expecting to leave their job in the early stages of economic recovery. For instance, this proportion increases from 18 per cent in 1983 to 26 per cent in 1984, and from 24 per cent in1993 to 26 per cent in 1994.

These sorts of data are often difficult to interpret and so we have calculated an 'inertia' index designed to summarise the data better.[5] In essence, a lower index means lower inertia, and hence greater movement in the labour market. The index shows that inertia has indeed declined over time, and that the most recent recovery period (1993 to 1995) has been marked by lower inertia than the previous recovery period of 1983 to 1986.

Likelihood of leaving current employer over next year

	1983	1984	1985	1986	1989	1990	1991	1993	1994	1995
	%	%	%	%	%	%	%	%	%	%
Likely	18	26	23	22	23	24	25	24	26	27
Not likely	81	74	77	78	76	76	74	76	72	7
Base	817	778	857	1532	1462	1307	1236	1144	1447	1449
Inertia index	110	83	88	92	91	85	81	89	75	74

Why might people expect to leave their job? Labour market economists traditionally divide reasons for leaving into two categories - involuntary (such as redundancy) and voluntary (such as going to another employer or becoming self-employed). Voluntary resignations have always been the most common reason for expecting to leave an employer. They also vary more than involuntary moves across the economic cycle. For instance, moving "to a new job" rose from 40 per cent of those expecting to leave to 58 per cent between 1983 and 1989 (as the jobs market became more buoyant). Consequently, the numbers planning to leave their jobs move in line with the business cycle, with the inertia index moving in the reverse direction. Labour market experts are well aware of this relationship when it comes to actual job movement, but it is remarkable to see it featuring so clearly in people's employment plans and expectations.

It should also be noted that this analysis reveals little evidence of increasing anxiety about redundancy. Numerically, the percentages citing redundancy or factory closure as reasons for leaving an employer are small, and have been declining since the early 1980s. They also fell back in 1995 as the economy strengthened. Indeed the figure of 13 per cent for 1995 is no higher than that seen in 1989, at the height of the Lawson boom.[6]

% giving as reason for leaving current employer

	1983	1984	1985	1986	1989	1990	1991	1993	1994	1995
Redundancy	23	20	18	19	13	9	18	14	17	13
New job	40	46	48	44	58	56	42	44	46	53
Self-employment.	7	8	5	10	9	9	4	6	6	6
Base	147	194	199	331	339	312	309	272	398	396

Base: all those "very" or "quite" likely to leave current employer

An insecure majority?

Having examined people's experience of, and expectations regarding, employment, we now turn to their experience of *unemployment* over the previous five years. Further, in order to examine the Borrie Commission's claim that we are all affected by employment insecurity, we examine recent experience of unemployment in terms of the social class of the individual. As the next table shows, the proportion of respondents touched by unemployment has remained stable over the past decade - at around one in five - partly reflecting the fact that the five year reference period to which the question refers helps smooth any economic cycle effects. Experience of unemployment does, however, differ according to social class, with social classes I and II (those from professional and managerial backgrounds) being substantially less likely than any other group to report it. Thus, in 1995, nearly one in three (29 per cent) of those in social classes IV and V (semi-skilled and unskilled manual workers) reported experience of unemployment in the previous five years, over double the comparable proportion among social classes I and II (14 per cent of whom had experienced unemployment during this period). Further, the experience of social classes I and II is fairly consistent over the past ten years, unlike that of other groups (particularly manual ones) who have been subject to considerable fluctuation. The considerable attention paid to the 'shake-out' of professional and managerial workers fails, so far as these figures are concerned, to have any firm foundations.

Employees' experience of unemployment in last five years, by Social Class

	1983	84	85	86	87	89	90	91	93	94	95	base range
I+ II	14	14	15	14	14	14	17	16	15	16	14	*203-523*
III non-manual	19	24	27	23	24	22	23	18	25	24	20	*190-405*
III manual	21	27	20	19	25	18	20	28	17	21	21	*189-337*
IV + V	19	28	29	24	27	29	28	21	30	26	29	*168-345*
Total	18	23	22	20	21	20	21	19	21	21	20	*778-1532*

A workaholic culture?

Is it the case that workers, especially those at the top, are increasingly having to work longer and harder to hold onto their jobs (Cooper, 1996)? True, official data on the number of hours people work shows a recent *decline* in hours worked.[7] Against this, however, the *British Social Attitudes* data on self-reported hours worked suggest that people think that they are working progressively *more* hours as the years roll by. As one might expect, the hours worked by professional and managerial (Social Classes I+II) and blue collar workers (Social Class III) are significantly higher than those worked by the rest of the workforce.

  Once again, it is interesting to examine the cyclical behaviour of the data. In all major economies it is common that the number of hours worked moves in step, or perhaps ahead of, the economic cycle. In the next table this phenomenon is clearly reflected in the fall in the proportion of people working 40 hours or more a week, from 30 per cent at the economic peak in 1989 to 26 per cent in 1991, the first year of recession. The cyclical recovery sees a jump in hours worked, as employers try to boost output without risking the hiring and firing costs associated with new staff. A similar, but more marked, pattern is evident when considering the hours worked by full-time employees only.

Hours worked per week (employees)

	1985	1986	1987	1989	1990	1991	1993	1994	1995
40 hours or more	26	26	27	30	28	26	27	29	31
60 hours or more	2	2	2	3	1	1	2	3	3
Base	*857*	*1532*	*1381*	*1462*	*1307*	*1236*	*1144*	*1447*	*1449*

Confidence in the future

Clearly, a further measure of insecurity concerns people's expectations of the future. We asked all employees:

> *Over the coming year do you expect your workplace to be increasing its number of employees, reducing its number of employees, or will the number of employees stay about the same?*

As shown in the next table, pessimists outnumbered optimists in the early 1990s. By 1995, however, they were neck and neck, mirroring almost exactly the position in 1987 (but not quite reaching the optimistic heights seen during the Lawson boom in 1989).

Employees' expectations about workplace jobs

	1983	1984	1985	1986	1987	1989	1990	1991	1993	1994	1995
	%	%	%	%	%	%	%	%	%	%	%
Number of jobs:											
Will increase	16	18	22	21	23	26	23	18	19	20	23
Stay the same	54	51	52	54	52	53	50	54	53	51	54
Will reduce	29	29	24	23	22	20	25	26	26	27	22
Base	*817*	*778*	*857*	*1532*	*1381*	*1462*	*1307*	*1236*	*1144*	*1447*	*1449*
'Increase' minus 'reduce'	-13	-11	-2	-2	+1	+6	-2	-8	-7	-7	+1

It is remarkable that *consumer* confidence began to pick up at about the same time as *employee* confidence about workplace size. The standard Gallup indicator, which shows the balance of people expecting their financial prospects to improve minus those expecting a deterioration, remained depressed - with more pessimists than optimists - until the spring of 1994. However, optimists overtook pessimists in 1994 and, although this takes us beyond the period covered by our data, the Gallup confidence results for the summer of 1996 are as strong as those seen at the height of the Lawson years in 1989.

Nevertheless, both the consumer and employee confidence balances have responded relatively slowly during this recovery. The contrast with the last recovery is particularly surprising when seen against the background of the headline unemployment figures. There was a marked improvement in employee confidence between 1984 and 1985, despite a continued rise in the official unemployment count. This time, however, people were much more sceptical, remaining pessimistic throughout 1993 and 1994 despite falling unemployment. Whatever influences consumer and employee confidence, it is not newspaper headlines.

A number of points emerge from our analysis so far. Firstly, although there has been a high degree of turnover in the labour market, there remains stability of tenure for a considerable group. Secondly, our data indicate that professional and managerial groups have not escaped the experience of unemployment, but remain substantially less prone to this than other groups. Finally, responses to our question on workplace jobs indicate that the economic recovery has at last resulted in optimism about workplace jobs, hand-in-hand with a more general recovery in consumer confidence.

Income inequality, wage differentials and social justice

We turn now to the second area seen to have been affected by the liberalisation of the labour market - income inequality.   We start by examining whether British attitudes towards income differentials have changed over time:

> *Thinking of income levels generally in Britain today, would you say that the **gap** between those with high incomes and those with low incomes is too large, about right, or too small?*

In 1983, when we first asked this question, 72 per cent thought that the gap was "too large" - an overwhelming majority. Nonetheless, this proportion rose over the next decade, increasing sharply in 1993 to 85 per cent and reaching an all-time high of 87 per cent in 1995. This is not, perhaps, surprising given the public discussion in recent years over pay (and, in particular, City salaries and managerial remuneration). However, delving deeper into the data reveals a more surprising picture. Firstly, if we focus on the 1995 responses, there is a remarkable unanimity across all social groups that the gap between high and low incomes is too large. It does not matter how we 'cut' the 1995 numbers - whether we display them by economic activity, social group, or educational attainment, we still see a similar percentage saying that the gap is too large. Yet this remarkable consensus has not always existed. Earlier in the survey's history, for instance, those in higher income groups or in social groups I and II were substantially less likely than average to say that the income gap was "too large". However, it is amongst this group that concern about inequality has increased the most. Consequently, they are both now in line with general consensus.

Perception of gap between high and low incomes

	1983	1984	1985	1986	1987	1989	1990	1991	1993	1994	1995
	%	%	%	%	%	%	%	%	%	%	%
Too large	72	75	77	78	79	80	81	80	85	85	87
About right	22	19	17	16	17	15	15	16	11	11	8
Too small	3	4	4	3	2	3	3	2	2	2	2
Base	1761	1675	1804	3100	2847	3029	2797	1445	1461	1167	1234

As well as asking about general inequality, we also ask employees about pay levels at their own place of work:

> *Thinking about the **highest** and **lowest** paid people at your place of work, how would you describe the **gap** between their pay, as far as you know?*

As the next table shows, a smaller proportion of people think that the income gap at their workplace is too large than think the income gap in society as a whole is too large. One reason for this is the high proportion of people who answered "don't know" to the question (around six to ten per cent in each year), presumably reflecting the fact that a lot of employees simply do not know the incomes of others within their workplace. Nonetheless, the results are broadly in line with those we would expect, with growing proportions saying that the pay gap at their workplace is too large.

Employees' perception of gap between highest and lowest paid at work

	1983	1984	1985	1986	1987	1989	1990	1991	1993	1994	1995
	%	%	%	%	%	%	%	%	%	%	%
Too big	40	38	39	39	41	45	47	44	46	52	50
About right	45	49	48	48	46	43	41	43	44	38	42
Too small	5	4	4	4	4	3	3	5	3	3	2
Base	817	778	857	1532	1381	1462	1307	1236	1144	1447	1449

Of course, it is one thing to feel that the 'income gap' is too large, but quite another to admit that one's own salary is too high! For this reason, we ask:

> *How would you describe the wages or salary you are paid for the job you do - on the low side, reasonable, or on the high side?*

It comes, perhaps, as no surprise to find that people generally think their pay is too low. However, the proportion of employees who feel that their pay is

"too low" dipped in the early 1990s (as the recession approached), perhaps because some employees regarded themselves as lucky to have any job at all.[8]

Employees' perception of own pay

	1983	1984	1985	1986	1987	1989	1990	1991	1993	1994	1995
	%	%	%	%	%	%	%	%	%	%	%
Very low	13	10	13	11	12	11	10	9	10	11	11
A bit low	28	31	27	29	30	28	25	20	21	25	24
Reasonable	54	55	56	55	54	56	59	63	60	56	58
On high side	5	4	4	4	5	5	6	9	8	9	7
Base	*817*	*778*	*857*	*1532*	*1381*	*1462*	*1307*	*1236*	*1144*	*1447*	*1449*

If we repeat this exercise for different income and social groups, we find an increasing gap between the answers given by different income groups, which is exactly what we would expect at a time of increasing inequality.[9] The most low paid group remain very disgruntled with their pay, while middle and higher income groups become progressively less dissatisfied. Indeed in the last two surveys, the readings for the high income group indicate that as a group, high earners express a broad degree of satisfaction with their remuneration.

Indirect evidence of increasing income inequality can also be found if we examine employees' expectations regarding pay. We asked:

> *If you stay in this job, would you expect your wages or salary over the coming year to rise by **more** than the cost of living, rise by the **same** as the cost of living, rise by less than the cost of living, or not to rise at all?*

Responses to this question are shown in the next table. In essence, it seems that the proportions of people expecting to fare either well or badly in the earnings league have both been increasing, whilst those expecting their pay to rise in line with inflation have both fallen. If we compare data from similar stages of the economic cycle this is shown quite clearly. For instance, in 1983, 27 per cent of employees thought their salary would rise by *less* than the cost of living - and nine per cent that it would not rise at all. By 1993, however, these figures stood at 29 per cent and 15 per cent respectively, an overall rise of eight percentage points.

However, the most striking feature of this table is the general degree of pessimism about pay trends. The 1980s saw a sustained rise in real wages - yet, even during the Lawson expansion, only around a fifth of employees thought their pay would move ahead of inflation (with a larger proportion expecting the opposite). Expectations regarding pay, therefore, have become severely depressed, helping to explain the non-inflationary growth

phenomenon of recent years. The 1995 figures are, however, less pessimistic than those recorded in 1993 and 1994, these having marked the greatest level of pessimism about wages ever recorded in the series (Hedges, 1994).

Employees' expectations regarding own pay

	1983	1984	1985	1986	1987	1989	1990	1991	1993	1994	1995
	%	%	%	%	%	%	%	%	%	%	%
Wages will rise by:											
More than cost of living	15	13	15	20	18	15	16	19	13	14	17
Same as cost of living	46	47	44	45	52	44	48	47	41	37	38
Less than cost of living	27	26	30	22	19	30	27	24	29	29	29
Will not rise at all	9	10	8	10	8	8	6	7	15	19	13
Base	*817*	*778*	*857*	*1532*	*1381*	*1462*	*1307*	*1236*	*1144*	*1447*	*1449*

Conclusion

Our data contain a mixed message for government and opposition. On the one hand, there is little evidence of substantial job insecurity. Despite a high degree of turnover in the labour market, there remains stability of tenure for a considerable group. People now appear to feel more confident about holding onto their jobs - and this improvement seems to have been reflected in a more general recovery in consumer confidence.

On the other hand, at a time when the labour market is becoming increasingly polarised, the *British Social Attitudes* survey reveals that the overwhelming majority of people think that the gap between high and low incomes is excessive. This consensus has, if anything, become more pronounced over time. Furthermore, although pay expectations appear to have been severely depressed, there is little evidence of any deep-rooted change in people's attitudes towards employment - suggesting that government attempts to win over the hearts and minds of British workers to more flexible working patterns have not yet paid dividends.

Notes

1. Evidence for the latter is, however, surprisingly weak. For instance, the OECD (1996) find that collective bargaining, minimum wage controls and the like are indeed associated with a stable income distribution, but find no significant evidence that this hits employment prospects for unskilled workers.
2. Hutton draws the implication that, contrary to the Galbraith thesis of a blocking majority, there is now 60:40 majority support for the welfare state formed by a coalition of the two 30 per cent groups. Taylor-Gooby (1995) uses the results of the 12th British Social Attitudes survey to examine this thesis.

3. These figures show that although Britons tend to work longer hours than do workers in other European countries, these have been on a declining trend. Indeed, one of the strangest aspects of the current recovery revealed by official surveys is that the average hours worked which usually move up sharply in the initial stages of recovery have failed to respond this time (Curtice and Spencer, 1994).

4. Gregg and Wadsworth disaggregate their data by gender, but find convergence between the two in their recent time series data. Reflecting this, we find surprisingly little male/female difference once the full/part time distinction is allowed for.

5. Our inertia index is calculated by scoring responses as follows: those who say it is "not at all likely" that they will leave their current employer over the next year score 2; those who are "not very likely" score 1; those who are "quite likely" score -1; and those who are "very likely" score - 2.

6. The other reasons (with 1995 figures given in brackets) were: firm will close (four per cent), reaching retirement age (four per cent); early retirement (three per cent); contract expiry (eight per cent); returning to education (four per cent); and family responsibilities (eight per cent).

7. Curtice and Spencer (1994), commenting on the unusual weakness of the official hours data during the recent recovery, suggested that the failure of overtime working to provide the usual signal of economic recovery on the shopfloor had confused the workforce and so cancelled or at least postponed the recovery in job security and consumer confidence. The recent recovery in workplace employment expectations and confidence suggests that this effect is now wearing off.

8. It is certainly hard to rationalise this in terms of standard measures of real take-home pay (such as the gap between the growth in average earnings and the tax and price index), which were looking weak at this time. Indeed, real earnings for those remaining in work rose more quickly in 1992 and 1993, as inflation fell and earnings failed to adjust quickly to this, when if anything employees become more disgruntled about pay.

9. Social Groups I and II were as dissatisfied with their remuneration as the rest of the workforce during the mid 1980s, but then became less dissatisfied between 1987 and 1989, perhaps in response to the reduction in the top rate of tax from 60 to 40 per cent in the 1988 budget.

References

Atkinson, A.B. (1997, forthcoming), 'Bringing income distribution in from the cold', *Economic Journal*, 1996 Royal Economic Society Conference volume.

Buck, N., Gershuny, J., Rose, D. and Scott, J. (1994), *Changing Households: The British Household Panel Survey, 1990-92*, Colchester: ESRC Research Centre on Micro-social change, University of Essex.

Burgess, S., and Rees, H. (1996), 'Job tenure in Britain 1975-1991', *Economic Journal*, **106**, 334-45.

Commission on Social Inequality (1993), *Social Inequality and Justice in a Changing World*, June, London: Institute for Public Policy Research.

Cooper, C. (1996), 'Hot under the collar', *Times Higher Educational Supplement*, June 21.

Curtice J. and Spencer, P. (1994), *Labour Flexibility and the Feelgood Factor*, London,: Kleinwort Benson.

Department of Social Security (1994), *Households Below Average Incomes, 1979-1992*, London: HMSO.

Galbraith, J.K. (1993), *The Culture of Contentment*, London: Penguin.

Gregg, P and Wadsworth, J. (1995), 'A short history of labour turnover, job tenure and job security', *Oxford Review of Economic Policy*, **11: 1**, 3-90.

Hedges, B. (1994), 'Work in a changing climate', in Jowell, R., Curtice, J., Brook, L. and Ahrendt, D. (eds.), *British Social Attitudes, the 11th Report*, Aldershot: Dartmouth.

Hills, J. (1995), *Joseph Rowntree Foundation Inquiry into Income and Wealth*, **II,** York: Joseph Rowntree Foundation.

Hutton, W. (1995), *The State We're In*, London: Jonathan Cape.

Jowell, R. and Park, A. (1996, forthcoming), 'Questioning British attitudes', in Taylor B. and Thomson K., (eds.), *Understanding Change in Social Attitudes*, Aldershot: Dartmouth.

Katz, L.M. and Murphy, K.M. (1992), 'Changes in relative wages 1963-87', *Quarterly Journal of Economics*, **107:1,** 35-79.

OECD (1996), *Employment Outlook*, July.

Robinson, P. (1995), *Change, Insecurity and Inequality: a Crisis of Work?* mimeo, London: Centre for Economic Performance, LSE.

Taylor-Gooby, P. (1995), 'Comfortable, marginal and excluded: who should pay higher taxes for a better welfare state?', in Jowell, R., Curtice J., Park A., Brook L. and Ahrendt, D. (eds.), *British Social Attitude: the 12th Report*, Aldershot: Dartmouth

Wood, A. (1994), *North-South Trade, Employment and Inequality: Changing Fortunes in a Skill-Driven World,* Oxford: Clarendon Press.

Acknowledgement

SCPR is grateful to the Department for Education and Employment whose financial support for the survey since 1984 has enabled us to continue to ask questions on labour market, workplace and education issues.

5 Illegal drugs: liberal and restrictive attitudes

Arthur Gould, Andrew Shaw and Daphne Ahrendt *

Introduction

Few would dispute that illegal drug use in the United Kingdom has risen over the past few decades. The number of registered addicts has increased from around 1,000 in 1970 to almost 30,000 in 1993, while seizures of drugs by customs and the police have risen from 11,000 in 1974 to nearly 70,000 in 1992 (Plant, 1987; ISDD, 1994). In 1993 around three in ten (31 per cent) of 16 year olds were found to have used an illegal drug.[1] The British policy response to this situation is mixed. Police forces are often taking a less tough line on some drug offences - such as possession of cannabis - and letting off offenders with a caution. On the other hand, the Home Secretary recently increased the fine for possession of cannabis to £2,500, much to the dismay of some senior police officers.

Meanwhile, a policy of 'harm reduction' dominates drug agencies throughout the country. Drug agency workers are virtually united in rejecting abstention as a policy, believing that this is not only unrealistic but that it has proved counterproductive in the past. Much better, they argue, to accept that drug use will occur and warn those doing so of the risks they take. To this end, syringe exchange schemes have been set up to encourage those injecting to do so with clean needles; methadone is prescribed to those dependent upon

* Arthur Gould is Senior Lecturer in the Department of Social Sciences at Loughborough University; Andrew Shaw is a Senior Researcher at SCPR; Daphne Ahrendt is an Associate Project Director at International Survey Research Limited.

heroin; advice is given on the dangers of adulteration and of using drugs in particular combinations.[2]

In such a fluid situation it is important to be able to gauge accurately the *public* mood. There are policy issues over which politicians are forced, rightly, to give in to public demands and pressures. Alternatively, it can be important that the public be educated in the light of expert opinion. Either way, policy-makers at least need to be aware of the extent to which their goals and assumptions have public backing. With public support there may be much they can achieve; without it they may be severely limited. How far, for instance, can a Home Secretary go in the 'war against drugs'? Does the public want tougher action, as may seem to be the case after a well-publicised 'Ecstasy death', or does it want a more tolerant approach from the authorities?[3]

We begin our chapter by considering how we might best conceptualise attitudes towards drugs. We then examine whether attitudes towards drugs have changed over time, and consider the key characteristics associated with what we shall term 'liberal' and 'restrictive' attitudes towards drugs. Our results suggest that, while the public as a whole remains hostile to drugs, certain groups are more liberal than others in their attitudes. Moreover, there is greater tolerance of cannabis than heroin - and this tolerance seems to have increased over time. We also find that there is a link between attitudes towards drugs, authoritarian attitudes generally, and attitudes towards a range of other issues (such as nationalism and immigration).

'Liberal' and 'restrictive' attitudes towards drugs

Most European countries are signatories to the international conventions which prohibit the production, sale and possession of narcotics and psychotropic drugs. However, the failure of prohibition to prevent the spread of drug use has prompted a variety of innovative policy responses to the issue. In Switzerland, for instance, there has been an experiment with the creation of a zone for heroin injectors in a Zürich park. Meanwhile, the Dutch have, to a large extent, decriminalised the use of cannabis and have, along with the British, introduced a range of harm reduction measures. Within these and other countries there are also those who argue for the legalisation of drugs altogether.

These attempts to approach drug use in a more 'liberal' way stand in stark contrast to what is termed 'the restrictive line' adopted in Sweden. There, the aim adopted by government is that of a drug-free society, its rationale being that failure to stop *all* drug use will result in such use spreading, epidemic-like, throughout society. Consequently, policies prioritising the arrest and punishment of suppliers are insufficient - consumers must be targeted and young people, in particular, need to be closely supervised in order to curtail drug habits (Bejerot and Hartelius, 1984). To this end, adult and young

'misusers' can be compulsorily taken into care, and being under the influence of drugs is now an imprisonable offence (Gould, 1989, 1994a). Countries which have taken a more liberal line are regarded by the Swedish authorities as having capitulated to the drugs problem. Even syringe exchange schemes - a harm reduction measure aimed at stopping the spread of HIV infection - have been prohibited in most Swedish counties (Gould, 1993 and 1994b).

In essence, therefore, a restrictive perspective is one which sees drugs as dangerously addictive and which emphasises abstinence on the part of the individual, and prohibition on the part of policy-makers. Drug use and misuse are viewed as a major threat to individuals and society. Conversely, a liberal perspective is more likely to accept that individuals can, and do, exert control over their use of drugs, that drug use is not necessarily harmful *per se* and that prohibition creates as many problems as it solves. Often other social problems are seen as greater threats to individuals and society than drug-taking.

This distinction between 'liberal' and 'restrictive' perspectives towards drugs is of considerable use when considering attitudes towards drugs. In many instances, the two positions represent the mirror image of one another. In Sweden, for instance, the belief might be that 'we must aim for a drug-free society', with the British equivalent being 'we must accept that we live in a drug-taking society'. Swedish experts would say that 'all use of drugs is misuse'. In contrast, British experts in the 1980s were accepting the fact that some use of drugs was 'non-problematic' (ACMD, 1982). Major British reports had testified to the relatively harmless nature of cannabis (Justice, 1991), whereas in Sweden one would read that cannabis was as dangerous a narcotic as heroin. This difference was quite clearly illustrated when, in 1994, we selected a number of liberal and restrictive statements from the British and Swedish literature on drugs and asked drug agency workers in both countries to rate how much they agreed with them. The results could not have been more polarised. All the British workers were at the liberal end of the spectrum and almost all the Swedes were at the restrictive end.[4]

Changing attitudes over time?

We begin by examining the extent to which attitudes towards two specific drugs (cannabis and heroin) have changed over time. We also consider variations in attitudes according to a range of socio-demographic variables (such as age, gender, education, social class and religion), party identification[5] and region.

Attitudes towards cannabis

On several occasions since 1983 we have asked respondents to the *British Social Attitudes* survey whether they agree or disagree that "smoking cannabis should be legalised". In 1995, just over three in ten agreed with this statement, compared with just under six in ten who disagreed. This marks a considerable change over time, with the British public steadily becoming less apprehensive of the drug. Although the majority still believes that smoking cannabis should be illegal, this proportion has fallen from 78 per cent in 1983 to 58 per cent some twelve years later.

Smoking cannabis should be legalised

	1983	1993	1995
	%	%	%
Agree	12	20	31
Neither agree nor disagree	10	17	12
Disagree	78	62	58
Base	*1610*	*1261*	*1041*

As seen in the next table, there are substantial age differences in attitudes towards the legalisation of cannabis. Only a third of the under-25s believe that cannabis should remain illegal, compared with over two-thirds of those aged 45 or over. Education, too, makes a difference. Those who had left school by the age of 15 are much more likely than those who remained in education until they were at least 19 to think that cannabis should remain illegal (70 per cent and 44 per cent respectively). Political party identification also matters, as does religious affiliation.

  Are some social groups leading the way when it comes to changing attitudes towards the legalisation of cannabis? As the next table shows, the declining belief that cannabis should remain illegal has occurred among all age-groups, but is most notable among those aged under 45. In particular, amongst young adults in our surveys (those aged between 18 and 24), the percentage who believe that smoking cannabis should be illegal has nearly halved since 1983. Similar sorts of changes are apparent among other social groups, though they are rarely as marked (the exception being a similarly dramatic change in the attitudes of those who remained in education until they were at least 19).

Smoking cannabis should be legalised
% disagreeing

	1983	1995	% point change	Base (1983)	Base (1995)
All	78	58	-20	1613	1041
Age group					
18-24	60	33	-27	209	91
25-34	65	44	-21	303	235
35-44	80	51	-29	311	198
45-54	86	71	-15	248	168
55+	83	70	-13	537	347
Terminal education age					
19 plus	65	44	-20	140	161
15 or under	80	70	-11	882	393
Party identification					
Labour	75	51	-24	530	445
Conservative	82	67	-15	627	273
Religious affiliation					
None	66	49	-17	504	422
Church of England	82	65	-17	652	343

Of course, the debate about the legalisation of cannabis is a complex one. To take account of some of the key issues, we asked people in 1993 and 1995 to choose between three possible positions governing the use of cannabis. As shown in the next table, this reveals a small shift in a liberal direction even in the short time since 1993 with around a third in 1995 opting for the legalisation of cannabis. Once again, the age difference is large, with over half of young adults (54 per cent) - and only one in seven older people (15 per cent) - favouring legalisation in one form or another. However, responses to these statements did not vary greatly by the other social characteristics discussed previously.

The legal status of cannabis

	1993 %	1995 %
Taking cannabis...		
... should be legal, without restrictions	5	6
... should be legal, but it should only be available from licensed shops	25	28
... should remain illegal	67	64
Base	*1484*	*1221*

What should happen to those who break the law as it stands? A large majority of the public (78 per cent overall), including all major sub-groups, agree that "people who sell cannabis should always be prosecuted". However, there is considerable variation in opinion over whether those "possessing small amounts of cannabis for their own use" should be prosecuted. Around four in ten (41 per cent) think they should not be prosecuted compared with around five in ten (49 per cent) who think they should. The majority of young people (52 per cent), graduates (62 per cent) and Londoners (65 per cent) agree with the non-prosecution of those possessing cannabis. This last finding possibly reflects the cosmopolitan nature of the capital, with the population of London being more used to, and more accepting of, a wider range of living styles than those in other parts of the country.

We also asked respondents whether they agreed or disagreed with the following two statements:

- *cannabis is a cause of crime and violence*
- *cannabis isn't nearly as damaging as some people think*

Those disagreeing with the first statement increased five percentage points between 1993 and 1995 (with 28 per cent disagreeing in 1995). However, there was no real change in the proportion agreeing with the latter statement (around a third doing so in 1993 and 1995), indicating that most people still perceive risks in using cannabis.

Overall, therefore, our results point towards a very small shift towards more liberal views over the short period since 1993 and a larger shift since 1983, but there remains a majority with restrictive attitudes towards cannabis.

Changing attitudes

Why might attitudes towards cannabis have changed? One possibility is that the liberal shift we have identified may partly reflect an increase in *perceptions* of cannabis use. If more people are perceived to have experimented with a drug, and its effects are not judged to be detrimental, then its use is perhaps more likely to be tolerated. Certainly, a majority of people believe that cannabis use is on the increase - two-thirds agree, for instance, that "there are more people taking cannabis in Britain now than there were five years ago" and 58 per cent think there will be more people taking cannabis in five years time compared with the present day.

Of course, the liberal shift may also reflect an actual increase in cannabis *use*. In 1995, when asked "have you yourself ever tried cannabis", just over one in five (21 per cent) said that they had. This marks an increase of five percentage points on the comparable figure from 1993 (when 16 per cent reported cannabis use). This is a large difference over a relatively short

period of time, and suggests that public policy is failing to prevent growth in the numbers of people who try this drug. This increase in 'users' does account for much of the shift we have identified towards more liberal views - as we shall see, there is a strong correlation between having used cannabis and holding liberal views about the drug.

Use of cannabis

Use of cannabis is clearly related to age - nearly four in ten of those aged between 18 and 34 have tried cannabis, compared with less than three per cent of those aged 55 and over.

% with experience of cannabis, by age

	%	Base
All	21	1220
Age		
18-24	37	104
25-34	38	274
35-44	28	220
45-54	14	207
55-64	2	152
65+	3	263

Education also makes a difference, with 45 per cent of graduates having tried cannabis. There are also regional variations, 36 per cent of those in London having tried the drug compared with only eight per cent of those in the Midlands. Of those who had tried cannabis, only a small minority (13 per cent) had done so 'often', while a majority (60 per cent) had tried it 'hardly ever' or 'only once'. However, two-thirds (67 per cent) of young users said they had tried cannabis 'occasionally' or 'often'.

Not surprisingly, 'triers' and 'abstainers' differ substantially in their attitudes towards cannabis. For instance, 'abstainers' are three times more likely than 'triers' to agree that "cannabis is a cause of crime and violence" (60 per cent and 20 per cent respectively). Similarly, 63 per cent of 'triers' agree that "cannabis isn't nearly as damaging as some people think" compared with just under a fifth of 'abstainers'.

On the question of legalising cannabis, the views of 'triers' and 'abstainers' are even more polarised, with three-quarters of 'triers' favouring legislation, and a similar proportion of 'abstainers' opposing it.

	'Trier'	'Abstainer'
Taking cannabis	%	%
... should be legal, without restrictions	14	3
... should be legal, but it should only be available from licensed shops	63	19
... should remain illegal	22	77
Base	*252*	*960*

Of note, however, is that the majority of 'triers' believe that cannabis should only be available from licensed shops, rather than being sold without restriction.

Attitudes towards heroin

Compared with attitudes towards cannabis, views on heroin are much more restrictive. Even cannabis 'triers' are not, in this respect, very unusual in their views on heroin. Thus, only one per cent of both cannabis 'triers' and 'abstainers' believe that taking heroin should be legal without restrictions. A huge majority - unchanged since 1993 - think that taking heroin should remain illegal.

	1993	1995
Taking heroin ...	%	%
... should be legal, without restrictions	1	1
... should be legal, but it should only be available from licensed shops	10	10
... should remain illegal	86	86
Base	*1484*	*1221*

It is not surprising to find that nearly nine in ten people want heroin to remain illegal. An equally large proportion of the public believes that heroin is "a cause of crime and violence", while less than a quarter believe that the drug is "not nearly as damaging to users as some people think". There is little change here compared with 1993.

While most people (72 per cent) agree that legalising heroin would result in many more people becoming addicts, the minority that disagrees is not negligible (17 per cent). Unusually, responses are *not* related to age. Rather, it is education which matters, with 58 per cent of graduates (compared with 78 per cent of those without a qualification) believing that legalising heroin would result in more addicts.

The public takes a tough stance on the sale and possession of heroin. There is near unanimous agreement (around 95 per cent) that "people who sell heroin always be prosecuted', while 70 per cent favour the prosecution of

those "possessing small amounts of heroin for their own use". Young people, graduates and Londoners, however, are less likely to favour prosecution for possession.

People should not be prosecuted for possessing small amounts of heroin

		Agree	Neither agree nor disagree	Disagree	Base
All	%	21	9	70	1224
Under 25s	%	25	14	61	104
Graduates	%	32	10	58	123
Londoners	%	37	14	49	130

Attitudes towards heroin do not vary much by sex, religion or political party identification. Even the young do not differ greatly in their attitudes compared with older age groups. However, whereas only ten per cent of the public think that heroin should be legal but only available from licensed shops, 26 per cent of graduates hold this view.

Cannabis and heroin

There is a clear relationship between views towards the legalisation of cannabis and heroin, though it should be noted that the majority of those who favour cannabis legalisation *oppose* this for heroin. Of the small group wishing to see the legalisation of cannabis without restriction, 15 per cent would want this for heroin too, while a further 32 per cent would accept heroin under a licensing system. Of those who support supply of cannabis under licence, 29 per cent favour the same law for heroin.

It is evident then that opinions relating to cannabis are much more evenly divided than is the case for heroin. There are some links between attitudes towards the two drugs, but it seems that many people both distinguish clearly between cannabis and heroin, and have different attitudes towards them. So, for example, nearly a quarter of all respondents think that heroin is a cause of crime and violence, but that cannabis is not. Moreover, the vast majority of those who do not think that "cannabis is a cause of crime and violence" (85 per cent) think precisely the opposite when it comes to heroin.

Liberal and restrictive attitudes towards illegal drugs

We have seen that, over the last few years, there has been a liberalising of attitudes towards cannabis. Moreover, considerable differences exist between the views of certain social groups on both cannabis and heroin.

The next section builds on these findings by analysing the responses to a number of statements which were included for the first time in the 1995 *British Social Attitudes* survey. These statements were based upon a liberal-restrictive scale previously administered to British and Swedish drug agency workers.[6] Although the scale had worked well in terms of validity, it had been designed with professional respondents in mind. For the *British Social Attitudes* survey, it was necessary to make the items more intelligible to a lay audience.

The illegal drugs scale

To assess people's attitudes towards illegal drugs, we asked them how strongly they agreed or disagreed with a number of statements about drugs. Roughly half the statements are liberal and half restrictive. Together they address a number of key issues, these ranging from the use of drugs and their legal status to individual freedom, morality and deviance.[7]

The advantage of this approach is that, by including a number of different statements about drugs, we can construct an attitude *scale* - a composite summary measure based on more than one item. This allows us to 'cancel out' some of the variations in response that might be due to, say, wording or context (see, for instance, Schuman and Presser, 1981; deVellis, 1991). The construction of the scale is discussed in detail in the Appendix to this chapter.

The statements used to build our scale are shown below. They show clearly that the general public can be described as *restrictive* in its attitude towards drugs. The liberal statements, for instance, all have levels of disagreement around, or in excess of 50 per cent. Disagreement is strongest on the question of whether adults should be free to take "any drug they wish" (with nearly eight in every ten disagreeing). Only the most libertarian is willing to go quite this far. However, the evidence suggests that on all the other items, liberal opinion consists of between a quarter and a third of the population. Thus, 27 per cent agree that illegal drug use "can sometimes be beneficial" and 32 per cent accept that illegal drugs are "a normal part of some people's lives".

Attitudes towards illegal drugs

Liberal statements:		Agree	Neither agree nor disagree	Disagree	Base
We need to accept that using illegal drugs is a normal part of some people's lives	%	32	19	49	1008
Smoking cannabis should be legalised	%	31	12	58	1041
Taking illegal drugs can sometimes be beneficial	%	27	23	51	1004
Adults should be free to take any drug they wish	%	9	13	78	1005
Restrictive statements:					
All use of illegal drugs is misuse	%	60	18	21	1004
Taking drugs is always morally wrong	%	53	25	22	1003
The best way to treat people who are addicted to drugs is to stop them from using drugs altogether	%	53	24	23	1009
The use of illegal drugs always leads to addiction	%	49	22	29	1008

Note: the base for each statement excludes those who did not answer it.

A similar, but less marked, conclusion can be drawn from responses to the restrictive statements. Thus, six in ten agree that "all use of illegal drugs is misuse" and around half agree with the three remaining statements. Liberal opinion remains steady at around 20 per cent for the rest. The highest liberal score (29 per cent) is for rejection of the statement that drug use "always leads to addiction".

These responses suggest that - on a range of individual items - between 70 and 80 per cent of the whole population hold restrictive views and between 20 and 30 per cent are liberal in their attitudes. Of course, people may have restrictive views on some items and liberal views on others, which is why a scale based on several items is useful.

Scale scores were calculated so that the most liberal possible position was scored 1.0, while the most restrictive score was scored 5.0. The mean score was 3.53, showing that, overall, attitudes in Britain tend to be slightly restrictive. If we group these scores into five categories from the most liberal to the most restrictive, the results are as follows:

Description	Score range	Percentage in range
Very liberal	1.00 - 1.99	4
Liberal	2.00 - 2.50	10
Moderate	2.51 - 3.49	29
Restrictive	3.50 - 4.00	30
Very restrictive	4.01 - 5.00	28
Base		*995*

Socio-economic influences on attitudes towards illegal drugs

Scale scores were calculated for a range of socio-economic groups. The mean scores for men (3.54) and women (3.52) are almost identical. However, men are more likely than women to have extreme scores, with a higher proportion of men than women in the very restrictive group (33 per cent of men and 23 per cent of women) *and* in the liberal and very liberal groups (17 per cent of men and 12 per cent of women).

Other social groups differ significantly in their scores on the scale. Given our earlier findings it is not surprising that scale scores increase substantially (that is, they become more restrictive) with age. The average score among those aged under 35 is 3.17, compared to a mean of 3.56 among 35 to 54 year olds and one of 3.88 among those 55 and over. Furthermore, as the next table shows, younger people are split fairly evenly between those with liberal views, moderate views and restrictive views. By contrast, over three-quarters of older people have restrictive outlooks.

Liberal, moderate and restrictive scale scores, by age

		Liberal score (1.0-2.5)	Moderate score (2.51-3.49)	Restrictive score (3.5-5.0)	*Base*
All	%	14	29	57	*995*
Age					
18-34	%	26	35	39	*315*
35-54	%	13	30	57	*353*
55 and over	%	3	20	77	*326*

Education is also an important influence on scale scores. The mean score among degree holders is *below* 3.0 and there are more liberals than those with restrictive views. In contrast, most of those in other qualification groups hold restrictive views, though the majorities are slender among those with A and O level qualifications.

Liberal, moderate and restrictive scale scores, by educational qualification

Highest qualification:		Liberal score (1.0-2.5)	Moderate score (2.51-3.49)	Restrictive score (3.5-5.0)	Base
Degree level	%	33	39	28	105
Other higher education	%	13	30	57	141
A level or equivalent	%	21	24	53	154
O level or equivalent	%	14	33	53	203
CSE level	%	7	27	66	82
None	%	6	24	70	300

A number of other socio-economic characteristics were associated with high or low scores on the drugs scale. For instance, those belonging to a religion have higher - more restrictive - scores than those who do not. There may also be a regional effect, since the mean score in Greater London (3.25) is noticeably *lower* than in other regions.

Clearly some of the differences in scores that we have found may be simply a reflection of others. For example, the lower - more liberal - scores among graduates may simply reflect the higher concentration of the young among those with degrees (this stemming from the comparatively recent expansion of higher education). In order to take account of this, we used an analysis technique - regression - which enables us to differentiate the effects of different characteristics upon, in this case, a person's score on the illegal drugs scale. This technique first selects the variable most strongly associated with scale score. Then it tests the extent to which others variables explain the remaining variance in scores and selects that which explains most. And so forth (Ahrendt and Young, 1994: 82).[8]

This analysis confirms the primary importance of age and, then, of holding a degree. This suggests that the relationship between age and attitudes does not simply reflect an 'age effect' (that is, that attitudes towards drugs will harden as people grow older). Rather, as higher education seems to have a liberalising effect even when age is taken into account, we might expect to see a marked increase in liberal attitudes towards drugs over the coming years.

Two other characteristics emerged as significant in our analysis. Living in London, as opposed to anywhere else in Great Britain, was associated with a slightly more liberal score on the drugs scale, as was not belonging to a religion (as opposed to belonging to one).[9] Gender and social class are confirmed to have no impact on mean scale scores.

Party identification

Earlier we found that Conservative Party identification was associated with having restrictive attitudes towards illegal drugs. The results of our scale back this up, although the variation between those identifying with different parties is comparatively small once other factors such as age are taken into account.[10]   Certainly, within all parties, those with restrictive attitudes far outnumber those with liberal ones.

Liberal, moderate and restrictive scale scores, by political party identification

		Liberal score (1.0-2.5)	Moderate score (2.51-3.49)	Restrictive score (3.5-5.0)	Base
Party identification:					
Conservative	%	10	23	67	*263*
Labour	%	18	30	53	*424*
Liberal Democrat	%	12	37	51	*146*
None	%	13	25	62	*87*

Authoritarian and libertarian attitudes

Attitudes towards certain issues are, quite clearly, related to traditional political distinctions between 'left' and 'right'. For instance, people's attitudes towards the welfare state, taxation and the redistribution of income and wealth are likely to vary according to whether one is left-wing or right-wing politically. But on some issues - such as capital punishment, censorship, punishment and acceptance of authority - the distinction between left-wing and right-wing values tells us little. Often, those at either the 'libertarian' or 'authoritarian' end of the spectrum may be drawn from both the political left *and* right. Attitudes towards drugs may well fall into this category of issues.[11] For instance, calls for a more liberal approach to drugs unite the Labour MPs Clare Short and Tony Banks, Liberal Democratic Party conferences and Professor Patrick Minford, the monetarist economist who has acted as an advisor to successive Conservative governments. Articles calling for legalisation of certain drugs are as likely to appear in the Economist as the New Statesman (Economist, 1988, New Statesman and Society, 1993).

The *British Social Attitudes* surveys include a set of questions which aim to measure where people stand on the libertarian-authoritarian and left-right value dimensions (both are explained fully in Appendix I of this Report). Our results certainly suggest that attitudes towards drugs *are* associated with how authoritarian or libertarian people are in their social and political attitudes.[12] This is illustrated in the next table, which groups scores on the libertarian-authoritarian scale into four categories. We also take into account

age, since this is related to scores on both scales. In contrast, a person's score on the left-right scale was not related to their score on the drugs scale.

As the next table shows (although the numbers in each group are rather small) among every age group the mean score on the drugs scale increases - that is, it becomes more restrictive - as we move from those with libertarian values, through those with moderate values, to those with authoritarian values. In particular, young libertarians have distinctively liberal views on drugs with a mean score of only 2.4 (although it should be noted that this group includes only 55 people). In contrast, mean scores on the drugs scale exceed 3.5 (and even 4) among authoritarian respondents.

Mean drugs scale score, by age and libertarian-authoritarian scale category

	Age					
	18-34		35-54		55 and over	
Libertarian-authoritarian scale position:		Base		Base		Base
Libertarian	2.4	55	3.0	58	3.1	32
Moderate	3.0	90	3.3	76	3.6	51
Authoritarian	3.5	103	3.6	124	3.9	102
Very authoritarian	3.6	66	4.0	94	4.2	139

National identity and immigrants

A number of writers on drug issues have commented upon the links between attitudes towards 'foreigners', or immigrants, and drugs. In the early years of the century, the media showed young British women as being the prey of 'evil orientals' who would use drugs to seduce and corrupt them (Kohn, 1992). The United States provides numerous illustrations of Mexicans, Blacks and Chinese portrayed as corrupting American youth and values (Musto, 1987). And Swedish concern about drugs has been accompanied by a concern about the damage being done to the Swedish way of life and national identity (Tham, 1991). As the 'influx' of immigrants is often portrayed as a threat to a nation's culture, so the importation of foreign drugs can be seen as having the same effect.

In 1995, a number of relevant questions were included on the *British Social Attitudes* survey. These substantiate this apparent link between attitudes to drugs and attitudes towards immigration and national identity. The results are shown in the next table and demonstrate a strong tendency for those with a liberal attitude towards drugs to be tolerant of the foreign and for those with a restrictive attitude to be intolerant. Thus, those with a restrictive attitude towards drugs are much more likely to believe that Britain is superior to other countries; that ethnic groups should adapt to the larger society; that immigrants cause crime; and that the European Union is a threat to British

traditions. Those with a liberal attitude towards drugs are not only less likely to agree with these sorts of statement, but are more likely to feel that Britain benefits from immigration and that the number of immigrants should be increased or remain the same.

  Of course, none of these relationships are absolute. For example, among both liberals and restrictivists more people share the view that it is better if ethnic groups adapt and blend in than think it is better if groups maintain their customs. Furthermore, age influences attitudes to both drugs and 'the foreign'. Yet within age groups the pattern remains clear: for a substantial minority of the population liberal-restrictive attitudes towards drugs are mirrored by liberal-restrictive attitudes towards what is foreign. This opens up the possibility that movement towards more insular attitudes to the foreign and to immigration might be associated with increasingly restrictive attitudes towards drugs (and, conversely, that more open attitudes towards the foreign might be associated with a liberalisation of attitudes towards drugs).

Attitudes towards 'the foreign' by attitudes towards drugs

	Liberal score (1.0-2.5)	Moderate score (2.51-3.49)	Restrictive score (3.5-4.0)	Very restrictive score (4.01-5.0)
% agreeing:				
The world would be a better place if people from other countries were more like the British	15	19	30	45
Immigrants increase crime rates	10	18	28	36
The number of immigrants should be increased or remain the same	54	34	27	21
Immigrants make Britain more open to new ideas and cultures	73	56	50	39
Lots of good traditions will be given up if we stay in the EU	21	36	46	53
% whose view closest to:				
It is better for society if (ethnic) groups maintain their distinct customs and traditions	35	12	15	11
% whose view closest to:				
It is better if (ethnic) groups adapt and blend into the larger society	51	68	65	72
Base	*134*	*274*	*305*	*268*

Attitudes towards specific drugs

Earlier we saw that attitudes towards drugs can depend upon the drug in question. How, then, do the results of our general drugs scale tally with questions about specific drugs - in this case, cannabis and heroin?

As the next table shows, the majority of liberals are *not* particularly liberal when it comes to the legalisation of heroin or its consequences. However, not surprisingly, their views are generally less strong than those with restrictive attitudes towards drugs. Only 46 per cent of liberals thought that the legalisation of heroin would increase the number of addicts, compared with 85 per cent of the most restrictive respondents. Differences were most apparent on the issue of prosecuting people for possession. Over half (52 per cent) of liberals thought they should not be prosecuted, in marked contrast to all other groups where less than 20 per cent agreed. Those with liberal attitudes are also less likely than those with restrictive ones to think that heroin use has increased over the last five years.

Attitudes towards heroin by drugs scale categories

	Liberal score (1.0-2.5)	Moderate score (2.51-3.49)	Restrictive score (3.5-4.0)	Very restrictive score (4.01-5.0)
% agreeing:				
Heroin use is greater now than five years ago	59	68	73	82
Heroin is a cause of crime and violence	83	87	92	98
Heroin isn't nearly as damaging as some think	14	10	8	7
If you legalise heroin many more people will become addicts	46	64	78	85
People should not be prosecuted for possessing small amounts of heroin for their own use	52	19	16	12
People who sell heroin should always be prosecuted	87	95	99	99
Base	*134*	*274*	*305*	*268*

The differences between those with liberal and restrictive attitudes towards drugs are exceptionally large when it comes to the issue of cannabis.[13] True, there is no great disagreement between these groups over whether cannabis use has grown in the last five years (with a clear majority in each group thinking that it has). But, on all the other statements, there were considerable differences. When it comes to the prosecution of those selling cannabis, for instance, those in the most restrictive camp were nearly twice as likely as

those in the most liberal camp to think that prosecution should always occur. Few liberals think cannabis is a cause of crime, compared with most of those with restrictive attitudes - and fewer than one liberal in five thinks that cannabis use will increase the number of addicts, compared with around four-fifths of those with more restrictive attitudes.

Attitudes towards cannabis by drugs scale categories

	Liberal score (1.0-2.5)	Moderate score (2.51-3.49)	Restrictive score (3.5-4.0)	Very restrictive score (4.01-5.0)
% agreeing:				
Cannabis use is greater now than five years ago	66	60	64	73
Cannabis is a cause of crime and violence	12	34	61	77
Cannabis isn't nearly as damaging to users as some think	69	43	22	13
If you legalise cannabis more people will become addicts	17	44	76	85
People should not be prosecuted for possessing small amounts	83	56	29	16
People who sell cannabis should always be prosecuted	47	69	90	95
Base	*134*	*274*	*305*	*268*

When comparing views on whether heroin and cannabis should be legalised, licensed or kept illegal, we find a similar pattern. Liberals are less likely to want heroin to remain illegal (58 per cent) than those with restrictive attitudes (well over 90 per cent of whom favour this option). Moreover, 40 per cent of liberals favour a licensing system for heroin compared with less than five per cent of those with restrictive attitudes. As far as cannabis is concerned, very few liberals (six per cent) want to see it remain illegal compared to nearly all (90 per cent) of those in the restrictive camp.

If we compare attitudes towards cannabis with those towards heroin, it is clear that liberals are considerably more liberal about the former than they are about the latter. For instance, around half (47 per cent) of those in the liberal camp think that people who sell cannabis should always be prosecuted. When it comes to selling heroin, however, nearly double (87 per cent) adopt this stance. Among those in the most restrictive camp, however, practically unanimous proportions (over 95 per cent in both cases) think that those selling cannabis or heroin should always be prosecuted. In conclusion, therefore, those with liberal attitudes towards drugs appear to have a somewhat relativist stance, with the type of drug in question making a difference to their attitudes. By contrast, those with restrictive attitudes adopt

an absolute stance - with the type of drug under consideration making little difference to their overall attitudes.

Conclusions

We began this chapter by pointing out that British drug policy is a mixed bag, with tough punitive measures on the one hand, and a softer 'harm-reduction' approach on the other. We have a Home Secretary who has raised the maximum fine for cannabis offences - and police and magistrates who condemn him. We have psychiatrists who want to prescribe drugs fairly liberally, while others seek to keep maintenance prescriptions within tight limits (Marks, 1995, Johns, 1995).

Previous research in Britain has suggested that professionals working in the field generally have a very liberal approach towards drugs. However, our liberal-restrictive drugs scale suggests that the public adopt a more restrictive stance. There would seem, therefore, to be a big divide between the attitudes of professionals and the public. However, when people's attitudes are examined in more detail we can see that certain groups - most notably, young people and those with degrees - are much more likely than average to have liberal attitudes. Further, although it might be tempting for some to imagine that the young will change their minds and become more restrictive as they grow older, our evidence suggests that attitudes are moving in a liberal direction.

There is a clear relationship between attitudes towards drugs and the use of drugs, with those who have 'tried' cannabis being more liberal than those who have not. And, as cannabis use appears to be increasing, it would hardly be surprising if attitudes become more tolerant. Moreover, since having a degree is positively associated with liberal attitudes towards drugs, and increasing numbers of young Britons are going to university, this too suggests a more liberal trend in the future.

What about the task faced by the medical and social personnel who work for drug agencies up and down the country? This would still appear to be a difficult one. Enlightened ministers and civil servants have backed harm reduction as a policy more likely to improve public health than not. And this policy has not been given a high public profile, thus escaping media bashing. But such a policy can have only limited success if its messages always have to err on the side of caution. Perhaps health educationists, alongside drug agency workers, should take a more proactive role in an attempt to close the gap between professional and public attitudes. This may, however, prove difficult if, as has been shown, hostility towards drugs is closely related to British xenophobia.

What lessons can policy makers and politicians learn? It would certainly be premature for them to rush into the streets and declare the war against drugs as over and argue for blanket legalisation. But, if a sizeable minority of the

public supports a more tolerant approach to drug issues, it might also be foolhardy to clamp down too much on recreational drug use. No political party can afford to offend greatly its restrictive majority, but it might be equally dangerous to alienate the liberal minority - especially if it is growing. The one certainty seems to be that heroin is almost universally disapproved of - by young and old, highly educated and poorly educated, men and women from all social strata. Even cannabis users can be relied upon to adopt an anti-heroin stance. What liberal opinion there is seems to favour a softer line when it comes to 'soft' drugs, and a hard one when it comes to 'hard' drugs.

Notes

1. Exeter University's annual survey of school students (as cited in ISDD, 1994).
2. This approach, first mooted in the Advisory Council on the Misuse of Drugs in 1982 was finally endorsed in its 1988 Report *Drugs and AIDS* (ACMD, 1982 and 1988).
3. The 1995 survey was carried out before the press publicity surrounding the Ecstasy-related death of Leah Betts.
4. Eighty drug agency workers and employees in statutory and voluntary drug organisations in Sweden and forty in Britain were asked to respond to an equal number of liberal and restrictive statements about drugs. Mean scores of, respectively, 1.0 and 5.0 represented the most liberal and restrictive positions possible. The mean scores for the Swedes was 3.8 while for the British it was 2.0. Only three Swedes scored less than 3 (the mid-point of the scale) and no British respondents scored more than 3. One Swede had the highest score of 4.8 and a British respondent had the lowest - 1.0!
5. Party identification is explained fully in the Appendix I of this Report.
6. This research is discussed in note 4 above.
7. The full set of statements, and the responses to them, can be found in Appendix III (self-completion questionnaire version A, questions A2.51a-p).
8. We used stepwise regression techniques. Regression is explained in detail in the Appendix to this Report.
9. Together, age, education, region and religion account for 19 per cent of the variation in scale scores. In the context of predictive equations in social research, this is much less modest than it appears.
10. When party identification is included in the regression analysis it adds a little to the predictive power (the proportion of variance explained increases to 20 per cent). This suggests a weak - but detectable - link between party and attitudes to illegal drugs.
11. For instance, Ahrendt and Young suggest that attitudes towards drugs may form an additional fifth dimension to the four authoritarian dimensions identified as making up *The Authoritarian Personality* (the four being conformism, punitiveness, anti-welfarism and sexual repressiveness) (see Ahrendt and Young, 1994).
12. There was a high correlation between the liberal-restrictive drug scale and scores on the libertarian-authoritarian scale ($r = 0.541$).
13. It should be borne in mind that a statement regarding the legalisation of cannabis is one of the eight items which form the drugs scale (and hence that some correlation between the scale and individual questions on cannabis is not surprising).

References

ACMD (1982), *Treatment and Rehabilitation,* London: HMSO.

ACMD (1988), *AIDS and Drug Misuse I,* London: HMSO.

Ahrendt, D. and Young, K. (1994) 'Authoritarianism updated' in Jowell, R., Curtice, J, Brook L and Ahrendt, D. (eds.), *British Social Attitudes: the 11th Report*, Aldershot: Dartmouth.

Bejerot, N. and Hartelius, J. (1984), *Missbruk och Motåtgärder,* Stockholm: Ordfront.

DeVellis, R.F. (1991), 'Scale development: theory and applications', *Applied Social Research Methods,* Series **26**, Newbury Park: Sage.

Economist (1988), 'Getting gangsters out of drugs', 2nd April, *The Economist.*

Evans, G. and Heath, A. (1995), 'The measurement of left-right and libertarian-authoritarian values: a comparison of balanced and unbalanced scales', *Quality and Quantity,* **29**, 191-206.

Gould, A. (1989), 'Cleaning the people's home: addiction policy in Sweden', in *British Journal of Addiction,* **3**: **2**.

Gould, A. (1993), 'Opposition to syringe exchange schemes in the UK and Sweden', in *Journal of European Social Policy,* **84**: **7**.

Gould, A. (1994a), 'Pollution rituals in Sweden: the pursuit of a drug-free society', in *Scandinavian Journal of Social Welfare,* **3**: **2**.

Gould, A. (1994b), 'Sweden's syringe exchange debate', in *Journal of Social Policy,* **23**:2.

ISDD (1994), *Drug misuse in Britain*, London: Institute for the Study of Drug Dependence.

Johns, A. (1995), 'Is there really a London connection?', in *Druglink*, London: Institute for the Study of Drug Dependence, **10**: **5**.

Justice (1991), 'Drugs and the law', in *Justice*, London.

Kohn, M. (1992), *Dope Girls,* London: Lawrence and Wishart.

Marks, J. (1995), 'Who killed the British system?', in *Druglink,* London: Institute for the Study of Drug Dependence, **10**: **4**.

Musto, D.F. (1987), *The American Disease: Origins of Narcotic Control*, Oxford: Oxford University Press.

New Statesman and Society (1993), 'Legalise it', *New Statesman and Society,* 12th November.

Plant, M. (1987), *Drugs in Perspective*, London: Hodder and Stoughton.

Schuman, H and Presser, S. (1981), *Questions and Answers in Attitude Surveys: Experiments on Question Form, Wording and Context,* San Diegò: Academic Press Inc.

Spector, P.E. (1992), 'Summated rating scale construction: an introduction', *Quantitative Applications in the Social Sciences,* **82**, Newbury Park: Sage.

Tham, H. (1991), 'Narkotikakontroll som nationellt projekt', in *Nordisk Alkoholtidskrift,* **9**: **2**.

Thomson, K. and Chetwynd, M. (1996), *Discrimination Against Gay Men and Lesbians: Technical Report*, London: SCPR.

Acknowledgement

We are grateful to the Economics and Social Research Council for funding the drug items in this year's survey (Grant number R000 221601).

Appendix

The drugs scale

The development of the drugs scale was guided by Thomson's derivation of an index of prejudice against homosexuals (Thomson and Chetwynd, 1996) and by Spector (1992) and DeVellis (1991).

Sixteen items on illegal drugs were included in self-completion version A, which was 'completed' by 1058 respondents (question numbers A2.51a to A2.51p). However, there was significant non-completion of these items (which came towards the end of the questionnaire), most of which was concentrated in 44 people who simply did not answer the question. The median rate of non-response to the 16 items was 4.9 per cent. Scale development was based upon 962 respondents (978 after weighting) who answered all 16 items, though scale scores are calculable for those with limited missing data.

A simple check was made to detect 'uniform' responding - always selecting "agree" (whether strongly or not), "disagree" or a neutral position. Only 4 respondents (9 when weighted) agreed with all 16 items, none disagreed with all and 9 (10 weighted) always choose a neutral option.

The item scores were standardised to a liberal-restrictive direction, by inverting the scores on restrictive items. "Can't choose" answers were recoded as "neither agree nor disagree".

One scale?

All items were designed to relate to a single (hypothesised) liberal-restrictive dimension on attitudes to drugs. A Cronbach's alpha score for all 16 items of 0.88 suggests a highly reliable scale, but shows neither that it is optimal nor that only one dimension underlies the data. Factor analysis (principal axis factoring) did show that only one factor explains a sizeable part (33.6 per cent) of the variance amongst the 16 items. Two other factors had eigenvalues greater than 1. It would be misleading, though, to conclude that there are three underlying dimensions. First, the proportion of the variance explained by the second and third factors (5.2 and 2.8 per cent) does not warrant this conclusion. Secondly, even within the orthogonal solution it is clear that several variables have some loading on the main factor. An oblique rotation shows that only two variables correlate very weakly with the main factor while a further two have relatively weak correlations.

The factor analysis distinguished between liberal and restrictive items in the first two factors. This is a common feature of factor analyses of single-sided but balanced attitude batteries (Evans and Heath, 1995). This suggests some acquiescence effect, though extremely high levels of disagreement with certain items should also be noted. Consequently, it was decided to maintain a balance between liberal and restrictive items within the scale.

Developing the scale

The sample was halved randomly prior to detailed development of a final scale. This was to enable the scale developed to be tested upon a second sample.

The alpha for the 16 item scale within the selected half-sample was 0.89. However, as the factor analysis indicated, some items have relatively low correlations with the scale. We proceeded iteratively, removing the lowest correlated item, re-assessing the scale and then removing a further item (most likely but not necessarily the lowest correlated item which remains).

Four items with low correlations to scale scores were removed in turn:

- *All illegal drugs should be made legal*
- *People who are addicted to drugs should decide for themselves whether they have treatment*
- *All adults have a duty to prevent young people from using illegal drugs*
- *Doctors must be allowed to prescribe drugs for those who are addicted to them*

A scale of the remaining twelve items had very high reliability (alpha = 0.89) but was highly unbalanced. Only three liberal items remained, two of which correlated least well with scale scores. With further omission of liberal items precluded, the two least well correlating restrictive items were removed:

- *The legalisation of drugs would lead to a considerable increase in misuse*
- *The only way to help addicts is to make them have treatment*

Reliability was barely affected (alpha=0.87) but a further seven restrictive items would have had to be removed to re-balance the scale. Therefore, including the separate item on legalisation of cannabis was considered. Clearly this is not an item about drugs generally and, in technical terms, is based on a slightly different response set. However, these concerns were overridden by the high salience and wider importance of this issue question, together with need for a further suitable liberal item. Other non-statistical criteria also merited consideration at this stage:

- the content, wording and importance of individual items;
- the scope of the items;
- the variance of items (and hence of the scale);
- the frequency of "can't choose" responses; and
- the preferred number of items, the required level of reliability and the balance between these.

High reliability and a broad range of topics were key criteria. Minimising the number of items was much less important (or even undesirable since the objective of using the scale in comparative research suggests the inclusion of sufficient items to minimise any translation effects). We decided to omit the following items:

- *Britain should aim to become a drug-free society*
- *The use of 'soft' drugs leads to the use of 'hard' drugs*
- *You can never trust someone who is addicted to drugs*

The final scale comprises these eight items:

Liberal items

- *Adults should be free to take any drug they wish*
- *Taking illegal drugs can sometimes be beneficial*
- *We need to accept that using illegal drugs is a normal part of some people's lives*
- *Smoking cannabis (marijuana) should be legalised*

Restrictive items

- *The best way to treat people who are addicted to drugs is to stop them using drugs altogether*
- *The use of illegal drugs always leads to addiction*
- *Taking drugs is always morally wrong*
- *All use of illegal drugs is misuse*

Alpha reliability for this scale was 0.84. Within the random half-sample not used to develop the scale alpha also equalled 0.84.

Calculating scale scores

Scores were assigned to all who answered at least six of the eight items, unless the total number of "can't choose" and missing responses exceeded four. The sum of the scores on completed items was divided by the number of items in order to constrain scale scores to the range 1 through 5. This implies that missing data is set to the mean of other scores. A more sophisticated imputation method was judged to be unnecessary because of the low volume involved - only 39 imputed values within a total of 7,960.

6 Northern Ireland during the cease-fire

Geoffrey Evans[*]

The summer of 1996 has seen the re-emergence of bitter and sometimes violent conflict between nationalists and unionists in Northern Ireland. Yet since autumn 1994 Northern Ireland had enjoyed a cease-fire, adhered to by militants on both sides of the sectarian divide.[1] Many saw this cessation of armed conflict within the province as an opportunity to develop the sorts of positive economic and social initiatives which, under the right conditions, could provide a basis for stable relations between its two communities and a more prosperous future. The principal aim of this chapter is to discover whether or not there is evidence of lessening of the divisions between Protestants and Catholics in Northern Ireland during the cease-fire or whether, despite the end of formal hostilities, the two communities have remained as distant and as sceptical as before with regard to community relations, the Northern Irish political *impasse* and the prospects for its resolution.

We also address the more general question of how responsive Northern Irish people are to political manoeuvres, and the extent to which they are prepared to accept the compromises without which a political settlement of 'the Troubles' seem a forlorn hope. The notion that it is the political elites or militant extremists, rather than the mass public, that fuel the continued conflict in the province has had influential proponents (for instance Boyle and Hadden, 1994).[2] Recently, however, we have seen 'elite' dialogues such as the Hume/Adams negotiations, the joint British-Irish Downing Street Declaration of December 1993 and, of course, the cease-fire itself announced

---

[*] Geoffrey Evans is Fellow in the Centre for European Studies at Nuffield College, Oxford.

by the unionist and nationalist militant hierarchies: all these, in their different ways, have shown that both politicians and terrorists are prepared - in principle at least - to compromise. Has this apparent 'opening-up' of relations been mirrored in the views of ordinary people in Northern Ireland? Regardless of the fate of the cease-fire itself, public perceptions of community divisions in the period following its announcement will provide important pointers as to the effectiveness of political negotiations in alleviating tensions in the province.

To this end, we compare the state of inter-communal relations as indicated by responses to the *Northern Ireland Social Attitudes* survey, carried out in late spring and early summer 1995, with the situation prevailing in 1994, immediately preceding the cease-fire. Where necessary we examine evidence from earlier surveys, as reported by Curtice and Gallagher (1990) and by Gallagher (1991, 1992) in earlier volumes in the *British Social Attitudes* Report series.[3] Where appropriate we also examine attitudes held by those on the British side of the Irish sea towards some of these issues; and in addition we explore responses to some new questions on expectations and preferences concerning the future of Northern Ireland.

Finally, we examine more closely differences - and similarities - between various social groups within the Catholic and Protestant communities with a view to providing pointers as to the future of the province. By assessing differences in support for dismantling barriers between the communities (according to age, education and religious observance and so on), we hope to throw light on longer-term prospects for community relations, arising perhaps from the changing composition of the Northern Irish population.

As will become apparent, the cease-fire (at least in its first year) brought with it signs of a remarkable optimism, especially among the Catholic population, but it is also clear that popular beliefs about the reality of the everyday relations between the two communities were far more mixed. More importantly still, such optimism in no sense translated into a narrowing of the gap between the communities with respect to their differing political aspirations and views on what political arrangements for Northern Ireland might be acceptable. These tensions, deriving from core disputes about the constitutional status of the province, are likely to continue to provide a resilient basis for communal divisions.

Perceptions of change in community relations

There had been nine months or so of freedom from terrorist acts whe⌐ fieldwork on the 1995 *British Social Attitudes* and *Northern Ireland Sociaı Attitudes* surveys began. So the very least that might have been expected was a rise in the proportion of people thinking that relations between the two communities had improved in recent times. This is certainly the view taken by respondents on the British side of the Irish sea, where close to three in five

(58 per cent) of responses are positive in tone. And sure enough, among Northern Irish respondents too we see a marked change compared with widespread scepticism evident in earlier years.

% of Northern Irish respondents thinking that community relations have improved compared to five years ago

	1989	1991	1993	1994	1995
Protestant	20	29	25	26	51
Catholic	23	31	27	26	62

Whereas in 1994 only one quarter of respondents thought relations had improved, just one year later more than 60 per cent of Catholics and half of Protestants were of this view. This dramatic shift is clearly attributable to the cease-fire. That the cease-fire had induced optimism as regards prospects for community relations is clear from the next table:

% of Northern Irish respondents thinking that community relations will have improved in five years' time

	1989	1991	1993	1994	1995
Protestant	22	30	27	30	52
Catholic	30	40	32	36	78

On this measure too, 1995 saw a marked increase in bullishness over the future of community relations. This was most marked among Catholics, but majorities in both the main religious groups also expressed optimism about the future. This is not to say, however, that people in Northern Ireland were expecting religious differences themselves to disappear. When asked about the enduring impact of religion in Northern Irish life, respondents - both Catholic and Protestant - showed little sign of changing their long-held view that religion "will always make a difference to the way people in Northern Ireland feel about each other". At most, there were signs that Catholics were a little less convinced of this than in earlier years.

% of Northern Irish respondents agreeing that religion will always make a difference to the way people feel about each other in Northern Ireland

	1989	1991	1993	1994	1995
Protestant	88	85	87	87	88
Catholic	83	79	81	83	74

That religious differences matter is not in itself surprising, nor should it necessarily be problematic. After all, Catholics and Protestants remain

distinct in countries such as the Netherlands, and their distinctiveness does not give rise to marked social tension, let alone violent conflict. The ubiquitous nature of religious differences in the province is widely recognised. Nonetheless, we see that perceptions of the quality of community relations - both at present and in the future - were much more positive than they had been since the *Northern Ireland Social Attitudes* series began.

It is interesting to note, however, that Catholic respondents were clearly more positive than Protestants in their assessments of both retrospective and, particularly, of prospective relations between the communities. One obvious reason for this difference in the 'peace bonus' in future expectations could be the different political aims of the two groups. As we can see from the next table, the proportion of the sample believing that Northern Ireland will eventually become part of a united Ireland increased by eleven percentage points between 1994 and 1995. Among Protestants there had already been a similar increase between 1993 and 1994 - possibly in response to the Downing Street declaration and events surrounding it. As the likelihood of a united Ireland grows, perhaps Protestant optimism about the future has been tempered, so increasing the 'siege mentality' sometimes attributed to hard-line unionists (Bruce, 1994).

% of Northern Irish respondents agreeing that a united Ireland within the next 20 years is "very" or "quite likely"

	1989	1991	1993	1994	1995
Protestant	23	21	24	34	45
Catholic	21	23	21	24	35

Although having *prima facie* appeal, the evidence in favour of this somewhat cynical interpretation is not as clear-cut as at first glance it seems. The notion of increased wariness among Protestants is not confirmed, for example, by answers to the standard *Northern Ireland Social Attitudes* question on whether the British army should leave the province:

% of Northern Irish respondents saying troops should be withdrawn

	1989	1991	1993	1994	1995
Protestant	18	12	10	13	21
Catholic	55	50	48	51	67

The proportions of both Protestants and Catholics wanting the troops to leave have risen since 1994. Although the majority of Protestants are clearly not convinced that the cease-fire will obviate the need for a continued British military presence, the significant increase in the proportion who wanted

British troops to leave (at a higher level than in any previous *Northern Ireland Social Attitudes* survey) suggests some relaxing of their concerns about the disintegration of social order in the province.

Further analysis also suggests that the less pronounced increase in optimism among Protestants about the future of community relations in the province was *not* derived from a belief that the republican aim of incorporating the North into a greater Ireland will meet with success.   There was no relationship, for example, between Protestants' beliefs in the likelihood of Irish unification and their views on the future of community relations: 55 per cent of Protestants who thought a united Ireland is likely believed that relations will get better, compared with 51 per cent of those who thought unification unlikely to happen.   Nor, for that matter, is there evidence to suggest that Catholics who expect to see a united Ireland are more likely to be *positive* in their assessment of future relations between the two communities: the corresponding figures were 82 per cent for nationalists and 77 per cent for non-nationalists.[4]

We do, unsurprisingly, find evidence that pessimism among Protestants is associated with a commitment to the union with Britain - 20 per cent of those who described themselves as "very strongly unionist" expected relations to get worse, compared with only seven per cent of those who described themselves as "not very strongly unionist" - while "very strong" nationalists were a little more optimistic about the future of community relations than were other Catholics. However, we can see below that these differences pre-dated the cease-fire and the negotiations leading up to it. The increase in optimism *within each of the two communities* was similar among nationalists, unionists and those who subscribed to neither view.

% of Northern Irish respondents thinking community relations will have improved in five years time, by unionist and nationalist identity

	1994	1995	Change 1994-1995
Protestant			
Unionist	27	50	+23
Non-Unionist	39	61	+22
Catholic			
Non-Nationalist	33	75	+42
Nationalist	38	82	+44

Thus the less optimistic prognosis for the future of the province among Protestants does not seem to stem from anticipation of unwanted changes. After all, even before the cease-fire unionists were more sceptical about prospects for community relations than were non-unionists, and (as we have seen) belief in the likelihood of unification was not related to optimism about the future. It is, of course, important to remember that levels of optimism increased differentially among the Catholics and Protestants as a result of the

cease-fire, but - equally importantly - the explanation for the greater degree of scepticism among Protestants does not appear to be simply a fear of Irish unification.

Perceptions of discrimination and prejudice

What we have found, then, is an optimism about the future alongside a generally widespread recognition of religion's continuing significance in Northern Ireland. Part of the reason for the latter can be found if we look beyond the relatively abstract sentiments examined in the questions about recent and future community relations, and examine beliefs about more specific aspects of everyday life in Northern Ireland. When we examine perceptions of, and attitudes towards, inter-communal prejudice, discrimination and segregation - which for many commentators (for example Smith and Chambers, 1991) have been the key problems which have continued to plague the province - we find much less evidence that the cease-fire has engendered a more positive outlook.

True, among Catholic respondents perceptions of levels of prejudice against both Catholics and Protestants declined by ten and five percentage points respectively between 1994 and 1995, while their belief that there are equal opportunities for members of both communities increased by six points. In both cases, positive appraisals reached new highs (at least over the period covered by the *Northern Ireland Social Attitudes* surveys).[5] Over the same period, Protestants' perceptions of prejudice against Catholics also dropped to a new low. However this was not the case in respect of Protestants' perceptions of prejudice against *Protestants*: the figure fell, but less sharply and then only to the 1993 level.

% agreeing that there is a lot of prejudice in Northern Ireland ...

	1989	1991	1993	1994	1995
... against Catholics					
Protestant respondents	27	21	18	23	15
Catholic respondents	38	38	35	36	26
... against Protestants					
Protestant respondents	27	21	19	24	20
Catholic respondents	15	16	15	17	12

% saying that the chances of Catholics and Protestants getting a job are the same

	1989	1991	1993	1994	1995
Protestant respondents	60	62	61	57	61
Catholic respondents	30	29	41	42	48

Moreover, as can be seen from the next table, among those Protestants who perceived religiously-based discrimination in the labour market, there was a marked swing towards seeing *Catholics* as the main beneficiaries. In earlier years their estimates had been more evenly balanced.[6]

If the chances are different, which group is more likely to get a job?

	1989	1991	1993	1994	1995
Protestant respondents:	%	%	%	%	%
Catholics more likely	43	49	41	41	52
Protestants more likely	34	26	28	30	20
Don't know/depends	22	25	31	29	29
Catholic respondents:	%	%	%	%	%
Catholics more likely	1	2	2	*	2
Protestants more likely	89	82	86	88	86
Don't know/depends	10	16	12	12	12

So although the proportions of respondents on both sides who thought that job discrimination *should* occur - and who were willing to say so - are extremely small (less than two per cent) the signs are that perceptions of discrimination - whomever it might be against - are likely to persist in one form or another, even when violent conflict is suspended.

So the picture as regards job opportunities is rather complex. In contrast, if we look at perceptions of the treatment of members of the two communities by the law enforcement and security authorities we see a more fixed pattern, with no marked change from before to after the cease-fire in the attitudes of people in either of the communities. Catholics remained considerably less likely than Protestants to believe that the two communities receive equal treatment by the Royal Ulster Constabulary (RUC), the Army, the Ulster Defence Regiment (now the Royal Irish Regiment[7]) and the courts.

Treatment of Catholics and Protestants by the authorities

	Protestants		Catholics	
% saying Catholics and Protestants get "treated equally" by:	1993	1995	1993	1995
Courts in treating those accused of non-terrorist offences	86	85	79	82
Courts in treating those accused of terrorist offences	79	80	53	59
Army in treating members of the public	70	68	43	41
RUC in treating members of the public	71	71	41	41
UDR/RIR in treating members of the public	60	62	30	27

Although Catholics have perceived an improvement in job opportunities for fellow-Catholics in recent years, it appears their perception of discrimination against them by the various law enforcement and security agencies has undergone little change. In many respects it was business as usual, despite the promise of change in the political situation, with beliefs about discrimination mirroring to a large degree the findings of earlier surveys. Despite the cessation of armed conflict, religious affiliation remains a significant social marker and is perceived to be a basis for treatment by others and by the authorities. Unsurprisingly then, the majority (57 per cent) of Northern Irish respondents continue to derive some social identity from their religion. The equivalent figure among British respondents is 42 per cent.[8] Similarly, political beliefs are a more important source of identity in Northern Ireland (42 per cent) than they are in Britain (33 per cent). Furthermore, when we compare these findings with those of Curtice and Gallagher (1990: 197), it becomes clear that the cease-fire has made no difference to the relative importance of these social attachments.

An increased commitment to integration?

The lack of marked changes in many of the indicators of inter-communal relations is perhaps not surprising, given the limited time for which the cease-fire had been in operation. If there is to be any reduction in the barriers between the two communities however, we should nonetheless hope to see some signs of a softening of attitudes in personal relationships and lifestyles, beyond the rhetoric of entrenched positions into the day-to-day life of individual communities. After all, scepticism about the current situation does not preclude a desire to change that state of affairs, and may even stimulate efforts to do so. Moreover, throughout the United Kingdom, people are more or less unanimous - 99 per cent of Northern Ireland Catholics, 94 per cent of Northern Ireland Protestants and 95 per cent of British respondents - in their belief that "better relations will come about through more mixing" (as opposed to more separation) - a view also expressed in earlier *Northern Ireland Social Attitudes* and *British Social Attitudes* surveys.[9] Given the importance that respondents attribute to integration as a source of harmony, it is vital to ask whether, rather than paying lip-service to an ideal, they themselves are willing to mix, and whether they support official measures to bring about greater mixing.

  First, consider the degree to which people report having friends from across the communal divide, and being willing to mix with members of the other community. If the barriers between Catholics and Protestants had in some way been reduced by the cease-fire, we might have expected a greater openness over that period. But as the next table shows, such movement as there has been is both minimal and patchy:

	Protestant			Catholic		
	1989	**1993**	**1995**	**1989**	**1993**	**1995**
% saying that "all" or "most" of their friends are of the same religion as themselves	53	53	59	54	52	57
% saying they would prefer a ...						
...mixed religion neighbourhood	68	67	73	76	82	83
... mixed religion workplace	83	87	89	86	94	94
... mixed religion school	53	53	59	54	52	57

True, there are small signs of an increase in Protestant preferences for an integrated neighbourhood and integrated schooling. Catholics also show signs of a shift towards greater integration with respect to schooling and friendships (their commitment to integrated work-places and neighbourhoods is so high that there is scarcely room for growth). However some at least of the narrowing of the gap between the communities appears to have occurred over the whole six years of the *Northern Ireland Social Attitudes* surveys, not just in the period immediately following the cease-fire.

Second, consider support for government initiatives to encourage integration. Again, with the exception of schooling, we find very high levels of support for integration, particularly among Catholics.[10] More importantly, however, we find little evidence of any increase which could be attributed to the conditions resulting from the cease-fire.

% saying the government and public bodies should do more to create integrated ...

	Protestant			Catholic		
	1989	**1993**	**1995**	**1989**	**1993**	**1995**
... housing	79	80	84	94	87	93
... workplaces	87	88	90	99	97	97
... schools	60	73	64	67	76	66

There have been net increases since 1993 among Protestants in support of integrated housing, workplaces and schooling, but these movements are small and follow no consistent pattern.

A similarly murky picture is evident when respondents are asked for their own views on whether, across a range of situations, "more mixing" should occur.

% of respondents in favour of more mixing in ...

	Protestant			Catholic		
	1989	1993	1995	1989	1993	1995
... primary schools	69	77	76	75	76	75
... secondary schools	70	80	78	79	81	81
... where people live	74	78	76	90	82	90
... workplace	77	83	81	94	96	95
... leisure and sports activities	82	85	85	93	94	94
... marriages	41	40	43	61	63	60

While respondents express clearly integrationist preferences, there is little if any evidence of an increase in integrationist sentiment since the cease-fire. Most of the observed increases in support for "more mixing" are to be found among Protestants between 1993 and 1994 - *before* the cease-fire. It is on the most personal level - mixed marriages - that there is least support for integration among both Catholics and Protestants, although Catholic respondents do tend to be rather more receptive to the idea than do Protestants.

Over the longer term, however, the evidence suggests that in recent years Protestants have become a little closer to Catholics in expressing an openness towards integration in at least some areas of everyday life. Expressed support for mixed schooling is now similar for both groups. Nonetheless, there is little evidence of changes in attitudes following the cease-fire. In the particularly sensitive area of intermarriage - posing perhaps the greatest threat to a person's religious identity and carrying the greatest social costs in the event of a return to intercommunal conflict - hostility to integration, especially among Protestants, remains relatively high.

The development of political trust?

A second arena in which one might look for positive change is that of politics. Political perceptions and attitudes can be divided into those focusing on the bodies that are likely to be involved in negotiations on the future of Northern Ireland, and those concerning the desired and expected constitutional arrangements for the province. We look first at the former. In the wake of the Hume/Adams talks, the Downing Street declaration, the cease-fire, and the negotiations expected to follow it, the question of who should be involved in decisions about Northern Ireland's future is likely to have assumed even greater salience than usual.

From responses to a question on who should decide Northern Ireland's long-term future, it is immediately apparent that openness to British involvement was little in evidence among either Protestants or Catholics: only one in ten in both communities believed that "Britain as a whole" should decide.

Despite their numerical minority, approaching half of Catholics believed the Northern Irish people should decide (although, of course, this does not mean that they necessarily endorse a simple majority vote). And Catholics are also far more likely than are Protestants to want to give the Republic a say in Northern Irish affairs.

Who has the right to decide Northern Ireland's long-term future?

	Protestant	Catholic
	%	%
Northern Irish people	78	44
Ireland, North and South	10	40
Northern Irish and British people	11	10
Britain, Northern Ireland and the Republic	0	4
Don't know	2	1

Protestant resistance to British involvement in deciding the future of Northern Ireland is noteworthy, and may well reflect their concern about British attitudes towards maintaining the Union. This concern is evident elsewhere, in response to questions intended to explore levels of trust in different types of government for Northern Ireland. Here there is a suggestion that trust by Protestants in British governments may well have declined further (from an already low level) between 1993 and 1995. Moreover, in the wake of the cease-fire, there is little sign among Protestants of increased trust in any of the three types of government asked about. Many would argue that there is little reason why it should have made a difference, given that Protestants would probably have most to lose in the negotiations that were expected to follow.

% of Northern Irish respondents saying that they would trust each type of government "just about always" or "most of the time"

	1989	1991	1993	1994	1995
Protestant respondents					
British government under direct rule	32	40	30	27	25
Stormont government under local assembly	67	73	65	64	64
Irish government in united Ireland	10	14	11	12	16
Catholic respondents					
British government under direct rule	15	22	19	17	22
Stormont government under local assembly	20	31	31	24	31
Irish government in united Ireland	36	45	37	38	45

In sharp contrast between 1994 and 1995, Catholic trust of British and prospective Irish and Stormont governments increases *across the board*, but only to the same levels already observed in 1991.

On the whole, then, what we are seeing appears to be little more than a *reprise* of the familiar patterns of community division, with patterns of trust - or, more accurately perhaps, mistrust - remaining well-entrenched.

Preferred and expected constitutional futures

We have shown the sometimes large divergences in attitudes between the Protestant and Catholic communities on who should have a say in decision-making, and in levels of trust in the various bodies that could well have a say. These can perhaps be more fully understood by examining their constitutional preferences and expectations. We also have evidence as to what the other involved parties - people in Britain and the Irish Republic - would like to see. In the province itself, preferences for various arrangements for Northern Ireland are (predictably) split along sectarian lines (see, for example, Curtice and Gallagher, 1990; Gallagher, 1995). In successive *British Social Attitudes* surveys, respondents in Britain have expressed just as much support for reunification of the North and South as have Northern Irish Catholics (Curtice and Gallagher, 1990: 204). There are clear differences of opinion too between, on the one hand, citizens of the Irish Republic and of Britain, and, on the other, Northern Irish Protestants (O'Leary, 1992; Hayes and McAllister, 1996). Unsurprisingly, in responses to the 1995 *Northern Ireland Social Attitudes* survey, we can again see the overwhelming strength of Protestant commitment to the Union, with the more mixed responses of Catholics tending on the whole to favour a united Ireland.

Opinions of Northern Irish respondents on what the long-term policy for the province should be

	1989	1991	1993	1994	1995
Protestant respondents	%	%	%	%	%
Remain part of the UK	93	93	89	89	86
Reunify with Ireland	3	4	6	6	7
Become an independent state	1	1	1	1	1
Other/don't know	3	2	5	4	5
Catholic respondents	%	%	%	%	%
Remain part of the UK	32	36	36	24	34
Reunify with Ireland	56	53	49	60	56
Become an independent state	0	0	0	1	1
Other/don't know	11	10	15	14	8

In this sense, Northern Irish Catholics closely mirror British respondents (of all denominations): in 1995, 52 per cent of the latter opted for re-unification and only 29 per cent for the maintenance of the Union (ten per cent replied "don't know").

The only noticeable difference in the pattern of responses to this question compared with earlier years is a decrease in 'unionist' responses among Protestants (down by eight percentage points since 1989). The accompanying small increase (four points over the same period) in the percentage of Protestants giving a 'pro-unification answer' could indicate a slight loosening of their commitment to the Union, but it is too early to make any inference about this apparent trend. The vagaries of survey measurement are such that it is important to have reasonably robust patterns of responses from which to draw inferences. Moreover, in this instance there is little evidence that the cease-fire itself had much impact on responses.

Settlement of the constitutional status of Northern Ireland is clearly vital to any attempt to resolve its conflicts. So for the 1995 surveys we decided to test and field further questions on constitutional preferences, going beyond the relatively limited choices offered to date (as shown in the previous table). The new questions incorporated several options which might prove relevant to future arrangements for the province. These included joint sovereignty, the choice of whether or not to have a Belfast parliament, issues which might possibly form part of any negotiations (see McGarry and O'Leary, 1995a). An explicit 'independence' option was also added, such as that advocated by the Scottish National Party (SNP) for Scotland. In this way, we are able to examine what effect the extension of the range of constitutional options presented to people in Northern Ireland and Britain would have on the pattern of responses. Would it produce an option that gained a reasonable level of support among both Protestants and Catholics? In addition, we changed the preamble to the question, placing greater emphasis on what respondents *themselves* would like to see happen in Northern Ireland, rather than asking respondents what they thought "the best long-term policy for Northern Ireland" would be. We hoped thereby to elicit answers which give relatively less weight to the *viability* of various options, and hence greater weight to respondents' own preferences.[11]

In the event however, and perhaps predictably, none of the new constitutional options offered had any noticeable cross-communal appeal. Protestants still opted for the unionist position - more often than not with a Belfast parliament - while Catholics were split fairly evenly between the nationalist and joint sovereignty options, which together were endorsed by 58 per cent of Catholics. One in five Catholics chose union with Britain, the majority of these turning down the option of a Belfast parliament.

The solidity of Protestant attachment to the Union is striking: even when a wide range of alternatives was offered - in itself likely to reduce the proportion of respondents opting for any one choice - there was only a very small drop in the proportion of Protestants choosing one or the other of the

unionist options. Almost no Protestants chose even the compromise option of joint sovereignty. Catholic preferences were, by comparison, far more fluid with the idea of joint sovereignty attracting the support of over a quarter. It is notable too that the numbers of "can't choose" responses increased noticeably in the face of the more complex array of choices presented.

% of respondents in Northern Ireland and Britain choosing different constitutional options

Northern Ireland should ...	Northern Irish		British
	Protestant	Catholic	
...remain part of the UK without a separate parliament in Belfast	29 ⌉	12 ⌉	11 ⌉
...remain part of the UK but with a separate parliament in Belfast	55 ⌟ 84	8 ⌟ 20	15 ⌟ 26
...become part of the Irish Republic without a separate parliament in Belfast	- ⌉	18 ⌉	14 ⌉
...become part of the Irish Republic with a separate parliament in Belfast	2 ⌟ 2	13 ⌟ 31	13 ⌟ 27
...be governed jointly by the UK and Irish Republic without own parliament in Belfast	1 ⌉	10 ⌉	3 ⌉
...be governed jointly by the UK and Irish Republic with own parliament in Belfast	4 ⌟ 5	18 ⌟ 28	13 ⌟ 16
...become an independent state with its own parliament separate from both the UK and Irish Republic	4	7	11
Can't choose	6	14	20

Again, British respondents are much more like Northern Irish Catholics than like Northern Irish Protestants, in spreading their preferences over more options and being more likely to say "can't choose" This concurrence between the views of the British and those of Northern Irish Catholics further highlights the isolated position of the unionists. But it has also caused some commentators to claim that British views derive from widespread ignorance about the Northern Irish situation in general, and the available constitutional options in particular. This, the argument goes, results from the bi-partisan approach adopted by British political parties which reduces the political significance and salience of the issue (see, for example, Hayes and McAllister, 1996). According to this perspective, the British simply want a change from the *status quo* - whatever that change might be - and when explicitly offered the option of full independence for Northern Ireland will choose that in preference to unification. As we can see, however, the British respondents in the *British Social Attitudes* survey express little enthusiasm

for an independent Northern Ireland, even when it is presented as an explicit option.   More British respondents favour joint sovereignty than favour independence, which *would* maintain a British involvement in the province.

Preferences are not expectations, however.   Regardless of what people would *like* to see in Northern Ireland, it might be even more informative to examine what sort of constitutional arrangement they *expect* to see in the near future. Do Protestants and Catholics differ in what they think will happen? Do Protestants have a 'siege mentality', convinced that they will be 'sold down the river'? Are Catholics similarly jaundiced about prospects for their political voice getting heard? We have already seen that in 1995, when questioned about the possibility that there could be a united Ireland in 20 years' time, quite high proportions of Protestants (45 per cent) and Catholics (35 per cent) respond in the affirmative. However, to preserve the time-series, that question did not present a range of alternative scenarios. A more balanced set of responses may be obtained by asking a question which compliments the one on constitutional *preferences*, but this time asking about *expectations* of likely constitutional outcomes over the next ten years.

% expecting the following constitutional outcomes "in, say, ten years' time"

	Northern Irish		
Northern Ireland should ...	**Protestant**	**Catholic**	**British**
... remain part of the UK without a separate parliament in Belfast	30 ⎤	23 ⎤	17 ⎤
... remain part of the UK but with a separate parliament in Belfast	32 ⎦ 62	12 ⎦ 36	18 ⎦ 35
... become part of the Irish Republic without a separate parliament in Belfast	5 ⎤	6 ⎤	7 ⎤
... become part of the Irish Republic with a separate parliament in Belfast	5 ⎦ 10	9 ⎦ 15	11 ⎦ 18
... be governed jointly by the UK and Irish Republic without own parliament in Belfast	8 ⎤	10 ⎤	6 ⎤
... be governed jointly by the UK and Irish Republic with own parliament in Belfast	8 ⎦ 16	15 ⎦ 25	8 ⎦ 14
... become an independent state with its own parliament separate from both the UK and Irish Republic	1	4	7
Can't choose	12	20	26

When presented with this range of possible outcomes, Protestant concerns about unification appear less marked than they did when asked in isolation. When asked baldly about the likelihood of Irish unification within the next 20 years, 48 per cent of Protestants thought that it was unlikely within the next 20 years. However, when asked in the context of other outcomes, over 60 per

cent are of the opinion that Northern Ireland will still be part of the UK in ten years' time, with only one in ten expecting unification with the Republic.[12] Of course, this still leaves a substantial minority believing that the Union as it stands now might not exist in ten years' time which, given that almost nine out of ten Protestants would choose to remain in the United Kingdom, leaves a sizeable gap among Protestants between desires and expectations.

Among Catholics, there is a similar gap between aspirations and expectations, in that more Catholics *expect* to remain part of the Union (36 per cent) than expect unification of Ireland (15 per cent), a reversal of the proportions *desiring* those outcomes (20 per cent and 31 per cent respectively). A fairly substantial proportion (20 per cent) of Catholics also remains uncertain about the future, and an even greater proportion (25 per cent) believes joint sovereignty is a possibility.

These observed discrepancies between expectation and preference could well sow the seeds of continued and considerable distrust, and indeed of unrest, with respect to the negotiations currently underway - and any further attempts to resolve Northern Ireland's constitutional disagreements. In terms of the hopes and fears of individuals, however, the extent of the gap between expectations and desires is less than it appears. This is because both nationalists and unionists display a disproportionate tendency to believe *their* preferred option is likely to win. Among Protestants committed to the maintenance of the Union, for example, no less than 69 per cent believe the Union is likely to be in existence in ten years' time. Conversely, among Catholics committed to unification with the Republic, 35 per cent think that unification is a likely outcome. Both of these figures are comfortably above the expectations of other groups. Nonetheless, this link between hopes and expected outcomes might itself eventually prove to be a poisoned chalice, as we can only speculate about how these optimistic nationalists and unionists would react should, in either case, that optimism be disappointed.

Longer-term prospects

On the whole, we have found only limited evidence of a change in attitudes towards community relations issues, and prospects for the future. In the short term, perhaps, this is to be expected. Nevertheless, we can obtain useful insights into the prospects for Northern Ireland in the longer term by looking at the attitudes, beliefs and values held by different sections within the two communities. This tells us not only to what extent attitudes towards issues such as integration and the constitution are shared by people within the two communities, but in some cases gives indications of what might happen to levels of support in the longer term. If levels of support for integration are higher among young people, for example, then as new cohorts arrive on the electoral register, overall levels of support for integration could increase. To take another example, if regular church attendance is associated with

opposition to integration, then a decline in levels of attendance could eventually lead to a greater flexibility of attitude. Similarly, if levels of support for "more mixing" of the two communities are higher among people with higher education qualifications, we might expect that as the proportion of the population with experience of higher educational increases, so in turn will levels of support for integration. A related logic applies to different occupational groups: the growth of a professional and geographically mobile middle class, for example, would militate against the perpetuation of old antagonisms (see McAllister and Rose, 1983; Evans and Duffy, 1996).[13]

To examine this idea in a preliminary and parsimonious manner, we constructed a multi-item scale of attitudes towards integration.[14] We also examined attitudes towards changes to current constitutional arrangements in Northern Ireland with a view to constructing a similar scale. In this case, however, we were thwarted since many of the available questions were simply not suitable for scaling to construct a 'for *versus* against' measure. We therefore selected, as an indicator of attitudes towards constitutional change, a question regarding the extent to which the Republic should have a say in how Northern Ireland is run:

> *How much say do you think an Irish government of any party should have in the way Northern Ireland is run?* [15]

We then used regression to examine, among both Catholic and Protestant communities, the relationship between certain socio-demographic characteristics (such as age and education) and attitudes to integration and to closer constitutional links between Northern Ireland and the Republic. (The statistical technique of regression is explained in more detail in Appendix I of this Report). The strength of association between each characteristic and these attitudes is shown in the next table.

Attitudes towards integration and constitutional change:
Coefficients for socio-demographic characteristics[16]

Characteristics	Attitudes towards integration		Attitudes towards constitutional change	
	Protestant	Catholic	Protestant	Catholic
Service class	.13*	.14*	-.02	-.03
Intermediate	.02	.11*	-.05	.06
Church attendance	-.16*	-.19*	-.04	.09
Educational qualifications	.04	.06	.07	-.12*
Age	.02	.02	-.09*	-.11*
R^2	.04	.07	.02	.03

Note: A positive coefficient indicates increased support for either integration or constitutional change; a negative coefficient, reduced support.
* Significant at the 5% level.

The first point to be noted from our analyses is that divisions *within* the two communities are relatively weak. However, it is clear that the divisions that do exist within the Catholics and Protestant communities in terms of attitudes towards integration are strikingly similar. For instance, pro-integrationists, whether Catholic or Protestant, tend to be middle class (as opposed to working class) and do not attend church very often. Differences in attitudes towards constitutional change also tend to cut across community boundaries, in that both younger Protestants and younger Catholics tend to be a little more in favour than their elders of the Republic having a say in the governance of Northern Ireland. When we come to look at education, however, the story is rather different: among Catholics, but not among Protestants, people with more educational qualifications tend to be less supportive of the Republic having a say in the affairs of Northern Ireland.

We can see then that attitudes towards integration and constitutional preferences have somewhat different social bases, suggesting that the two sets of issues are distinctive and should not be treated as different facets of the same issue. The finding that middle class people who display low levels of church attendance are more supportive of integration than are others is consistent with previous, more anecdotal, observations (see for example Bruce, 1994: 134), although the reasons for this openness have been questioned by sceptical commentators (see again Bruce, 1994; and McGarry and O'Leary, 1995). Are there then sufficient grounds for predicting that an increasingly middle class and more secular Northern Ireland might in time be more receptive to integration? Perhaps we should be cautious, given the relative weakness of the divisions within the two communities along age and class lines, the slowness with which the class structure changes its shape (Duffy and Evans, 1997) and the rate of secularisation. Any changes will, on our evidence, be gradual (see McAllister and Rose, 1983, for some estimates of how long they might take). Moreover, because the associations we have noted are not particularly strong, there could be many set-backs along the way, and a renewal of inter-communal violence would undoubtedly put a great strain upon any impetus towards integration.

With respect to the long-term prospects for support for constitutional change, we might further speculate that the more marked tendency among younger people to support change suggests a shift towards greater openness in attitudes towards the constitution in future years - although this inference must be particularly heavily qualified, not just because these effects are weak but because age differences themselves may change as people get older and pass through different stages of the life-cycle (for a discussion of this, see Evans and Duffy, 1996).

Increasing levels of education, however, do not lead us to predict an increased appetite for constitutional change. On the contrary, among Catholics it would suggest a more reserved attitude to the involvement of the Republic in Northern Ireland.

A more detailed assessment of the long-term implications of current demographic trends must await a more extensive analysis of this complex issue. For the time being, we can merely reiterate the possible benefits for community relations of growth in the size of the middle class and of the trend towards secularisation.[17]

Conclusions

By comparing prevailing social and political attitudes with those observed in earlier *Northern Ireland Social Attitudes* studies, we have been able to assess the impact of the cease-fire on cross-communal relations. In addition, we have considered, if only tentatively, the likely impact on social divisions of a future period of peace and stability in the region. We have also examined prospects for political reform, by asking respondents to choose between a wider range of options available to parties looking to construct a lasting political settlement.

Answers to this complex array of questions have indeed revealed pronounced signs of optimism in the advent of the cease-fire, with Catholics in particular - although not alone - displaying signs of what is now popularly called a 'feelgood factor'. At the same time, however, positive changes in feelings about the future of community relations and attitudes towards integration have been, at best, muted. Certainly, there have been small declines in levels of perceived discrimination, particularly against Catholics, and small shifts towards more support for integration in some areas. Nonetheless, the general impression on our evidence is that attitudes have remained relatively unaffected by the cessation of armed conflict in the province.

This immutability of attitudes is most marked with respect to any eventual political settlement. Here there was little evidence of any change accompanying the cease-fire. A stable majority of Catholics continued to endorse constitutional change, while the near-unanimous Protestant commitment to the United Kingdom remained more or less undiminished. The opposition among the large majority of Protestants to any British involvement in deciding the future of Northern Ireland has served to highlight the extent of their concern about the British government's commitment to the Union: a concern that would not be unrealistic if what we have seen of British public opinion were to be taken at face value.

As we have noted, attitudes towards the constitution are well entrenched, and there is no particular reason to expect people to change their preferences as to what an eventual settlement might bring simply because of a cessation of armed conflict. If anything, we might expect Protestants' attitudes to harden as the perceived likelihood of a united Ireland increases. Thus, even when offered no less than seven constitutional choices (including those of independence, joint sovereignty, and a separate Belfast parliament in a

unified Ireland), Protestant respondents showed no sign of wavering from their unionism. This entrenched commitment of Protestants to the Union contrasts markedly with the wide range of constitutional options that Catholics in the province seem willing to consider (and to a lesser degree their greater openness towards 'mixing'). But to understand this 'intransigence', as it has often been called, we need consider only that declarations, negotiations and peace talks, and pontifications about constitutional resolutions of the 'Northern Irish problem' all send out one clear signal to the Protestant community in Northern Ireland: that its hitherto dominant position is likely in some way to be found to be 'compromised'. In other words, the Protestant community may have to give up some of its political power. Compromise is likely in the first instance to benefit nationalists, and as such it can serve only to strip away some if not all of the remaining advantages accrued by unionists in the early part of this century (Bew *et al*, 1995). Under such weight of history, 'intransigence' is not remarkable.

So the obvious questions posed by these findings remain. Was the collapse of the cease-fire (a reality on the mainland, ambiguous still for Northern Ireland itself) 'inevitable', given the lack of either progress towards inter-party talks or change in attitudes in the aftermath of the IRA's 'cessation of hostilities'. Are the leaders of the different parties to the conflict the prisoners of public opinion, or (as some would claim) perpetuating the conflict to serve their own narrow political ambitions. Was the *débâcle* at Drumcree in summer 1996, and the other confrontations during that year's marching season, always on the cards? The divisions between the communities are such that under the 'right' conditions any politicians seeking to inflame sentiments are sure to succeed. But of course things are not that simple. The collapse of the cease-fire may have had more to do with divisions within the IRA leadership than with public impatience for progress towards a settlement. Moreover, there are many other instances where long-standing social divisions have been resolved by some sort of political or constitutional reform (see, for example, the instances cited by Horowitz, 1985).

What our findings do suggest, however, is that the political divisions between the nationalist and unionist communities in Northern Ireland are embedded in the beliefs of the population itself, and are not just the preserve of politicians and warring extremists. If they are changing, it is only slowly and the social sources of change in attitudes towards integration are rather different from those which might underlie changes in attitudes towards the constitution.

In conclusion we should say that arguments which place the primary blame on politicians for the protracted conflict in Northern Ireland seem to be unfounded (for example, Pollak, 1993). Equally suspect is the charge that the limited set of political choices offered to voters in Northern Ireland has served to perpetuate community divisions (Roberts, 1990).[18] The most recent

evidence suggests that, irrespective of the steps taken towards equal opportunity in the job market, and of whatever progress may be made towards integration, the political aspirations of nationalists - or fear of the unionists - will continue to provide a mass basis for political disputes.

Notes

1. There were, of course, two cease-fires - that called by the Provisional Irish Republican Army (PIRA) on 31 August 1994 and that called in response by the Combined Loyalist Military Command (CLMC) in October 1994. At the time of writing (August 1996), the CLMC cease-fire still holds. The PIRA cease-fire ended on 9 February 1996, although PIRA has distanced itself from 'nationalist' terrorist acts which had occurred in Northern Ireland (but not in Britain) since then.
2. This idea informed the content of the Opsahl Report (Pollak, 1993).
3. In this chapter we focus primarily on self-identified Protestants and Catholics, and omit examination of the attitudes of those Northern Irish respondents who profess no religious affiliation (a decision also made by Gallagher, 1995). This choice is made on grounds of limited space, and because only a small proportion (ten per cent of respondents, mainly lapsed Protestants) do not express a religious identity.
4. Among both Catholics and Protestants the correlation between answers to the two questions is a non-significant 0.04.
5. Evidence from previous analyses of *Northern Ireland Social Attitudes* surveys has also indicated that Catholics perceptions of discrimination against them declined following the Fair Employment Act of 1989 (see Gallagher, 1995).
6. Protestants are also more likely to see Catholics as benefiting from policies concerning unemployment and the implementation of the Fair Employment Act. When asked, for example, about whether the Fair Employment Commission treated Catholics and Protestants equally, only 60 per cent of Protestants agreed compared with no less than 86 per cent of Catholics. Almost all Protestants who did not agree saw the Commission as favouring Catholics. Beliefs about government unemployment schemes display a similar although less pronounced pattern (69 per cent and 78 per cent respectively, seeing them as less than even-handed).
7. The Ulster Defence Regiment (UDR) merged with the Royal Irish Rangers in July 1992, ostensibly as part of a programme of army cuts announced in 1991. The merged force was renamed the Royal Irish Regiment (RIR).
8. The questions on social identity are those used by Curtice and Gallagher (1990: 197). The question runs: "How close would you say you feel towards....people who have the same religious background as yours?....people who have the same political beliefs as you?" and so on.
9. This is not to assume that they are correct in such a belief. Some commentators have argued quite forcefully that integration may cause more trouble than it resolves (see, for example, McGarry and O'Leary, 1995b).
10. When interpreting these answers, it is important to note that the verbs used in the statements about the government's role in integration are *encourage* and *create*, neither of which carries much force. If stronger words, such as 'ensure' - or even 'enforce' - had been used, agreement may well have been more muted. It is also possible that attitudes towards government intervention *in general* might affect some respondents' views on the desirability of government efforts to increase mixing (see Sniderman *et al*, 1991), which may in part explain why Protestants, who are less supportive of government intervention in the economy (see Duffy and Evans, 1997, forthcoming), are more wary than Catholics of government action to enforce mixing. However, multivariate analysis shows that this accentuating effect is of minor consequence. The difference between Protestants and

Catholics cannot be explained away simply as a consequence of other ideological orientations.

11. Moreover, the new questions were included in the self-completion questionnaire, so that it was answered without an interviewer present. This tactic, it was hoped, would give respondents more time to ponder the available options and make a considered choice not necessarily mirroring that of the party to which they owed allegiance.

12. There is a substantial relationship between answers to the question on Irish re-unification and the new, more complex multiple option question on expected constitutional outcomes, which indicates that they do tap into the same concerns. The rather high level of affirmative responses given in answer to the Irish re-unification question, when compared with those offered in response to the new multiple option question, could derive from differences in the time span referred to in the two questions (20 years in the former and ten in the latter). However, other evidence strongly suggests that the time-span specified may not matter much after all. A version of the multiple option question (designed by Professor Brendan O'Leary and the author and co-funded by the BBC and RTE) was asked in an Ulster Marketing Services poll at the time of the May 30 1996 elections in Northern Ireland. This gave a 20-year time span, but responses were in fact rather similar to those given in the 1995 *Northern Ireland Social Attitudes* survey, where the question refers to a ten-year time span. A more likely cause of the high levels of agreement with the Irish re-unification question is the tendency for respondents who are faced with "agree/disagree" questions to agree more often than not, regardless of their actual position. This 'acquiescence response set' has been observed in numerous analyses of surveys and has been the topic of considerable debate by survey specialists. For a general review see 'The acquiescence quagmire' in Schuman and Presser (1981); for recent considerations of this topic in British surveys, see Evans and Heath (1995). Also, of course, the presentation of a range of possible outcomes to respondents is likely to make each option less salient than if it were asked in isolation and thus decrease the emphasis given to any particular option.

13. The growth of a non-religious group of respondents who do not identify themselves as either Catholic or Protestant is, of course, another potential source of change that we cannot examine in the space available to us.

14. The use of a multi-item scale helps to reduce bias resulting from such factors as the idiosyncrasies of particular questions and response options and their location in the questionnaire. Positions on such scales can therefore give a general estimate of an individual's position on the issue under consideration (see Nunnally and Bernstein, 1994).

15. This question had the merits both of being asked of the whole sample (unlike the question on "the best long-term policy for Northern Ireland"), and of clearly tapping into attitudes for or against the constitutional status quo. The response options were "a great deal", "some", "a little" and "no say at all". This item correlated highly with the various other measures of attitudes towards unification and trust in the Irish government.

16. Age, educational qualification and church attendance are treated here as continuous variables. Social class, based upon the Goldthorpe/Heath class schema (explained in detail in Appendix I of this Report) is used to create two dummy variables, comparing the effect of being in either the service or intermediate class against being in the working class.

17. See Curtice and Gallagher (1990) for evidence on the rate of secularisation in Northern Ireland, and Duffy and Evans (1997, forthcoming) for evidence on the changing class structure.

18. For a further refutation of this claim, see Duffy and Evans (1996).

References

Bew, P. Gibbon, P. and Patterson, H. (1995), *The State in Northern Ireland, 1921-94: Political Forces and Social Classes*, London: Serif.

Boyle, K. and Hadden, T. (1994), *Northern Ireland: the Choice*, Harmondsworth: Penguin.

Bruce, S. (1994), *The Edge of the Union: the Ulster Loyalist Political Vision*, Oxford: Oxford University Press.

Carmines, E.G. and Zeller, R.A. (1979), *Reliability and Validity Assessment*, Beverley Hills, Ca.: Sage.

Curtice, J. and Gallagher, T. (1990), 'The Northern Irish dimension', in Jowell, R., Witherspoon, S. and Brook, L. (eds.), *British Social Attitudes: the 7th Report*, Aldershot: Gower.

Duffy, M. and Evans, G. (1996), 'Building bridges: the political implications of electoral integration for Northern Ireland', *British Journal of Political Science*, 26, 123-40.

Duffy, M. and Evans, G. (1997, forthcoming), 'Class, sex and community relations', in Breen, R., Devine, P. and Dowds, L. (eds.), *Social Attitudes in Northern Ireland: the Sixth Report*, Belfast: Appletree Press.

Evans, G. and Duffy, M. (1996, forthcoming), 'Beyond the sectarian divide: the social bases and political consequences of unionist and nationalist party competition in Northern Ireland', *British Journal of Political Science*.

Evans, G. and Heath, A. (1995), 'The measurement of left-right and libertarian-authoritarian values: comparing balanced and unbalanced scales', *Quality and Quantity*, 29, 191-206.

Evans, G., Heath, A. and Lalljee, M.G. (1996), 'Measuring left-right and libertarian-authoritarian values in the British electorate', *British Journal of Sociology*, 47, 93-112.

Gallagher, T. (1991), 'Justice and the law in Northern Ireland' in Jowell, R., Brook, L. and Taylor, B. (eds.) *British Social Attitudes: the 8th report*, Aldershot: Dartmouth.

Gallagher, T. (1992), 'Community relations in Northern Ireland', in Jowell, R., Brook, L., Prior, G. and Taylor, B., *British Social Attitudes: the 9th report*, Aldershot: Dartmouth.

Gallagher, A.M. (1995), 'Equality, contact and pluralism: attitudes to community relations', in Breen, R., Devine, P. and Robinson, G. (eds.), *Social Attitudes in Northern Ireland: the fourth report*, Belfast: Appletree Press.

Hayes, B.C. and McAllister, I. (1996), 'British and Irish public opinion towards the Northern Ireland problem', *Irish Political Studies*, 11, 61-82.

Horowitz, D.L. (1985), *Ethnic Groups in Conflict*, Berkeley: University of California Press.

McAllister, I. and Rose, R. (1983), 'Can political conflict be resolved by social change?', *Journal of Conflict Resolution*, 27, 533-57.

McGarry, J. and O'Leary, B. (1995a), *Explaining Northern Ireland*, Oxford: Blackwell.

McGarry, J. and O'Leary, B. (1995b), 'Five fallacies: Northern Ireland and the liabilities of liberalism', *Ethnic and Racial Studies*, 18, 837-61.

O'Leary, B. (1992), 'Public opinion and Northern Irish futures', *Political Quarterly*, 63, 143-70.

Nunnally, J.C. and Bernstein, I.H. (1994), *Psychometric Theory*, New York: McGraw-Hill.

Pollak, A. (ed.) (1993), *A Citizens' Inquiry: The Opsahl Report on Northern Ireland*, Dublin: Lilliput Press.

Roberts, H. (1990), 'Sound stupidity: the British party system and the Northern Ireland question', in McGarry, J. and O'Leary, B. (eds.), *The Future of Northern Ireland*, Oxford: Clarendon Press.

Schuman, H. and Presser, S. (1981), *Questions and Answers in Attitude Surveys: Experiments on Question Form, Wording and Context,*. New York: Academic Press.

Smith, D.J. and Chambers, G. (1991), *Inequality in Northern Ireland*, Oxford: Oxford University Press.

Sniderman, P.M., Brody, R.A. and Tetlock, P.E. (1991), *Reasoning and Choice: Explorations in Political Psychology*, Cambridge: Cambridge University Press.

Acknowledgement

We are grateful to the Northern Ireland government departments for the funding that enables the *Northern Ireland Social Attitudes* survey to be conducted.

7 National identity

Lizanne Dowds and Ken Young[*]

Beyond the rhetoric of the New World Order lies a wide-spread unease, against a backcloth of failing empires, disintegrating nation-states, and new regional and ethnic claims to loyalty. The sense of identity traditionally derived from the old collectivities no longer claims special attention. And yet that sense of identity, of being 'among one's own', remains a powerful human need. The 1990s could be said to be a decade characterised by a search for a more elemental sense of identity than the years immediately preceding it; moreover, an identity made special by ties of 'blood and belonging' (Ignatieff, 1993). So, at least, goes one argument about our current predicament.[1]

But there are other, less regressive, constructions to be put upon this new order. One of these is to regard the nation-state as the quintessential product of modernity and to let it pass away unlamented. The passage into post-modernity is, it has been argued, one into a more transient and contingent world, of flux and paradox, in which a single or firm sense of identity - of who one is - is neither sought nor offered. Instead, *situational* identities are adopted, reflecting a wider range of life-experiences that cut across the concept of 'nationhood'. The prospect is held up of a life of multiple identities and shifting ties, in which the certitudes and loyalties of the nation-state are replaced at will from a whole range of new identities on offer. In

* Lizanne Dowds is a Research Fellow at the Centre for Social Research, Queen's University, Belfast. Ken Young is Professor of Politics and Vice-Principal at Queen Mary and Westfield College, University of London.

this moral emporium, few will choose to identify themselves with either nation or state and, if their attachment is in any way territorial, it is as likely as not to derive its rationale and vigour from the face-to-face community of local neighbourhoods.[2]

This *lateral* dispersion of identity may seem both over-fanciful in the kaleidoscope of identities it can offer, and romantic in its celebration of the local in the face of the global. Yet in Britain, we are currently witnessing unprecedented confusions of national consciousness, arising from the prospect of a *vertical* displacement of old loyalties by those widely believed to be demanded by an emerging European 'super-state'. On this reckoning, the old tales of solidarity within bounded territorial (but not ethnic) communities have not been forgotten but are being re-told on a supra-national scale appropriate to the emotionally powerful appeal of a united Europe (Schlesinger, 1992).[3] To the extent that people feel themselves to be citizens of this new Europe, they might be expected to be the weaker in their national attachments; indeed, it was just such a hope, after two devastating world wars, that underpinned the original European project. On this view, the gradual eclipse of national by European identity is both natural and welcome.[4]

These positions all provide plausible, if partial, accounts of the new uncertainties assailing people's sense of national identity. But they are essentially speculations, having at best a spasmodic connection with empirical evidence. Still less can they deal with the several components of identity: those things that, in varying mixes, go to make up an attachment to this community, to that nation-state, or to some other icon, be it regional, linguistic, religious or whatever. Furthermore, within the multi-state that is the United Kingdom - one which, perhaps uniquely, few of whose citizens would describe themselves as belonging to - an altogether different nationalism must be taken into account. To what extent do respondents living in the constituent parts of the United Kingdom *include themselves* by considering themselves to be 'British' at all? Do Scottish and Welsh respondents accept being asked about their 'pride' in British history and British sporting achievements? How do the Northern Irish respond to similar questions about the United Kingdom? Do they, rather, simply find it curious (or even offensive)? Do the English regard themselves as English first and British second?

In this chapter, then, we explore the dimensions of national identity among respondents of the constituent parts of the United Kingdom and note the position of those within the United Kingdom who regard themselves as indisputably 'outsiders' within this schema. We then go on to construct a typology of national identities and, in the light of this, consider one of the greatest constitutional challenges facing British people in the coming years: the re-articulation (or even the survival) of national identities in the face of what many view - some with enthusiasm, others with dismay - as a relentless drive towards European integration.

The questions in the 1995 *British Social Attitudes* and *Northern Ireland Social Attitudes* surveys on aspects of national identity have been asked in over twenty other countries, as part of the *International Social Survey Programme*. So this chapter can be only a very preliminary look at results from what should prove to be a rich and varied dataset.

Dimensions of identity

We begin by exploring the constituents of what we loosely call 'national identity', before going on to identify where its heartland is to be found. Inescapably, we are dealing here in the currency of 'nationalism' - a word with connotations, at least among the intelligentsia, evoking the excess of the regimes of Hitler and Mussolini, and finding echoes (for example) in some of the successor states of the former Yugoslavia. Hence it is difficult now, in mainland Britain, to speak approvingly of nationalism, as the term has become associated with xenophobia and bigotry. 'National identity' can perhaps be regarded as its acceptable face, something more inclusive than the imagined nation, with its stress on commonalities of language, experience and descent (Keane, 1995). But to restrict our usage of the term in this way would perhaps place too much weight upon the nuance, missing the point that, in popular discourse, nationalism is rarely seen as something shameful.

Why this ambivalence about nationalism? One possible reason is that its positive or 'inclusive' aspects (pride in the nation, in its achievements and institutions, readiness to admit others to the national community) is conflated with its negative or 'exclusive' aspects (bellicose perceptions of outsiders, unease in the face of difference, unwillingness to grant entry or concede assimilation). Both rest on the recognition of difference, on a clear distinction between what is British and what is not (Parekh, 1994). But they come at it from very different directions with (to give one obvious example) exclusive nationalism placing stronger emphasis on the maintenance of boundaries and national autonomy. Moreover, as we shall see, each of these two main aspects of nationalism has within it major strands and tensions.

Inclusive nationalism

The inclusive version of nationalism may be said to encompass two distinct elements: pride in national heritage and culture; and pride in the way the nation functions both at home, and in the wider world. Some would assert that the former is at root backward looking, a celebration of what has been handed down from the past (and a concomitant complacency about the future, engendering a reluctance to change). Remembrance of past glories on the battlefield and the continued celebration of great (and not so great) cultural

icons serve to buttress what might almost be termed the 'Pomp and Circumstance' version of national identity.[5]

Nonetheless, as the table below shows, the majority of people in Britain are distinctly proud of their heritage and culture. Over 80 per cent of English, Scottish and Welsh respondents feel proud of their history and proud of the armed forces.[6] There is little evidence here of a rejection of a 'British' identity among Scottish and Welsh respondents and the level of enthusiasm is, perhaps, surprising given not only the much-quoted cynicism of the 1990s, but also the rising popularity of the nationalist parties in Scotland and Wales.

However, while the English, Scottish and Welsh (by and large) appear to accept their 'Britishness', those in Northern Ireland appear distinctly more ambivalent. In fact, when distinguishing between those Northern Ireland respondents who consider themselves to be 'British' and those who consider themselves to be 'Irish'[7], a vast chasm in identity becomes apparent. For the Northern Ireland 'Irish', questions on the extent to which they felt pride in their country ("the United Kingdom" in the questionnaire fielded in Northern Ireland*) clearly left them somewhat at a loss. Only 22 per cent felt proud of the United Kingdom's history while a token 13 per cent said that they felt proud of its armed forces. A rather larger proportion (45 per cent) felt proud of its sporting achievements, though this may have more to do with the success of popular British football clubs than with any sense of pride in national team effort in international competition. However, what is also interesting about these results is the rather more subtle point that the Northern Ireland 'British' are exactly that: British in their outlook. Respondents in Northern Ireland who see themselves as British hold views that are entirely consistent with those of their Scottish, Welsh and English counterparts. This pattern can be seen time and again in all the constituent measures of national identity.

---

* Of course, many respondents in Northern Ireland would have had no difficulty in answering questions about 'pride in Britain'; but, since none of them - unionist, nationalist, or those with other loyalties, or none - live in mainland Great Britain, we decided to ask about "the United Kingdom".

% saying they are "very" or "somewhat" proud of Britain's heritage and culture

	England	Scotland	Wales	Northern Ireland (All)	Northern Ireland 'British'	Northern Ireland 'Irish'
Its history	85	83	85	56	75	22
Its armed forces	82	83	86	59	81	13
Its achievements in sports	71	65	69	62	68	45
Its achievements in the arts and literature	70	60	71	56	61	47
Base	*856*	*94*	*65*	*619*	*279*	*156*

Note: Northern Ireland respondents were asked about "the United Kingdom"

The second element of national identity is more forward-looking. Britain may hold a diminished place in today's world, but many continue to expect it to be held with distinction. British democratic institutions and practices, the British economy and Britain's influence in the world would, in this view, be matters for greater pride than past achievements. This domain of national identity is one in which nostalgic longing gets short shrift in the face of current competitive demands. Perhaps unsurprisingly, the proportions of those who say they feel pride in the way the nation functions are a great deal smaller than those who feel pride in its heritage and culture. The way in which democracy works is the most common source of pride (cited by over half of respondents in mainland Britain), but only around four in ten are prepared to say that they feel proud of Britain's economic achievements.

Once again the views of Northern Ireland 'British' respondents fall well within the range of those held by English, Scottish and Welsh respondents, while the 'Irish' in Northern Ireland are clearly a group apart.

% saying that they are "very" or "somewhat" proud of the way the nation functions

	England	Scotland	Wales	Northern Ireland (All)	Northern Ireland 'British'	Northern Ireland 'Irish'
The way its democracy works	61	56	59	45	54	25
Its political influence in the world	48	43	53	38	47	19
Its social security system	44	42	52	45	48	33
Its economic achievements	38	34	40	36	42	21
Base	*856*	*94*	*65*	*619*	*279*	*156*

Note: Northern Ireland respondents were asked about "the United Kingdom".

Exclusive nationalism

It would be too easy to see exclusive nationalism as not merely negative but as an undifferentiated reactionary impulse. However, we shall argue that there is an important distinction to be drawn between cultural and economic protectionism on the one hand, and raw xenophobia on the other. The first may be a pragmatic response to the threats posed, for example, by foreign cultural hegemony; a response particularly evident in the French government's protection of the language, or the limits placed on the import of American television programmes. Perhaps the recent campaign in Britain to preserve Radio 3 in its traditional form owes something to this kind of cultural conservatism. In the economic sphere, protectionism is a commonplace reaction to the damaging effects of import penetration, albeit one less easily attainable in a world of multilateral trade agreements. Support for protectionism varies quite markedly according to the measure proposed. While a comfortable majority of British respondents feel that there is a case for Britain to limit imports to protect the economy, only about a third would ban foreigners from buying land in Britain.

As for Northern Ireland, the familiar pattern resurfaces. The Northern Ireland 'Irish' are the least protectionist and the least culturally conservative of the national groupings, while the Northern Ireland 'British' are, if anything, more protectionist than their mainland counterparts.

Endorsement of protectionist measures

% "strongly agreeing" or "agreeing" that:	England	Scotland	Wales	Northern Ireland (All)	Northern Ireland 'British'	Northern Ireland 'Irish'
Britain should limit imports to protect the economy	62	68	61	63	71	49
Television should give preference to British programmes	34	34	48	29	38	16
Foreigners should not be allowed to buy land in Britain	31	40	29	29	37	18
Base	856	94	65	619	279	156

Note: Northern Ireland respondents were asked about "the United Kingdom".

Quite distinct from protectionist tendencies such as these lies a xenophobic urge which seeks to exclude *people* rather than *products*, and is arguably based on a fear of social contamination or pollution. With the loss of an Imperial role followed by two decades of immigration from the new Commonwealth, the sense of what it was to be distinctively British

underwent something of a shock. Racist politics flared briefly before being neutralised by the policies of successive governments to limit immigration. As a result, immigration is scarcely a live issue today, but retains a powerful political undertow in the guise of a fear of multi-culturalism and cultural dilution (Husbands, 1994). Here lies a xenophobic dislike of 'otherness' in general, and of the stranger in particular: a *heterophobia* which may - or may not - be coloured by enmity or degenerate into racism (Cohen, 1994). The truly xenophobic items in this scale receive only minority support. For instance, only around a quarter say that immigrants increase crime rates. Less overtly xenophobic concerns are more widespread - about half of mainland Britons think that immigrants take jobs away from people born in Britain and two thirds think that the number of immigrants should be reduced.

On some of these measures (but not all), the Northern Ireland 'British' emerge as rather less xenophobic than the British on the mainland - perhaps because there has been comparatively little new Commonwealth immigration to Northern Ireland. But their concern that immigrants take the jobs of those born in the United Kingdom is even greater than that of their mainland counterparts.

Endorsement of xenophobic sentiments

% who:	England	Scotland	Wales	Northern Ireland (All)	Northern Ireland 'British'	Northern Ireland 'Irish'
Disagree that immigrants are good for the economy	37	34	40	26	30	17
Agree that immigrants increase crime rates	25	16	31	22	25	15
Disagree that political refugees should be allowed to stay in Britain	25	26	31	12	16	.3
Disagree that immigrants make Britain open to new ideas and cultures	17	12	20	13	16	9
Disagree that schools should make more effort to teach foreign languages	5	4	5	5	5	3
Say that immigrants take jobs away from those born in Britain	48	52	48	52	61	41
Agree that the number of immigrants should be reduced	64	65	65	45	53	30
Base	*856*	*94*	*65*	*619*	*279*	*156*

Note: Northern Ireland respondents were asked about "the United Kingdom".

Constructing a typology of national identity

Unpacking the constituent elements of national identity provides us with some curious and some enlightening results - none of which has so far led us particularly close to that part of the population whose sense of national identity might justify their claim to be at 'the heart of Britain'. But perhaps the most useful approach - which may give us some insight into the really challenging contemporary policy issues - is to construct national identity 'types' based on its constituent elements, and see how those with widely differing composite national identities view issues to do with integration into Europe. Although there may be a common set of attitudes that tends to be associated with all aspects of national identity, correlations show that our two main strands of inclusive and exclusive nationalism remain fairly distinct.[8] We therefore constructed a typology of national identity according to how respondents in Britain scored on either of the two inclusive aspects of national identity (pride in heritage and culture and in the way the nation functions) and on either of the two exclusive aspects (which we have labelled as protectionism and xenophobia). Respondents who were in the top third of the sample according to their score on *either* of the inclusive aspects were considered to be high in national sentiment. Respondents who were in the top third of the sample according to their score on *either* of the two exclusive aspects of national identity were considered to be high in exclusiveness. On this basis, we categorised respondents into four groups:

1.   Low in exclusiveness and low in national sentiment
2.   Low in exclusiveness and high in national sentiment
3.   High in exclusiveness and low in national sentiment
4.   High in exclusiveness and high in national sentiment

We then identified, through modelling, the characteristics associated with each of these 'types' (see Appendix B of this chapter for full details of the logistic regression models used).

Group 1 may be labelled *supra-nationalists*. Low in exclusiveness and low in national sentiment, *supra-nationalists* tend to be unmoved by the symbols of nation. Generally respondents who fall into this category are likely to be libertarian,[9] better educated, younger, female and rather more likely to read *The Guardian* or *The Independent*. They are not very attached to their locality[10] and are rather unlikely to read the *Daily Express*.

Group 2, with their combination of low exclusiveness and high national sentiment, we term the *patriots*. In common with the first group, these respondents are likely to be well-educated and (fairly) libertarian; but they also, in contrast, tend to be strongly attached to their area. *Patriots* are likely to read the *Daily Telegraph*, *The Times*, or the *Daily Express*.

Group 3, defined by a combination of high exclusiveness and low national sentiment, we term the *belligerents*. Respondents falling into this category are likely to be male readers of *The Sun*, notably authoritarian in outlook and with few educational qualifications. They tend not to feel a sense of attachment to their area.

Group 4 we term the *John Bulls* for their combination of high exclusiveness and high national sentiment. Again these respondents tend to have few educational qualifications, and are likely to hold authoritarian values. They differ from the *belligerents* in that they are likely to be older, strongly attached to their area, and to read the *Daily Mail*.

These four national identity categories show that there are four distinct ways of 'being British'. Perhaps the first - the *supra-nationalists* - are the least distinctively British of the four, and might be reasonably said to have little sense of national identity. Not so the remainder. The fourth group - *John Bulls* - embody a widespread image (indeed, almost a caricature) of traditional proud and exclusive nationalism. They are antithetical to the *supra-nationalists*. But there is a second antithesis here too: that of the *patriots* and the *belligerents*. Their opposition is an orthogonal one, for where the first are high (on national sentiment), the second are low; and where they in turn are high (on exclusiveness), the first are low.

Patterns of party identification are as might be expected. In Britain the *supra-nationalists* are more likely on average to support the Labour Party, while the *patriots* and the *John Bulls* are more likely than average to support the Conservatives. The *belligerents* are notable in that they are rather more likely than other groups to support no party at all: 14 per cent did not, compared with about seven per cent for other groups.

So clearly demarcated are these four categories that the kind of people belonging to them might reasonably be expected to react differently to, and perhaps exercise a potent if divergent influence upon, the politics of European integration in the coming years. Moreover, this issue of national identity bears directly upon the much debated question of whether a distinctively European identity - a 'citizen's Europe' - is likely to arise (Odermatt, 1991; Papcke, 1992; Schlesinger, 1992).

National identities and Britain's position in Europe

Any exploration of the possible impact of national identity upon the development of attitudes to European integration must start from people's views about Britain's relationship with the European Union at present. The next table tends to confirm that Europe has gained renewed importance in British domestic politics. True, the shifts between 1994 and 1995 are not very large, but they are marked enough to pose the question of whether a new 'Eurosceptic' trend might be gathering strength both in Northern Ireland and

in mainland Britain. Longer-run comparisons are not available for several of
the items, because a different, more detailed set of questions about attitudes
to Europe was introduced only in 1994 (Evans, 1995). However, it is worth
noting that a long-standing question as to whether or not Britain should
withdraw from the European Union (formerly EEC or European
Community), asked from 1983 to 1991, has shown a marked downward trend
in favour of withdrawal, reaching a low of 17 per cent in 1991. We shall
have to wait for more years of results of the new questions, with their greater
range of options, to see whether the changes between 1994 to 1995 are a
chance fluctuation, or the beginning of a re-assertion of an anti-European
Union position that once commanded the support of more than two in five
respondents.

Britain's relationship with the European Union 1994-95

	Britain		Northern Ireland	
	1994	1995	1994	1995
Britain's relationship with the European Union ...	%	%	%	%
... should be closer	37	29	45	39
... should be less close	23	26	10	13
... is about right	34	39	37	38
Don't know	7	6	7	11
Britain should do all it can to ...	%	%	%	%
... unite fully with the European Union	40	32	48	45
... protect its independence from the European Union	53	60	41	41
Don't know	7	8	11	14
Britain's long-term policy should be to ...	%	%	%	%
... leave the European Union	11	14	6	7
... stay in the European Union and try to reduce European Union powers	25	23	24	17
... leave things as they are	20	20	23	25
... stay in the European Union and try to increase European Union powers	28	28	27	29
... work for the formation of a single European government	8	8	12	11
Don't know	7	6	7	11
Base	*1165*	*1227*	*762*	*738*

Returning now to the 1995 figures, we can explore attitudes to the Union by
analysing responses by the four distinct groups we have already identified:
the *supra-nationalists, patriots, belligerents,* and *John Bulls.*

It can be said at once that, as an issue, the European Union enjoys a similar salience among all four groups, although its level is fairly modest. We asked respondents how much they had "heard or read about" the European Union: 58 per cent said "a lot" or "quite a bit", with most of the remaining respondents (34 per cent) saying "not much". And at this point, as we examine responses to the discrete policy options for Britain that we offered, the ability of this four-fold categorisation to discriminate becomes apparent. *Supra-nationalists* and *patriots* are quite close in their response to the perceived benefits of European Union membership (58 and 52 per cent respectively think that Britain benefits from membership) and differ sharply from the *belligerents* and the *John Bulls*, whose adverse judgements (22 and 28 per cent) are also similar to one another. A similar pattern can be seen in responses to the proposition that Britain might leave the European Union.

Very different, however, are the patterns of response on other issues. *Supra-nationalists* are alone in their substantial degree of support for a closer relationship with the Union, at least on a generalised level; on the specific benefits (and obligations) of closer links, there is more of a continuum. *Supra-nationalists* are alone too in their remarkably high level of support - a bare majority - for 'uniting fully' with the European Union, a position which just a third of the *patriots* and less than a quarter of the other groups espouse. And while levels of support for a single currency are modest, it is here too that the *supra-nationalists* distinguish themselves. Hardly enthusiastic (with only 28 per cent in favour), nonetheless the proportion giving it their backing is around twice as high as that of any of the other main groups, all united in their deep distrust of such a move.

Turning to Northern Ireland respondents, it is again worth comparing those who identify themselves as 'Irish' with those who identify themselves as 'British', and we again come across a curiously distinctive result. The latter have far and away the most pro-European attitudes of any group in the sample: a full two-thirds believe that Britain should do all it can to unite with the European Union, while well over half think that closer links would make Britain stronger economically. But while common sense might suggest that a feeling of being 'European' may lead to weaker national attachments, in this case a reverse influence is almost certainly operating. It seems that unsatisfactory national attachments may foster an inclination towards a stronger role for Europe to replace a troubled sense of national identity. It is also significant in this context to recall that the Social Democratic and Labour Party in Northern Ireland sees a reduction of national sovereignty in a European setting as offering the best framework for the resolution of the conflict in Northern Ireland (Smith and Corrigan, 1995). Equally, while the 'Irish' in Northern Ireland may see a united Europe as a way round the thorny issue of sovereignty, the Northern Ireland 'British' are no more and no less pro-European than those on the mainland.

Britain's relationship with the European Union,
by different national identity groups

% saying:	Supra-nationalists	Patriots	Bellig-erents	John Bulls	Northern Ireland 'British'	Northern Ireland 'Irish'
They have heard or read "a lot" about the EU	23	23	16	19	14	14
Britain benefits from EU membership	58	52	22	28	34	53
Britain should leave the EU	9	8	20	20	10	2
Britain should unite with EU	51	32	23	21	29	67
Closer links with EU would make Britain stronger	45	34	26	24	34	58
Britain should be closer to EU	44	25	27	20	25	51
Closer links with EU would give Britain more influence in the world	34	28	22	23	31	49
There should be a single European currency	28	16	15	13	14	32
Base	275	239	202	299	324	204

We can now draw on these analyses to comment on the aggregate picture of attitudes towards Britain's relationship with European Union. The negative views of Britain's relationship with Europe are driven by the *belligerents* and the *John Bulls* on just about every issue. On the generalities of links with the European Union, and of the benefits derived from membership of it, the *patriots* join the *supra-nationalists*. On the more radical forms of integration, however - the single currency and full unification - they part company. These, then, are the fault-lines that are likely to run through the politics of Britain's relationship with the rest of the European Union in the coming years.

Conclusions

So where do we find the 'heart of Britain'? This has turned out to be a difficult hunt for an elusive quarry. This is quite possibly because the concept of Britain is itself elusive and because what could be termed 'sentimental Britain' has no single focus. This, perhaps, should not be a matter of surprise. Historically, *England* has enjoyed a clear identity as a nation within a *British* territorial state.[11] The main nationalist force in British politics has been a Conservative *and Unionist* Party whose image, historical

pedigree and electoral constituency has been England first, and the Union second.[12] Half a century ago, the term 'British' would have coupled more easily to Empire than to any specific society; Britain, it might now be said, has lost an Empire, and not yet found a nation.

Our own findings must be understood in the light of this distinction between *nation* and *state*. These separate words have been commonly used as interchangeable abbreviations for a much more specific entity - the *nation-state*. That hyphenated term was coined specifically to describe the case of a territorial-political unit (the state) whose borders coincided with the territorial distribution of a national group (the nation). Such nation-states are less common than is often imagined (Connor, 1978). And Britain is not among them.

It is no great surprise, then, that our findings reveal such a patchwork of different responses. The questionnaire module invited respondents to reply in terms of their identification with something - Britain - that is, arguably, for many not even a clear geographical entity; in some respects a state (within which all of us are subsumed, willingly or otherwise), and in others a nation (to which we may or may not belong). 'National identity', as we have presented it here, evokes responses that reflect that complexity.

We have identified four distinct types of orientation to British identity, labelled, for convenience, the *supra-nationalists*, the *patriots*, the *belligerents* and the *John Bulls*. Which, if any, can lay claim to the 'heart of Britain'? Many would probably agree that those who have no pride in British achievements and institutions rule themselves out of contention - the *supra-nationalists* and the *belligerents*. That leaves two groups who score high on the inclusive aspects of nationalism: the *patriots* and the *John Bulls*. The label we have chosen for the latter group quite deliberately reflects the narrow and exclusive view which this group brings to bear upon the world. As it is *British*, rather than *English*, identity of which we are in pursuit here, it must be conceded that the *Telegraph*-reading *patriots* have the strongest claim - for better or worse - to the 'heart of Britain'.

Many would agree that a strong and positive sense of national identity is already an anachronism; but if it does have a legitimate place, then a combination of pride and an absence of exclusionary fear provides a reasonable enough working definition. In the British context, *patriots* bring a confident and positive approach to European integration, place high value on the benefits of British membership of the European Union, and are utterly committed to continuing membership; yet they are hostile to unification, chary of a single currency and no more willing than most to forge "closer links". Most importantly, perhaps, our findings uncover subtle distinctions of 'national identity' that reveal the media characterisation of 'Europhiles' and 'Eurosceptics' to be an unhelpful over-simplification.

Nonetheless, it is worth noting that, in other historical contexts, the views of the *supra-nationalists* and the *John Bulls* could well have lain claim to represent the 'heart of Britain'. The *supra-nationalists* articulate a set of

values quite consistent with those of Edmund Burke and other 18th century Parliamentarians in their view of Europe and their acknowledgement of interdependence between Britain and its colonies. The *John Bulls*, on the other hand, could be seen as representing a view that became consolidated in the first decades of the 19th century, in the wake of Britain's victory in the Napoleonic wars, and lasted into the Victorian and Edwardian eras, sustained by the increasing perception of a threat from a united and powerful Germany. The *patriots* could be said to exemplify the attitudes of a generation who, after victory in the Second World War, saw their lot thrown in with the rest of Europe in the face of cold war threats from further afield. The *belligerents*, though, may well be an evolving 20th century phenomenon and for this alone they would deserve special consideration as representing the heart of Britain today. It may be that the precursors of this group developed with a loss of dominance that accompanied the loss of Empire, and also perhaps from the loss of Britain's position and status in Europe after half a century of relative economic decline. With little pride and much exclusiveness they may well feel that their birthright has been taken from them, and attempt to define themselves through their sense of loss and negativity.

The purpose of this analysis, however, is neither the award of an accolade nor the revelation of the fault-lines in the emerging British politics of European integration. The *patriots* in our sample are outnumbered both by the *supra-nationalists* who are insouciant in their support for full unification, and by the *John Bulls*, who see few benefits from membership. When the *belligerents* are taken into account, it becomes clear that the moderate line - of pragmatic pursuit of the benefits of membership of the European Union within a sturdy framework of national sovereignty - is the position of a beleaguered minority.

Notes

1. For an important argument that the 'ethnic nation' is not a different category from that of the 'civic nation', but rather represents the failure to achieve an inclusive political community, see Schnapper (1995).
2. In fact, the evidence on local attachment shows it to be generally very weak, and to stem almost exclusively from the characteristics of people themselves, rather than those of the places in which they live. Indeed, the largest single group of respondents (almost a third of the total) in a recent large study of local identity in shire England (carried out by MORI) professed no attachment to either village, town or county. The definition of attachment was, however, differently constructed from that used here (Young *et al,* 1996).
3. This is not to say that the very concept of identity itself should be taken for granted. Rather, it is coming increasingly to be questioned as a dangerous fiction, with national identity itself an ideological device to give substance to exclusionary myths (see Gillis, 1994).
4. This is, of course, a distinctively Franco-German view of the dichotomy between national and European patriotism. Elsewhere in Europe, for example in Catalonia, a different discourse is being developed (see Cardus and Estruch, 1995).

5. This nostalgic strand of national identity has been attacked as a restrictive preoccupation, holding back the modernisation of British society and economy.
6. It should be noted that the number of Scottish and, in particular, Welsh *British Social Attitudes* respondents is rather small, so the figures should be treated as having fairly wide confidence intervals.
7. A question asking respondents whether they considered themselves to be... 'British, Irish, Ulster, or Northern Irish' has been asked routinely in each of the six successive Northern Ireland Social Attitudes Surveys. (Unfortunately a similar question is not asked in Britain.) The results for Northern Ireland given in the body of this report focus on two groups - those who describe themselves as 'British' and those who describe themselves as 'Irish'. Not only are they the largest groups; they also tend to occupy opposite ends of the national identity continuum. Those who describe themselves as 'Northern Irish' tend to have views that fall in the middle, while those with an 'Ulster' identity tend to have views that are very close to those who describe themselves as 'British'.
8. In mainland Britain the correlations were as follows:

Protectionism and xenophobia	.41
Pride in culture and pride in the nation	.29
Protectionism and pride in culture	.20
Protectionism and pride in nation	.10
Xenophobia and pride in culture	.09
Xenophobia and pride in nation	.00

9. See Appendix I of this Report for the construction of the libertarian-authoritarian scale.
10. In the sense of "feeling close to" their neighbourhood or their town/city.
11. This distinction was better understood in the past. Geoffrey Gorer could launch his relentless exploration of *English* character in a *British* newspaper in 1950, with so little sense of incongruity that the issue escaped mention altogether (Gorer, 1955).
12. A strong sense of national identity is, of course, not the prerogative of those on the right of the political spectrum. When, however, it has emerged on the left, in such writers as Orwell, it has been quintessentially English, rather than British, in character, and uneasy at best with the notion of a 'British' state.

References

Cardus, S. and Estruch, J. (1995), 'Politically correct anti-nationalism', *International Journal of the Social Sciences*, **144**, 347-52.

Cohen, R. (1994), Frontiers of Identity: the British and Others, Harlow: Longman.

Connor, W. (1978), 'A nation is a nation, is a state, is an ethnic group, is a ...', *Ethnic and Racial Studies*, **1: 4**, 379-88.

Evans, G (1995), 'The state of the Union: attitudes towards Europe', in Jowell, R., Curtice, J., Park, A., Brook, L. and Ahrendt, D. (eds.), *British Social Attitudes: the 12th Report*, Aldershot: Dartmouth.

Gillis, J.R. (1994), *Commemorations: the Politics of National Identity*, Princeton, N.J.: Princeton University Press.

Gorer, G. (1995), *Exploring English Character*, London: The Cresset Press.

Husbands, C. (1994), 'Crises of national identity as the 'new moral panics': political agenda-setting about definitions of nationhood', *New Community*, **20: 2**.

Ignatieff, M. (1993), *Blood and Belonging: Journeys into the New Nationalism*, London: Chatto and Windus.

Keane, J. (1995), 'Nations and nationalism: a reply to Cardus and Estruch', *International Journal of the Social Sciences*, **144**, 353-55.

Odermatt, P. (1991), 'The use of symbols in the drive for European integration', in Leersen, J.Th. and Spiering, M. (eds.), *National Identity: Symbol and Representation*, Amsterdam: Rodopi.

Papcke, S. (1992), 'Who needs European identity and what could it be?', in Nelson, B., Roberts, D. and Veit, W. (eds.), *The Idea of Europe: Problems of National and Transnational Identity,* Oxford: Berg.

Parekh, B. (1994), 'Discourses on national identity', *Political Studies*, **40:3**, 492-504.

Schlesinger, P. (1992), 'Europeanness: a new cultural battlefield', *Innovation*, **5: 1.**

Schnapper, D. (1995), 'The idea of nation', *Qualitative Sociology*, **18: 2**, 177-87.

Smith, M.L. and Corrigan, J. (1995), 'Relations with Europe', in Breen, R., Devine, P. and Robinson, G. (eds.), *Social Attitudes in Northern Ireland: the Fourth Report,* Belfast: Appletree.

Young, K., Gosschalk, B. and Hatter, W. (1996), *In Search of Community Identity,* York: York Publishing.

Acknowledgement

Since 1989, the ESRC has helped ensure SCPR's continuing participation in the *International Social Survey Programme* (ISSP), through its funding (until 1994) of the Joint Centre for the Study of Social Trends (JUSST) and currently its successor, the Centre for Research into Elections and Social Trends (CREST). We are grateful to the Council for its financial support.

Appendix A: Constructing scales of national identity

Factor analyses were carried out on 23 (the majority) of the items in the national identity module, separately for respondents living in mainland Britain, for those living in Northern Ireland who described their identity as British (279), and those living in the province who described their identity as 'Irish' (156). Details of the factor analysis technique are given in Appendix I of this volume.

While the results of the factor analyses for the British in Britain and the 'British' in Northern Ireland were very similar indeed, those for the Northern Ireland 'Irish' were completely different, and thus ultimately precluded this group from the national identity scales. Because the other two groups were so similar we took the unorthodox decision to combine them and construct scales of the constituent parts of national identity that would work for both samples.

We labelled the exclusive dimensions *xenophobia* and *protectionism**, the first being made up of items dealing with immigration and linguistic identity, the second cultural and economic exclusion. The inclusive dimensions we labelled *pride in the way the nation functions* and *pride in heritage and culture*. The following table shows the dimensions that emerged from the factor analysis of the combined British and Northern Ireland 'British' sample.

The fifth dimension that emerged we called *attachment to place*. It was derived from a series of questions asking respondents how close they felt to their town or city/county/neighbourhood/country. Although we use this scale as an independent variable in modelling our different national identity types, we did not feel that it was a constituent of national identity itself, rather aspects of national identity were mediated through people's sense of attachment to place.

---

* Items were used in the construction of scales only if they had a factor loading of 0.5 or more. In the event, using just the three items shown here to form the 'Protectionism' scale resulted in a reliability coefficient that was rather low (0.64) for the overall sample. So, for this scale only, we included two extra items which had rather lower factor loadings (0.46 and 0.46) but which resulted in an adequate reliability coefficient (as shown here). The two items were: "Britain should follow its own interests, even if this leads to conflict with other nations", and "It is impossible for people who do not share British customs and traditions to become fully British" (with the question wording adapted appropriately for respondents in Northern Ireland). Both these items loaded n.ore heavily on the 'Protectionism' factor than on any other. These five factors accounted for 45 per cent of the overall variance.

Varimax rotated factor loadings showing dimensions of national identity
(British and Northern Ireland 'British')

	Xeno-phobia	Pride in the way the nation functions	Pride in heritage and culture	Protec-tionism	Attach-ment to place
Immigrants good for economy	.68				
Immigrants increase crime rate	-.65				
Political refugees should be allowed to stay	.63				
Immigrants make UK open to new ideas and culture	.63				
Schools make more effort to teach foreign languages	.62				
Immigrants take jobs away from people born here	-.61				
Number of immigrants should be increased	.60				
Proud of political influence in the world		.68			
Proud of the social security system		.68			
Proud of the way democracy works		.67			
Proud of economic achievements		.61			
UK/Britain is a better country than most others		.57			
Proud of armed forces			.72		
Proud of history			.72		
Proud of achievements in sports			.71		
Proud of achievements in arts and literature			.52		
UK should limit imports to protect its economy				.70	
Television should give preference to UK programmes				.66	
Foreigners should not be allowed to buy land in UK				.65	
Feels close to own town or city					.84
Feels close to own county					.81
Feels close to own neighbourhood or village					.73
Feels close to Britain/Northern Ireland					.63
Cronbach's alpha (GB)	.8	.7	.7	.7[13]	.8
Cronbach's alpha (NI)	.8	.8	.8	.6	.8

Appendix B: Logistic regression models

Modelling different national identity 'types': *supra-nationalists*
(low exclusiveness/low national sentiment)

	Model chi square	Change in chi square	Final wald statistic	R (partial correlation)	Signifi-cance
Libertarian	72.124	72.124	34.5995	-.1684	.0000
More educational qualifications	104.251	32.127	16.7912	-.1135	.0000
Not highly attached to area	121.665	17.413	11.6961	.0919	.0006
Doesn't read the *Daily Express*	129.663	7.998	5.1683	-.0525	.0230
Female	136.107	6.444	5.9000	.0583	.0151
Reads *The Guardian*	142.655	6.548	7.6351	.0700	.0057
Reads *The Independent*	148.293	5.638	5.7692	-.0573	.0163
Younger	153.221	4.928	4.8990	-.0502	.0269

Modelling different national identity 'types': *patriots*
(low exclusiveness/high national sentiment)

	Model chi square	Change in chi square	Final wald statistic	R (partial correlation)	Signifi-cance
More educational qualifications	17.917	17.917	10.8445	-.0903	.0010
Highly attached to area	35.947	18.030	16.6079	-.1161	.0000
Reads *The Daily Telegraph*	43.256	7.309	9.7904	.0848	.0018
Reads *The Daily Express*	48.825	5.569	6.2517	.0626	.0124
Libertarian	54.551	5.726	6.3012	-.0630	.0121
Reads *The Times*	58.232	3.681	3.8635	.0415	.0493

Appendix B (contd.)

Modelling different national identity 'types': *belligerents*
(high exclusiveness/low national sentiment)

	Model chi square	Change in chi square	Final wald statistic	R (partial correlation)	Signifi- cance
Reads *The Sun*	9.306	9.306	5.0698	.0555	.0243
Not highly attached to area	20.087	10.781	15.3630	.1157	.0001
Authoritarian	28.962	8.875	5.4233	.0586	.0199
Male	36.480	7.519	9.2030	-.0849	.0024
Fewer educational qualifications	44.279	7.799	7.6564	.0753	.0057

Modelling different national identity 'types': *John Bulls*
(high exclusiveness/high national sentiment)

	Model chi square	Change in chi square	Final wald statistic	R (partial correlation)	Signifi- cance
Fewer educational qualifications	71.966	71.966	35.2451	.1671	.0000
Authoritarian	117.089	45.123	37.3223	.1722	.0000
Highly attached to area	126.412	9.323	6.8531	-.0638	.0088
Reads the *Daily Mail*	131.530	5.118	4.5565	.0463	.0328
Older	135.393	3.864	3.8493	.0394	.0498

8 Matters of life and death: attitudes to euthanasia

David Donnison and Caroline Bryson [*]

Introduction

What is euthanasia? Literally it means "a good death", but this seems more propaganda than definition. It is more helpful to begin to define it as one person deliberately bringing another person's life to an end. This may be done in several ways: by treatment which shortens life; by the withdrawal of treatment; by the decision not to offer treatment which might prolong life; or by suicide assisted by someone else - usually a doctor, relative or friend. Euthanasia may be either voluntary - with the person making the request understanding what will happen; or non-voluntary - with the person not being competent either to make any request or to understand what was happening.[1]

This chapter explores the subject of euthanasia in three stages. We start by describing and distinguishing the different circumstances which may amount to 'euthanasia', or which are associated with it, and consider why they have attracted growing attention in recent years.

In the second part of the chapter we report our findings on public attitudes to euthanasia. First we ask whether people understand the law as it presently stands. We explore the degree of support for changes in the law, and the sorts of circumstances in which people would support and oppose change. Next we show the characteristics which distinguish supporters of euthanasia from their opponents, and the ways in which the feelings of both are related to

[*] David Donnison is Professor Emeritus of the University of Glasgow. Caroline Bryson is a Senior Researcher at SCPR and Co-director of the *British Social Attitudes* survey series.

other attitudes and loyalties. Finally, we consider whether we can make any forecast of the direction in which attitudes are likely to move in future.

Our task is to report public attitudes, not to change them. However, we try in the third part of the chapter to suggest some of the conclusions which a range of different interested groups may draw from our findings.

Why attitudes to euthanasia matter

Defining euthanasia more closely

We have already offered a broad definition of 'voluntary euthanasia' and shall use this term fairly freely throughout this chapter. But although it may seem easy to define, the concept is a very slippery one. Our wishes are never formulated without a thought for the world in which we live. Indeed, they are shaped partly by the constraints imposed on us by that world. For instance, if we 'decide' to end our lives because of fears about our future health, or about the burdens our continued existence may lay on ourselves or others, are we acting 'voluntarily'? Would our action still be voluntary if our doctors or relatives had greatly exaggerated these burdens and we had mistakenly believed them? Or what if the burdens were real enough, but could readily have been lightened by good nursing and community care, had they been available? So the word 'voluntary' always poses questions about the circumstances which shape a decision and the scope for changing these circumstances.

The distinction between voluntary and involuntary euthanasia is further complicated by the small, but growing, practice of preparing 'advance directives', sometimes also called living wills or - a more recent development - 'values histories'. They provide the means by which patients who have become incapable of communicating for themselves can provide helpful evidence for doctors and relatives about what they would wish to be done for them in various circumstances. Such statements can in some cases be legally binding.[2]

Euthanasia, then, may be voluntary or non-voluntary (or somewhere in between). Those involved may be medical staff, relatives or friends of patients, or the patients themselves. They may administer or withhold drugs, food or water, or connect or disconnect apparatus. Public attitudes to euthanasia, as we shall show, depend heavily on who does what.

The condition of the patients may also vary. They may be helplessly and irreversibly unconscious; or unconscious with some chance of recovery. A recent case has reminded us that even the experts may find it difficult to distinguish between these conditions.[3] Patients may be conscious, and suffering from a terminal illness in severe pain; or suffering from a terminal illness but with no pain. Others, without any physical burdens, may simply feel that life is no longer worth living and seek help in ending it. Again, the

judgements which people make about euthanasia depend critically upon the circumstances that apply.[4]

Growing concern about euthanasia

Euthanasia has always been practised. Socrates was a famous early case of assisted suicide. But, until recently, people have usually seemed content to leave decisions about death and dying to doctors. In the last few years, however, death and the medical decisions bearing upon it have rarely been out of the headlines or off the television screens for long.

In only one place, the Northern Territory of Australia, has voluntary euthanasia been made legal, and there only in restricted and clearly defined circumstances. That was in 1995. In the United States, the state of Oregon has moved towards legalisation, but again only in the most restricted circumstances.   Its *Death With Dignity Act* of 1994 is essentially a prescribing measure which deals with assisted suicide. Legal challenges were lodged immediately in both countries, and it will take time to determine how workable these measures will be in practice. The courts of Michigan recently found Dr. Kevorkian - a frank practitioner of assisted suicide - not guilty of assisting in two cases of this kind. This seems to demonstrate that American juries are not prepared to convict practitioners who honestly try to help patients with good reasons for wishing to die to achieve what they want. Such 'jury nullification' (to use the technical term) does not change the law but does suggest that change will soon be on the way. Moreover, American judges have always been more willing than their British colleagues to go back to first principles and assert the citizen's freedom of choice and expression. In a carefully reasoned judgement given in March 1996, a Federal Appeals Court determined that "there is a constitutionally protected interest in determining the time and manner of one's own death".[5] If confirmed in the Supreme Court, to which this judgement is likely to be taken, this will go a long way towards legalising euthanasia in the United States.

The Netherlands has the longest and most widely quoted experience of euthanasia. There, euthanasia remains a crime. But if doctors follow the prescribed procedures - gaining repeated requests from patients, ascertaining that their suffering is unrelievable and unacceptable, seeking independent medical opinions and making the proper reports to the local medical examiner - then no action is taken against them (Admiraal, 1996). But for several reasons these procedures cannot easily be adopted by other countries.[6]

There have been surveys of public opinion in many countries, including Britain, which show growing public support for voluntary euthanasia in defined circumstances.[7] In Britain, however, successive governments have shown no inclination to change the law. There have been two private members' bills for the legalisation of euthanasia, both unsuccessful. Meanwhile, more and more cases dealing with medical decisions at the end of

life are being brought to the courts (McLean, 1996). Court decisions, often tolerating but not publicly endorsing euthanasia, have tended to throw responsibility back onto the doctors.

Why has there been this recent growth of interest in euthanasia in so many Western countries? There are strong reasons to believe that it is no passing craze, and indeed that interest will continue to grow. In the past, death normally took place in the home, at a point determined by nature. Today, death itself is becoming harder to define, and the progress of medical technology, capable of keeping people alive for very long periods, brings death increasingly into hospitals. For instance, in Britain there are thought, at any one time, to be as many as a thousand people in a persistent vegetative state for more than six months after an 'acute insult' of some kind, such as a motor-cycle accident. There are probably as many more in a similar condition resulting from other causes, such as Alzheimer's disease (Jennett, 1996). And, although many would prefer to die in their own homes, the number doing so appears to be falling. The great majority of us will die in hospital (BMA, 1993; Charlton et al, 1995). Not surprisingly then, doctors and nurses are being increasingly drawn into the decision-making process. Patients - and potential patients - therefore want their voices to be heard too.

The growing debate about euthanasia can also be seen in the context of an ageing population, increased geographical mobility and a decline in family size. Nowadays there are fewer younger people living nearby to take responsibility for looking after frail, elderly relatives. Thus people who can no longer manage on their own may be compelled to move into the homes of younger relatives, rather than rely on the daily visits which in the past were easier to make. There is evidence too that many younger people are unwilling to shoulder such burdens, and see caring for the elderly as the responsibility of the state (Diba, 1995). The threat of dementia, afflicting one in four of those over the age of 85, then becomes still more pressing for potential sufferers, and for those who may have to care for them. For many people, the quality of life in their last years, and the timing of death, have become increasingly sensitive issues.

In addition, the spread of AIDS has brought a young and articulate group of people into the debates about death and dying. Initially hostile to the whole idea of euthanasia, fearing perhaps that others might be tempted to see it as a 'solution' to their problems, in recent years many of those involved appear to have reassessed their position. Indeed, in the Netherlands, it is claimed that over one in ten AIDS patients die through 'active euthanasia', a disproportionately large share compared to other disease groups (Seale and Addington-Hall, 1994).

Meanwhile, increasing care has been taken to make many widely-available drugs safer. It used to be fairly easy to kill oneself with an overdose of sleeping pills, but - without the help of a doctor or pharmacist - suicide is now much harder than it used to be. Many of those who join the societies

pressing for the legalisation of voluntary euthanasia do so because they offer information about the range of methods for ending one's life.

Increasing debate about euthanasia should also be seen as a part and parcel of the move towards the 'empowerment' of the general public. People generally have become increasingly confident about questioning professional authority in all fields, and medical professionals have certainly not been exempt from this. Moreover, the creation of internal markets within the hospitals, coupled with the high costs of units providing intensive care, mean that the public is becoming more alert to 'priority setting' or 'rationing' in the health service. Certainly, if people were ever reluctant to talk about euthanasia, evidence from the *British Social Attitudes* survey strongly suggests that they are not so any more.[8]

The debate

Those who oppose euthanasia on religious grounds tend to present the simplest and clearest case. God, they believe, is the giver of all life; and God alone is entitled to reclaim the human soul at the end of life. The Roman Catholic church is consistent in extending this prohibition to abortion, suicide, and chemical or mechanical means of birth control. Opponents of euthanasia fear that any relaxation in the law, even if confined to special cases, will place society on a 'slippery slope'. Rather, they would argue for much improved palliative care, and the development of more hospices to provide it, to help control the pain suffered by many people towards the end of their lives. Some would say that such progress is less likely to be made if euthanasia comes widely to be seen as an easier, cheaper solution. And if some suffer as a result of the prohibition of euthanasia, they would argue that such a price is worth paying as a means of achieving a greater good - that of maintaining the moral standards of the wider society. Authorities speaking for many faiths - the Church of Scotland[9], the Church of England, the Greek and Russian Orthodox Churches, the Mormons, Jehovah's Witnesses, Muslims and, for quite different reasons, the Buddhists and Hindus - are united in opposing voluntary euthanasia. The Presbyterians and Unitarians are among the few Churches to maintain that euthanasia may sometimes be defended as having a legitimate role in modern medical treatment and care.

At the other end of the spectrum are those who adopt an essentially libertarian stance, stressing individual human rights and arguing that anyone seeking to end his or her life is entitled to claim professional advice and help, without having to justify their decision in any way (Radcliffe Richards, 1994). But most, probably, would not go this far. More common are voluntary societies in many Western countries which press for legislation to make voluntary euthanasia legal in certain circumstances. They distribute information about advance directives or living wills, and may also provide information for their members about 'departing drugs', and safe and effective

methods of 'deliverance' (see, for instance, Mair, 1981; Docker, 1993). Their members approach the subject of euthanasia from various standpoints but generally share a conviction that, in a world where death increasingly depends on human decisions, patients are entitled to a hearing about the timing and manner of their passing. In practice many doctors do give them that hearing. But the patient cannot rely on this, and doctors may well endanger their careers by trying to help patients who want to end their lives. In fact, the argument of many of those who press for changes to the law is much like that deployed by those who support abortion in certain defined circumstances. If euthanasia were recognised, discussed, reported and properly controlled (they say), it would be easier to safeguard moral standards.

The professions most directly involved - doctors, nurses and lawyers - are scattered at various points across this wide spectrum.

In Britain, different kinds of cases go to different kinds of courts, these paying little attention to each others' decisions, and thus not producing authoritative guidelines. Some feel this has led to inconsistency, and even hypocrisy (McLean, 1996). Proponents of euthanasia argue that patients fit enough to understand their situation, and to act and speak for themselves, are entitled to end their lives by suicide or by refusing treatment. But since they may not legally ask anyone else to help them commit suicide, they will be unable to decide the point of their death because they will have to wait until they become helpless. Then, when permanently and wholly unconscious, non-voluntary euthanasia may be legally available. Some people believe that patients may be driven into suicides which would not have taken place, had they been confident that a doctor would help them to die if they were to make that final request.[10]

In this country, the courts have generally left to doctors the principal responsibility for deciding what to do. Doctors are entitled to refuse patients treatment if 'best practice' - which means what respected members of the profession normally do - suggests this would not be in the patient's 'best interests'. But once a treatment has begun it cannot legally be withdrawn unless it has demonstrably failed. There may be a psychological difference between refusing to offer, and withdrawing, a life-saving treatment, but most philosophers would say there is no moral difference if the consequences of both decisions are known to be the same.

These are some of the unresolved issues which worry those unhappy about present arrangements in Britain. For instance, should society regard it as acceptable that many doctors, having been asked by their patients to hasten their deaths, acquiesce[11] and so endanger their careers (and compromise their professional dignity and security) in engaging in an activity that could result in a criminal prosecution? Advocates of voluntary euthanasia also question whether it is right that the courts should have the final say on whether a patient should live or die. Some judges (for instance, Lord Mustill and Lord Brown-Wilkinson) have remarked that the issues are getting beyond the

capacity of the courts to resolve, and that they should all be comprehensively reviewed by Parliament.[12] Parliament, both Lords and Commons, has so far declined to take up this invitation. Private members' bills have been brushed aside. The House of Lords' Select Committee on Medical Ethics spent two years studying these problems and concluded that no change should be made. On the available evidence, MPs' attitudes to euthanasia are more volatile than on comparable issues (such as abortion and the death penalty). However, only a minority favours reform.[13]

Public attitudes towards euthanasia

Questions addressed

From this brief review of a complex subject a number of key questions emerge. Do the British people understand the main provisions of the laws governing euthanasia? What are their attitudes towards euthanasia? Have these changed over time? More specifically, is there a demand for changes to the laws governing euthanasia? And, if change is desired, what changes and within what limits? Once we have addressed these questions, we can then explore the motives, loyalties and experiences underlying present attitudes. Finally, insofar as the survey evidence allows us to do so, we can speculate as to how public attitudes are likely to change in the future.

Knowledge of the present law

What do people understand as being the present law governing euthanasia? We gave two examples, and asked whether the law allows doctors to end life in these circumstances. The responses are shown in the next table.

Knowledge of the present law

Does the law allow doctors to end the life of a person with ...		Law allows	Law does not allow	Don't know/ refused
... an incurable and painful illness from which they will die, for example, someone dying of cancer?	%	3	93	4
... an incurable illness which leaves them unable to make a decision about their own future, for instance, a person in a coma on a life support machine who is never expected to regain consciousness?	%	44	49	7

Base: 1234

The great majority of people appear to understand the law in the first of these cases very well. The greater uncertainty which people express when it comes to the case of a patient in a coma is understandable. It is here that the law itself is more uncertain.

Changes in attitudes over time

There is evidence from previous *British Social Attitudes* surveys of widespread and increasing support for the legalisation of euthanasia in certain circumstances. Thus, in the decade between 1984 and 1994 there was a seven percentage point increase in the proportion thinking that doctors should be able to end the life of someone with a painful incurable disease. By 1994, more than eight out of ten people thought that euthanasia should be an option in these circumstances. We asked:

Suppose a person has a painful incurable disease. Do you think that doctors should be allowed by law to end the patient's life, if the patient requests it?

	1984	1989	1994
	%	%	%
Yes, the law should allow it	75	79	82
No, the law should not allow it	24	20	15
Base	*1562*	*1274*	*1000*

Under what circumstances, if any, should euthanasia be legal?

In 1995, the *British Social Attitudes* survey was able to focus on the issue of euthanasia in more depth than before, allowing us to address many of the issues central to informed debate. These include the degree of the subject's dependency, their level of pain, their likelihood of recovery and whether they are capable of speaking for themselves. As we shall see, these sorts of issues are crucial when it comes to people's attitudes towards euthanasia.

We constructed seven scenarios and asked respondents whether in these circumstances a doctor should *ever* be allowed by law to end a patient's life or not. These scenarios, and people's responses to them, are shown in the next table.

**% who think euthanasia should "definitely" or "probably"
be allowed by law for a person...**

... who has an incurable illness which leaves them unable to make a decision about their **own** future, for instance, imagine a person in a coma on a **life support machine** who is never expected to regain consciousness (if their relatives agree)	86
... who has an incurable and painful illness from which they will die, for example, someone dying of cancer	80
... in a coma, never expected to regain consciousness, but who is **not** on a life support machine (if their relatives agree)	58
... who is **not** in much pain, **nor** in danger of death, but becomes permanently and completely **dependent** on relatives for all their needs, for example, someone who cannot feed, wash or go to the toilet by themselves	51
... with an incurable illness from which they will die, but which is **not** very painful, as might be the case for someone dying from leukaemia	44
... with an incurable and painful illness from which they will **not** die, for example, someone with severe arthritis	42
... someone who is not ill or close to death, but who is **simply tired of living** and wishes to die - for example, someone who is extremely lonely and no longer enjoys life	12

Base: 1234

Note: The items have been reordered to reflect the level of support for legalisation of euthanasia in each case.

This shows that there are varying levels of support for euthanasia, and that these depend on the particular circumstances involved. For instance, support for euthanasia is generally higher when the case involves someone never expected to regain consciousness than it is when the case involves a conscious patient. People do not, therefore, regard euthanasia, and decisions about its legalisation, as a one-dimensional issue. But perhaps we have over-complicated matters by drawing attention to quite so many factors? It may be that people's attitudes to euthanasia are determined by fewer issues than those included in the seven scenarios - for example, solely by whether a person is expected to regain consciousness, or by whether their condition is curable. To ascertain whether or not this was the case, we used factor analysis.[14] In the event, no underlying factor or factors emerged. This confirms that each of the seven scenarios measures a different aspect of a person's attitudes to euthanasia.

Developing a 'euthanasia scale'

In order to identify the sorts of characteristics associated with support for, or opposition to, euthanasia, we gave each respondent a 'score' based on the

number of scenarios for which he or she thought that euthanasia should be legal. Thus, if someone supports doctors being allowed to end life in all seven scenarios, it is fair to say they are pro-euthanasia, compared to someone who thinks that euthanasia should be allowed in only one or two cases.

The most 'pro-euthanasia' score on our scale is eight, and the most 'anti-euthanasia' score is one. The scale produces a fairly normal distribution, close to a 'bell-shaped curve'. This tells us that we are not living in a society where large numbers of people are either pro- or anti-euthanasia. Whilst small minorities of people disagree or agree with euthanasia in all circumstances, most feel that euthanasia should be permissible under some, but by no means all, conditions.

Euthanasia score - number of scenarios for which euthanasia should "definitely" or "probably" be allowed

Score	%
One	5
Two	8
Three	11
Four	17
Five	19
Six	17
Seven	16
Eight	7
Base	*1185*

Supporters and opposers of euthanasia

By using the scale we are able to say how strongly people support or oppose the legalisation of euthanasia. We can then examine in detail the sorts of characteristics associated with a pro- or anti-euthanasia outlook. We focus on two types of characteristics that might be linked to attitudes to euthanasia - socio-demographic characteristics (such as age or education) and attitudes towards other 'moral' issues (such as abortion or capital punishment). The latter should help us shed light on whether attitudes towards euthanasia form a 'subset' of attitudes towards the sanctity of life in general.

We begin by calculating the mean score for a number of different groups. The higher the score, the greater this group's support for euthanasia, and *vice-versa*. This shows that certain demographic groups do indeed have quite distinct attitudes towards euthanasia. For instance, the young (those aged between 18 and 34) are more pro-euthanasia than those who are older. Attitudes towards euthanasia also vary according to marital status, education, ethnic group, region and religion. The scores for all these groups can be found in the Appendix to this chapter.

Attitudes towards euthanasia also seem linked to attitudes towards other 'moral' issues such as abortion and capital punishment. For instance, those who are anti-abortion are more opposed to euthanasia than those who are supportive of abortion. And, not surprisingly, those who think that suicide is "never justified" are much more anti-euthanasia than those who think that it might be justifiable in certain circumstances.

Although looking at mean scores is helpful, it is limited by the fact that many of the characteristics we are interested in are closely related to one another. So, for instance, although age and religion are both linked to attitudes towards euthanasia, they may not be *independently* linked. Rather, it could be that religion is the key determinant of attitudes towards euthanasia and that age only *seems* to be important because the young are simply less likely to attend religious services. Such problems can be overcome by using regression, a statistical modelling technique which establishes the independent importance of relationships between various factors and attitudes to euthanasia (a more detailed description of regression techniques can be found in Appendix I of this report).

We start by looking at the relationship between certain socio-demographic characteristics (such as sex and age) and attitudes towards euthanasia. Having done this, we then examine the relationship between attitudes towards euthanasia and attitudes towards other moral issues. Socio-demographic characteristics were included for their substantive interest, but were also chosen to ensure precise estimates of the association between attitudes to euthanasia and attitudes to similar moral issues (which we consider later on).

First, socio-demographic characteristics. The characteristics we included in the model are shown below and those which had a statistically significant relationship with attitudes towards euthanasia are shown in bold. The remainder did not prove to have an independent link with attitudes to euthanasia once those shown in bold had been accounted for. A more detailed account of this model can be found in the Appendix to this chapter.

**Model 1: Attitudes towards euthanasia
and socio-demographic characteristics**

> **Ethnicity**
> Sex
> Age
> **Disability**
> Marital status
> **Region**
> **Qualifications**
> **Church attendance**

This shows that a number of characteristics are associated with attitudes towards euthanasia. Perhaps the most important finding, however, is the *failure* of age to have any significant bearing on attitudes towards euthanasia.

In fact, the apparent relationship between attitudes towards euthanasia and age seems merely to reflect the importance of religious attendance - which itself varies strongly with age.[15]   When it comes to attitudes towards euthanasia, then, age acts simply as a proxy for a set of traditional values bound up with religious attendance and belief.[16]

How exactly do the characteristics listed previously relate to attitudes towards euthanasia?   First, religion. Put simply, low levels of religious attendance (that is, attending church or an equivalent less than once a month) are strongly associated with pro-euthanasia sentiment (it is among this group that a disproportionate number of young people are found - hence the apparant importance of age). There was no significant difference in attitudes between those who attend church infrequently and those with no religion whatsoever.   We may speculate that those attending religious services regularly are more likely to think of life as God-given, and so something that individuals have no right to end. Given the growing secularisation of Britain, these findings suggest that support for the legalisation of euthanasia will increase over time. We return to this issue later in the chapter.

Ethnicity also matters - with white respondents being more pro-euthanasia than respondents from other ethnic groups. Regional differences also exist, with those in Scotland being more anti-euthanasia than those in England or Wales.   This difference exists even when regional variations in religious attendance are taken into account.

Those with a disability are more pro-euthanasia than those who are able-bodied.   A possible explanation for this is that disabled people are more inclined to sympathise with those in pain or suffering, or with those wholly dependent upon others, who wish to end their own lives.   However, this 'disability effect' applies only among the young - among older respondents being disabled has no significant link with attitudes towards euthanasia.

Previous *British Social Attitudes* studies have found a strong relationship between educational qualifications and liberal attitudes towards certain moral issues, such as abortion.   So we might expect to see a similar pattern in respect of euthanasia.   In the event, our results lend only limited support to this idea: it is only those whose highest educational qualification was A-levels who are significantly more likely to support euthanasia than those without qualifications. A relationship noted between having a degree and being pro-euthanasia was not significant (this may, however, simply reflect the small number of graduates in our sample).

If concern for the protection of partners and children, or worries about the impact on others of taking one's own life, had been important considerations, then we might have expected marital status to have an association with attitudes towards euthanasia.   In fact, marital status had no significant influence on attitudes.[17]

What of the possible relationship between attitudes to euthanasia and attitudes toward other issues?   To test the possible relationship between attitudes to euthanasia and sanctity of life issues, we used data from a series

of questions covering attitudes to abortion and capital punishment.   To
supplement these, we also considered people's responses to two further
statements which tap 'right to life' issues - "suicide is never justifed no
matter how bad things are" and "advances in medical science will give
doctors too much power to decide when to end people's lives".   Finally, to
tap more pragmatic attitudes towards ending life, we looked at responses to
the following question:

> How much do you trust hospital doctors always to put the interests of
> their patients above the convenience of the hospital?

Clearly, if euthanasia is considered acceptable for people in extreme ill-
health, then there must be confidence in the diagnosis.
   The characteristics we included in our second model are shown below. As
before, only those marked in bold had a statistically significant relationship
with attitudes to euthanasia.

**Model 2: Attitudes towards euthanasia, socio-demographic
characteristics and other social attitudes**

Ethnicity
Sex
Age
Disability
Marital status
Region
Qualifications
Church attendance
Trust in doctors
Attitudes to abortion
Attitudes to capital punishment
Attitudes to suicide
Attitudes to medical advances and power of doctors

This model found a very strong association between attitudes towards
euthanasia and attitudes towards other 'life and death' issues, supporting the
hypothesis that euthanasia is a 'sanctity of life' issue, as well as a medical
one.   Thus, being 'anti-suicide' or 'anti-capital punishment' is strongly
associated with being anti-euthanasia. Further, as expected, those who worry
about the potential power doctors might have in the future also oppose
euthanasia.   And those who do *not* wholeheartedly trust doctors to put
patients' interests above those of their hospital are more supportive of
euthanasia than those who do.
   When the effects of these attitudes are added into our model, education no
longer has a significant effect, suggesting there is an association between
attitudes to 'life and death issues' and educational attainment. Religious
attendance, however, continues to have a significant independent effect on

attitudes towards euthanasia, even when its strong association with attitudes to issues such as abortion is taken into account. The effects of ethnic origin, disability and region also remain significant. This model is shown in more detail in the Appendix to this chapter.

Should instructions to carry out euthanasia be followed?

So far we have considered a number of scenarios within which euthanasia might be allowed by law. This does not, however, address the issue of 'living wills', which we described to respondents as:

> *A document which some people draw up saying what they would wish to happen if they have an incurable illness which leaves them unable to make a decision about their own future.*

We then asked:

> *Suppose that someone's 'living will' includes an instruction that doctors should **not** keep them alive if they have a painful illness from which they will die. Do you think the law should allow doctors to decide to end a patient's life on the instruction of the 'living will', or not?*

Nearly three-quarters (74 per cent) of people thought a doctor should be *allowed* to end a patient's life in these circumstances. However, when asked whether a doctor should be *required* to carry out such instructions in a living will, a smaller proportion agreed. However, at 62 per cent, those opting for this approach still represent a comfortable majority. In fact, the law does, in some circumstances, require doctors to act on the instructions in a living will.

Only two per cent of our sample had actually made a living will; but if the 12 per cent who said they had considered making one have serious intentions, this is a proportion that may soon rise.

How might attitudes towards euthanasia change?

Our earlier analyses revealed that attitudes to euthanasia vary with age, mainly because church attendance (which is strongly associated with attitudes to euthanasia) is much more common among older generations than it is among younger ones. The difference between young and old in this respect is shown in the next table.

Religion and religious observance, by age

	18-34	35-54	55 +
% attending religious ceremony once a month or more	12	19	28
% saying have 'no religion'	20	5	4
Base	*371*	*411*	*451*

Unless the young dramatically change as they grow older, it seems probable that religion and religious attendance will have a diminishing importance for future generations. Consequently, support for the legalisation of euthanasia seems likely to increase. Further, the importance of education in our models suggests that 'pro-euthanasia' attitudes will increase as the population becomes better educationally qualified.

The association between attitudes to euthanasia and attitudes to other 'sanctity of life' issues hints at a future that may be more 'pro-euthanasia'. Censure of euthanasia is associated with opposition to abortion, suicide and capital punishment. True, older generations are *more* likely than younger ones to support capital punishment - but support for abortion, and a reluctance to condemn suicide, are much stronger than average among the young, and they may retain much of this support as they grow older. Further, when it comes to the issue of abortion, society as a whole has become substantially more liberal over the last decade (Heath and McMahon, 1992; Jowell and Park, 1996).[18] However, levels of support for capital punishment have changed little over this period.

Conclusions

The most consistent argument marshalled by advocates of voluntary euthanasia is based on respect for individual human liberty, which includes the right of everyone to end their lives at a time and in a manner of their own choosing (Radcliffe Richards, 1994). Equally principled is the standpoint of their opponents, who assert that - whatever the consequences for individuals - for the good of society nothing should be done to bring life to an end so long as it is possible to preserve it. The state therefore has a duty to preserve life, and this duty cannot be overridden by concerns for the individual. Clear though both doctrines may seem in theory, each is doomed to fail in practice, for the great majority of our respondents will accept neither.

While there are people with strong views about euthanasia, our survey shows that most fall somewhere between the two extremes. So perhaps those in both the pro- and anti-euthanasia pressure groups should recognise that, for the majority, pragmatism rather than principle rules. Our research confirms the finding of earlier surveys that, in certain limited circumstances, there is overwhelming public support for euthanasia - for the patient in an irreversible coma on a life-support machine (if their relatives agree) and for people with

incurable and painful illnesses who have requested euthanasia. There is also strong support for the notion that patients should be able to rely on doctors to end their lives on the basis of written instructions, such as those in 'living wills'. For the four other scenarios we presented, people are much more evenly divided, and for one (if a person is simply 'tired of living') they are overwhelmingly opposed to euthanasia.

One striking finding is that it is above all the *medical profession* that people would turn to for help in making the final decision. Of the three scenarios which attracted the greatest support for euthanasia, two involved patients in irreversible comas who were wholly dependent on doctors and nurses. In neither of these situations could euthanasia be described as 'voluntary'. The British Medical Association urges fuller and franker communication between doctors and their patients as death approaches, and stresses the patient's right to 'autonomy and choice' at this point (BMA, 1993). Our survey suggests that most people trust doctors. They are presumably ready to discuss these issues with them.

Most people also think that living wills should be given legal authority. However, it has been fairly convincingly demonstrated that there are many cases in which this would be very difficult to apply in any workable and consistent fashion.[19]

There is strong evidence from surveys among doctors that euthanasia in Britain and elsewhere is already a fairly widespread practice, sought by patients and assisted by doctors. Public opinion seems less and less likely to condemn it. We are, it seems, well down the 'slippery slope' often quoted by opponents of the practice. Proponents of euthanasia argue, as did those advocating a woman's right to choose abortion, that errors and abuses are the more likely to occur precisely because, being illegal, it cannot be discussed, regulated or monitored. Rapid changes in medical practice and technology, they say, accompanied by changes in beliefs and values, cannot easily be reversed. If those arguments are accepted they suggest that opponents of euthanasia, rather than fighting a long but ultimately doomed rearguard action, might do better to focus on issues they may be best equipped to deal with - such as defining and enforcing the proper limits of practice, protecting the most vulnerable patients, and vigilantly monitoring and commenting critically on the effects of any change that may be introduced.

Nonetheless, this study does suggest that, although opponents of euthanasia who campaign under the 'right to life banner' are a small minority, they have identified a deep seam of values, cutting across boundaries of politics and class, which perhaps constitute a fault-line in British public opinion. Opposition to abortion and euthanasia, a censorious view of suicide, and opposition to the death penalty (the latter, however, is not quite so clear-cut) forge a powerful alliance, and gain institutional strength through the religious beliefs and observance that many 'pro-life' advocates share.

The issue divides all parties in rather similar ways. Surveys of Parliament show what may be rather anxious fluctuations in opinion among Members

and there is no majority for reform in sight. And since our own survey shows no strong party-political allegiances likely to mobilise for reform, if the law is to be changed it will be only through a private member's bill - much as was the case with proposed reforms to the laws governing abortion. That means that the work of preparing the ground for reform and drafting bills will have to be largely done by outsiders, with little help from the civil service. On 'living wills', too, and their practical application, there is work to be done before they could safely be given stronger legal force.

There is massive public support for a limited measure of legalisation. That would be much easier, politically, than abolishing the death penalty. But such change, if it comes, would be likely to create new inconsistencies as well as resolving old ones - leaving scope for continuing argument between advocates and opponents of reform. Meanwhile the timing and manner of death will increasingly become a matter for human decision, rather than a natural process. Only one thing is certain. If nothing is done, the issue is not going to go away.

Notes

1. Some would add, as a third category, involuntary euthanasia: the person could have made such a request but was not given the opportunity to play any part in the decision; but that is beyond the scope of our discussion. Most people would classify this as murder.
2. The British Medical Association (BMA) has recommended that 'living wills' be respected where possible, and the Council of the BMA has said that it would support legislation to clarify the somewhat confused situation which has arisen through the evolution of common law (British Medical Association, 1993). Societies advocating the legalisation of euthanasia often argue that 'living wills' should be given the force of law when patients are unable to speak for themselves, and should be interpreted, when necessary, by a nominated proxy who knows the patient well. However, it is in practice very difficult to provide instructions that will help (or indeed reach) a doctor working in an intensive care unit in the middle of the night. (For an account of these and other difficulties, see Pace, 1996; Sommerville, 1996; Docker, 1996.)
3. "A man who for seven years was thought to be in the same permanent unconscious state as the 'right to die' Hillsborough victim, Tony Bland, has become aware of his surroundings and is communicating with hospital staff ... The case ... puts a huge question mark over experts' ability to diagnose such cases reliably...". *The Guardian*, March 16, 1996.
4. Some cases can be fairly simply described, and thus provide the 'scenarios' we asked respondents to consider. But they do not exhaust the possibilities. We have said nothing, for example, about society's treatment of foetuses and infants with severe physical or mental handicaps, a subject posing further difficult questions which pressure upon questionnaire space prevented us from addressing.
5. The case, *Compassion in Dying vs State of Washington, No. 94-35534*, is discussed by Cheryl K. Smith, one of the drafters of the Oregon legislation (Smith, 1996).
6. Procedures such as those used in the Netherlands depend both upon there being a public prosecutor - which there is in Scotland but not in the rest of the UK - and, many believe, upon primary medical care of a quality which few people in Britain receive.
7. For example, the Roper polls, 1986, 1988, 1990 and 1991 in the USA; NOP polls, 1976, 1985, 1989 and 1993 in England, Scotland and Wales; Gallup polls, 1968, 1974, 1979,

1984, 1989 and 1990 in Canada; a 1987 MORI poll in Britain; annual Roy Morgan Research Centre polls in Australia, and many others.

8. When the questions in our survey were first pilot-tested, we warned the interviewers that some respondents might find the subject painful and that they should omit the rest of the questions in that module, should any respondent show signs of reluctance to answer or become distressed. On the contrary, they reported that people were not in the least unwilling to talk - indeed, it was often difficult to bring interviews to a close. To be sure, this is no more than anecdotal evidence, but the vast majority of respondents to the main survey do not appear to have found the questions unacceptable.

9. The Board of Social Responsibility of the Church of Scotland (1995) provides a recent and full statement which members of many Churches would accept.

10. That may explain why a Dutch doctor experienced in euthanasia, Peiter Admiraal, has said (in the course of a conference discussion) that he believes that voluntary euthanasia may be less common in the Netherlands since it became an accepted medical practice.

11. Sixty per cent of those responding to a survey carried out for the *British Medical Journal* had been asked by patients to hasten death, and 32 per cent of those asked had done so (Ward and Tate, 1994). Moreover, 79 per cent of those responding to a survey conducted on behalf of the magazine *Doctor* said that voluntary euthanasia was "an accepted part of medical practice" (*Doctor*, Press Release, February 1995).

12. See the case of *Airedale NHS Trust vs Bland,* 1993, 1 All ER 8821, quoted by McLean (1996).

13. Their *House Magazine* reported that "in 1992 a study showed that 36 per cent of MPs supported euthanasia in principle, falling back to 18 per cent in 1992 and now [1995] we are back up to 27 per cent". (House of Commons, July 17, 1995).

14. For an explanation of factor analysis, see Appendix I of the Report.

15. The dataset includes a number of variables concerned with religion, among them belief in God, religious affiliation and church attendance. Our initial analyses found that the best indicator of attitudes was attendance at church (or another place of worship), hence this was the variable adopted for the final analyses.

16. In an earlier model that excluded religious attendance but included the other demographic variables, age was found to be significant.

17. In earlier models we also found the following variables were not significant: household size and responsibility for caring for others.

18. In 1983, 55 per cent of people *disagreed* with a statement that the law should allow abortion in cases where "the woman decides on her own that she does not wish to have the child". By 1993, this proportion had dropped to 41 per cent (see Jowell and Park, 1996).

19. In fact, 'values histories', which provide a fuller and more helpful account of the patient's expectations of life, leave doctors scope to interpret that account in particular cases (for an argument in favour of this approach, see Docker, 1996.)

References

Admiraal, P. (1996), 'Voluntary euthanasia: the Dutch way', in McLean, S. (ed.), *Death, Dying and the Law,* Aldershot: Dartmouth.

Board of Social Responsibility of the Church of Scotland (1995), *Euthanasia: a Christian Perspective*, Edinburgh: St. Andrew's Press.

British Medical Association (1995), *Advance Statements About Medical Treatment*, London: B.M.J. Publishing Group.

British Medical Association (1993), *Medical Ethics Today: its Practice and Philosophy,* London: B.M.J. Publishing Group.

Charlton, R., Dovey, S., Mizushima, Y. and Ford, F. (1995), 'Attitudes to death and dying in the UK,New Zealand and Japan', *Journal of Palliative Care,* **11: 1**, 42-7.

Curtice, J. and Jowell, R. (1995), 'The sceptical electorate', in Jowell, R., Curtice J., Park, A., Brook L. and Ahrendt, D. (eds.), *British Social Attitudes: the 12th Report*, Aldershot: Dartmouth.

Diba, R. (1995), *Meeting the Costs of Continuing Care: Public Views and Perceptions*, York: York Publishing Services.

Docker, C. and Smith, C. (1993), *Departing Drugs*, Edinburgh: Voluntary Euthanasia Society for Scotland.

Docker, C. (1996), 'The way forward?', in McLean, S. (ed.), *Death, Dying and the Law*, Aldershot: Dartmouth.

Doctor (February 9, 1995), Press Release.

Heath, A. and McMahon, D. (1992), 'Changes in values', in Jowell, R., Brook, L., Prior, G. and Taylor, B. (eds.), *British Social Attitudes: the 9th Report*, Aldershot: Dartmouth.

House of Commons (1995), *The House Magazine*, London: House of Commons, 17 July.

House of Lords (1994), *Report of the Select Committee on Medical Ethics*, House of Lords Paper No.21, London: HMSO.

Jennett, B. (1996), 'Managing patients in a persistent vegetative state...', in McLean, S. (ed.), *Death, Dying and the Law*, Aldershot: Dartmouth.

Jowell, R. and Park, A. (1996, forthcoming), 'Questioning British attitudes', in Taylor, B. and Thomson, K. (eds.), *Understanding Change in Social Attitudes*, Aldershot: Dartmouth.

Mair, G. (1981), *How to Die with Dignity*, Edinburgh: Voluntary Euthanasia Society for Scotland.

McLean, S. (1996), 'Law at the end of life: what next?', in McLean, S. (ed.), *Death, Dying and the Law*, Aldershot: Dartmouth.

Pace, N. (1996), 'Law and ethics at the end of life: the practitioner's view', in McLean, S. (ed.), *Death, Dying and the Law*, Aldershot: Dartmouth.

Radcliffe Richards, J. (1994), 'Thinking straight and dying well', *Newsletter of Voluntary Euthanasia Society of Scotland*, September.

Seale, C. and Addington-Hall, J. (1994), 'Euthanasia: why people want to die earlier', *Social Science and Medicine*, **39: 5**,.647-54.

Sommerville, A. (1996), 'Are advance directives really the answer? And what was the question?', in McLean, S. (ed.), *Death, Dying and the Law*, Aldershot: Dartmouth.

Smith, C (1996), 'America gives green light to assisted suicide', *Newsletter of Voluntary Euthanasia Society of Scotland*, **16: 2**.

Ward, B. and Tate, P.(1994), 'Attitudes among NHS doctors to requests for euthanasia', *British Medical Journal*, **308**, 1332-33.

Acknowledgement

We wish to thank the Nuffield Foundation for the grant which enabled the questions on euthanasia to be asked. We also wish to thank Alex Bryson, Clive Payne and Rory Wolfe for their advice on statistical techniques.

Appendix

Euthanasia scale

Respondents who answered "don't know" or refused at more than two of the seven scenarios were not given a scale score. Respondents who did not answer the self-completion were excluded from the mean score analysis below (for comparability with the models).

The closer the score is to 8, the more 'pro-euthanasia' the group in question is, and the closer to 1, the more 'anti-euthanasia'. The scale is ordinal, where higher scores represent stronger support. The scale is not an interval scale, where a score of (for example) 4 would mean that someone is twice as supportive of the legalisation of euthanasia than someone who scores 2.

Mean scores for the euthanasia scale (1 to 8): socio-demographic and attitudinal characteristics

Variable	Mean score	Base
Age		
18-34	5.20	307
35-54	4.91	360
55+	4.56	359
Marital status		
Married	4.74	525
Living as married	5.27	58
Divorced/separated	5.41	133
Widowed	4.62	123
Never married	5.16	187
Ethnicity		
White	4.94	985
Non-white	3.88	41
Highest educational qualification		
Degree	5.13	98
Other higher education	4.71	148
A level or equivalent	5.41	122
O level/GCSE or equivalent	4.92	217
CSE or equivalent	4.67	75
No UK qualifications	4.74	366
Region		
England/Wales	4.95	927
Scotland	4.32	99
Religious attendance [a]		
Every week	3.95	132
At least once a month	4.51	78
At least once a year	4.85	179
Less often/never	5.08	548
No religion	5.53	89

[a] The full question asked people about attending church or other religious ceremonies.

Table (contd.)

Variable	Mean score	Base
Religion		
Church of England	4.94	343
Roman Catholic	4.04	84
Other Christian	4.45	170
Non-Christian	4.49	20
No religion	5.23	409
Belief in God		
Believer	4.53	465
Agnostic	5.22	377
Atheist	5.23	117
Data missing on belief	4.85	67
Attitudes to abortion [b]		
Pro-abortion	5.38	426
'Mid-view' on abortion	4.94	272
Anti-abortion	4.13	263
Data missing on abortion	4.55	65
Attitudes to suicide		
Suicide can be justified in some circumstances	5.30	532
Suicide never justified in any circumstances	4.46	494
Attitudes to capital punishment [c]		
Pro-capital punishment	5.21	549
Anti-capital punishment	4.53	477
Trust in NHS to act in patients' interest		
Trust all of the time	4.35	171
Trust most of the time	4.96	549
Trust some of the time	5.12	253
Trust just about never	4.98	32
Don't know about trust	4.50	21
Power of doctors to decide to end people's lives		
Doctors have too much power	4.43	199
Doctors do not have too much power	5.02	827

[b]   A scale on abortion was developed from a series of questions on whether abortion should be allowed in a particular circumstance. People were given a score based on the number of circumstances in which they thought it should be allowed. People who did not answer or answered "don't know" at more than two questions were excluded from the scale (and are shown above under the heading 'data missing'). Otherwise, people were grouped into 'pro' 'middle view' and 'anti' in three roughly equal groups.

[c]   A capital punishment 'score' was derived from three questions on whether capital punishment should be allowed in a particular circumstance. People were given a score based on the number of circumstances in which it should be allowed. People were then grouped into 'pro' and 'anti' camps.

Multivariate analysis

The statistical technique of regression is explained in more detail in Appendix I to this Report.

A positive coefficient means that the characteristic is associated with greater support for euthanasia than the comparison group; a negative coefficient that it is associated with less support.

Respondents who did not answer the self-completion were excluded from Model 1 (for comparability with Model 2).

Model 1: Attitudes to euthanasia and socio-demographic characteristics

Characteristic (comparison group in brackets)	Coefficient	Significance level
Ethnicity (non-white)		
White	1.01	0.00
Sex (man)		
Woman	0.10	0.38
Age (55 + years)		
18 - 34	0.28	0.13
35 - 54	0.24	0.11
Disability (able-bodied)		
Disabled	0.29	0.04
Marital status (single)		
Married/cohabiting	- 0.09	0.58
Divorced/separated	0.23	0.29
Widowed	0.04	0.86
Highest qualification (no qualification)		
Degree	0.38	0.07
Other higher education	-0.13	0.49
A-level (or equivalent)	0.48	0.02
O-level/GCSE (or equivalent)	0.11	0.49
CSE (or equivalent)	-0.20	0.39
Church attendance (at least once a month)		
At least once a year	0.79	0.00
Less than once a year/never	0.63	0.00
Has no religion	0.97	0.00
Region (England/Wales)		
Scotland	-0.72	0.00

Note: significance level of 0.01 or below = significant at 99% level. Significance level of 0.05 or below = significant at 95% level.

**Model 2: Attitudes to euthanasia, socio-demographic characteristics
and other social attitudes**

Characteristic (comparison group in brackets)	Coefficient	Significance level
Ethnicity (non-white)		
White	0.83	0.00
Sex (man)		
Woman	-0.01	0.96
Age (55 + years)		
18 - 34	0.14	0.46
35 - 54	0.16	0.30
Disability (able-bodied)		
Disabled	0.31	0.04
Marital status (single)		
Married/cohabiting	- 0.16	0.36
Divorced/separated	0.22	0.32
Widowed	0.08	0.74
Highest educational qualification (no qualification)		
Degree	0.34	0.13
Other higher education	-0.30	0.11
A-level (or equivalent)	0.28	0.19
O-level/GCSE (or equivalent)	0.03	0.86
CSE (or equivalent)	-0.11	0.64
Church attendance (at least once a month)		
At least once a year	0.39	0.01
Less than once a year/never	0.42	0.03
Has no religion	0.60	0.02
Region (England/Wales)		
Scotland	-0.76	0.00
Trust doctors to act in patients interests rather than those of hospital (always)		
Most of the time	0.59	0.00
Only some of the time	0.59	0.00
Just about never	0.45	0.18
Don't have an opinion	0.05	0.91
Abortion (pro-abortion)		
Middle ground	-0.30	0.04
Anti-abortion	-0.98	0.00
Missing data	-0.61	0.01
Capital punishment (anti-capital punishment)		
Pro-capital punishment	0.73	0.00
Suicide (suicide is sometimes justifiable)		
Suicide is never justifiable	-0.59	0.00
Medical advances may give doctors too much power to end life (disagree)		
Agree	-0.29	0.04

Note: significance level of 0.01 or below = significant at 99% level. Significance level
        of 0.05 or below = significant at 95% level.

9 Public spending and taxation

Lindsay Brook, John Hall and Ian Preston[*]

The 1992 general election, as most elections do, focused heavily on the stances of the two main political parties on taxation and public spending. While opinion polls, and indeed the *British Social Attitudes* survey series itself, suggest that the public favours higher public spending, it is never clear that the electorate is willing to 'put its money where its mouth is'. In this chapter we attempt to shed light on this important issue of public policy.

We address three separate but related sets of questions. First, how much do demands for higher public spending depend on the expected targeting of the tax increases necessary to finance them? In particular, are people still willing to support increases in spending to the same extent once the tax consequences for *themselves* become apparent?

Second, to what extent is popular support for the welfare state based on perceptions of self-interest as opposed to notions of the wider public good? At a time in which private welfare provision is becoming increasingly important, this question has implications for the very survival of the welfare state itself. This leads us to our third question: whether or not the take-up of private sector alternatives to state provision influences people's support for the welfare state.

The answers to these questions will tell us a great deal about the extent to which the welfare state can be expected to cope with increasing demands

[*] Lindsay Brook is a Research Director at SCPR and Co-director of the *British Social Attitudes* survey series; John Hall is a Senior Research Officer in the Public Finances Sector of the Institute for Fiscal Studies; Ian Preston is a Research Fellow at the Institute for Fiscal Studies and Lecturer in Economics at University College London.

upon it caused by an ageing population, changing technology and ever-growing expectations of its role. If individuals are prepared to contemplate higher levels of taxation for themselves, and if the growth of private alternatives fails to undermine popular support for the welfare state, then its future may be relatively secure. If not, it is at risk of being starved of resources and may end up by providing little more than a safety-net for the wholly dependent.

In this chapter we offer first a brief summary of the background to the debate and then turn to whether perceptions of self- *versus* public interest differ appreciably between individuals. We then report on the extent to which people's support for higher public spending survives a rise in their own tax bills that such extra spending would entail. We ask which groups in society are in practice most sympathetic to higher levels of public spending and look in particular at the characteristics of those who are covered by private medical insurance or who choose to educate their children privately. Do these (usually richer) individuals exhibit lower levels of support for the welfare state than the rest of the population? Finally, we examine the factors that influence attitudes towards aspects of state welfare.

Trends in attitudes to tax and spending

Since its first survey in 1983, the *British Social Attitudes* series has included questions about attitudes to a variety of public spending programmes. Some of these questions refer to priorities for extra public spending. Others try to establish people's willingness to pay for increases, or to accept decreases, in spending. In the table below we show the proportions of respondents who chose each of four spending programmes as one of their two highest priorities for additional public spending over the years. Not only do education and health consistently attract the highest levels of support (in each case over 50 per cent in every year of the survey) but support for extra spending on them is substantially higher in 1995 than it was in 1983. In contrast, support for more spending both on help for industry and on defence has declined over the period. We show only four of the annual readings in the table, but they represent the general trend.

Trends in spending priorities, 1983-1995

% support for extra spending on:	1983	1987	1991	1995
Health	63	78	74	77
Education	50	55	62	66
Defence	8	4	4	3
Help for industry	29	11	10	9
Base	*1761*	*2847*	*2918*	*1234*

While these questions may be helpful in determining the relative popularity of various areas of spending, they tell us little about public attitudes to *overall* levels of public spending and taxation. Every year of the *British Social Attitudes* survey we have asked people about their willingness to pay for extra provision, linking expenditure on health, education and welfare benefits. Since 1983, respondents have been asked whether they would like to see an increase or decrease in the level of spending *and* tax on these three items. As the next table shows, when the two are explicitly linked in this way, the majority of respondents consistently opts for higher taxes *and* higher spending. Indeed, the majority has shifted over the years from support for the *status quo* to a desire for higher spending *and* higher taxes.

Tax and spending preferences for health, education and social benefits, 1983-95

	1983	1987	1991	1995
	%	%	%	%
Increased taxes and more spending on health, education and social benefits	32	50	65	61
Keeping taxes and spending on these services the same as now	54	42	29	31
Reducing taxes and less spending on these services	9	3	3	5
Base	*1761*	*2847*	*2918*	*1234*

The series also introduced in 1985 a series of detailed questions about public spending on health, education, law and order, defence, environment, the arts, pensions and unemployment benefit. As a means of discouraging capricious 'overspending' by respondents, however, the introduction to this series of questions explicitly says that if they vote for much higher spending on any of the programmes, it might require a tax increase to pay for it. Despite this warning against choosing higher spending, in 1994 almost three quarters of respondents, for instance, expressed a preference for an increase in state spending on pensions. On the other hand, there were wide variations between the different programmes on offer. Around two in five people, for instance, opted for *lower* public spending on culture and the arts. Preferences for individual spending areas also varied over time: those in favour of higher spending on law and order grew from less than one half of all respondents in 1985 to almost three-quarters (72 per cent) in 1994.

Since rises in overall public spending do indeed imply rises in taxes (at least in the longer term), the series has also looked at trends in public attitudes to taxation. The answers to some of these questions on tax do, however, seem to contradict the answers to some of the questions on spending. The fact is that most individuals feel that their own taxes are already high enough. Each year, for instance, respondents are asked whether they think that taxes for

those on high incomes, middle incomes and low incomes are too high or too low. Then they are asked which of these groups they believe themselves to be in. In 1995, for instance, only four per cent of those who say they are middle income and three per cent of those who claim to be low income felt that their *own* taxes were too low. Indeed, fewer than three per cent of the sample described themselves as having a high income. So it is hardly surprising that most people want any extra tax burdens to fall on the highest income groups, and that almost nobody - a minority even of those describing themselves as high-income - thinks that their *personal* tax level is too low. It is *other people's* taxes that most people feel should go up.

We therefore decided to rectify the omission of previous years of the series and to include in 1995 a series of questions which made more specific the size and incidence of possible tax increases that would be needed to sustain increases in public spending. We tried to make explicit the size of the change in the tax bills that would result from particular spending choices.

As will be seen later in this chapter, different individuals exhibit very different preferences both between different public spending programmes, and on the overall balance between public spending and levels of taxation. This is to be expected. Individual respondents should theoretically take into account, among other things, the direct benefit to their household from a particular spending programme and the amount their household is likely to pay in higher taxes for that benefit. Individual views might, however, also be coloured by perceptions of the national interest. Hence, any individual's response may well reflect a vague amalgam of self-interest and public interest, and part of our task is to identify the balance between these two elements.

The factors that help to identify and explain the relative popularity of various programmes of public spending will certainly have implications for the future financing of these services. If, for instance, people support welfare spending mainly out of self-interest, then programmes aimed at relatively small segments of the population, such as single parents or students in higher education, are likely to be more vulnerable to cuts over time, than are programmes of universal provision, such as the NHS and schools.

But the factors underlying the private costs and benefits of public spending to an individual are complex. Individuals differ in their ability to pay and, other things being equal, better-off households might be expected to be more willing to pay for improvements to public services for that reason. On the other hand, if spending increases are financed through income-related taxes, as the better-off may reasonably fear, then richer households will expect to pay a higher share of the cost of any spending increase and this may inhibit their willingness to pay. So the purely financial calculus for any household is itself very complicated. The benefits arising from different sorts of spending may also differ between individuals. Even in broader terms, it is often difficult to determine how the benefits from public spending are distributed across the population. Demographic factors are likely to influence the

pattern. Parents with young families might, for instance, expect their children to benefit directly from higher spending on education, just as the retired may expect to benefit directly from an increase in state pensions. But individuals with different levels of household income will in practice have unequal access to *private alternatives* to state provision, whether in education, pensions or health. Apart from these factors which affect people's interests directly, answers to these questions will also vary according to their personal philosophies and values, which in turn are often related to their social and educational background.

So, in 1995 we asked about seven spending programmes (health, police, education, defence, the environment, public transport, culture and the arts), and asked respondents to say separately for each one which would be best for "you and your household" and which would be best for "the country as a whole". In addition, we explicitly stated the tax consequences of each of the expenditure choices, presenting half of the sample with an income-related tax consequence and the other half with a flat rate charge or 'refund'. This allows us to determine whether rich households are less likely to support spending increases when they are financed through more progressive tax instruments.   In the following sections, we describe and interpret the responses.

National interest *versus* self-interest

The next table shows support for a tax-financed spending increase on each of the seven programmes perceived to be of direct benefit to respondents themselves and their household, to the country as a whole, and to both.[1] For some, notably health and education, increases in spending were more likely to be viewed as good for the country as a whole than as good for their family in particular. Nonetheless there is plainly considerable consonance between perceptions of private and national interests in general, as shown by the similarity in the ordering of programmes in the first two columns of the table, and there is also considerable *overlap* between perceptions of household and national interests, as shown in the third column. It is not surprising that this overlap of interest should be seen to exist for a spending area such as defence where the distinction between private and public interest is conceptually unclear, and which economists refer to as a 'public good'. What is more striking is that there is also such clear alignment between perceptions of private and national interest in spending on an item such as education, where most of spending, though publicly funded, is on specific services of benefit to particular individuals.

The largest discrepancy between the first two columns - perceptions of public *versus* private interest - is in relation to education, where a particularly large proportion of the population see higher spending as good for the country but not for themselves. Reassuringly, 83 per cent of the respondents

who expressed that view were in households with no children currently in the household (compared with 66 per cent of the total sample who were in households without children).

% saying that tax-financed spending increase on each programme would be ...

	... good for own household	... good for country as a whole	... good for own household *and* for country
Health	65	74	59
Education	55	72	50
Police	38	39	30
The environment	28	31	22
Public transport	27	32	22
Defence	8	9	5
Culture and the arts	8	7	5

Base: 1218

By making this distinction between personal benefit and what would be for the good of 'the country as a whole', we were assuming that individuals could distinguish their own self-interest from that of the nation, but these answers do not tell us which of these two factors had the most influence on their general attitudes. One way of examining whether people's priorities are motivated more by self-interest or more by national interest is to compare the spending priorities of those respondents who think spending increases are in *both* their own interest and the national interest with those who believe such increases would benefit either only themselves or only the nation at large.

In each case we found that particular spending programmes were more likely to get a higher priority when they were seen as *both* personally and nationally beneficial - further confirmation that public support for the main pillars of the welfare state derives from a combination of self-interest and some notion of the public good.[2]

Do perceptions of tax consequences matter?

Our questions in the 1995 survey attempted to specify the tax consequences for individuals of choosing a higher or lower level of public expenditure. We decided to split the sample into two equal-sized random subsamples, thus allowing us to link the respondent's choice for levels of expenditure on each spending programme to a *different* type of tax change. Thus, one half of respondents were presented with tax consequences expressed as one penny in the pound of income tax for extra or less public expenditure on the programme, while the other half were presented with tax consequences expressed as a flat £35 annual change in the tax payments of each adult in the

respondent's household. These two amounts are linked in that £35 is the average increase in the tax bill for each adult as a consequence of raising income tax by a penny in the pound.[3] We also wanted to know whether or not respondents were clear about the cost to their household of their responses to our questions on public spending, so we asked them to estimate (within bands) the cost to them of a penny in the pound on income tax.

Since the relative popularity of individual spending programmes tends to vary over time, it would have been ideal to have asked the *same* sample of people the two sets of public spending questions, one where the tax consequences were made explicit and one where they were not. However, the best we can do for the moment (see the next table) is to compare responses given in 1994 with those we obtained in 1995, and for 1995 to show separately the responses of those who see spending increases as in their own and the country's interests under the different tax scenarios. The contrast is clear and consistent. Once the tax consequences of higher spending are spelled out - whether we base comparisons on expressions of personal or of perceived national interest - the popularity of increases in public spending falls markedly (in some cases by up to one half). This holds true for every one of the areas of spending we posited. Moreover, in four of the spending areas it did not make much difference according to whether we spelled out the tax consequences in terms of a change in the basic rate of income tax or as a flat rate. The exceptions were health and education where an income tax rise was somewhat less of a discouragement than was a flat rate tax.

% opting for higher public spending with and without tax consequences specified

	1994 No tax consequences	1995 Flat rate tax		1995 Progressive tax	
		Country	Self	Country	Self
Health	87	68	62	76	66
Education	73	64	53	72	51
Police	72	40	38	40	39
The environment	48	29	28	31	27
Defence	19	10	8	9	10
Culture and the arts	12	8	8	7	9
Base	*971*	*610*		*608*	

Note: Only the six spending programmes which were asked about in both 1994 and 1995 are shown above.

It is highly unlikely that the size of these changes can be explained in terms of shift in public attitudes between the two years, especially since - as we have shown - attitudes towards welfare spending overall have been relatively constant over the same period. One explanation could be that although

respondents in 1994 did appreciate that spending changes would have an impact on their taxes, they simply envisaged smaller increases in expenditure than those we specified in the 1995 survey. This might be particularly the case for smaller spending programmes, such as culture and the arts, where a penny in the pound on income tax would finance an extremely large percentage increase in current budgets. But a more likely explanation is that, in the absence of its being spelled out, respondents either underestimated the true tax cost to them of their spending choices, or assumed (sometimes with good reason) that the tax consequences of extra public spending would fall on someone else.

In either case, our evidence suggests that failing to specify the tax consequences of changes in the level of public expenditure can lead to significant over-estimates of the popularity of such increases. On the other hand it also remains the case that, even when the personal tax consequences of spending choices *are* clearly spelled out, some two in every three people still say they would be willing to pay more in tax to support improvements in the NHS, a majority (albeit a smaller one) would be prepared to pay more taxes to improve education, and a substantial minority (40 per cent) would pay more in taxes to improve policing.

We specified the tax consequences of a rise or cut in government spending, but did respondents appreciate what difference it might make in terms of their own income? To find out, we asked respondents how much they thought a penny in the pound increase in income tax would cost them. Since we had information on the number of adults living in each household, we were able to identify those respondents who appeared to expect their household to pay more tax under the income tax rise than under the flat rate of £35 per head.[4] Reassuringly, perhaps, responses suggest that the better-off did indeed appreciate that a rise in income tax was more expensive for them: 59 per cent of those with annual gross household incomes above £18,000 expected to pay more under the income tax option, while only 17 per cent of those with incomes below £8,000 did so.

We can use this split sample to examine whether support for public spending differs between groups of individuals with similar characteristics according to the specified size of the tax burden on their households. We would expect respondents who think they would face a higher tax bill to be less in favour of increases in spending, when the method of financing them was *via* income tax, when compared with *similar* respondents faced with a flat rise of £35. Since these respondents are typically better off, another way of putting this is that proposals for higher spending through rises in income tax should be less successful in winning the support of the affluent than proposals to do so by means of a flat-rate levy.

The next table illustrates the effect of tax instrument on choices of spending in the three most popular areas. It shows clearly that people who expected to pay more under an income tax rise than under a flat rate charge were not less

but *more* likely to support public spending increases when they were posited in terms of an income tax rise.[5]

Effect of tax instrument on spending choices of the better-off

% opting for higher spending on ...

	... health	... education	... police/law enforcement	Base.
Expect to pay *more* if income tax were increased and higher spending paid for by ...				
... a progressive income tax	70	60	42	*174*
... a flat rate charge	60	53	32	*189*

In summary then, it is plain that tax consequences matter. Making them explicit sharply reduces the willingness of people to support increases in public spending. On the other hand, the popularity of certain increases in spending (such as on health, education and crime prevention) remains at a high level even when the tax consequences *are* made clear. Moreover, there is little evidence that the rich are inhibited from supporting increases in public spending despite their realisation that they will bear a greater tax burden to pay for them. On the contrary, increases in public spending attract greater support even from the well-off when the method of financing them is more progressive (that is, related to individual household's income) than when it is less so (that is, shared equally between households).[6]

Who wants higher public spending?

As with other goods, demand for those supplied by the state will be heavily influenced by individual circumstances and tastes. People differ in how much tax they pay as well as in how much they benefit personally from particular types of public spending. Just as richer people demand and buy more or better quality private goods, such as cars and holidays, so we would expect them to demand more or better public services. Likewise, demographic circumstances influence individual demands for public services. The NHS effectively transfers resources from the healthy to the sick just as the education service transfers them from older to younger people.[7] We would therefore expect attitudes to public spending to differ by income and age, as well as by other individual and household characteristics.

The next table illustrates the different tendencies of different sorts of people (without yet controlling for the possible influence of other factors) to support higher spending on the three most popular spending programmes: health, education and the police.[8] As can be seen, the two-thirds of respondents who expressed a preference for higher health spending are in fact fairly uniformly spread amongst most groups. However, we should note the lower levels of

support among younger adults, who are of course least likely to be heavy users of the NHS, and among Conservative identifiers, who are less likely to be advocates of higher public spending anyway. Not surprisingly, support for higher education spending is strongest among those with children aged under 18 in the household, and weakest by far among older respondents, while support for spending on law and order is strongest among older people. Not surprisingly, Labour identifiers are more sympathetic than Conservative identifiers to public spending increases on health and education; but interestingly the difference disappears when it comes to spending on law and order.

% in each group opting for more public spending on ...

	... health	... education	... police/law enforcement	Base
Socio-economic characteristics:				
Manual worker	65	53	40	565
Educated past age 18	66	58	39	272
Owner-occupier	65	51	38	782
Demographic characteristics:				
Female	65	54	38	699
With children aged under 18	66	72	34	407
Age:				
18-29	58	53	32	256
60+	61	39	49	372
Party identification:				
Labour	67	58	39	555
Liberal Democrat	75	52	45	160
Conservative	55	45	39	314
All	64	52	39	1218

We now take a more detailed look at the role of household income in determining attitudes. We divided respondents into three broad income bands (each representing roughly one third of the sample), and within each band look at the proportions who regard increases in public spending on each of the seven programmes as in their personal interest or in the national interest. Because of the markedly different incidence of tax payments across income bands, we show here only the responses from the subsample who were asked to consider a *flat* increase in tax payments. The most striking pattern to emerge from this analysis is that self-interest and the national interest seem to be much more compatible for poorer people than for richer people. With the exception of higher spending on culture and the arts, richer people are more inclined to view higher spending as beneficial to the nation as a whole rather than to them and their households. This variation between

the preferences of richer and poorer individuals expresses itself most strongly in their perceptions of what is in the national interest.

	Income group		
	Low	Middle	High
% saying that higher spending on each programme is in ...			
...their own interests			
Health	67	62	69
Education	55	53	59
Police/law enforcement	44	38	37
Public transport	33	24	28
Environment	30	26	30
Culture and the arts	10	5	9
Defence	17	8	5
...the national interest			
Health	69	74	79
Education	65	67	82
Police/law enforcement	41	39	39
Public transport	30	26	41
Environment	31	28	34
Culture and the arts	10	6	7
Defence	12	11	5
Base	*406*	*328*	*346*

This analysis reinforces our earlier finding that there is a fair degree of support from the better-off for core government spending programmes. It could be that, at the very least, the 'comfortable' top third recognises that a country which neglects its health service, schools, police forces and so on could well become an increasingly uncomfortable one in which to live - not only for those who largely depend on state provision, but also for those who have the means to opt out of the welfare state (and those who have chosen to do so). It is to a closer examination of this latter group that we now turn.

How does use of private sector services affect attitudes?

Since individual preferences for public spending seem to be driven at least partially by perceptions of self-interest, we might expect those who 'exit' to the private sector for some services to differ substantially in their views from those who depend solely on the state sector.[9] A wide range of services is provided by both state and private sectors, among them housing, health, pensions and education. We focus here on the two most popular programmes, health and education, provided by the state free at the point of

use. Individuals who choose to use private sector health care and education are in effect paying 'a second time' for an alternative to the service which they may see themselves as already having 'paid for' through their taxes. The size of the private sector in both health and (especially) education is, of course, very modest in comparison with the dominant state provider.

Before examining the public spending preferences of individuals who 'go private', we pause to consider which groups opt for private sector provision in the first place. One important consideration must, of course, be household income, since it is only those who can afford to pay private school fees[10] and private medical insurance premiums who effectively have a choice to do so. The next table shows the proportions within different income groups who have either purchased private medical cover individually or have it paid for by an employer, as opposed to those who are reliant solely on the NHS. It is all too apparent that those with higher incomes are more likely to be covered by both forms of private insurance than those on low or medium incomes.

Penetration of private medical insurance by income group

	Income group		
	Low	Middle	High
	%	%	%
No private medical insurance	95	91	73
With private medical insurance ...			
... paid for by self	5	7	9
... paid for by employer	-	2	18
Base	*406*	*328*	*346*

A similar picture emerges in respect of education, where eight per cent of those on high incomes have ever had any of their children privately educated, as against four per cent of those on low incomes. When we focus on those households with children currently attending a private school, the ratio is 4:1 in favour of those with high incomes as opposed to those on middle or low incomes.

However, attributes other than household income are also associated with the decision to opt for education or health care in the private sector. As shown in Besley *et al* (1996), those with private health insurance are also likely to be richer, better educated and more inclined to identify with the Conservative Party than those without such cover.[11] They are also more likely to live in areas with the longest waiting times for an NHS operation. There is also a pronounced association between private education of children and parents: over one in five of those who themselves went to private schools have chosen to educate at least one child privately, as against only one in twenty of the remainder.

The next table summarises those characteristics which are most closely related to consumption of private education or health.

| | % in each group ... | | | |
	... currently covered by private health insurance	Base	... whose children have ever used private education	Base
Socio-economic characteristics:				
Manual worker	8	565	4	395
Educated past age 18	19	272	17	161
Owner-occupier	17	782	10	511
Demographic characteristics:				
Female	12	699	8	497
With children	16	407	6	319
Age:				
18-29	11	256	2	59
60+	7	372	13	292
Party identification:				
Labour	8	555	3	389
Liberal Democrat	20	160	15	205
Conservative	24	314	18	96
All	14	1218	8	800

Note: The bases for the second column of percentages are lower than those for the first, since they relate only to those who have ever had any children.

As noted, these respondents may see themselves as paying twice for health and education services and thus may be more likely to resist increasing state spending. Indeed, as Besley *et al* (1996) found, BSA respondents with private medical insurance were significantly less likely than those without to support extra health spending. Naturally, people with private health insurance tend nonetheless still to rely on the state sector for some medical services, such as accident and emergency and, depending on their particular policy, often for many other services too. Even so, those with private health insurance are less inclined to see higher public health spending as in their own interests (54 per cent, as opposed to 67 per cent of those without private cover[12], although it is important to note that those with private health insurance who favoured extra spending on the NHS were in the majority.)[13] The proportions who see such increases as being in the *national* interest are, however, similar (at 71 per cent and 73 per cent respectively), as are the proportions who nominate health as the top priority for extra state spending (at 46 per cent and 50 per cent respectively).

In contrast, respondents whose children had been placed in private education differed little from their counterparts who relied solely on state education in

the extent to which they regarded extra public spending on education as being in their own or the national interest.   Surprisingly, however, they were significantly *more* likely to see education as the top priority for extra public spending (46 per cent as against 31 per cent).[14] This could reflect either self-interest or some notion of the public good or, more plausibly perhaps, a bit of both. One possibility is that they are reluctant members of the private sector and that, had state education been better, they would have preferred to save the cost and inconvenience of educating their children privately. In addition, since children in private schools are likely (indeed more likely than their counterparts in state schools) to go on to study within the state higher education system, their parents retain a clear vested interest in higher education funding. On the other hand, they may be expressing the high value they place on education as, say, employers of labour. Or they may simply be expressing strong support for the notion that a good education should be available to all children.   All we can say with certainty is that the relationships between the use people make of private sector alternatives and their preferences for increased public spending are much less straightforward than we might have anticipated.

Social security spending

Social security spending is classically an area in which perceptions of self-interest vie with notions of the common good. Most people expect to receive certain universal benefits, such as the state pension or child benefit, at some stage during their lives, but do not necessarily expect to receive targeted benefits, such as unemployment benefit or income support.   Are people especially likely to support spending on social security benefits which they either receive themselves or expect to receive at some stage during their lifetimes?   Or are attitudes towards such benefits more likely to reflect people's value judgements, such as their notions of the 'deserving' and 'undeserving' poor? If so, we would expect certain benefits - such as those for single parents, which tend to receive a great deal of hostile media attention - to be less popular candidates for extra spending than other less controversial ones.

We listed five benefits - the state pension, unemployment benefit, child benefit, single parent benefit, and benefits for the disabled - and asked respondents to choose two of them as priorities for extra spending.   The pattern of responses, shown in the next table, suggests that the universality of the benefit is not the main point at issue. Pensions, for instance, and benefits for groups with high levels of public sympathy - such as disabled people - both attract wide public support. In contrast, benefits for single parents are the first or second priority of only one in ten respondents, and the universally available child benefit is chosen as a priority by only one in three.

Social security benefits as priorities for extra public spending

**% naming each benefit as
first or second priority**

State pension	68
Benefits for the disabled	58
Child benefit	33
Unemployment benefit	25
Benefits for single parents	12
Base	*1234*

Of course these ratings may to an extent reflect people's perceptions of whether these benefits are 'objectively' high or low at present, but those perceptions are themselves likely to colour their underlying attitudes. To examine why else certain social security benefits attract higher levels of public support than others, we need to look at the characteristics of those who named the (universal) state pension as their top priority as against the much smaller proportion who gave top priority to the (targeted) unemployment benefit.

Overall, nearly five times the proportion of people name the state pension as name unemployment benefit as their top priority and, indeed, among none of the groups considered below is unemployment benefit the popular of the two.

Ratios of those who give priority to pensions *versus* unemployment benefit

	% naming as top spending priority ...			
	... state pension	... unemployment benefit	**Ratio**	*Base*
Self-employed	57	3	20.9	*1144*
Aged 60+	68	5	14.8	*372*
Owner-occupier	50	9	5.5	*782*
Aged 40-59	52	10	5.0	*347*
Low income household	51	12	4.2	*406*
Full-time worker	43	10	4.2	*374*
Aged 30-39	39	10	3.8	*280*
Children in household	35	11	3.3	*407*
Full-time education past 18	42	13	3.3	*272*
Individuals with a disability	35	11	3.1	*106*
Labour identifiers	44	14	3.1	*555*
Single adult household	20	10	2.1	*91*
All	47	10	4.7	*1218*

But, as the table above shows, there are striking differences between the 'supporters' of each. The self-employed, for instance, are more than twenty times more likely to choose the state pension than a benefit which they themselves would typically not receive. Similarly, respondents aged 60 or over were fourteen times more likely to choose pensions rather than benefits for the unemployed. Unemployment benefit was relatively more likely to be named as a priority by people below retirement age, Labour Party identifiers, those in full-time education, and people in single adult households. Some of these characteristics, such as the respondent's age, seem firmly rooted in self-interest. Others, such as political views, which are still important even after controlling for each of the other factors, suggest that people's underlying values are also important.

Once again, it seems that people are neither wholly individualistic nor wholly altruistic in their attitudes to welfare.

Conclusions

Although people are less likely to advocate large increases in public expenditure when the personal tax consequences are spelled out to them in detail, a comfortable majority nonetheless supports increases in spending on at least one or more of the core areas of health, education and universal welfare benefits. There is no evidence either that richer people are less in sympathy than poorer ones with increases in public spending, even if they are asked to pay a higher share of the tax burden to finance them. Indeed, supposedly against their interests, they appear to be more inclined to favour increases in expenditure when financed through progressive rather than regressive tax instruments.

Health and education spending are the overwhelming priorities for extra public expenditure. There are differences in popularity between selective benefits, driven partly perhaps by perceptions of how 'deserving' various groups in the population are, and partly perhaps by different perceptions of which tax and spending changes would be of greatest personal benefit and, for that matter, of greatest benefit to the nation. Individual priorities were clearly driven by a combination of self-interest and altruism.

We examined the extent to which the recent growth in the consumption of private health and education is likely to undermine the public consensus in favour of extra state provision in these areas. There is tentative evidence that this may happen to a small degree in the case of the NHS, but there is no evidence for it in the case of education. On the contrary, parents who send their children to private schools seem to be the most supportive of improvements to the state education system, perhaps because they have opted only reluctantly for the private sector, feeling they have been faced with little choice.

Notes

1. The figures in this table, and others in this section, combine answers to spending financed through different tax instruments.
2. Lipsey (1994) has pointed out that "people are ... much more likely to favour the benefits from which they or their families expect to gain directly than those from which they perceive little immediate self-advantage". Hudson and Jones (1994) have argued, on the other hand, "that 'public concern' may be more important than self-interest in the preferences that voters reveal".
3. Whilst it was convenient to keep the same magnitude of change for all spending programmes, this would, of course, represent a rather more substantial change in the budgets assigned to some programmes than to others.
4. As answers were given in bands the comparison is necessarily somewhat coarse. Respondents are characterised as expecting to pay more under one tax than the other if their expected tax payments lay in different bands for the two tax instruments.
5. The 'anchoring' effect whereby suggested magnitudes are established in the mind of the respondent as a reasonable benchmark is empirically well established (see Green et al, 1995; Tversky and Kahneman, 1974) and could well be a plausible factor reducing the impact of the implied tax burden on willingness to pay.
6. Roberts et al (1994) note that "respondents generally agree that people with higher incomes should pay more taxes."
7. Evandrou et al (1993) assess the incidence of public spending benefits according to evidence on use. They find that benefits in kind from education, health and housing subsidies are "worth most in the middle of the distribution."
8. This sort of table cannot, of course, tell us the effects of any of these variables conditional on the effects of the others.
9. Hirschman (1970) discusses 'exit' as a way of expressing discontent with public policy.
10. Although the means-tested Assisted Places Scheme pays at least part of the school fees of some children who attend non-state schools.
11. Propper (1989, 1993) finds similar socio-economic and attitudinal influences in other British datasets.
12. These numbers combine the subsamples told to expect payment through different tax instruments.
13. Taylor-Gooby (1991) has observed that "even secure access to private medicine does not appear to lead people to abandon their allegiance to the NHS".
14. We get similar results if we confine the analysis to those with children currently in the household.

References

Besley, T., Hall, J. and Preston, I. (1996), *Private Health Insurance and the State of the NHS*, The Institute for Fiscal Studies, Commentary No. **52**, London: IFS.

Evandrou, M., Falkingham, J., Hills, J. and Le Grand, J. (1993), 'Welfare benefits in kind and income distribution', *Fiscal Studies*, **14**, 1.

Green, D., Jacowitz, K., Kahneman, D. and McFadden, D. (1995), 'Referendum contingent valuation, and willingness to pay for public goods', paper presented at Econometric Society 7th World Congress, Tokyo.

Hirschman, A. (1970), *Exit, Voice and Loyalty,* Cambridge, Mass: Harvard University Press.

Hudson, J. and Jones, P.R. (1994), 'The importance of the 'ethical voter': An estimate of 'altruism'', *European Journal of Political Economy,* **10**.

Lipsey, D. (1994), 'Do we really want more public spending?', Jowell, R., Curtice, J., Brook, L. and Ahrendt, D. (eds.), *British Social Attitudes: the 11th Report*, Aldershot: Dartmouth.

Propper, C. (1989), 'An econometric analysis of the demand for private health insurance in England and Wales', *Applied Economics,* **21**.

Propper, C. (1993), 'Constrained choice sets in the UK demand for private medical insurance', *Journal of Public Economics*, **51**.

Roberts, M., Hite, P. and Bradley, C. (1994), 'Understanding attitudes towards progressive taxation', *Public Opinion Quarterly*, **58**.

Taylor-Gooby, P. (1991), 'Attachment to the welfare state.', in Jowell, R., Brook, L. and Taylor, B. (eds.), *British Social Attitudes: the 8th Report*, Aldershot: Gower.

Tversky, A. and Kahneman, D. (1974), 'Judgment under uncertainty: heuristics and biases', *Science*, **185**.

Acknowledgements

We are grateful for the comments and suggestions of John Curtice, Andrew Dilnot, Paul Johnson and Katarina Thomson. This research project is being carried out with funding from the ESRC under its Economic Beliefs and Behaviour Programme (grant number L 122 521 004). We are grateful to the Council for its financial support.

Appendix I
Technical details of the surveys

British Social Attitudes

As in 1994, three versions of the 1995 *British Social Attitudes* questionnaire were fielded. Each 'module' of questions is asked either of the full sample (around 3,600 respondents) or of a random two-thirds or one-third of the sample. The structure of the questionnaire (versions A, B and C) is shown at the beginning of Appendix III.

Sample design

The *British Social Attitudes* survey is designed to yield a representative sample of adults aged 18 or over. Since 1993, the sampling frame for the survey has been the Postcode Address File (PAF), a list of addresses (or postal delivery points) compiled by the Post Office.[1]

For practical reasons, the sample is confined to those living in private households. People living in institutions (though not in private households at such institutions) are excluded, as are households whose addresses were not on the Postcode Address File.

The sampling method involved a multi-stage design, with three separate stages of selection.

Selection of sectors

At the first stage, postcode sectors were selected systematically from a list of all postal sectors in Great Britain. Before selection, any sectors with fewer than 500 addresses were identified and grouped together with an adjacent sector; in Scotland all sectors north of the Caledonian Canal were excluded (because of the prohibitive costs of interviewing there). Sectors were then stratified on the basis of:

- Registrar General's Standard Region
- Population density (persons per hectare) with variable banding used according to region, in order to create three equal-sized strata per region
- Ranking by percentage of homes that were owner-occupied, from the 1991 Census figures.

Two hundred postcode sectors were selected, with probability proportional to the number of addresses in each sector.

Selection of addresses

Thirty addresses were selected in each of the 200 sectors. The sample was therefore 200 x 30 = 6,000 addresses, selected by starting from a random point on the list of addresses for each sector, and choosing each address at a fixed interval. The fixed interval was calculated for each sector in order to generate the correct number of addresses.

The Multiple-Output Indicator (MOI) available through PAF was used when selecting addresses. MOI shows the number of accommodation spaces sharing one address. Thus, if the MOI indicates more than one accommodation space at a given address, the chances of the given address being selected from the list of addresses would increase so that it matched the total number of accommodation spaces. As would be expected, the vast majority (97 per cent) of MOIs had a value of one. The remainder, which ranged between two and thirty three, were incorporated into the weighting procedures (described below).

Selection of individuals

Interviewers called at each address selected from PAF and listed all those eligible for inclusion in the sample - that is, all persons currently aged 18 or over and resident at the selected address. The interviewer then selected one respondent using a computer-generated random selection procedure. Where there were two or more households or 'dwelling units' at the selected address,

interviewers first had to select one household or dwelling unit using the same random procedure. They then followed the same procedure to select a person for interview.

Weighting

Data were weighted to take account of the fact that not all the units covered in the survey had the same probability of selection. The weighting reflected the relative selection probabilities of the individual at the three main stages of selection: address, household and individual.

First, because addresses were selected using the Multiple Output Indicator (MOI), weights had to be applied to compensate for the greater probability of an address with an MOI of more than one being selected, compared to an address with an MOI of one. Secondly, data were weighted to compensate for the fact that dwelling units at an address which contained a large number of dwelling units were less likely to be selected for inclusion in the survey than ones which did not share an address. The reason we use this procedure is that in most cases these two stages will cancel each other out, resulting in more efficient weights. Thirdly, data were weighted to compensate for the lower selection probabilities of adults living in large households compared with those living in small households.

The distribution of weights used is shown below:

Weight	No.	%	Scaled weight	Weight	No.	%	Scaled weight
0.13	12	0.3	0.0670	0.90	1	0.0	0.4821
0.17	12	0.3	0.0893	0.92	1	0.0	0.4945
0.20	1	0.0	0.1071	1.00	1150	31.7	0.5357
0.25	3	0.1	0.1339	1.06	1	0.0	0.5681
0.27	1	0.0	0.1461	1.20	1	0.0	0.6428
0.29	1	0.0	0.1530	1.33	3	0.1	0.7142
0.33	4	0.1	0.1786	1.50	1	0.0	0.8035
0.38	2	0.1	0.2009	2.00	1911	52.6	1.0713
0.50	7	0.2	0.2678	3.00	345	9.5	1.6070
0.60	1	0.0	0.3214	4.00	128	3.5	2.1427
0.63	1	0.0	0.3348	5.00	26	0.7	2.6783
0.67	4	0.1	0.3571	6.00	4	0.1	3.2140
0.75	2	0.1	0.4017	7.00	2	0.1	3.7497
0.80	1	0.0	0.4285	8.00	1	0.0	4.2853
0.86	1	0.0	0.4591	12.00	5	0.1	6.4280

All weights fell within a range between 0.125 and 12. The average weight applied was 1.9. The weighted sample was scaled down to make the number of weighted productive cases exactly equal to the number of unweighted productive cases (n = 3,633).

All the percentages presented in this Report are based on weighted data. Tables show unweighted bases.

Questionnaire versions

Each address in each sector (sampling point) was allocated to either the A, B or C third of the sample. The first address in the sampling point was allocated the A version, the second the B version, the third the C version and so on. Each version was thus assigned to 2,000 addresses.

Fieldwork

Interviewing was mainly carried out during May, June and July 1995, with a small number of interviews taking place in August.

Fieldwork was conducted by interviewers drawn from SCPR's regular panel and conducted using face-to-face computer-assisted interviewing.[2] Interviewers attended a one-day briefing conference to familiarise them with the selection procedures and questionnaires.

The average interview length was 61 minutes for version A of the questionnaire, 58 minutes for version B and 63 minutes for version C. The final response achieved is shown below:

	No.	%
Addresses issued	6,000	
Vacant, derelict and other out of scope	749	
In scope	5,251	100.0
Interview achieved	3,633	69.2
Interview not achieved	1,618	30.8
Refused [1]	1,372	26.1
Non-contacted [2]	110	2.1
Other non-response	136	2.6

1   'Refusals' comprise refusals before selection of an individual at the address, refusals to the office, refusal by the selected person, 'proxy' refusals (on behalf of the selected respondent) and broken appointments after which the selected person could not be recontacted.

2   'Non-contacts' comprise households where no one was contacted and those where the selected person could not be contacted.

The A versions of the questionnaire achieved a response rate of 71 per cent; for the B version it was 67 per cent; and for version C, 70 per cent.

As in earlier rounds of the series, respondents were asked to fill in a self-completion questionnaire which, whenever possible, was collected by the interviewer. Otherwise, the respondent was asked to post it to SCPR. If necessary, up to three postal reminders were sent to obtain the self-completion supplement.

A total of 498 respondents (14 per cent of those interviewed) did not return their self-completion questionnaire.   Version A of the self-completion questionnaire was returned by 86 per cent of respondents to the face-to-face interview, version B by 87 per cent and version C by 85 per cent. As in previous rounds, we judged that it was not necessary to apply additional weights to correct for non-response.

Advance letter

Letters describing the purpose of the survey and the coverage of the questionnaire were posted to sampled addresses approximately one week before the start of fieldwork on the 1995 survey.[3]

Analysis variables

A number of standard analyses have been used in the tables that appear in this report. The analysis groups requiring further definition are set out below. For further details, see Brook *et al* (1997, forthcoming).

Region

The Registrar General's ten Standard Regions have been used, except that we have distinguished between Greater London and the remainder of the South-East.   Sometimes these have been grouped into what we have termed 'compressed region': 'Northern' includes the North, North-West, Yorkshire and Humberside. East Anglia is included in the 'South', as is the South-West.

Standard Occupational Classification

Respondents are classified according to their own occupation, not that of the 'head of household'. Their spouses or partners are similarly classified. The main Social Class variables used in the analyses in this report are the Registrar General's Social Class and Socio-economic Group (SEG).

  Since 1991, the OPCS *Standard Occupational Classification* (SOC) has been used for the occupation coding of the BSA survey.[4] SOC has a hierarchical structure, consisting of 371 Unit Groups which can be aggregated into 77 Minor Groups, 22 Sub-major Groups and nine Major Groups.

Registrar General's Social Class

Each respondent's Social Class is based on his or her current or last occupation. Thus, all respondents in paid work at the time of the interview, waiting to take up a paid job already offered, retired, seeking work, or looking after the home, have their occupation (present, past or future, as appropriate) classified into Occupational Unit Groups according to SOC. The combination of occupational classification with employment status generates the following six Social Classes:

I	Professional, etc. occupations	
II	Managerial and technical occupations	'Non-manual'
III (Non-manual)	Skilled occupations	
III (Manual)	Skilled occupations	
IV	Partly skilled occupations	'Manual'
V	Unskilled occupations	

They are usually collapsed into four groups: I & II, III Non-manual, III Manual, and IV & V.

The remaining respondents are grouped as "never had a job" or "not classifiable". For some analyses, it may be more appropriate to classify respondents according to their current social class, which takes into account only their present economic position. In this case, in addition to the six social classes listed above, the remaining respondents not currently in paid work fall into one of the following categories: "not classifiable", "retired", "looking after the home", "unemployed" or "others not in paid occupations".

Socio-economic Group

As with Social Class, each respondent's Socio-economic Group (SEG) is based on his or her current or last occupation. SEG aims to bring together people with jobs of similar social and economic status, and is derived from a combination of employment status and occupation. The full SEG classification identifies 18 categories, but these are usually condensed into six groups:

- Professionals, employers and managers
- Intermediate non-manual workers
- Junior non-manual workers
- Skilled manual workers
- Semi-skilled manual workers
- Unskilled manual workers

As with Social Class, the remaining respondents are grouped as "never had a job" or "not classifiable".

Goldthorpe schema

The Goldthorpe schema classifies occupations by their 'general comparability', considering such factors as sources and levels of income, economic security, promotion prospects, and level of job autonomy and authority. The Goldthorpe schema was derived from the SOC unit groups combined with employment status. Two versions of the schema are coded: the full schema has 11 categories; the 'compressed schema' combines these into the five classes shown below.

- Salariat (professional and managerial)
- Routine non-manual workers (office and sales)
- Petty bourgeoisie (the self-employed, including farmers, with and without employees)
- Manual foremen and supervisors
- Working class (skilled, semi-skilled and unskilled manual workers, personal service and agricultural workers)

There is a residual category comprising those who have never had a job or who gave insufficient information for classification purposes.

Industry

All respondents whose occupation could be coded were allocated a Standard Industrial Classification (SIC 1992). For comparison with previous years, the 1995 *British Social Attitudes* data has also been coded to the older SIC 1980 classification. Two-digit class codes are used. As with Social Class, SIC may be generated on the basis of the respondent's current occupation only, or on his or her most recently-classifiable occupation.

Party identification

Respondents can be classified as identifying with a particular political party on one of three counts: if they consider themselves supporters of that party, as closer to it than to others, or as more likely to support it in the event of a general election (responses are derived from Qs. 33-43). The three groups are generally described respectively as *partisans, sympathisers* and *residual identifiers*. In combination, the three groups are referred to in as 'identifiers'.

Attitude scales

Since 1986, the *British Social Attitudes* surveys have included two attitude scales which aim to measure where respondents stand on certain underlying value dimensions - left-right and libertarian-authoritarian.   Since 1987 (except 1990), a similar scale on 'welfarism' has been asked.[5]

A useful way of summarising the information from a number of questions of this sort is to construct an additive index (DeVellis, 1991; Spector, 1992). This approach rests on the assumption that there is an underlying - 'latent' - attitudinal dimension which characterises the answers to all the questions within each scale. If so, scores on the index are likely to be a more reliable indication of the underlying attitude than the answers to any one question.

Each of these scales consists of a number of statements to which the respondent is invited to "agree strongly", "agree", "neither agree nor disagree", "disagree", or "disagree strongly".

The items are:

Left-right scale

>   The government should redistribute income from the better-off to those who are less well off. *[Redistrb]*
>
>   Big business benefits owners at the expense of workers.*[BigBusnN]*
>
>   Ordinary people do not get their fair share of the nation's wealth. *[Wealth]* [6]
>
>   There is one law for the rich and one for the poor. *[RichLaw]*
>
>   Management will always try to get the better of employees if it gets the chance. *[Indust4]*

Libertarian-authoritarian scale

>   Young people today don't have enough respect for traditional British values. *[TradVals]*
>
>   People who break the law should be given stiffer sentences. *[StifSent]*
>
>   For some crimes, the death penalty is the most appropriate sentences. *[DeathApp]*
>
>   Schools should teach children to obey authority. *[Obey]*
>
>   The law should always be obeyed, even if a particular law is wrong. *[WrongLaw]*
>
>   Censorship of films and magazines is necessary to uphold moral standards. *[Censor]*

Welfarism scale

> The welfare state makes people nowadays less willing to look after themselves. *[WelfResp]*
>
> People receiving social security are made to feel like second class citizens. *[WelfStig]*
>
> The welfare state encourages people to stop helping each other. *[WelfHelp]*
>
> The government should spend more money on welfare benefits for the poor, even if it leads to higher taxes. *[MoreWelf]*
>
> Around here, most unemployed people could find a job if they really wanted one. *[UnempJob]*
>
> Many people who get social security don't really deserve any help. *[SocHelp]*
>
> Most people on the dole are fiddling in one way or another. *[DoleFidl]*
>
> If welfare benefits weren't so generous, people would learn to stand on their own two feet. *[WelfFeet]*

The indices for the three scales are formed by scoring the leftmost, most libertarian or most pro-welfare position as 1 and the rightmost, most authoritarian or most anti-welfarist position as 5. The "neither agree nor disagree" option is scored as 3. The scores to all the questions in each scale are added and then divided by the number of items in the scale giving indices ranging from 1 (leftmost, most libertarian, or most pro-welfare) to 5 (rightmost, most authoritarian, most anti-welfare). In 1995, scores on the three indices have been placed on the dataset.[7]

The scales have been tested for reliability (as measured by Cronbach's alpha). The Cronbach's alpha for the scales in 1995 are 0.84 for the left-right and 'welfarism' scales and 0.74 for the libertarian-authoritarian scale. This level of reliability can be considered "respectable" for the left-right scale and "very good" for the other two scales (DeVellis, 1991: 85).

Other analysis variables

These are taken directly from the questionnaire and to that extent are self-explanatory. The principal ones are:

Sex (Q.15)	Highest educational qualification
Age (Q.770)	obtained (Q.895-917)
Household income (Q.1015)	Marital status (Q.763)
Economic position (Q.111)	Benefits received (Q.993-1006)
Religion (Q.733)	

Sampling errors

No sample precisely reflects the characteristics of the population it represents because of both sampling and non-sampling errors. If a sample were designed as a random sample (if every adult had an equal and independent chance of inclusion in the sample) then we could calculate the sampling error of any percentage, p, using the formula:

$$s.e.\ (p) = \sqrt{\frac{p(100-p)}{n}}$$

where n is the number of respondents on which the percentage is based. Once the sampling error had been calculated, it would be a straightforward exercise to calculate a confidence interval for the true population percentage. For example, a 95 per cent confidence interval would be given by the formula:

$$p \pm 1.96 \times s.e.(p)$$

Clearly, for a simple random sample (srs), the sampling error depends only on the values of p and n. However, simple random sampling is almost never used in practice because of its inefficiency in terms of time and cost.

As noted above, the *British Social Attitudes* sample, like that drawn for most large-scale surveys, was clustered according to a stratified multi-stage design into 200 postcode sectors (or combinations of sectors). With a complex design like this, the sampling error of a percentage giving a particular response is not simply a function of the number of respondents in the sample and the size of the percentage; it also depends on how that percentage response is spread within and between sample points. The complex design may be assessed relative to simple random sampling by calculating a range of design factors (DEFTs) associated with it, where

$$DEFT = \sqrt{\frac{\text{Variance of estimator with complex design, sample size n}}{\text{Variance of estimator with srs design, sample size n}}}$$

and represents the multiplying factor to be applied to the simple random sampling error to produce its complex equivalent. A design factor of one means that the complex sample has achieved the same precision as a simple random sample of the same size. A design factor greater than one means the complex sample is less precise than its simple random sample equivalent. If the DEFT for a particular characteristic is known, a 95 per cent confidence interval for a percentage may be calculated using the formula:

$$p \pm 1.96 \times complex\ sampling\ error\ (p)$$

$$= p \pm 1.96 \times DEFT \times \sqrt{\frac{p(100-p)}{n}}$$

Calculations of sampling errors and design effects were made using the World Fertility Survey 'Clusters' programme.

The following table gives examples of the confidence intervals and DEFTs calculated for a range of different questions, some fielded on all three versions of the questionnaire and some on one only; some asked on the interview questionnaire and some on the self-completion supplement. It shows that most of the questions asked of all sample members have a confidence interval of around plus or minus two to three per cent of the survey proportion. This means that we can be 95 per cent certain that the true population proportion is within two to three per cent (in either direction) of the proportion we report. The confidence intervals calculated for questions asked of only a third the sample tend to be greater than those calculated for questions asked of the entire sample.

It should be noted that the design effects for certain variables (notably those most associated with the area a person lives in) are greater than those for other variables. This is particularly the case for party identification and housing tenure. For instance, Labour identifiers and local authority tenants tend to be concentrated in certain areas; consequently the design effects calculated for these variables in a clustered sample are greater than the design effects calculated for variables less strongly associated with area, such as attitudinal variables.

		% (p)	Complex standard error of p (%)	95 per cent confidence interval	DEFT
Classification variables					
DV*	**Party identification**				
	Conservative	26.4	1.0	24.4 - 28.3	1.33
	Liberal Democrat	12.3	0.7	10.8 - 13.7	1.37
	Labour	44.4	1.3	41.9 - 47.0	1.54
DV*	**Housing tenure**				
	Owns	68.5	1.5	65.5 - 71.6	1.97
	Rents from local authority	18.1	1.4	15.4 - 20.8	2.13
	Rents privately	12.5	1.2	10.2 - 14.8	2.11
DV*	**Religion**				
	No religion	40.4	1.1	38.2 - 42.5	1.33
	Church of England	31.9	0.9	30.0 - 33.7	1.19
	Roman Catholic	8.9	0.6	7.6 - 10.1	1.29
Q.795	**Age of completing continuous full-time education**				
	16 or under	66.6	1.1	64.4 - 68.8	1.40
	17 or 18	16.7	0.8	15.2 - 18.2	1.22
	19 or over	13.5	0.7	12.1 - 15.0	1.29

* DV = Derived variable

Attitudinal variables		% (p)	Complex standard error of p (%)	95 per cent confidence interval	DEFT
C.62	Benefits for the unemployed are …				
	… too low	51.1	1.7	47.6 - 54.5	1.21
	… too high	29.7	1.5	26.7 - 32.8	1.17
A.363	Importance of continuing to have a monarchy				
	Very important	30.5	1.4	27.7 - 33.4	1.09
	Quite important	35.1	1.7	31.7 - 38.5	1.23
	Not very important	18.2	1.3	15.6 - 20.7	1.15
	Not at all important	6.9	0.9	5.1 - 8.7	1.22
	Abolish monarchy	8.8	0.9	7.0 - 10.5	1.09
B.494	How serious a problem is traffic congestion in towns and cities				
	Very serious	50.2	1.8	46.6 - 53.8	1.23
	Serious	43.7	1.7	40.3 - 47.0	1.16
	Not very serious	4.7	0.7	3.4 - 6.1	1.10
	Not a problem at all	0.4	0.2	0.0 - 0.8	1.16
	Don't know	0.9	0.2	0.4 - 1.4	0.90
C.566	In a year from now, respondent expects unemployment to have gone up	41.3	1.9	37.5 - 45.0	1.33
A2.37 B2.25 C2.25	Britain is worse than most of its competitors in training employers in new skills	32.9	0.9	31.1 - 34.7	1.06
A2.30	Strongly agree or just agree that cannabis should be legalised	30.3	1.6	27.0 - 33.5	1.15
B2.40b	Attitudes to government spending on building more roads				
	Spend much more	3.7	0.7	2.3 - 5.0	1.17
	Spend more	16.7	1.1	14.4 - 19.0	0.98
	Spend the same as now	36.2	1.6	33.1 - 39.4	1.05
	Spend less	23.4	1.4	20.6 - 26.2	1.07
	Spend much less	9.6	0.9	7.8 - 11.5	0.99
	Can't choose	6.1	0.7	4.6 - 7.6	0.99
C2.33a	Death penalty for murder in course of a terrorist act …				
	… in favour	67.0	1.4	64.1 - 69.8	0.98
	… against	26.5	1.4	23.7 - 29.3	1.03

These calculations are based on the total sample from the 1995 survey (3,633 respondents to the main questionnaire and 3,135 returning self-completion questionnaires); on the A version respondents (1,227 for the main questionnaire and 1,058 for the self-completion); on the B version respondents (1,172 and 1,023 respectively); or on the C version respondents (1,234 and 1,054 respectively). As the examples above show, sampling errors for proportions based only on respondents to just one of the three versions of the questionnaire, or on subgroups within the sample, are somewhat larger than they would have been had the questions been asked of everyone.

Analysis techniques

Regression

Regression analysis aims to summarise the relationship between a 'dependent' variable and one or more 'independent' variables. It shows how well we can estimate a respondent's score on the dependent variable from knowledge of their scores on the independent variables.   It is often undertaken to support a claim that the phenomena measured by the independent variables cause the phenomenon measured by the dependent variable. However, the causal ordering, if any, between the variables cannot be verified or falsified by the technique.   Causality can only be inferred through special experimental designs or through assumptions made by the analyst.

All regression analysis assumes that the relationship between the dependent and each of the independent variables takes a particular form.   In *linear regression*, the most common form of regression analysis, it is assumed that the relationship can be adequately summarised by a straight line. This means that a one point increase in the value of an independent variable is assumed to have the same impact on the value of the dependent variable on average irrespective of the previous values of those variables.

Strictly speaking the technique assumes that both the dependent and the independent variables are measured on an interval-level scale, although it may sometimes still be applied even where this is not the case. For example, one can use an ordinal variable (e.g. a Likert scale) as a *dependent* variable if one is willing to assume that there is an underlying interval level scale and the difference between the observed ordinal scale and the underlying interval scale is due to random measurement error. Categorical or nominal data can be used as *independent* variables by converting them into dummy or binary variables; these are variables where the only valid scores are 0 and 1, with 1 signifying membership of a particular category and 0 otherwise.

The assumptions of linear regression can cause particular difficulties where the *dependent* variable is binary.   The assumption that the relationship

between the dependent and the independent variables is a straight line means that it can produce estimated values for the dependent variable of less than 0 or greater than 1. In this case it may be more appropriate to assume that the relationship between the dependent and the independent variables takes the form of an S-curve, where the impact on the dependent variable of a one-point increase in an independent variable becomes progressively less the closer the value of the dependent variable approaches 0 or 1. *Logistic regression* is an alternative form of regression which fits such an S-curve rather than a straight line. The technique can also be adapted to analyse multinomial non-interval level dependent variables, that is, variables which classify respondents into more than two categories.

The two statistical scores most commonly reported from the results of regression analyses are:

A measure of variance explained: This summarises how well all the independent variables combined can account for the variation in respondent's scores in the dependent variable. The higher the measure, the more accurately we are able in general to estimate the correct value of each respondent's score on the dependent variable from knowledge of their scores on the independent variables.

A parameter estimate: This shows how much the dependent variable will change on average, given a one unit change in the independent variable (while holding all other independent variables in the model constant). The parameter estimate has a positive sign if an increase in the value of the independent variable results in an increase in the value of the dependent variable. It has a negative sign if an increase in the value of the independent variable results in a decrease in the value of the dependent variable. If the parameter estimates are standardised, it is possible to compare the relative impact of different independent variables; those variables with the largest standardised estimates can be said to have the biggest impact on the value of the dependent variable.

Regression also tests for the statistical significance of parameter estimates. A parameter estimate is said to be significant at the five per cent level, if the range of the values encompassed by its 95 per cent confidence interval (see also section on sampling errors) are either all positive or all negative. This means that there is less than a five per cent chance that the association we have found between the dependent variable and the independent variable is simply the result of sampling error and does not reflect a relationship that actually exists in the general population.

Factor analysis

Factor analysis is a statistical technique which aims to identify whether there are one or more apparent sources of commonality to the answers given by respondents to a set of questions. It ascertains the smallest number of *factors*

(or dimensions) which can most economically summarise all of the variation found in the set of questions being analysed. Factors are established where respondents who give a particular answer to one question in the set, tend to give the same answer as each other to one or more of the other questions in the set. The technique is most useful when a relatively small number of factors is able to account for a relatively large proportion of the variance in all of the questions in the set.

The technique produces a *factor loading* for each question (or variable) on each factor. Where questions have a high loading on the same factor then it will be the case that respondents who give a particular answer to one of these questions tend to give a similar answer to the other questions. The technique is most commonly used in attitudinal research to try to identify the underlying ideological dimensions which apparently structure attitudes towards the subject in question.

Northern Ireland Social Attitudes

In 1995, for the sixth year, the *British Social Attitudes* survey was extended to include Northern Ireland, supported by funding from all the Northern Ireland Departments. As in 1994 two versions of the questionnaire were fielded to accommodate a greater number of questions, with a total target sample size of around 1,500 respondents. As in previous years, the questionnaire consisted of 'core' questions (asked of all respondents in both Britain and Northern Ireland), some (but not all) of the other modules fielded on the mainland, and a special module mainly concerned with community relations in Northern Ireland. For most topic areas, therefore, users of the data have the opportunity to compare the attitudes of respondents in Northern Ireland to those of respondents in Britain.

The Central Survey Unit of the Northern Ireland Statistics and Research Agency (NISRA) (formerly the Policy Planning and Research Unit) in Belfast carried out the sampling and fieldwork on behalf of SCPR. Researchers from SCPR and NISRA together planned the survey timetable and documentation, and - with the help of the Centre for Social Research at the Queen's University of Belfast - designed the questionnaire modules. As with previous NISA surveys, final responsibility for the questionnaire rested with SCPR.

The results of the *Northern Ireland Social Attitudes* surveys are presented and discussed in a series of annual books, edited by researchers at the Centre for Social Research. The volume reporting on the results of the 1995 *Northern Ireland Social Attitudes* survey will appear in early 1997 (see Breen *et al*, 1997, forthcoming). For further information about the technical details of the 1995 *Northern Ireland Social Attitudes* survey, see McClelland in the Appendices to Breen *et al* (1997, forthcoming).

International Social Survey Programme

The *International Social Survey Programme* is run by a group of research organisations, each of which undertakes to field annually an agreed module of questions on a chosen topic area. Since 1985, an *International Social Survey Programme* module has been included in one of the *British Social Attitudes* self-completion questionnaires.   Each module is chosen for repetition at intervals to allow comparisons both between countries (currently standing at 27) and over time.   In 1995, the chosen subject was National Identity.   The 1995 *International Social Survey Programme* module comprises Qs. 2.01 to 2.21 of the A version of the self-completion questionnaire.

For further details see Brook *et al* (1997, forthcoming).

Notes

1. Until 1991 all *British Social Attitudes* samples were drawn from the Electoral Register (ER). However, following concern that this sampling frame might be deficient in its coverage of certain population subgroups, a 'splicing' experiment was conducted in 1991. We are grateful to the Market Research Development Fund for contributing towards the costs of this experiment. Its purpose was to investigate whether a switch to PAF would disrupt the time-series - for instance, by lowering response rates or affecting the distribution of responses to particular questions. In the event, it was concluded that the change from ER to PAF was unlikely to affect time trends in any noticeable ways, and that no adjustment factors were necessary. Since significant differences in efficiency exist between PAF and ER, and because we considered it untenable to continue to use a frame that is known to be biased, we decided to adopt PAF as the sampling frame for future British Social Attitudes surveys. For details of the PAF/ER 'splicing' experiment, see Lynn and Taylor (1995).
2. In 1993 it was decided to mount a split-sample experiment designed to test the applicability of Computer-Assisted Personal Interviewing (CAPI) to the *British Social Attitudes* survey series. CAPI has been used increasingly over the past decade as an alternative to traditional interviewing techniques. As the name implies, CAPI involves the use of lap-top computers during the interview, with interviewers entering responses directly into the computer. One of the advantages of CAPI is that it significantly reduces both the amount of time spent on data processing and the number of coding and editing errors. Over a longer period, there could also be significant cost savings. There was, however, concern that a different interviewing technique might alter the distribution of responses and so affect the year-on-year consistency of *British Social Attitudes* data.

    Following the experiment, it was decided to change over to CAPI completely in 1994 (the self-completion questionnaire still being administered in the conventional way). The results of the experiment are discussed in the *11th Report* (Lynn and Purdon, 1994).
3. An experiment was conducted on the 1991 *British Social Attitudes* survey, which showed that sending advance letters to sampled addresses before fieldwork begins has very little impact on response rates. However, interviewers do find that an advance letter helps them to introduce the survey on the doorstep, and a majority of respondents have said that they preferred some advance notice. For these reasons, advance letters have been used on the *British Social Attitudes* surveys since 1991.
4. Before 1991, occupational coding was carried out according to the OPCS *Classification of Occupations 1980* (CO80). However, analysts can be confident that the change to

SOC does not affect year-on-year comparability of Social Class variables in the *British Social Attitudes* survey. For further details see Appendix I in Jowell *et al* (1992).

5. Because of methodological experiments on scale development, the exact items detailed below have not been asked on all versions of the questionnaire each year. However, in 1995, these items were asked on all three versions.

6. In 1994, this item was replaced by:
   Ordinary people get their fair share of the nation's wealth. *[Wealth1]*

7. In constructing the scale, a decision had to be taken on how to treat missing values ("Don't knows" and refused/not answered). Respondents who had more than two missing values on the left-right scale and more than three missing values on the libertarian-authoritarian and welfare scale were excluded for that scale. For respondents with just a few missing values, "Don't knows" were recoded to the midpoint of the scale and not answered/refused were recoded to the scale mean for that respondent on their valid items.

References

Breen, R., Devine, P. and Dowds, L. (eds.) (1997, forthcoming), *Social Attitudes in Northern Ireland: the Sixth Report*, Belfast: Appletree.

Brook, L. *et al* (1997, forthcoming), *British Social Attitudes 1995 survey: Technical Report*, London: SCPR.

DeVellis, R.F. (1991), 'Scale development: theory and applications', *Applied Social Research Methods Series*, **26**, Newbury Park: Sage.

Jowell, R., Brook, L., Prior, G. and Taylor, B. (1992), *British Social Attitudes: the 9th Report*, Aldershot: Dartmouth.

Lynn, P. and Purdon, S. (1994), 'Time-series and lap-tops: the change to computer-assisted interviewing', in Jowell, R., Curtice, J., Brook, L. and Ahrendt, D. (eds.) *British Social Attitudes: the 11th Report*, Aldershot: Dartmouth.

Lynn, P and Taylor, B (1995), 'On the bias and variance of samples of individuals: a comparison of the Electoral Registers and Postcode Address File as sampling frames', *The Statistician*, **44**, 173-94.

Spector, P.E (1992), 'Summated rating scale construction: an introduction', *Quantitative Applications in the Social Sciences*, **82**, Newbury Park: Sage.

Appendix II
Notes on the tabulations

1. Figures in the tables are from the 1995 *British Social Attitudes* survey or the 1995 *Northern Ireland Social Attitudes* survey, unless otherwise indicated.
2. Tables are percentaged as indicated.
3. In tables, '*' indicates less than 0.5 per cent but greater than zero, and '-' indicates zero.
4. When findings based on the responses of fewer than 100 respondents are reported in the text, reference is generally made to the small base size.
5. Percentages equal to or greater than 0.5 have been rounded up in all tables (e.g. 0.5 per cent = one per cent, 36.5 per cent = 37 per cent).
6. In many tables the proportions of respondents answering "Don't know" or not giving an answer are omitted. This, together with the effects of rounding and weighting, means that percentages will not always add to 100 per cent.
7. The self-completion questionnaire was not completed by all respondents to the main questionnaire (see Appendix I). Percentage responses to the self-completion questionnaire are based on all those who completed it.
8. Where tables show the base (the number of respondents who answered the question), this is printed in small italics. The bases are *un*weighted, unless otherwise stated.

Appendix III
The questionnaires

As explained in Appendix I, three different versions of the adults' questionnaire (A, B and C) were administered, each with its own self-completion supplement. The diagram that follows shows the structure of the questionnaires and the topics covered (not all of which are reported on in this volume).

The three interview questionnaires reproduced on the following pages are derived from the Blaise program in which they were written. For ease of reference, each item has been allocated a question number. Gaps in the numbering system indicate items that are essential components of the Blaise program but which are not themselves questions, and so have been omitted. In addition, on all six questionnaires we have removed the keying codes and inserted instead the percentage distribution of answers to each question. We have also included the SPSS variable name, bracketed and in italics, beside each question. Above the questions we have included routeing instructions. A routeing instruction should be considered as staying in force until the next routeing instruction. Percentages for the core questions are based on the total weighted sample, while those for questions in versions A, B or C are based on the appropriate weighted subsamples. We reproduce first version A of the interview questionnaire in full; then those parts of version B and version C that differ. The three versions of the self-completion questionnaire follow, with those parts fielded in more than one version reproduced in one version only.

The percentage distributions do not necessarily add up to 100 because of weighting and rounding, or for one or more of the following reasons:

(i)   Some sub-questions are filtered - that is, they are asked of only a proportion of respondents.   In these cases the percentages add up (approximately) to the proportions who were asked them.   Where, however, a series of questions is filtered, we have indicated the weighted base at the beginning of that series (for example, all employees), and throughout have derived percentages from that base.

(ii)   If fewer than 50 respondents (unweighted) are asked a question, frequencies (the number of people giving each response) are shown, rather than percentages.

(iii) At a few questions, respondents were invited to give more than one answer and so percentages may add to well over 100 per cent. These are clearly marked by interviewer instructions on the questionnaires.

As reported in Appendix I, the *British Social Attitudes* self-completion questionnaire was not completed by 14 per cent of respondents who were successfully interviewed. To allow for comparisons over time, the answers in the supplement have been repercentaged on the base of those respondents who returned it (for version A: 1,079 weighted; for version B: 1,032 weighted; and for version C: 1,035 weighted). This means that the figures are comparable with those given in all earlier reports in this series except in *the 1984 Report*, where the percentages for the self-completion questionnaire in Appendix III need to be recalculated if comparisons are to be made.

BRITISH SOCIAL ATTITUDES: 1995 SURVEY

Main questionnaire plan

A	B	C
	1. Newspaper readership Party identification	
	2. Public spending, welfare benefits and health care	
	3. Economic activity, labour market, training and disabled people	
4. Fear of crime; 'self-policing'		4. Economic prospects
5. Constitutional issues	5. Countryside/environment	5. Taxation/public spending
6. Education	6. Transport	6. Charitable giving
7. Drugs	7. Taste and decency	7. Welfare/social security
8. Northern Ireland		8. Euthanasia
	9. Short housing	
	10. Religion and ethnic origin Classification (incl. pension provision - version C)	

Self-completion questionnaire plan

A	B	C
1. ISSP National identity	1. Family networks	
2a. Immigration	2. Family attitudes	
2b. Constitutional issues		
	3. Health care	
	4. Labour market	
5. Northern Ireland	5. Countryside/environment	5. Taxation/public spending
6. Education	6. Transport	6. Charitable giving
7. Drugs	7. Taste and decency	7. Welfare/social security
		8. Euthanasia
		9. North/South differences
	10. Attitude scales	

British Social Attitudes 1995:

Interview questionnaire

Contents page

INTRODUCTION

n=3633

Q1 **ASK ALL**
[Serial]
Serial
Range: 70001 ... 79200

Q5 *[Version]*
VERSION

%
34.5 **A**
32.5 **B**
33.0 **C**

[First]
INTERVIEWER: FOR YOUR INFORMATION ... you are in the
Questionnaire for -
Serial number: (serial number)
You should have a light green/gold/mauve coloured ARF and
self-completion questionnaire

- TO RETURN TO THE MENU, PRESS <Esc>
- TO GO DIRECTLY TO 'ADMIN', PRESS <Ctrl + Enter>
- OTHERWISE TO CONTINUE WITH THE INTERVIEW PRESS '1' AND
<Enter>

Q9 *[IntNum]*
Please type in your interviewer number
Range: 1 ... 9997

Q10 *[StrtTime]*
Start Time
Open Question (Maximum of 8 characters)

NEWSPAPER READERSHIP AND PARTY IDENTIFICATION

n=3633

Q15 *[RSex]*
INTERVIEWER CHECK : PLEASE CODE SEX OF RESPONDENT
%
46.0 Male
54.0 Female
-    (Don't Know)
-    (Refusal/NA)

Q16 *[ReadPap]*
Do you normally read any daily **morning** newspaper at least
3 times a week?
%
62.2 Yes
37.8 No
-    (Don't Know)
-    (Refusal/NA)

Q17 **IF 'Yes' AT [Readpap]**
[WhPaper]
Which one do you normally read?
IF MORE THAN ONE ASK: Which one do you read **most**
frequently?
%
CODE ONE ONLY
5.3   (Scottish) Daily Express
7.8   Daily Mail
13.3 Daily Mirror/Record
1.6   Daily Star
16.3 The Sun
1.8   Today
4.7   Daily Telegraph
0.3   Financial Times
2.4   The Guardian
1.0   The Independent
2.7   The Times
4.0   Morning Star
      Other Irish/Northern Irish/Scottish regional or local
      daily morning paper **(WRITE IN)**
0.2   Other **(WRITE IN)**
0.4   (More than one paper read with equal frequency)
-    (Don't Know)
0.0   (Refusal/NA)

Q22 **VERSION B: ASK ALL**   n=1180
[TVHrsWk]
How many hours of television do you normally watch on an
ordinary day or evening during **the week**, that is, Monday
to Friday?
INTERVIEWER: ROUND UP TO NEAREST HOUR
IF DOES NOT WATCH TELEVISION ON WEEKDAYS, CODE 0
IF NEVER WATCHES TELEVISION AT ALL, CODE 97
Range: 0 ... 97
Median: 3 hours
0.2   (Don't Know)
-    (Refusal/NA)

IF WATCHES TELEVISION n=1180

Q23 *[TVHrsWke]*
How many hours of television do you normally watch on an ordinary day or evening **at the weekend**?
INTERVIEWER: ROUND UP TO NEAREST HOUR
IF DOES NOT WATCH TELEVISION AT WEEKENDS, CODE 0
Range: 0 ... 97
Median: 3 hours
0.2 (Don't Know)
0.2 (Refusal/NA)

VERSION B: ASK ALL

Q24 *[Satellit]*
Do you have a satellite dish or are you connected to a cable network in your own home?
INTERVIEWER: EXCLUDE DISHES NO LONGER WORKING OR NO LONGER CONNECTED

%	
12.7	Yes, satellite
8.8	Yes, cable
0.4	Yes, both
78.1	No
-	(Don't Know)
-	(Refusal/NA)

Q25 *[Video]*
Do you have a video recorder in your own home?

%	
82.7	Yes
17.3	No
-	(Don't Know)
-	(Refusal/NA)

IF 'Yes' AT [Video]

Q26 *[Vidfilm]*
CARD
How often nowadays do you personally watch a rented or bought video?

VERSION B: ASK ALL

Q27 *[CineOft]*
CARD AGAIN
How often do you go to the cinema nowadays?

	[Vidfilm] %	*[CineOft]* %
Once a week or more	9.7	1.0
Less often than once a week, but at least once a month	16.5	7.8
Less often than once a month, but at least once a year	28.6	31.3
Less often than once a year	27.9	59.9
(Don't Know)	-	-
(Refusal/NA)	-	-

3

VERSION A: ASK ALL n=1253

Q28 *[AtTVSpor]*
CARD
How much attention do you generally pay to stories on television or in the newspapers about sport?

Q29 *[AtTVPol]*
CARD AGAIN
How much attention do you generally pay to stories on television or in the newspapers about what goes on in politics?

Q30 *[AtTVRoy]*
CARD AGAIN
How much attention do you generally pay to stories on television or in the newspapers about the Royal Family?

Q31 *[AtTVCrim]*
CARD AGAIN
How much attention do you generally pay to stories on television or in the newspapers about crime?

Q32 *[AtTVSex]*
CARD AGAIN
How much attention do you generally pay to stories on television or in the newspapers about sex scandals?

	[AtTVSpor] %	*[AtTVPol]* %	*[AtTVRoy]* %
A great deal of attention	13.7	9.4	5.4
Quite a bit of attention	17.3	27.8	14.2
Some attention	18.1	25.4	30.9
A little attention	30.5	22.5	30.8
No attention at all	20.4	14.9	18.7
(Don't Know)	-	-	-
(Refusal/NA)	-	-	-

	[AtTVCrim] %	*[AtTVSex]* %
A great deal of attention	21.3	3.5
Quite a bit of attention	48.7	9.7
Some attention	22.2	25.5
A little attention	6.4	35.1
No attention at all	1.4	26.2
(Don't Know)	-	-
(Refusal/NA)	-	-

ASK ALL n=3633

Q33 *[SupParty]*
Generally speaking, do you think of yourself as a supporter of any one political party?

%	
43.2	Yes
56.6	No
0.2	(Don't Know)
0.0	(Refusal/NA)

4

n=3633

Q34 IF 'No' AT [SupParty]
[ClosePty]
Do you think of yourself as a little closer to one political party than to the others?
%
26.7 Yes
29.7 No
0.1 (Don't Know)
0.2 (Refusal/NA)

Q35 IF 'Yes' AT [SupParty] OR 'Yes/No' AT [ClosePty]
[PartyID1]
IF 'Yes' AT [SupParty] OR AT [ClosePty]: Which one?
IF 'No' AT [ClosePty]: If there were a general election tomorrow, which political party do you think you would be most likely to support?
CODE ONE ONLY
%
26.4 Conservative
44.4 Labour
12.3 Liberal Democrat
1.3 Scottish Nationalist
0.6 Plaid Cymru
0.9 Green Party
0.4 Other party (WRITE IN)
0.3 Other answer (WRITE IN)
9.0 None
3.2 (Don't Know)
1.2 (Refusal/NA)

Q43 IF ANY PARTY AT [PartyID1]
[Idstrng]
Would you call yourself very strong (party given at [PartyID1]) fairly strong, or not very strong?
%
10.3 Very strong (party at [PartyID1])
28.2 Fairly strong
47.4 Not very strong
0.2 (Don't Know)
4.9 (Refusal/NA)

n=1253

Q44 VERSION A: ASK ALL
[MembPolP]
Are you a member of a political party?
IF YES, PROBE: Which one?
DO NOT PROMPT
%
96.5 No, not member
Yes - Conservative 1.9
   - Labour 1.2
   - Liberal Democrat 0.4
   - Scottish Nationalist/Plaid Cymru 0.0
   - Other (WRITE IN) -
(Don't Know) -
(Refusal/NA) -

5

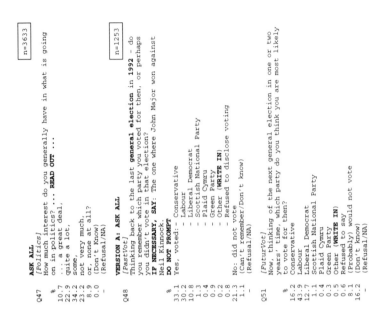

n=3633

Q47 ASK ALL
[Politics]
How much interest do you generally have in what is going on in politics? ... READ OUT ...
%
10.7 ... a great deal,
22.9 quite a lot,
34.2 some,
23.2 not very much,
8.9 or, none at all?
0.0 (Don't Know)
- (Refusal/NA)

Q48 VERSION A: ASK ALL
[PastVot]
Thinking back to the last **general election** in **1992** - do you remember which party you voted for then, or perhaps you didn't vote in that election?
IF NECESSARY, SAY: The one where John Major won against Neil Kinnock.
DO NOT PROMPT
%
Yes, voted:- Conservative 33.1
         - Labour 30.2
         - Liberal Democrat 10.8
         - Scottish National Party 1.3
         - Plaid Cymru 0.4
         - Green Party 0.9
         - Other (WRITE IN) 0.2
         - Refused to disclose voting 0.8
No: did not vote 21.3
(Can't remember/Don't know) 1.1
(Refusal/NA) -

n=1253

Q51 [FuturVot]
Now, thinking of the next general election in one or two years' time, which party do you think you are most likely to vote for then?
%
16.2 Conservative
43.9 Labour
12.7 Liberal Democrat
1.1 Scottish National Party
0.4 Plaid Cymru
0.3 Green Party
0.5 Other (WRITE IN)
0.6 Refused to say
8.1 (Probably) would not vote
16.2 (Don't know)
- (Refusal/NA)

6

PUBLIC SPENDING, WELFARE BENEFITS AND HEALTH CARE

n=1199

VERSION C: ASK ALL

Q58 [Spend1]
CARD
Here are some items of government spending. Which of them, if any, would be your highest priority for **extra** spending? Please read through the whole list before deciding.
ENTER ONE CODE ONLY FOR HIGHEST PRIORITY

Q59 [Spend2]
CARD AGAIN
And which next?
ENTER ONE CODE ONLY FOR NEXT HIGHEST

	[Spend1]	[Spend2]
	%	%
Education	32.1	33.4
Defence	0.8	1.6
Health	49.0	27.5
Housing	4.7	9.6
Public transport	1.5	5.1
Roads	0.8	5.1
Police and prisons	2.9	6.6
Social security benefits	3.9	7.1
Help for industry	3.6	5.1
Overseas aid	0.0	0.4
(None of these)	0.4	0.6
(Don't Know)	0.2	0.2
(Refusal/NA)	-	0.1

Q60 [SocBen1]
CARD
Thinking now only of the government's spending on **social benefits** like those on the card. Which, if any, of these would be your highest priority for extra spending?
ENTER ONE CODE ONLY FOR HIGHEST PRIORITY

Q61 [SocBen2]
CARD
And which next?
ENTER ONE CODE ONLY FOR NEXT HIGHEST

	[SocBen1]	[SocBen2]
	%	%
Retirement pensions	46.2	21.8
Child benefits	13.3	19.5
Benefits for the unemployed	9.8	14.8
Benefits for disabled people	23.2	34.6
Benefits for single parents	5.6	5.9
(None of these)	1.1	2.1
(Don't Know)	0.8	1.3
(Refusal/NA)	-	-

Q62 [Dole]
Opinions differ about the level of benefits for unemployed people. Which of these two statements comes closest to your own view? ... **READ OUT** ...

%
51.1 ..benefits for unemployed people are **too low** and cause hardship,
29.7 or, benefits for unemployed people are **too high** and discourage them from finding jobs?
(Neither)
10.7 Both: Unemployment Benefit causes hardship but can't be higher or there would be no incentive to work
0.8
1.0 Both: Unemployment Benefit causes hardship to some, while others do well out of it
0.0 About right/in between
3.1 Other answer (**WRITE IN**)
3.6 (Don't Know)
- (Refusal/NA)

ASK ALL

Q65 [TaxSpend]
CARD
Suppose the government had to choose between the three options on this card. Which do you think it should choose?

n=3633

%
4.8 Reduce taxes and spend **less** on health, education and social benefits
30.6 Keep taxes and spending on these services at the **same** level as now
60.8 Increase taxes and spend **more** on health, education and social benefits
2.9 (None)
1.0 (Don't Know)
- (Refusal/NA)

Q66 [NHSSat]
CARD
All in all, how satisfied or dissatisfied would you say you are with the way in which the National Health Service runs nowadays? Choose a phrase from this card.

Q67 [GPSat]
CARD
From your own experience, or from what you have heard, please say how satisfied or dissatisfied you are with the way in which each of these parts of the National Health Service runs nowadays.
First, local doctors or GPs?

Q68 [DentSat]
CARD
(And how satisfied or dissatisfied are you with the NHS as regards ...)
... NHS dentists?

Q69 [InPatSat]
CARD
(And how satisfied or dissatisfied are you with the NHS as regards...)
... Being in hospital as an **in-patient**?

n=3633

Q70 [OutPaSat]
CARD
(And how satisfied or dissatisfied are you with the NHS as regards ...)
... Attending hospital as an **out-patient**?

	[NHSSat]	[GPSat]	[DentSat]
	%	%	%
Very satisfied	7.8	31.9	18.8
Quite satisfied	29.2	46.7	36.2
Neither satisfied nor dissatisfied	17.7	9.5	17.3
Quite dissatisfied	24.8	8.3	13.0
Very dissatisfied	20.1	3.0	9.5
(Don't know)	0.4	0.5	5.3
(Refusal/NA)	0.0	0.0	0.0

	[InPatSat]	[OutPaSat]
	%	%
Very satisfied	21.2	14.4
Quite satisfied	35.5	40.7
Neither satisfied nor dissatisfied	18.0	17.0
Quite dissatisfied	11.8	15.0
Very dissatisfied	5.2	7.4
(Don't know)	8.2	5.4
(Refusal/NA)	0.0	0.0

Q71 [PriMed]
Are you covered by a private medical health insurance scheme, that is an insurance scheme that allows you to get private medical **treatment**?
ADD IF NECESSARY: For example, BUPA or PPP.

	%
Yes	15.4
No	84.4
(Don't Know)	0.2
(Refusal/NA)	0.1

IF 'Yes' AT [PrivMed]
Q72 [PrivPaid]
Does your employer (or your partner's employer) pay the majority of the cost of membership of this scheme?

	%
Yes	7.8
No	7.3
(Don't Know)	0.3
(Refusal/NA)	0.2

ASK ALL
Q73 [NHSLimit]
It has been suggested that the National Health Service should be available **only to those with lower incomes**. This would mean that contributions and taxes could be lower and most people would then take out medical insurance or pay for health care. Do you support or oppose this idea?
IF 'SUPPORT' OR 'OPPOSE': **A lot or a little?**

9

---

n=1199

VERSION C: ASK ALL
Q74 [SchLimit]
In the same way, state schools could be **free** only for children from low income families. This would mean that taxes could be lower and most people would pay towards their children's schooling. Do you support or oppose this idea?
IF 'SUPPORT' OR 'OPPOSE': **A lot or a little?**

Q75 [PenLimit]
It has also been suggested that state pensions should only be paid **to those with lower incomes**. This would mean that taxes could be lower and most people, and their employers, would pay towards their pensions. Do you support or oppose this idea?
IF 'SUPPORT' OR 'OPPOSE': **A lot or a little?**

	[NHSLimit]	[SchLimit]	[PenLimit]
	%	%	%
Support a lot	7.9	6.0	11.4
Support a little	14.6	11.1	16.9
Oppose a little	16.4	13.8	21.0
Oppose a lot	58.7	67.3	46.8
(Don't Know)	2.3	1.7	4.0
(Refusal/NA)	0.0	-	-

n=3633

ASK ALL
Q76 [InPat1]
CARD
Now, suppose you had to go into a local NHS hospital for observation and maybe an operation. From what you know or have heard, please say whether you would think the hospital doctors would tell you all you feel you need to know.

Q77 [InPat2]
CARD AGAIN
(And please say whether you think...)
...the hospital doctors would take seriously any views you may have on the sorts of treatment available?

Q78 [InPat3]
CARD AGAIN
(And please say whether you think...)
...the operation would take place on the day it was booked for?

Q79 [InPat4]
CARD AGAIN
(And please say whether you think...)
...you would be allowed home only when you were really well enough to leave?

Q80 [InPat5]
CARD AGAIN
(And please say whether you think...)
...the nurses would take seriously any complaints you may have?

Q81 [InPat6]
CARD AGAIN
(And please say whether you think...)
...the hospital doctors would take seriously any complaints you may have?

10

Q82 [InPat7]
CARD AGAIN
(And please say whether you think ...)
...there would be a particular nurse responsible for dealing with any problems you may have?

n=3633

	[InPat1]	[InPat2]	[InPat3]	[InPat4]
	%	%	%	%
Definitely would	20.5	12.5	10.3	15.8
Probably would	48.3	46.2	47.0	37.6
Probably would not	22.0	30.2	30.0	33.4
Definitely would not	7.1	6.5	8.3	11.2
(Don't Know)	2.1	4.5	4.0	2.0
(Refusal/NA)	0.0	0.0	0.0	0.0

	[InPat5]	[InPat6]	[InPat7]
	%	%	%
Definitely would	26.8	19.4	15.9
Probably would	56.9	57.6	38.1
Probably would not	11.4	16.9	31.9
Definitely would not	2.7	3.6	5.5
(Don't Know)	2.2	2.5	8.5
(Refusal/NA)	0.0	0.0	0.0

Q83 [OutPat1]
CARD AGAIN
Now suppose you had a back problem and your GP referred you to a hospital out-patients' department. From what you know or have heard, please say whether you think you would get an appointment within three months?

Q84 [OutPat2]
CARD AGAIN
(And please say whether you think ...)
...when you arrived, the doctor would see you within half an hour of your appointment time?

Q85 [OutPat3]
CARD AGAIN
(And please say whether you think ...)
...if you wanted to complain about the treatment you received, you would be able to without any fuss or bother?

Q86 [WhchHosp]
CARD AGAIN
Now suppose you needed to go into hospital for an operation. Do you think you would have a say about which hospital you went to?

	[OutPat1]	[OutPat2]	[OutPat3]	[WhchHosp]
	%	%	%	%
Definitely would	11.9	7.5	13.2	6.2
Probably would	33.3	28.7	42.6	18.5
Probably would not	35.4	39.9	28.6	44.3
Definitely would not	15.0	21.6	9.7	26.7
(Don't Know)	4.3	2.6	5.9	4.4
(Refusal/NA)	0.0	0.0	0.0	0.0

Q87 [GPChange]
Suppose you wanted to change your GP and go to a different practice how difficult or easy do you think this would be to arrange? Would it be ... READ OUT ...

%	
6.2	very difficult,
21.2	fairly difficult,
35.7	not very difficult,
30.6	or, not at all difficult?
6.2	(Don't Know)
0.0	(Refusal/NA)

n=3633

Q88 VERSIONS A AND B: ASK ALL
[NHS5yrs]
CARD
Please say how much better or worse you think each of these things has been getting over the last five years.
.....the general standard of health care on the NHS?

n=2434

Q89 [WtOp5Yrs]
CARD AGAIN
(Please say how much better or worse you think each of these things has been getting over the last five years)
....the time most people wait to get operations in NHS hospitals?

Q90 [WtAp5Yrs]
CARD AGAIN
(Please say how much better or worse you think each of these things has been getting over the last five years)
....the time most people wait to get outpatients' appointments in NHS hospitals?

Q91 [WtCo5Yrs]
CARD AGAIN
(Please say how much better or worse you think each of these things has been getting over the last five years)
...the time most people wait in outpatients' departments in NHS hospitals before a consultant sees them?

Q92 [WtGP5Yrs]
CARD AGAIN
(Please say how much better or worse you think each of these things has been getting over the last five years)
..the time most people wait at their GP's surgery before a doctor sees them?

	[NHS5yrs]	[WtOp5yrs]	[WtAp5yrs]	[WtCo5yrs]	[WtGP5yrs]
	%	%	%	%	%
Much better	3.0	2.0	1.8	2.4	5.9
Better	14.5	15.1	15.5	15.5	23.2
About the same	32.2	26.0	38.0	39.2	49.0
Worse	39.0	38.6	30.5	30.5	16.8
Much worse	10.2	13.9	8.2	7.9	4.5
(Don't Know)	1.0	4.5	5.2	4.4	1.6
(Refusal/NA)	0.0	0.0	0.0	0.0	0.0

Q93 **ASK ALL**
[SickPay1]
CARD
Please say, from this card, who you think should be **mainly** responsible for ensuring that people who are off work because they are sick continue to get paid?

Q96 *[SickPay2]*
CARD AGAIN
And if someone was off work sick for six months, who do you think should be **mainly** responsible for ensuring that they continue to get paid.

n=3633

	[SickPay1]	[SickPay2]
	%	%
Mainly the government	29.6	53.3
Mainly the employer	28.7	14.1
Shared equally	38.2	25.7
Some other arrangement (**WRITE IN**)	0.5	1.6
It depends	1.6	2.8
(Individual should make own private arrangement)	0.5	1.1
(Don't Know)	0.8	1.3
(Refusal/NA)	-	-

Q99 **VERSION A: ASK ALL**
[AIDSXpel]
CARD

n=1253

Please look at this card and tell whether schools should or should not have the legal right to expel children who have AIDS?

%	
8.7	Definitely should
11.2	Probably should
25.7	Probably should not
50.7	Definitely should not
3.6	(Don't Know)
0.0	(Refusal/NA)

Q100 *[AIDSSymp]*
Please say whether you agree or disagree with this statement:
People who have AIDS get much less sympathy from society than they ought to get:
PROBE: Strongly or a little?

%	
38.4	Strongly agree
33.7	Agree a little
15.5	Disagree a little
8.3	Strongly disagree
4.1	(Don't Know)
-	(Refusal/NA)

Q101 **VERSION B: ASK ALL**
[PMS]
CARD

n=1180

Now I would like to ask you some questions about sexual relationships. If a man and woman have sexual relations before marriage, what would your general opinion be?

Q102 *[ExMS]*
CARD AGAIN
What about a **married person** having sexual relations with someone other than his or her partner?

Q103 *[HomoSex]*
CARD AGAIN
What about sexual relations between two adults of the same sex?

	[PMS]	[ExMS]	[HomoSex]
	%	%	%
Always wrong	8.5	54.1	43.6
Mostly wrong	9.1	28.2	11.3
Sometimes wrong	15.8	11.5	9.6
Rarely wrong	10.3	1.6	7.1
Not wrong at all	50.8	1.4	22.3
(Depends/ varies)	4.1	2.2	3.7
(Don't Know)	0.7	0.4	1.6
(Refusal/NA)	0.6	0.5	0.7

Q104 **VERSION C: ASK ALL**
[NHSTrust]
CARD

n=1199

How much do you trust hospital doctors always to put the interests of their patients above the convenience of the hospital?

%	
16.6	Always
51.9	Most of the time
25.7	Only some of the time
3.1	Just about never
2.7	(Don't Know)
-	(Refusal/NA)

Q105 *[InfCare]*
May I just check, is there anyone **in your household** who is sick, disabled or elderly who you look after or give special help to (for example, a relative, husband/wife, child, friend)?

%	
10.3	Yes
89.7	No
0.0	(Don't Know)
-	(Refusal/NA)

Q106 **IF 'NO' OR 'Don't Know' AT [InfCare]**
[EvInfCar]
Have you **ever** had anyone **in your household** who was sick, disabled or elderly who you looked after or gave special help to?

%	
20.4	Yes
69.3	No
-	(Don't Know)
-	(Refusal/NA)

ECONOMIC ACTIVITY, LABOUR MARKET, TRAINING AND DISABLED PEOPLE

n=3633

Q111 **ASK ALL**
[REconAct]
CARD
Which of these descriptions applies to what you were doing last week, that is, in the seven days ending last Sunday?
CODE ALL THAT APPLY
PROBE: Which others?
Multicoded (Maximum of 10 codes)

%	
3.4	In full-time education (not paid for by employer, including on vacation)
0.4	On government training/employment programme (e.g. Employment Training, Youth Training, etc.)
51.8	In paid work (or away temporarily) for at least 10 hours in week
0.4	Waiting to take up paid work already accepted
4.5	Unemployed and registered at a benefit office
0.8	Unemployed, **not** registered, but actively looking for a job
0.4	Unemployed, wanting a job (of at least 10 hrs per week) but **not** actively looking for a job
4.6	Permanently sick or disabled
18.2	Wholly retired from work
14.2	Looking after the home
1.4	(Doing something else) (WRITE IN)
-	(Don't know)
-	(Refusal/NA)

Q112 **ASK ALL IN PAID WORK (FOR 10+ HOURS A WEEK)**
[REmploye]
In your (main) job are you ... **READ OUT** ...

%	
83.4	... an employee,
16.6	or, self-employed?
-	(Don't know)
0.0	(Refusal/NA)

n=1881

Q113 **ASK ALL EMPLOYEES (IF 'employee' or 'Don't Know' AT [REmployee])**
[EmploydT]
For how long have you been continuously employed by your present employer?
ENTER NUMBER. THEN SPECIFY MONTHS OR YEARS
Range: 1 ... 60
Median: 60 months

0.1	(Don't Know)
0.0	(Refusal/NA)

n=1568

Q115 *[ESrJbTim]*
In your present job, are you working ... **READ OUT** ...
RESPONDENT'S OWN DEFINITION

%	
78.6	... full-time,
21.3	or, part-time?
-	(Don't Know)
0.0	(Refusal/NA)

Q116 *[EJbHours]*
How many hours a week do you **normally** work in your (main) job?
IF RESPONDENT CANNOT ANSWER, ASK ABOUT LAST WEEK.
ROUND TO NEAREST HOUR.
CODE 95 FOR 95+
Range: 10 ... 95
Median: 38 hours

0.2	(Don't Know)
0.0	(Refusal/NA)

n=1568

Q117 *[EJbHrCat]* **(NOT ON SCREEN)**
HOURS WORKED - CATEGORISED

%	
5.2	10-15 hours a week
8.8	16-23 hours a week
5.9	24-29 hours a week
79.8	30 or more hours a week
0.2	(Don't Know)
0.0	(Refusal/NA)

Q118 *[WageNow]*
How would you describe the wages or salary you are paid for the job you do - on the low side, reasonable, or on the high side?
IF LOW: Very low or a bit low?

%	
11.4	Very low
23.5	A bit low
58.3	Reasonable
6.5	On the high side
0.2	Other answer (WRITE IN)
-	(Don't Know)
0.1	(Refusal/NA)

Q121 *[PayGap]*
CARD
Thinking of the **highest** and the **lowest** paid people at your place of work, how would you describe the **gap** between their pay, as far as you know?
Please choose a phrase from this card.

%	
20.3	Much too big a gap
29.8	Too big
42.0	About right
1.7	Too small
0.2	Much too small a gap
5.8	(Don't Know)
0.1	(Refusal/NA)

Q122 *[WageXpct]*
If you stay in this job, would you expect your wages or salary over the coming year to ... **READ OUT** ...

%	
17.1	... rise by **more** than the cost of living,
38.4	rise by the **same** as the cost of living,
29.4	rise by **less** than the cost of living,
13.0	or, not to rise at all?
1.0	(Will not stay in job)
1.2	(Don't Know)
0.0	(Refusal/NA)

n=1568

Q123 [WageDown]
IF 'Not rise at all' AT [WageXpct]
Would you expect your wages or salary to stay the same, or in fact to go down?

%
Go down 12.0
Stay the same 1.0
(Don't Know) -
(Refusal/NA) 1.2

Q124 [NumEmp]
ASK ALL EMPLOYEES
Over the coming year do you expect your workplace to be
... READ OUT ...

%
... increasing its number of employees, 22.7
reducing its number of employees, 22.4
or, will the number of employees stay about the same 53.6
Other answer (WRITE IN) 0.3
(Don't Know) 1.0
(Refusal/NA) 0.0

Q127 [LeaveJob]
Thinking now about your own job. How likely or unlikely is it that you will leave this employer over the next year for any reason? Is it ... READ OUT ...

%
... very likely, 14.5
quite likely, 12.9
not very likely, 28.5
or, not at all likely? 43.3
(Don't Know) 0.6
(Refusal/NA) 0.0

Q128 [WhyGoFW]
IF 'very likely' OR 'quite likely' AT [LeaveJob]
CARD
Why do you think you will leave? Please choose a phrase from this card or tell me what other reason there is.
CODE ALL THAT APPLY
Multicoded (Maximum of 9 codes)

%
Firm will close down [WhyGo1] 1.0
I will be declared redundant [WhyGo2] 3.5
I will reach normal retirement age [WhyGo3] 1.1
My contract of employment will expire [WhyGo4] 2.1
I will take early retirement [WhyGo5] 0.7
I will decide to leave and work for another employer [WhyGo6] 14.7
I will decide to leave and work for myself, as self-employed [WhyGo7] 1.8
I will leave to look after home/children/relative [WhyGo10] 2.2
(Return to education- likely to leave employment) [WhyGo11] 1.0
Other answer (WRITE IN) [WhyGo8] 2.5
(Don't know) 0.6
(Refusal/NA) 0.0

17

n=1568

Q140 [ELookJob]
ASK ALL EMPLOYEES
Suppose you lost your job for one reason or another - would you start looking for another job, would you wait for several months or longer before you started looking, or would you decide **not** to look for another job?

%
Start looking 88.0
Wait several months or longer 4.9
Decide not to look 6.6
(Don't Know) 0.4
(Refusal/NA) 0.0

Q141 [EFindJob]
IF 'Start looking' AT [ELookJob]
How long do you think it would take you to find an acceptable replacement job?
IF 'NEVER' PLEASE CODE 96
ENTER NUMBER. THEN SPECIFY MONTHS OR YEARS
Range: 1 ... 96
Median: 2 months

%
(Never) 2.0
(Don't Know) 8.6
(Refusal/NA) 0.5

Q143 [ERetrain]
IF '3 months or more' 'Never' OR 'DK' AT [EFindJob]
How willing do you think you would be in these circumstances to retrain for a different job ... READ OUT ...

%
...very willing, 23.5
quite willing, 15.4
or - not very willing? 7.3
(Don't Know) 0.2
(Refusal/NA) 0.5

Q144 [EUnemp]
ASK ALL EMPLOYEES
During the last **five years** - that is since May 1990 - have you been unemployed and seeking work for any period?

%
Yes 19.8
No 80.2
(Don't Know) -
(Refusal/NA) 0.0

Q145 [EUnempT]
IF 'Yes' AT [EUnemp]
For how many months in total during the last five years?
ENTER NUMBER OF MONTHS
Range: 0 ... 60
Median: 4 months

%
(Don't know) -
(Refusal/NA) 0.0

18

n=1568

Q146 **ASK ALL EMPLOYEES**
[MpUnions]
At your place of work are there unions, staff associations, or groups of unions recognised by the management for negotiating pay and conditions of employment?
IF YES, PROBE FOR UNION OR STAFF ASSOCIATION
IF 'BOTH', CODE '1'

%
50.4   Yes : trade union(s)
4.6   Yes : staff association
42.9   No, none
2.0   (Don't Know)
0.0   (Refusal/NA)

Q147 [IndRel]
In general how would you describe relations between management and other employees at your workplace ... **READ OUT** ...

%
30.2   ... very good,
44.6   quite good,
17.8   not very good,
6.6   or, not at all good?
0.7   (Don't Know)
0.1   (Refusal/NA)

Q148 [WorkRun]
And in general, would you say your workplace was ... **READ OUT** ...

%
23.0   ... very well managed,
53.9   quite well managed,
22.9   or, not well managed?
0.2   (Don't Know)
0.0   (Refusal/NA)

Q149 [EmpEarn]
Now for some more general questions about your work. For some people their job is simply something they do in order to earn a living. For others it means much more than that. On balance, is your present job ... **READ OUT** ...

%
34.7   ... just a means of earning a living,
64.7   or, does it mean much more to you than that?
0.6   (Don't Know)
0.0   (Refusal/NA)

IF 'A means of earning a living' AT [EmpEarn]
Q150 [EmpLiv]
Is that because ... **READ OUT** ...

%
11.5   ... there are no better jobs around here,
10.2   you don't have the right skills to get a better job,
10.5   or, because you would feel the same about **any** job you had?
2.6   (Don't Know)
0.6   (Refusal/NA)

19

---

n=1568

Q151 **ASK ALL EMPLOYEES**
[EPrefJob]
If without having to work, you had what you would regard as a reasonable living income, do you think you would still prefer to have a paid job or wouldn't you bother?

%
68.5   Still prefer paid job
29.0   Wouldn't bother
2.4   Other answer (**WRITE IN**)
0.3   (Don't Know)
0.0   (Refusal/NA)

Q154 [EWkHrd]
CARD
Which of these statements best describes your feelings about your job? In my job :

%
8.0   I only work as hard as I have to
42.0   I work hard, but not so that it interferes with the rest of my life
49.9   I make a point of doing the best I can, even if it sometimes does interfere with the rest of my life
0.1   (Don't Know)
0.0   (Refusal/NA)

Q155 [ECourse]
In the last **two** years, have you been on any courses or had other formal training, which was part of your work or helpful to your work?
ANY TRAINING WHICH IS RELATED TO RESPONDENT'S PAST, PRESENT OR FUTURE WORK MAY BE COUNTED, BUT DO NOT INCLUDE LEISURE COURSES OR HOBBIES WHICH ARE NOT JOB RELATED

%
58.2   Yes, had training related to work
41.7   No, had none
-   (Don't Know)
0.0   (Refusal/NA)

ASK ALL WHO HAVE HAD TRAINING RELATED TO WORK IN LAST TWO YEARS   n=914
Q156 [ECourseT]
All in all, about how many full days have you spent in this kind of training over the last two years?
Range: 0 ... 997
Median: 8 days
1.3   (Don't Know)
0.1   (Refusal/NA)

Q157 [ECrsWhen]
And did you do this training **entirely** in your own time, entirely in work time, or partly one and partly the other? Please include any 'homework' you might have done in your own time.

%
13.4   Entirely in own time
55.4   Entirely in work time
31.1   Partly one / partly other
-   (Don't Know)
0.1   (Refusal/NA)

20

n=914

Q158 [ECrsPay]
CARD
From this card, please say who paid the **fees** for this training?
Multicoded (Maximum of 5 codes)

%	
8.9	No fees [ECPNoFee]
9.3	Self / family / relative [ECPSelf]
81.6	Employer / potential employer [ECPEmplo]
1.6	Training for Work / YT / ET [ECPTW]
0.3	Training Credit [ECPTC]
2.2	Other (WRITE IN) [ECPOth]
0.2	(Don't know)
0.4	(Refusal/NA)

ASK ALL EMPLOYEES n=1568

Q161 [ExpCours]
IF 'Yes' AT [Ecourse]: Over the **next** two years, do you
expect to have any more courses or training for your work?
IF 'No', 'Don't Know' OR 'Refusal/NA' AT [Ecourse]: Over
the **next** two years, do you **expect** to have any courses or
training for your work?

%	
53.4	Yes, expect to
41.0	No, don't expect to
5.1	(It depends)
0.5	(Don't Know)
0.0	(Refusal/NA)

Q162 [ElkCours]
IF 'Yes' AT [Ecourse]: And apart from what you expect, would
you like to have any more courses or formal training for your
work in the next two years, or are you not that bothered?
IF 'No', 'Don't Know' OR 'Refusal/NA' AT [Ecourse]: And
apart from what you expect, would you **like** to have any
courses or formal training for your work in the next two
years, or are you not that bothered?

%	
55.7	Yes, would like to
41.2	No, not that bothered
2.9	(It depends)
0.1	(Don't Know)
0.0	(Refusal/NA)

Q163 IF 'Yes, would like to' AT [ElkCours]
[EYTrain1]
CARD
Here are some possible benefits of training. Which, if any,
is the **main** reason why you would like to do more training?

Q164 IF ANSWER GIVEN AT [EYTrain1]
[EYTrain2]
CARD AGAIN
And which next?

	[EYTrain1]	[EYTrain2]
	%	%
To make work more interesting	6.3	15.7
To earn more money	4.8	10.3
To improve chances of promotion	8.6	7.8
To improve chances of getting a better job	8.6	8.5
To learn new sorts of skills	25.1	10.0
Other reason (WRITE IN)	1.7	1.8
(None of these)	0.4	1.1
(Don't Know)	0.1	-
(Refusal/NA)	0.1	0.1

n=1568

ASK ALL EMPLOYEES
Q165 [ELearn1]
In the last two years, have you done any of the following
things in connection with your work? Please just answer
yes or no.
Have you been asked to do anything just for **practice** in
order to learn the work?

Q166 [ELearn2]
Have your been given any special talks or lectures about
the work?

Q167 [ELearn3]
Have you been placed with more experienced people to see
how the work should be done?

Q168 [ELearn4]
Have you been sent round to different parts of the
organisation to see what sort of work is done?

Q169 [ELearn5]
Have you been asked to read things to help you learn about
the work?

Q170 [ELearn6]
Have you been taught or trained by anybody while you were
actually doing the work?

Q171 [ELearn7]
Have you been sent on any courses to introduce you to new
methods of working?

	[Elearn1]	[Elearn2]	[Elearn3]	[Elearn4]
	%	%	%	%
Yes	38.1	54.1	34.8	28.7
No	61.9	45.8	65.1	71.2
(Don't Know)	-	-	-	-
(Refusal/NA)	0.1	0.1	0.1	0.1

	[Elearn5]	[Elearn6]	[Elearn7]
	%	%	%
Yes	56.7	48.5	37.4
No	43.3	51.4	62.6
(Don't Know)	-	-	-
(Refusal/NA)	0.1	0.1	0.0

Q172 [ECHkAge]
Can I just check, what was your age last birthday?
Range: 18 ... 97
Median: 38 years
- (Don't Know)
0.2 (Refusal/NA)

ASK EMPLOYEES BELOW FIVE YEARS ABOVE RETIREMENT AGE n=1558

Q173 [ERedun]
During the last two years - that is, since May 1993 - have you been made redundant?

%	
5.9	Yes
94.1	No
-	(Don't Know)
0.0	(Refusal/NA)

ASK EMPLOYEES WHO HAVE BEEN MADE REDUNDANT IN LAST TWO YEARS n=92

Q174 [ERedPay]
Did you, or will you, receive any redundancy payments as a result of this?

%	
52.8	Yes
46.6	No
-	(Don't Know)
0.6	(Refusal/NA)

IF 'Yes' AT [ERedPay]

Q175 [ERedPyA]
How would you describe the amount of redundancy pay you received, or will receive - on the low side, reasonable, or on the high side?
IF LOW: Very low or a bit low?

%	
13.3	Very low
7.5	A bit low
28.4	Reasonable
3.5	On the high side
-	Other answer (WRITE IN)
-	(Don't Know)
0.6	(Refusal/NA)

ASK EMPLOYEES WHO HAVE BEEN MADE REDUNDANT IN THE LAST TWO YEARS

Q178 [ERedFr]
All things considered, do you think your redundancy was handled fairly by your employer?

%	
56.9	Yes - handled fairly
41.4	No - not handled fairly
1.2	Other answer (WRITE IN)
-	(Don't Know)
0.6	(Refusal/NA)

ASK ALL EMPLOYEES n=1568

Q181 [EOthWk]
At present, apart from your main job, do you ever do **any** other work for which you are paid?

%	
14.8	Yes
85.2	No
-	(Don't Know)
0.0	(Refusal/NA)

ASK EMPLOYEES WHO DO NOT HAVE A SECOND JOB n=1336

Q182 [EWdWk]
If you were offered some other work for 10 hours a week or less, and the earnings you would make were reasonable, how seriously would you consider it? ... **READ OUT** ...

%	
19.2	...very seriously,
22.6	fairly seriously,
15.2	not very seriously,
41.2	or not at all seriously?
1.8	(It depends)
-	(Don't Know)
0.1	(Refusal/NA)

ASK EMPLOYEES WHO HAVE A SECOND JOB n=233

Q183 [EChkWk]
Did you do any of this other work in the seven days ending last Sunday?

%	
59.0	Yes
40.8	No
-	(Don't Know)
0.2	(Refusal/NA)

Q184 [EFreqWk]
And do you do this other work ... **READ OUT** ...
IF MORE THAN ONE TYPE OF WORK DONE, ASK ABOUT MOST FREQUENT.
IF EQUALLY FREQUENT, ASK ABOUT MOST RECENT.

%	
47.5	...at least once a week,
19.7	at least once a month,
32.6	or less often?
-	(Don't Know)
0.2	(Refusal/NA)

Q185 [EHrsWk] ([ETimWk] gives hours per month)
How many hours a (week/month/year) do you **normally** do this other work?
IF RESPONDENT CANNOT ANSWER, ASK ABOUT LAST WEEK/MONTH.
ROUND TO NEAREST HOUR.
Range: 1 .. 200
Median: 13 hours per month

3.0	(Don't Know)
0.2	(Refusal/NA)

Q186 [EPayWk]
Considering the number of hours you spend doing this other work, would you say the money you earn is on the high side, reasonable, or on the low side?
IF LOW: Very low or a bit low?

%	
20.3	Very low
19.8	A bit low
44.9	Reasonable
14.8	On the high side
-	Other answer (WRITE IN)
-	(Don't Know)
0.2	(Refusal/NA)

Q189 [EImpWk]
And if it were no longer possible for you to do this other work, how much would it matter to you? ...READ OUT ...
%
32.0 ...a lot,
26.6 a little,
41.2 or not at all?
\- (Don't Know)
0.2 (Refusal/NA)

n=233

Q190 [ETaxWk]
Would you still do this other work if you had to pay tax on your earnings, or do you already pay tax on them?
CODE ONE ONLY
%
69.0 Already pay tax
19.7 Yes - would still work
10.4 No - would not work
0.7 (It depends)
\- (Don't Know)
0.2 (Refusal/NA)

Q191 [EWhyWk]
CARD
On this card are some of the reasons that people give for having more than one job. Thinking of the job we have just been talking about, please choose the reason that best explains why you first started doing it.
%
21.2 I needed the money to get by
23.6 I wanted the money for extras
6.0 To learn new skills
1.6 To meet people
3.5 To keep up with old skills
19.3 I found it interesting
14.3 The chance just came up
10.4 Other reason (WRITE IN)
\- (Don't Know)
0.2 (Refusal/NA)

ASK ALL EMPLOYEES
Q194 [EDisPrb]
Now some questions about health problems and disabilities.
Firstly, do you have any health problems or disabilities which limit the kind of paid work you can do?
%
9.2 Yes
90.6 No
\- (Don't Know)
0.1 (Refusal/NA)

n=1568

ASK EMPLOYEES WHO HAVE HEALTH PROBLEM OR DISABILITY

n=147

Q195 [EDisTm]
Do you expect this health problem or disability to last for more than a year?
%
93.8 Yes
3.7 No
1.1 (Don't Know)
1.5 (Refusal/NA)

Q196 [EDisTyp]
CARD
Which of these health problems or disabilities do you have?
PROBE: Any others?
CODE ALL THAT APPLY
Multicoded (Maximum of 13 codes)
%
48.6 Problem or disability connected with your arms, legs, hands, feet, back or neck (including arthritis or rheumatism) [EDTArm]
10.3 Difficulty in seeing [EDTSee]
4.0 Difficulty in hearing [EDTHear]
11.7 Skin conditions or allergies [EDTSkin]
24.2 Chest or breathing problems, asthma, bronchitis [EDTChes]
9.3 Heart, blood pressure or blood circulation problems [EDTBloo]
5.1 Stomach, liver, kidney or digestive problems [EDTStom]
3.7 Diabetes [EDTDiab]
2.2 Depression, bad nerves [EDTDepr]
4.0 Epilepsy [EDTEpil]
0.7 Severe or specific learning difficulties (mental handicap) [EDTLDif]
2.2 Mental illness or phobia, panics or other nervous disorders [EDTMent]
6.6 Other health problems or disabilities (WRITE IN) [EDTOth]
\- (Don't know)
5.8 (Refusal/NA)

n=147

IF MORE THAN ONE CODED AT [EDisTyp]
[EDisWst]
CARD AGAIN
Q199 Which of these health problems or disabilities affects you the most?
%
9.5 Problem or disability connected with your arms, legs, hands, feet, back or neck (including arthritis or rheumatism)
0.8 Difficulty in seeing
1.1 Difficulty in hearing
1.8 Skin conditions or allergies
6.2 Chest or breathing problems, asthma, bronchitis
1.1 Heart, blood pressure or blood circulation problems
0.7 Stomach, liver, kidney or digestive problems
\- Diabetes
0.4 Depression, bad nerves
2.2 Epilepsy
1- Severe or specific learning difficulties (mental handicap)
1.8 Mental illness or phobia, panics or other nervous disorders
0.7 Other health problems or disabilities (WRITE IN)
\- (Don't know)
1.5 (Refusal/NA)

n=147

Q200 ASK EMPLOYEES WHO HAVE A HEALTH PROBLEM OR DISABILITY
[EDisAff]
CARD
On this card are some of the ways that health problems or disabilities can affect the sorts of **paid** work that people are able to do. Which of these, if any, apply to you?
Multicoded (Maximum of 11 codes)

%
- I cannot do any paid work at all [EDANoWk]
6.9 I cannot work full-time [EDANoFt]
6.6 I can be off work for 20 or more days a year [EDA20dy]
5.1 I have to stop work several times a day for 10 minutes or more [EDA10mi]
9.1 It can be difficult to travel to work [EDATrav]
4.4 I need help with my job at least some of the time [EDAHelp]
47.5 I cannot do certain types of job [EDATypJ]
2.6 I find it difficult to communicate effectively with other people [EDAComm]
1.5 I need special equipment to do my job [EDAEqui]
7.8 It is difficult for me to work in certain sorts of buildings [EDABui]
12.8 My health problem or disability causes other difficulties (WRITE IN) [EDAOth]
28.3 (None apply)
5.5 (Don't know)
7.3 (Refusal/NA)

n=1568

ASK ALL EMPLOYEES

Q203 [EDisPrj]
Generally speaking, do you think there is a lot of prejudice in Britain against people with disabilities, a little, hardly any, or none?

Q204 [EDisJob]
And when it comes to **getting a job**, do you think there is a lot of prejudice in Britain against people with disabilities, a little, hardly any, or none?

	[EDisPrj]	[EDisJob]
	%	%
A lot	35.7	45.2
A little	50.6	45.4
Hardly any	8.7	5.0
None	3.3	2.3
(Don't Know)	1.6	2.0
(Refusal/NA)	0.0	0.0

Q205 [EDisExp]
As far as you know, have you ever had a co-worker or colleague with a health problem or disability that limited the kind of paid work that they could do?
%
33.4 Yes
66.3 No
0.2 (Don't Know)
0.1 Refusal/NA

n=1568

Q206 IF 'Yes' AT [EDisExp]
[EDisHlp]
And did this co-worker or colleague have any special provision at work to help them do their job? This includes special equipment, adaptations or specific help from other colleagues or co-workers.
%
17.4 Yes
15.8 No
0.1 (Don't Know)
0.3 (Refusal/NA)

ASK ALL EMPLOYEES

Q207 [EDisCon]
IF 'Yes' AT [EDisExp]: And, as far as you know, do you have any other regular contact with anyone who has a health problem or disability that limits the kind of paid work that they can do?
IF 'No', 'Don't Know' OR 'Refusal/NA' AT [EDisExp]: And, as far as you know, do you have any regular contact with anyone who has a health problem or disability that limits the kind of paid work that they can do?
%
30.6 Yes
69.2 No
0.1 (Don't Know)
0.1 (Refusal/NA)

n=313

ASK ALL SELF-EMPLOYED (IF 'self-employed' AT [REmploye] (Q112))

Q208 [SSrJbTim]
In your present job, are you working ... READ OUT ...
RESPONDENT'S OWN DEFINITION
79.9 ... full-time,
19.4 or, part-time?
0.5 (Don't Know)
0.2 (Refusal/NA)

Q209 [SJbHours]
How many hours a week do you **normally** work in your (main) job?
IF RESPONDENT CANNOT ANSWER, ASK ABOUT LAST WEEK.
ROUND TO NEAREST HOUR
CODE 95 FOR 95+
Range: 10 ... 95
Median: 45 hours
0.5 (Don't Know)
0.2 (Refusal/NA)

Q210 [SJbHrCat] (NOT ON SCREEN)
SELF-EMPLOYED HOURS WORKED - CATEGORISED
%
7.0 10-15 hours a week
6.3 16-23 hours a week
4.0 24-29 hours a week
82.0 30 or more hours a week
0.5 (Don't Know)
0.2 (Refusal/NA)

n=313

Q211 [SUnemp1]
During the last five years – that is since May 1990 – have you been unemployed and seeking work for any period?

%
24.0 Yes
75.8 No
  - (Don't Know)
 0.2 (Refusal/NA)

IF 'Yes' AT [SUnemp]
Q212 [SUnempT]
For how many months in total during the last five years (have you been unemployed)?
ENTER NUMBER OF MONTHS
Range: 0 ... 60
Median: 6 months
0.3 (Don't Know)
0.2 (Refusal/NA)

ASK ALL SELF-EMPLOYED
Q213 [SEmplee]
Have you, for any period in the last five years, worked as an employee as your main job rather than as self-employed?

%
27.4 Yes
72.4 No
  - (Don't Know)
 0.2 (Refusal/NA)

IF 'Yes' AT [SEmplee]
Q214 [SEmpleeT]
In total for how many months during the last five years have you been an employee?
ENTER NUMBER OF MONTHS
Range: 1 ...60
Median: 24 months
0.3 (Don't Know)
0.2 (Refusal/NA)

IF 'No', 'Don't know' OR 'Refusal/NA' AT [SEmplee]
Q215 [SEmplSer]
How seriously in the last five years have you considered getting a job as an employee?... READ OUT ...

%
 4.1 ... very seriously,
 8.6 quite seriously,
 8.4 not very seriously,
51.3 or, not at all seriously?
  - (Business not in existence then)
 0.2 (Refusal/NA)

ASK ALL SELF-EMPLOYED
Q216 [Bus1OK]
Compared with a year ago, would you say your business is doing ... READ OUT ...

%
15.1 ... very well,
19.6 quite well,
46.9 about the same,
13.4 not very well,
 1.7 or, not at all well?
 3.1 (Business not in existence then)
 0.2 (Refusal/NA)

---

n=313

Q217 [Bus1Fut]
And over the coming year, do you think your business will do ... READ OUT ...

%
29.5 ... better,
53.8 about the same,
11.2 or, worse than this year?
 3.3 Other answer (WRITE IN)
 2.1 (Don't Know)
 0.2 (Refusal/NA)

Q220 [SPartnrs]
In your work or business, do you have any partners or other self-employed colleagues?
NOTE: DOES NOT INCLUDE EMPLOYEES

%
45.7 Yes, has partner(s)
54.1 No
  - (Don't Know)
 0.2 (Refusal/NA)

Q221 [SNumEmp]
And in your work or business, do you have any employees, or not?
NOTE: FAMILY MEMBERS MAY BE EMPLOYEES ONLY IF THEY RECEIVE A REGULAR WAGE OR SALARY

%
31.3 Yes, has employee(s)
68.5 No
  - (Don't Know)
 0.2 (Refusal/NA)

Q222 [SEmpEarn]
Now for some more general questions about your work. For some people their job is simply something they do in order to earn a living. For others it means much more than that. On balance, is your present job ... READ OUT ...

%
30.1 ... just a means of earning a living,
69.7 or, does it mean much more to you than that?
  - (Don't Know)
 0.2 (Refusal/NA)

IF 'a means of earning a living' AT [SEmpEarn]
Q223 [SEmpLiv]
Is that because ... READ OUT ...

%
 5.5 ... there are no better jobs around here,
 7.9 you don't have the right skills to get a better job,
14.7 or, because you would feel the same about any job you had?
 2.1 (Don't Know)
 0.2 (Refusal/NA)

ASK ALL SELF-EMPLOYED
Q224 [SPrefJob]
If without having to work, you had what you would regard as a reasonable living income, do you think you would still prefer to do paid work or wouldn't you bother?

%
67.8 still prefer paid job
28.3 Wouldn't bother
 3.5 Other answer (WRITE IN)
 0.5 (Don't Know)
 0.2 (Refusal/NA)

Q227 [SWkHrd]
CARD
Which of these statements best describes your feelings about your job? In my job :

%
8.3   I only work as hard as I have to
23.6   I work hard, but not so that it interferes with the rest of my life
67.6   I make a point of doing the best I can, even if it sometimes does interfere with the rest of my life
0.3   (Don't Know)
0.2   (Refusal/NA)

n=313

Q228 [SChkAge]
Can I just check, what was your age last birthday?
Range: 18 ... 97
Median: 43 years
0.5   (Don't Know)
0.2   (Refusal/NA)

ASK SELF-EMPLOYED BELOW FIVE YEARS ABOVE RETIREMENT AGE
Q229 [SRedun]
During the last two years - that is, since May 1993 - have you been made redundant?
%
3.3   Yes
96.5   No
-   (Don't Know)
0.2   (Refusal/NA)

n=310

ASK SELF-EMPLOYED WHO HAVE BEEN MADE REDUNDANT IN THE LAST TWO YEARS
Q230 [SRedPay]
Did you, or will you, receive any redundancy payments as a result of this?
Number
8   Yes
2   No
-   (Don't Know)
1   (Refusal/NA)

n=11

IF 'Yes' AT [SRedPay]
Q231 [SRedPyA]
How would you describe the amount of redundancy pay you received, or will receive - on the low side, reasonable, or on the high side?
IF LOW: Very low or a bit low?
Number
3   Very low
3   A bit low
2   Reasonable
1   On the high side
-   Other answer (WRITE IN)
-   (Don't Know)
1   (Refusal/NA)

ASK SELF-EMPLOYED WHO HAVE BEEN MADE REDUNDANT IN THE LAST TWO YEARS
Q234 [SRedFr]
All things considered, do you think your redundancy was handled fairly by you employer?
Number
5   Yes - handled fairly
5   No - not handled fairly
-   Other answer (WRITE IN)
1   (Refusal/NA)

n=11

ASK ALL SELF-EMPLOYED
Q237 [SOthWk]
At present, apart from your main job, do you ever do **any** other work for which you are paid?
%
13.5   Yes
86.3   No
-   (Don't Know)
0.2   (Refusal/NA)

n=313

ASK SELF-EMPLOYED WHO DO NOT HAVE A SECOND JOB
Q238 [SWdWk]
If you were offered some other work for 10 hours a week or less, and the earnings you would make were reasonable, how seriously would you consider it? ... **READ OUT** ...
%
12.7   ...very seriously,
16.8   fairly seriously,
10.5   not very seriously,
57.0   or, not at all seriously?
2.8   (It depends)
-   (Don't Know)
0.2   (Refusal/NA)

n=270

ASK SELF-EMPLOYED WHO HAVE A SECOND JOB
Q239 [SChkWk]
Did you do any of this work in the seven days ending last Sunday?
Number
24   Yes
19   No
-   (Don't Know)
1   (Refusal/NA)

n=43

Q240 [SFreqWk]
And do you do this other work ... **READ OUT** ...
IF MORE THAN ONE TYPE OF WORK DONE, ASK ABOUT MOST FREQUENT. IF EQUALLY FREQUENT, ASK ABOUT MOST RECENT.
Number
17   ...at least once a week,
11   at least once a month,
14   or less often?
-   (Don't Know)
1   (Refusal/NA)

Q241 *[SHrsWk]* (*[StimWk]* gives hours per month)
How many hours a (week/month/year) do you **normally** do this other work?
IF RESPONDENT CANNOT ANSWER, ASK ABOUT LAST WEEK/MONTH.
ROUND TO NEAREST HOUR.
Range: 1 .. 200
Median: 10 hours per month

Number
1 (Don't Know)
1 (Refusal/NA)

n=43

Q242 *[SPayWk]*
Considering the number of hours you spend doing this other work, would you say the money you earn is on the low side, reasonable, or on the high side?
IF LOW: Very low or a bit low?

Number
4 Very low
5 A bit low
25 Reasonable
7 On the high side
1 Other answer (**WRITE IN**)
- (Don't Know)
1 (Refusal/NA)

Q245 *[SImpWk]*
And if it was no longer possible for you to do this other work, how much would it matter to you? ... **READ OUT** ...

Number
12 ... a lot,
12 a little,
19 or not at all?
- (Don't Know)
1 (Refusal/NA)

Q246 *[STaxWk]*
Would you still do this other work if you had to pay tax on your earnings, or do you already pay tax on them?
CODE ONE ONLY

Number
27 Already pay tax
6 Yes - would still work
7 No - would not work
2 (It depends)
- (Don't Know)
1 (Refusal/NA)

Q247 *[SWhyWk]*
CARD
On this card are some of the reasons that people give for having more than one job. Thinking of the job we have just been talking about, please choose the reason that best explains why you **first** started doing it.

Number
9 I needed the money to get by
4 I wanted the money for extras
3 To learn new skills
3 To meet people
4 To keep up with old skills
12 I found it interesting
3 The chance just came up
3 Other reason (**WRITE IN**)
1 (Don't Know)
1 (Refusal/NA)

33

ASK ALL SELF-EMPLOYED
[SDisPrb]
Now some questions about health problems and disabilities.
Firstly, do you have any health problems or disabilities which limit the kind of paid work that you can do?

n=313

%
9.9 Yes
89.9 No
- (Don't Know)
0.2 (Refusal/NA)

Q250

ASK SELF-EMPLOYED WHO HAVE A HEALTH PROBLEM OR DISABILITY
Q251 *[SDisTm]*
Do you expect this health problem or disability to last for more than a year?
IF ALREADY LASTED FOR MORE THAN A YEAR, CODE 1.

n=32

Number
30 Yes
1 No
- (Don't Know)
1 (Refusal/NA)

Q252 *[SDisTyp]*
CARD
Which of these health problems or disabilities do you have?
PROBE: Any others?
CODE ALL THAT APPLY

Number
16 Multicoded (Maximum of 13 codes)
Problem or disability connected with your arms, legs, hands, feet, back or neck (including arthritis or rheumatism) *[SDTArm]*
3 Difficulty in seeing *[SDTSee]*
2 Difficulty in hearing *[SDTHear]*
3 Skin conditions or allergies *[SDTSkin]*
2 Chest or breathing problems, asthma, bronchitis *[SDTChes]*
7 Heart, blood pressure or blood circulation problems *[SDTBloo]*
3 Stomach, liver, kidney or digestive problems *[SDTStom]*
1 Diabetes *[SDTDiab]*
1 Depression, bad nerves *[SDTDepr]*
1 Epilepsy *[SDTEpil]*
- Severe or specific learning difficulties (mental handicap) *[SDTLDif]*
1 Mental illness or phobia, panics or other nervous disorders *[SDTMent]*
6 Other health problems or disabilities (**WRITE IN**) *[SDTOth]*
- (Don't know)
2 (Refusal/NA)

34

n=32

Q255   IF MORE THAN ONE CODED AT [SDisTyp]
[SDisWst]
CARD AGAIN
Which of these health problems or disabilities affects you
the most?

Number
4   Problem or disability connected with your arms, legs, hands,
       feet, back or neck (including arthritis or rheumatism)
1   Difficulty in seeing
1   Difficulty in hearing
2   Skin conditions or allergies
2   Chest or breathing problems, asthma, bronchitis
-      Heart, blood pressure or blood circulation problems
-      Stomach, liver, kidney or digestive problems
-      Diabetes
1   Depression, bad nerves
1   Epilepsy
-      Severe or specific learning difficulties (mental handicap)
-      Mental illness or suffer from phobia, panics or other
       nervous disorders
-      Other health problems or disabilities
1   (Don't Know)
1   (Refusal/NA)

Q256   ASK SELF-EMPLOYED WHO HAVE A HEALTH PROBLEM OR DISABILITY
[SDisAff]
CARD
On this card are some of the ways that health problems or
disabilities can affect the sorts of **paid** work that people
are able to do. Which of these, if any, apply to you?
PROBE: Any others?
CODE ALL THAT APPLY
Multicoded (Maximum of 11 codes)

Number
-      I cannot do any paid work at all [SDANoWk]
4   I cannot work full-time [SDANoFt]
2   I can be off work for 20 or more days a year [SDA20dy]
3   I have to stop work several times a day for 10 minutes
       or more [SDA10min]
-      It can be difficult to travel to work [SDATrav]
2   I need help with my job at least some of the time [SDAHelp]
19   I cannot do certain types of job [SDATyp]
1   I find it difficult to communicate effectively with other
       people [SDAComm]
1   I need special equipment to do my job [SDAEqui]
1   It is difficult for me to work in certain sorts of
       buildings [SDABuil]
1   My health problem or disability causes other difficulties
       (WRITE IN) [SDAOth]
3   (None apply)
-      (Don't know)
2   (Refusal/NA)

n=313

Q259   ASK ALL SELF-EMPLOYED
[SDisPrj]
Generally speaking, do you think there is a lot of
prejudice in Britain against people with disabilities, a
little, hardly any, or none?

n=313

Q260   [SDisJob]
And when it comes to **getting a job**, do you think there is
a lot of prejudice in Britain against people with
disabilities, a little, hardly any, or none?

	[SDisPrj]	[SDisJob]
	%	%
A lot	32.3	44.5
A little	50.6	47.0
Hardly any	8.6	5.0
None	7.2	2.6
(Don't Know)	1.2	0.9
(Refusal/NA)	0.2	0.2

Q261   [SDisExp]
As far as you know, have you ever had a co-worker or
colleague with a health problem or disability that limited
the kind of paid work that they could do?
%
25.9   Yes
74.0   No
-      (Don't Know)
0.2   (Refusal/NA)

            IF 'Yes' AT [SDisExp]
Q262   [SDisHlp]
And did this co-worker or colleague have any special
provision at work to help them do their job? This includes
special equipment, adaptations or specific help from other
colleagues and co-workers.
%
9.1   Yes
16.8   No
-      (Don't Know)
0.2   (Refusal/NA)

            ASK ALL SELF-EMPLOYED
Q263   [SDisCon]
IF 'Yes' AT [SDisExp]: And, as far as you know, do you
have any other regular contact with anyone who has a
health problem or disability that limits the kind of paid
work that they can do?
IF 'No', 'Don't Know' OR 'Refusal/NA' AT [SDisExp]: And,
as far as you know, do you have any regular contact with
anyone who has a health problem or disability that limits
the kind of paid work that they can do?
%
27.7   Yes
72.1   No
-      (Don't Know)
0.2   (Refusal/NA)

            ASK ALL LOOKING AFTER THE HOME (IF 'Looking after
            the home' AT [REconAct] (Q111))
Q264   [EverJob]
Have you, during the last five years, ever had a full- or
part-time job of 10 hours or more a week?
%
34.5   Yes
65.5   No
-      (Don't Know)
-      (Refusal/NA)

n=516

n=516

Q265 **IF 'No' AT [EverJob]**
[FtJobSer]
How seriously in the past five years have you considered getting a **full-time job?**
PROMPT, IF NECESSARY: Full-time is 30 or more hours a week
... **READ OUT** ...

Q266 **IF 'Not very seriously' OR 'Not at all seriously' AT [FtJobSer]**
[PtJobSer]
How seriously, in the past five years, have you considered getting a **part-time** job ... **READ OUT** ...

	[FtJobSer]	[PtJobSer]
	%	%
... very seriously,	3.4	1.8
quite seriously,	4.3	2.6
not very seriously,	4.2	5.1
or, not at all seriously?	53.6	48.3
(Don't Know)	-	-
(Refusal/NA)	-	-

n=205

ASK ALL UNEMPLOYED (IF 'Unemployed and registered', 'Unemployed, not registered' OR 'Unemployed, not actively looking' AT [REconAct] (Q111))
[UnempT]
Q267 In total how many months **in the last five years** - that is, since May 1990 - have you been unemployed and seeking work?
Range: 1 .. 60
Median: 24 months
1.6 (Don't Know)
- (Refusal/NA)

Q268 [CurUnemp]
How long has this **present** period of unemployment and seeking work lasted so far?
ENTER NUMBER THEN SPECIFY MONTHS OR YEARS
Range: 1 .. 60
Median: 12 months
0.5 (Don't Know)
- (Refusal/NA)

Q270 [JobQual]
How confident are you that you will find a job to match qualifications? ... **READ OUT** ...
%
13.9 very confident,
28.6 quite confident,
31.4 not very confident,
25.6 or, not at all confident?
0.5 (Don't Know)
- (Refusal/NA)

Q271 [UFindJob]
Although it may be difficult to judge, how long **from now** do you think it will be before you find an acceptable job?
ENTER NUMBER THEN SPECIFY MONTHS OR YEARS
CODE 96 FOR NEVER
Range: 1 ... 96
Median: 4 months
11.8 (Never)
28.8 (Don't Know)
- (Refusal/NA)

Q273 **IF 3 MONTHS OR MORE, NEVER OR DK**
[URetrain]
How willing do you think you would be in these circumstances to retrain for a different job ... **READ OUT** ...
%
34.5 ... very willing,
27.6 quite willing,
20.0 or, not very willing?
0.5 (Don't Know)
- (Refusal/NA)

ASK ALL UNEMPLOYED
Q274 [ConMove]
Have you ever **actually** considered moving to a different area - an area other than the one you live in now - to try to find work?
%
40.7 Yes
59.3 No
- (Don't Know)
- (Refusal/NA)

Q275 [UJobChnc]
Do you think that there is a real chance nowadays that you will get a job in this area, or is there **no real chance** nowadays?
%
48.3 Real chance
46.8 No real chance
5.0 (Don't Know)
- (Refusal/NA)

Q276 [UnemEarn]
For some people work is simply something they do in order to earn a living. For others it means much more than that.
In general, do you think of work as ... **READ OUT** ...
%
39.4 ... just a means of earning a living,
59.2 or, does it mean much more to you than that?
1.3 (Don't Know)
- (Refusal/NA)

Q277 **IF 'a means of earning a living' AT [UnemEarn]**
[UnempLiv]
Is that because ... **READ OUT**
%
14.0 ... there are no good jobs around here,
11.8 you don't have the right skills to get a good job,
13.4 or, because you would feel the same about **any** job you had?
0.3 (Don't Know)
1.3 (Refusal/NA)

n=661

ASK ALL RETIRED[1]
Q278 [REmplPen]
Do you receive a pension from any past employer?
%
54.3 Yes
45.0 No
0.1 (Don't Know)
0.6 (Refusal/NA)

Q279 [MsCheck][2]
May I just check, are you ... **READ OUT** ...
%
63.3 ... married,
36.4 or, not married?
0.1 (Don't Know)
0.2 (Refusal/NA)

IF 'married' AT [MsCheck]
Q280 [SEmplPen]
Does your (wife/husband) receive a pension from any past employer?
%
20.7 Yes
42.3 No
0.1 (Don't Know)
0.5 (Refusal/NA)

ASK ALL RETIRED
Q281 [PrPenGet]
And do you receive a pension from any **private** arrangements you have made in the past, that is **apart** from the state pension or one arranged through an employer?
%
8.0 Yes
91.2 No
0.1 (Don't Know)
0.7 (Refusal/NA)

IF 'married' AT [MsCheck]
Q282 [SPrPnGet]
And does your (wife/husband) receive a pension from any **private** arrangements (she/he) has made in the past, that is **apart** from the state pension or one arranged through an employer?
%
2.3 Yes
60.5 No
0.3 (Don't Know)
0.5 (Refusal/NA)

ASK ALL RETIRED[3]
Q283 [RetAge]
(Can I just check) are you over (65/60)?
%
86.2 Yes
12.3 No
1.5 (Don't Know)
(Refusal/NA)

[1] On Version C these questions were asked after the Classification section - see Q1023-1039.
[2] On Version C: derived from [Marstat]
[3] On Version C: derived from [RAge]

39

IF 'Yes' AT [RetAge]
Q284 [RPension]
On the whole would you say the present **state** pension is on the low side, reasonable, or on the high side?
IF 'ON THE LOW SIDE': Very low or a bit low?
%
40.9 Very low
25.5 A bit low
18.7 Reasonable
0.1 On the high side
0.6 (Don't Know)
1.8 (Refusal/NA)

Q285 [RPenInYr]
Do you expect your state pension in a year's time to purchase **more** than it does now, **less**, or about the **same**?
%
3.9 More
54.2 Less
25.6 About the same
2.3 (Don't Know)
1.6 (Refusal/NA)

ASK ALL RETIRED
Q286 [RetirAg2]
At what age did you retire from work?
NEVER WORKED, CODE: 00
Range: 0   80
Median: 60 years
1.8 (Never worked)
0.4 (Don't Know)
0.6 (Refusal/NA)

n=28

ASK ALL ON GOVERNMENT SCHEME (IF 'On government training/employment programme' AT [REconAct] (Q111))
Q287 [WgUnemp]
During the last five years - that is since May 1990 - have you been unemployed **and** seeking work for any period?
Number
16 Yes
12 No
- (Don't Know)
- (Refusal/NA)

Q288 [WgEarn]
For some people work is simply something they do in order to earn a living. For others it means much more than that. In general, do you think of earning a living ...
Number
9 ... just a means of earning a living,
16 or, does it mean much more to you than that?
2 (Don't Know)
1 (Refusal/NA)

IF 'a means of earning a living' AT [WgEarn]
Q289 [WgLiv]
Is that because ... **READ OUT**
Number
2 ... there are no good jobs around here,
1 you don't have the right skills to get a good job,
5 or, because you would feel the same about **any** job you had?
3 (Don't Know)
(Refusal/NA)

40

Q290 ASK ALL NOT IN PAID WORK (FOR 10+ HOURS A WEEK) (ALL EXCEPT 'in paid work', 'Don't Know', 'Refusal/NA' AT [REconAct] (Q111))   n=1752
[NPChkAge]
Can I just check, what was your age last birthday?
Range: 18 ... 97
Median: 58 years
- (Don't Know)
0.3 (Refusal/NA)

Q291 ASK ALL NOT IN PAID WORK (FOR 10+ HOURS A WEEK) BELOW RETIREMENT AGE PLUS 5 YEARS   n=1232
[NPRedun]
During the last two years - that is, since May 1993 - have you been made redundant?
%
6.6 Yes
93.2 No
- (Don't Know)
0.2 (Refusal/NA)

Q292 ASK THOSE NOT IN PAID WORK (FOR 10+ HOURS A WEEK) WHO HAVE BEEN MADE REDUNDANT IN LAST TWO YEARS   n=84
[NPRedPay]
Did you, or will you, receive any redundancy payments as a result of this?
%
54.5 Yes
41.7 No
- (Don't Know)
3.8 (Refusal/NA)

Q293 IF 'Yes' AT [NPRedPay]
[NPRedPyA]
How would you describe the amount of redundancy pay you received, or will receive - on the low side, reasonable, or on the high side?
IF LOW: Very low or a bit low?
%
17.9 Very low
6.4 A bit low
26.9 Reasonable
3.2 On the high side
3.8 Other answer (WRITE IN)
- (Don't Know)
- (Refusal/NA)

Q296 ASK THOSE NOT IN PAID WORK (FOR 10+ HOURS A WEEK) WHO HAVE BEEN MADE REDUNDANT IN LAST TWO YEARS
[NPRedFr]
All things considered, do you think your redundancy was handled fairly by your employer?
%
58.3 Yes - handled fairly
32.1 No - not handled fairly
7.1 Other answer (WRITE IN)
- (Don't Know)
2.6 (Refusal/NA)

Q299 ASK ALL NOT IN PAID WORK (FOR 10+ HOURS A WEEK)   n=1752
[NPOthWk]
At present, do you ever do any work for which you are paid?
%
12.2 Yes
87.6 No
- (Don't Know)
0.2 (Refusal/NA)

Q300 ASK THOSE NOT IN PAID WORK (FOR 10+ HOURS A WEEK) WHO DO NOT HAVE A JOB OF LESS THAN 10 HOURS   n=1538
[NPWkWk]
If you were offered some work for 10 hours a week or less, and the earnings you would make were reasonable, how seriously would you consider it? ... READ OUT
%
17.0 ...very seriously,
15.0 fairly seriously,
6.0 not very seriously,
58.2 or, not at all seriously?
3.5 (It depends)
0.2 (Refusal/NA)

Q301 ASK THOSE NOT IN PAID WORK (FOR 10+ HOURS A WEEK) WHO HAVE A JOB OF LESS THAN 10 HOURS   n=217
[NPChkSWk]
Did you do any of this work in the seven days ending last Sunday?
%
66.1 Yes
32.4 No
- (Don't Know)
1.5 (Refusal/NA)

Q302 [NPFreqWk]
And do you do this work ... READ OUT ...
IF MORE THAN ONE TYPE OF WORK DONE, ASK ABOUT MOST FREQUENT.
IF EQUALLY FREQUENT, ASK ABOUT MOST RECENT.
%
70.9 ...at least once a week,
11.5 at least once a month,
15.1 or less often?
1.0 (Don't Know)
1.5 (Refusal/NA)

Q303 [NPHrsWk] ([NPTimWk] gives hours per month)
How many hours a (week/month/year) do you normally do this work?
IF RESPONDENT CANNOT ANSWER, ASK ABOUT LAST WEEK/MONTH.
ROUND TO NEAREST HOUR.
Range: 1 ... 200
Median: 26 hours per month
5.2 (Don't Know)
1.5 (Refusal/NA)

Q304 [NPPayWk]   n=217
Considering the number of hours you spend doing this work, would you say the money you earn is on the low side, reasonable, or on the high side?
IF LOW: Very low or a bit low?
%
22.8 Very low
12.2 A bit low
51.1 Reasonable
11.3 On the high side
1.0 Other answer (WRITE IN)
- (Don't Know)
1.5 (Refusal/NA)

ASK THOSE NOT IN PAID WORK (FOR 10+ HOURS A WEEK) WHO HAVE A JOB OF LESS THAN 10 HOURS

Q307 [NPImpWk]
And if it was no longer possible for you to do this work, how much would it matter to you? ... READ OUT ...
%
50.6 ...a lot,
27.7 a little,
20.2 or not at all?
- (Don't Know)
1.5 (Refusal/NA)

Q308 [NPTaxWk]
Would you still do this work if you had to pay tax on your earnings, or do you already pay tax on them?
CODE ONE ONLY
%
30.2 Already pay tax
30.1 Yes - would still work
33.3 No - would not work
3.7 (It depends)
0.7 (Don't Know)
2.0 (Refusal/NA)

ASK ALL NOT IN PAID WORK (FOR 10+ HOURS A WEEK)   n=1752

Q309 [NPDisPrb]
Now some questions about health problems and disabilities. Firstly, do you have any health problems or disabilities which limit the kind of paid work that you can do?
%
39.8 Yes
60.0 No
- (Don't Know)
0.2 (Refusal/NA)

ASK THOSE NOT IN PAID WORK (FOR 10+ HOURS A WEEK) WHO HAVE A HEALTH PROBLEM OR DISABILITY   n=701

Q310 [NPDisTm]
Do you expect this health problem or disability to last for more than a year?
IF ALREADY LASTED FOR MORE THAN A YEAR, CODE 1.
%
94.7 Yes
3.8 No
1.0 (Don't Know)
0.5 (Refusal/NA)

Q311 [NPDisTyp]   n=701
CARD
Which of these health problems or disabilities do you have?
PROBE: Any others?
CODE ALL THAT APPLY
Multicoded (Maximum of 13 codes)
%
60.7 Problem or disability connected with your arms, legs, hands, feet, back or neck (including arthritis or rheumatism) [NPDTArm]
15.9 Difficulty in seeing [NPDTSee]
12.2 Difficulty in hearing [NPDTHear]
6.5 Skin conditions or allergies [NPDTSkin]
23.9 Chest or breathing problems, asthma, bronchitis [NPDTChes]
33.5 Heart, blood pressure or blood circulation problems [NPDTBloo]
11.8 Stomach, liver, kidney or digestive problems [NPDTStom]
7.8 Diabetes [NPDTDiab]
8.6 Depression, bad nerves [NPDTDepr]
1.8 Epilepsy [NPDTEpil]
1.2 Severe or specific learning difficulties (mental handicap) [NPDTLDif]
3.3 Mental illness or phobia, panics or other nervous disorders [NPDTMent]
10.9 Other health problems or disabilities (WRITE IN) [NPDTOth]
- (Don't know)
5.5 (Refusal/NA)

IF MORE THAN ONE CODED AT [NPDisTyp]
Q314 [NPDisWst]
CARD AGAIN
Which of these health problems or disabilities affects you the most?
%
21.5 Problem or disability connected with your arms, legs, hands, feet, back or neck (including arthritis or rheumatism)
4.2 Difficulty in seeing
0.7 Difficulty in hearing
1.1 Skin conditions or allergies
7.9 Chest or breathing problems, asthma, bronchitis
7.9 Heart, blood pressure or blood circulation problems
1.4 Stomach, liver, kidney or digestive problems
1.5 Diabetes
2.1 Depression, bad nerves
0.1 Epilepsy
- Severe or specific learning difficulties (mental handicap)
0.5 Mental illness or suffer from phobia, panics or other nervous disorders
3.3 Other health problems or disabilities
0.5 (Don't Know)
0.7 (Refusal/NA)

Q315   **ASK THOSE NOT IN PAID WORK (FOR 10+ HOURS A WEEK)**   [n=701]
       WHO HAVE A HEALTH PROBLEM OR DISABILITY
       [NPDisAff]
       CARD
       On this card are some of the ways that health problems or disabilities can affect the sorts of **paid** work that people are able to do. Which of these, if any, apply to you?
       PROBE: Any others?
       CODE ALL THAT APPLY
       Multicoded (Maximum of 11 codes)

%	
45.7	I cannot do any paid work at all *[NPDANoWk]*
13.8	I cannot work full-time *[NPDANoFt]*
5.6	I can be off work for 20 or more days a year *[NPDA20dy]*
8.7	I have to stop work several times a day for 10 minutes or more *[NPDA10mi]*
6.0	It can be difficult to travel to work *[NPDATrav]*
1.2	I need help with my job at least some of the time *[NPDAHelp]*
23.9	I cannot do certain types of job *[NPDATypJ]*
1.5	I find it difficult to communicate effectively with other people *[NPDAComm]*
1.8	I need special equipment to do my job *[NPDAEqui]*
3.3	It is difficult for me to work in certain sorts of buildings *[NPDABui]*
7.8	My health problem or disability causes other difficulties (WRITE IN) *[NPDAOth]*
14.6	(None apply)
4.8	(Don't know)
5.5	(Refusal/NA)

Q318   **ASK ALL NOT IN PAID WORK (FOR 10+ HOURS A WEEK)**   [n=1752]
       [NPDisPrj]
       Generally speaking, do you think there is a lot of prejudice in Britain against people with disabilities, a little, hardly any, or none?

Q319   *[NPDisJob]*
       And when it comes to **getting a job**, do you think there is a lot of prejudice in Britain against people with disabilities, a little, hardly any, or none?

	[NPDisPrj]	[NPDisJob]
	%	%
A lot	32.3	44.6
A little	46.4	44.8
Hardly any	11.9	4.9
None	6.6	2.5
(Don't Know)	2.7	3.1
(Refusal/NA)	0.1	0.1

Q320   *[NPDisExp]*
       As far as you know, have you ever had a co-worker or colleague with a health problem or disability that limited the kind of paid work that they could do?

%	
19.3	Yes
80.1	No
0.6	(Don't Know)
0.1	(Refusal/NA)

Q321   **IF 'Yes' AT [NPDisExp]**   [n=1752]
       [NPDisHlp]
       And did this co-worker or colleague have any special provision at work to help them do their job? This includes special equipment, adaptations or specific help from other colleagues and co-workers.

%	
7.9	Yes
11.1	No
0.2	(Don't Know)
0.7	(Refusal/NA)

Q322   **ASK ALL NOT IN PAID WORK (FOR 10+ HOURS A WEEK)**
       [NPDisCon]
       IF 'Yes' AT [NPDisExp]: And, as far as you know, do you have any other regular contact with anyone who has a health problem or disability that limits the kind of paid work that they can do?
       IF 'No', 'Don't Know' OR 'Refusal/NA' AT [NPDisExp]: And, as far as you know, do you have any regular contact with anyone who has a health problem or disability that limits the kind of paid work that they can do?

%	
26.8	Yes
72.9	No
0.2	(Don't Know)
0.1	(Refusal/NA)

FEAR OF CRIME (VERSIONS A AND B)

n=2434

VERSION A AND B: ASK ALL

[Victim]

Q326 Now some questions about crime. Do you ever worry about the possibility that you or anyone else who lives with you might be the victim of crime?

%
81.1 Yes
18.7 No
0.1 (Don't Know)
0.0 (Refusal/NA)

IF 'Yes' AT [Victim]

[VmWorry]

Q327 Is this ... READ OUT ...

%
28.0 ... a big worry,
34.9 a bit of a worry,
18.2 or - an occasional doubt?
 - (Don't Know)
0.2 (Refusal/NA)

VERSIONS A AND B: ASK ALL

[VicAtt5]

Q328 And now some questions about crimes that may have happened to you.

THE CRIME MAY HAVE HAPPENED MORE THAN ONCE OR SEVERAL CRIMES MAY HAVE HAPPENED ON THE SAME OCCASION.

In the past five years have you yourself been physically attacked?

Q329 [VicThr5]
(In the past five years have you yourself ...) ...been threatened?

Q330 [VicHmB5]
(In the past five years have you yourself ...) ... had your home burgled?

Q331 [VicCar5]
(In the past five years have you yourself ...) ...had a car belonging to you or another family member stolen, or had things stolen from a car?

Q332 [VicVan5]
(In the past five years have you yourself ...) ... had your home or a car damaged by vandals?

Q333 [VicOth5]
(In the past five years have you yourself ...) ... had something else stolen?

	[VicAtt5]	[VicThr5]	[VicHmB5]	[VicCar5]	[VicVan5]	[VicOth5]
	%	%	%	%	%	%
Yes	7.3	16.5	17.4	45.8	39.0	21.6
No	92.7	83.4	82.5	54.1	60.9	78.4
(Don't Know)	0.0	0.0	0.0	0.0	0.0	0.0
(Refusal/NA)	0.0	0.0	0.0	0.0	0.0	0.0

Q334 [VicNum]
(NOT ON SCREEN - DERIVED FROM [VicAtt5] to [VicOth5])
Number of types of victimisation

%
28.8 None
26.4 One
23.6 Two
13.0 Three
6.2 Four
1.4 Five
0.5 Six
0.1 Missing information

Q335 [AreaCrim]
Compared with the rest of Britain, how much crime would you say there is in your area ...READ OUT ...
IF ASKED WHAT WE MEAN BY 'AREA', SAY 'IT IS WHAT YOU THINK OF AS YOUR AREA'

%
12.9 ... a lot more in your area,
13.4 a bit more,
31.3 about the same,
26.8 a bit less,
14.3 or - a lot less in your area?
1.2 (Don't Know)
0.0 (Refusal/NA)

Q336 [AreaCrN]
And compared to two years ago would you say there is now ... READ OUT ...
IF ASKED WHAT WE MEAN BY 'AREA', SAY 'IT IS WHAT YOU THINK OF AS YOUR AREA'

%
21.1 ... a lot more crime in your area,
33.0 a bit more crime,
35.3 about the same,
5.6 a bit less crime,
1.2 or - a lot less crime in your area?
2.3 (Have lived in area less than 2 years)
0.0 (Don't Know)
0.0 (Refusal/NA)

Q337 [GoPolice]
During the past two years, have you ever reported a crime or accident to the police or gone to them for help?

%
43.9 Yes
56.0 No
0.1 (Don't Know)
0.0 (Refusal/NA)

IF 'Yes' AT [GoPolice]

Q338 [PCHelp]
On those occasions, how helpful have you found them in the way they dealt with you ... READ OUT ...

%
17.1 ... very helpful,
16.4 fairly helpful,
5.8 fairly unhelpful,
3.8 or - very unhelpful?
0.7 (Varied)
0.0 (Don't Know)
0.2 (Refusal/NA)

n=2434

Q339 **VERSIONS A AND B: ASK ALL**
[PCStop]
During the past two years, have you ever been stopped or asked questions by the police about an offence which they thought had been committed?
%
15.0 Yes
84.9 No
0.0 (Don't Know)
0.0 (Refusal/NA)

IF 'Yes' AT [PCStop]
Q340 *[PCPolite]*
On those occasions, how polite have you found them when they approached you ... **READ OUT** ...
%
7.5 ... very polite,
4.5 fairly polite,
1.2 fairly impolite,
1.6 or - very impolite?
0.1 (Varied)
- (Don't Know)
0.1 (Refusal/NA)

Q341 **VERSIONS A AND B: ASK ALL**
[PCArEff]
CARD
Taking everything into account, how effective would you say the police are in preventing crime in **your area**?
IF ASKED WHAT WE MEAN BY 'AREA', SAY 'IT IS WHAT YOU THINK OF AS YOUR AREA'

Q342 *[PCGBEff]*
CARD AGAIN
And in general, how effective would you say the police in Britain **as a whole** are in preventing crime?

	[PCArEff]	[PCGBEff]
	%	%
Very effective	7.1	5.6
Fairly effective	46.6	47.1
Not very effective	36.6	39.0
Not at all effective	6.5	5.7
(It depends)	0.6	1.2
(Don't Know)	2.5	1.2
(Refusal/NA)	0.0	0.1

Q343 *[PCContct]*
May I just check, have you, or someone you know, had any contact at all with the police in the past **two years**?
%
63.2 Yes
36.7 No
0.1 (Don't Know)
0.0 (Refusal/NA)

n=2434

Q344 *[NWSFav]*
CARD
Some people think that Neighbourhood Watch Schemes, that is schemes where neighbours get together to keep an eye on each other's properties, are a good way of preventing crime. Others say that we should leave this to the police. How much are you in favour of or against the idea of Neighbourhood Watch Schemes?
%
29.4 Strongly in favour
47.8 In favour
17.0 Neither in favour nor against
4.0 Against
1.3 Strongly against
0.5 (Don't Know)
0.0 (Refusal/NA)

Q345 *[NWSEff]*
CARD
And how effective do you think these schemes are as a way of preventing crime?
%
13.7 Very effective
58.8 Fairly effective
20.8 Not very effective
2.9 Not at all effective
1.2 (It depends)
2.5 (Don't Know)
0.1 (Refusal/NA)

Q346 *[NWSArea]*
Has a Neighbourhood Watch Scheme ever been set up in **your area** covering your address?
IF ASKED WHAT WE MEAN BY 'AREA', SAY 'IT IS WHAT YOU THINK OF AS YOUR AREA'
%
36.6 Yes
59.9 No
3.5 (Don't Know)
0.0 (Refusal/NA)

IF 'Yes' AT [NWSArea]
[NWSHHMb]
Q347 Do you consider your household to be a member of this scheme?
%
24.7 Yes
9.4 No
2.1 Scheme no longer operating
0.4 (Don't Know)
3.5 (Refusal/NA)

IF 'No', 'Don't know' or 'Refusal/NA' AT [NWSArea]
[NWSJoin]
Q348 Would you personally join a Neighbourhood Watch Scheme if there was one in **your area**?
IF ASKED WHAT WE MEAN BY 'AREA', SAY 'IT IS WHAT YOU THINK OF AS YOUR AREA'
%
46.7 Yes
14.2 No
2.5 (Don't Know)
0.0 (Refusal/NA)

Q349 **VERSIONS A AND B: ASK ALL**
[PatrlFav]
CARD
Some people think the general public should take a more active role in preventing crime such as by setting up 'street watch schemes', of local residents. Others say we should leave this to the police. How much are you in favour of or against the idea of such 'street watch schemes'?

%	
9.8	Strongly in favour
34.5	In favour
25.0	Neither in favour nor against
23.3	Against
6.4	Strongly against
1.0	(Don't Know)
0.0	(Refusal/NA)

Q350 [PatrlEff]
CARD
And how effective do you think a local 'street watch scheme' would be in preventing crime in **your area**?
IF ASKED WHAT WE MEAN BY 'AREA', SAY 'IT IS WHAT YOU THINK OF AS YOUR AREA'

%	
9.1	Very effective
46.2	Fairly effective
31.1	Not very effective
7.9	Not at all effective
2.4	(It depends)
3.4	(Don't Know)
0.0	(Refusal/NA)

Q351 [PatrlPrt]
And if a 'street watch scheme' were set up in **your area**, how likely would you **yourself** be to take part? Would you be ... **READ OUT** ...
IF ASKED WHAT WE MEAN BY 'AREA', SAY 'IT IS WHAT YOU THINK OF AS YOUR AREA'

%	
14.8	... very likely,
29.7	fairly likely,
24.7	not very likely,
27.0	or - not at all likely?
2.8	(It depends)
0.9	(Don't Know)
0.0	(Refusal/NA)

Q352 [SecurFav]
CARD
Some people say residents should be allowed to get together and hire **private** security patrols to help prevent crime in their area. How much are you in favour of or against this?

%	
3.9	Strongly in favour
16.8	In favour
23.4	Neither in favour nor against
33.8	Against
21.3	Strongly against
0.8	(Don't Know)
0.0	(Refusal/NA)

51

n=2434

Q353 [SecurEff]
CARD
And how effective do you think **private** security patrols would be in preventing crime in **your area**?
IF ASKED WHAT WE MEAN BY 'AREA', SAY 'IT IS WHAT YOU THINK OF AS YOUR AREA'

%	
8.7	Very effective
39.3	Fairly effective
31.5	Not very effective
13.1	Not at all effective
3.5	(It depends)
3.8	(Don't Know)
0.0	(Refusal/NA)

Q354 [SecurPrt]
CARD
And if a **private** security patrol were set up here, how much would you **yourself** be prepared to pay toward the costs each year?

%	
52.1	Nothing at all
13.1	Less than £10 a year
16.6	£10 or more but less than £25 a year
7.6	£25 or more but less than £50 a year
4.2	£50 or more but less than £100 a year
1.2	£100 or more a year
3.3	(It depends)
1.2	(Don't Know)
0.0	(Refusal/NA)

Q355 [SpConFav]
CARD AND READ OUT
In many police forces now, **uniformed unpaid volunteer** Special Constables are used to help patrol villages and local neighbourhoods. They do this in their spare time but have the same powers of arrest as any other police officer. These officers are called either Parish Constables or Neighbourhood Constables. How much are you in favour of or against the idea of using Parish or Neighbourhood Constables to help patrol their local area in their spare time?

%	
26.9	Strongly in favour
48.0	In favour
13.2	Neither in favour nor against
7.2	Against
3.7	Strongly against
0.9	(Don't Know)
0.0	(Refusal/NA)

Q356 [SpConEff]
CARD
And how effective do you think Parish or Neighbourhood Constables would be in preventing crime in **your area**?
IF ASKED WHAT WE MEAN BY 'AREA', SAY 'IT IS WHAT YOU THINK OF AS YOUR AREA'

%	
18.1	Very effective
58.5	Fairly effective
15.9	Not very effective
3.8	Not at all effective
1.4	(It depends)
2.4	(Don't Know)
0.0	(Refusal/NA)

n=2434

52

CONSTITUTIONAL ISSUES (VERSION A)

n=1253

VERSION A: ASK ALL

Q361 [Coalitin]
Which of the following do think is **generally** better for Britain ... **READ OUT** ...

%
45.5 ... to have a government formed by one political party
50.4 or, for two or more parties to get together to form a government?
4.1 (Don't Know)
0.1 (Refusal/NA)

Q362 [VoteSyst]
Some people say that we should change the voting system to allow smaller political parties to get a fairer share of MPs. Others say that we should keep the voting system as it is, to produce more effective government. Which view comes closest to your own ... **READ OUT** ...
IF ASKED, REFERS TO 'PROPORTIONAL REPRESENTATION'

%
37.4 ... that we should change the voting system,
58.1 or, keep it as it is?
4.5 (Don't Know)
- (Refusal/NA)

Q363 [Monarchy]
Now some questions about the monarchy or the royal family in Britain. Firstly, how important or unimportant do you think it is for Britain to continue to have a monarchy ... **READ OUT** ...

%
30.5' ... very important,
35.1 quite important,
18.2 not very important,
6.9 not at all important,
8.8 or, do you think the monarchy should be abolished?
0.6 (Don't Know)
- (Refusal/NA)

Q364 [RoyFamN]
Which do you think would be best for Britain now ... **READ OUT** ...

%
77.5 ... to continue to have the Queen,
19.7 or instead, to have a President elected by all the people every five years or so?
2.8 (Don't Know)
- (Refusal/NA)

IF 'to continue to have Queen' AT [RoyFamN]

Q365 [RoyFamF]
And what about when the present Queen's reign ends? Which do you think would be best for Britain then? Do you think Britain should .. **READ OUT** ...

%
66.8 ... continue to have a king or a queen who inherits the job by birth,
9.2 or instead, have a President elected by all the people every five years or so?
1.4 (Don't Know)
2.8 (Refusal/NA)

---

n=1253

VERSION A: ASK ALL

Q366 [ECGBCise]
Now a few questions about Britain's relationship with the European Union (sometimes still called the European Community). As a member state, would you say that Britain's relationship with the European Union should be ... **READ OUT** ...

%
29.2 ... closer,
26.3 less close,
38.6 or, is it about right?
5.9 (Don't Know)
0.0 (Refusal/NA)

Q367 [ECLnkInf]
Do you think that closer links with the European Union would give Britain ... **READ OUT** ...

%
26.8 ... **more** influence in the world,
17.1 **less** influence in the world,
50.7 or, would it make no difference?
5.4 (Don't Know)
0.0 (Refusal/NA)

Q368 [ECLnkStr]
And would closer links with the European Union make Britain ... **READ OUT** ...

%
32.2 ... **stronger** economically,
20.2 **weaker** economically,
38.6 or, would it make no difference?
9.0 (Don't Know)
0.0 (Refusal/NA)

Q369 [NIreland]
Do you think the long-term policy for Northern Ireland should be for it... **READ OUT** ...

%
28.5 ... to remain part of the United Kingdom,
51.9 or, to reunify with the rest of Ireland?
0.9 (Northern Ireland should be an independent state)
- (Northern Ireland should be split up into two)
6.2 (It should be up to the Irish to decide)
2.6 Other answer (**WRITE IN**)
9.8 (Don't Know)
0.1 (Refusal/NA)

Q372 [DecFutNI]
And who do you think should have the right to decide what the long-term future of Northern Ireland should be? Should it be... **READ OUT** ...

%
34.5 ... the people in Northern Ireland on their own,
45.2 or, the people of Ireland, both north and south,
16.1 or, the people both in Northern Ireland and in Britain
1.3 (Britain, Northern Ireland and the Irish Republic all three together)
0.5 Other answer (**WRITE IN**)
2.5 (Don't Know)
- (Refusal/NA)

n=1253

Q375 [TroopOut]
Some people think that government policy towards Northern Ireland should include a complete withdrawal of British troops. Would you personally **support** or **oppose** such a policy?
IF 'SUPPORT' OR 'OPPOSE', PROBE: Strongly or a little?

%
38.5 Support strongly
24.7 Support a little
11.5 Oppose a little
16.8 Oppose strongly
0.3 (Troops should be withdrawn in the long-term but not immediately)
0.4 (It should be up to the Irish to decide)
2.3 Other answer (WRITE IN)
5.4 (Don't Know)
- (Refusal/NA)

Q378 [Nation]
On the whole, do you think Britain's interests are better served by ... READ OUT ...

%
46.4 ... closer links with Western Europe,
20.4 or ... closer links with America?
20.6 (Both equally)
6.6 (Neither)
6.6 (Don't Know)
0.0 (Refusal/NA)

Q379 [UniteEC]
Which of these comes closer to your views ... READ OUT ...
31.6 ... Britain should do all it can to unite fully with the European Union,
59.8 or, Britain should do all it can to protect its independence from the European Union?
8.4 (Don't Know)
0.1 (Refusal/NA)

Q380 [ECPolicy]
CARD
Do you think Britain's long-term policy should be ...
READ OUT ...
CODE ONE ONLY
13.6 ... to leave the European Union,
23.3 to stay in the EU and try to **reduce** its powers,
20.3 to leave things as they are,
28.4 to stay in the EU and try to **increase** its powers,
8.1 or, to work for the formation of a single European government?
6.3 (Don't Know)
0.0 (Refusal/NA)

Q381 [EcuView]
CARD
And here are three statements about the future of the pound in the European Union. Which **one** comes closest to your view?
CODE ONE ONLY
18.1 **Replace** the pound by a single currency
17.5 Use **both** the pound and a new European currency in Britain
61.9 **Keep** the pound as the **only** currency for Britain
2.5 (Don't Know)
- (Refusal/NA)

---

n=1253

EDUCATION (VERSION A)

VERSION A: ASK ALL

Q386 [EdSpend1]
CARD
Now some questions about education. Which of the groups on this card, if any, would be your highest priority for **extra** government spending on education?
ONE CODE ONLY FOR **HIGHEST** PRIORITY

Q387 [EdSpend2]
CARD AGAIN
And which is your next highest priority?
ONE CODE ONLY FOR **NEXT HIGHEST**

	[EdSpend1]	[EdSpend2]
	%	%
Nursery or pre-school children	20.6	10.9
Primary school children	17.5	24.9
Secondary school children	32.2	19.7
Less able children with special needs	18.8	25.9
Students at colleges or universities	8.5	15.9
(None of these)	0.7	0.6
(Don't Know)	1.6	1.9
(Refusal/NA)	-	0.1

Q388 [PrimImp1]
CARD
Here are a number of things that some people think would improve education in our schools. Which do you think would be the **most** useful one for improving the education of children in **primary** schools - aged 5-11 years? Please look at the whole list before deciding.
CODE ONE ONLY

Q391 [PrimImp2]
CARD AGAIN
And which do you think would be the **next** most useful one for children in **primary** schools?
CODE ONE ONLY

	[PrimImp1]	[PrimImp2]
	%	%
More information available about individual schools	0.6	1.2
More links between parents and schools	8.8	11.0
More resources for buildings, books and equipment	18.7	27.5
Better quality teachers	15.8	12.7
Smaller class sizes	36.3	20.3
More emphasis on exams and tests	1.4	3.7
More emphasis on developing the child's skills and interests	15.6	21.3
Other (WRITE IN)	1.3	0.6
(Don't Know)	1.6	1.8
(Refusal/NA)	-	-

n=1253

Q394 [SecImp1]
CARD
And which do you think would be the **most** useful thing for improving the education of children in **secondary** schools - aged 11-18 years?
CODE ONE ONLY

Q397 [SecImp2]
CARD AGAIN
And which do you think would be the **next** most useful one for children in **secondary** schools?
CODE ONE ONLY

	[SecImp1] %	[SecImp2] %
More information available about individual schools	0.5	1.3
More links between parents and schools	3.9	5.6
More resources for buildings, books and equipment	18.4	19.7
Better quality teachers	19.0	9.8
Smaller class sizes	20.8	14.1
More emphasis on exams and tests	6.2	8.5
More emphasis on developing the child's skills and interests	12.8	17.4
More training and preparation for jobs	14.8	20.9
Other (**WRITE IN**)	1.1	0.3
(Don't Know)	2.4	2.5
(Refusal/NA)	-	-

Q400 [SchSelec]
Which of the following statements comes closest to your views about what kind of **secondary** school children should go to?
%
48.1 Children should go to a different kind of secondary school, according to how well they do at primary school
49.1 All children should go to the same kind of secondary school, no matter how well or badly they do at primary school
2.7 (Don't Know)
- (Refusal/NA)

Q401 [Advise16]
Suppose you were advising a 16 year old about their future. Would you say they should ... **READ OUT** ...
%
52.6 ... stay on in full-time education to get their GCE 'A' levels,
12.4 or, study full-time to get vocational, rather than academic, qualifications,
12.4 or, leave school and get training through a job?
22.2 (Varies/depends on the person)
0.5 (Don't Know)
- (Refusal/NA)

n=1253

Q402 [VocVAcad]
In the long-run, which do you think gives people more opportunities and choice in life ... **READ OUT** ...
%
43.0 ...having good practical skills and training,
31.7 or, having good academic results?
24.8 (Mixture/depends)
0.6 (Refusal/NA)
-

Q403 [PrivSch]
Generally speaking, what is your opinion about private schools in Britain? Should there be ... **READ OUT** ...
%
7.2 ...more private schools,
59.9 about the same number as now,
15.4 fewer private schools,
14.4 or no private schools at all?
3.1 (Don't Know)
0.1 (Refusal/NA)

Q404 [PrivEfct]
If there were **fewer** private schools in Britain today do you think, on the whole, that state schools would ... **READ OUT** ...
%
23.1 ...benefit,
18.1 suffer,
55.6 or would it make no difference?
3.2 (Don't Know)
0.1 (Refusal/NA)

Q405 [PrivPart]
Some people think private schools have an important part to play in the British education system. Others think they should not be allowed. What about you? Do you think private schools should ... **READ OUT** ...
%
38.6 ... definitely be allowed,
39.8 probably be allowed,
9.3 probably not be allowed,
10.4 or, definitely not be allowed?
1.8 (Don't Know)
0.2 (Refusal/NA)

Q406 [SegEdBoy]
If you had to advise an 11 year old **boy** on what sort of school he should go to, would you suggest a single-sex or a mixed-sex school?
%
18.3 Single-sex
73.4 Mixed-sex
5.7 (No preference)
2.2 (It depends)
0.3 (Don't Know)
0.1 (Refusal/NA)

IF 'single-sex' AT [SegEdBoy]

Q407 [SingleBo]
Is this because ... **READ OUT** ...
%
12.5 ...you think boys do better at their school work at single-sex schools,
4.9 boys are happier to be with other boys at that age,
0.8 or, for some other reason (**WRITE IN**)?
0.0 (Don't Know)
0.3 (Refusal/NA)

n=1253

Q410 **IF 'Mixed-sex' AT [SegEdBoy]**
[SegEdBoy]
Is this because ... **READ OUT** ...

2.6   ...you think boys do better at their school work at mixed sex schools,
69.4 boys and girls should learn to mix with each other,
1.2   or, for some other reason (**WRITE IN**)?
0.1   (Don't Know)
0.3   Refusal/NA)

VERSION A: ASK ALL

Q413 [SegEdGrl]
And what if you had to advise an 11 year old **girl** on what sort of school she should go to? Would you suggest a single-sex or a mixed-sex school?

%
21.9 Single-sex
70.5 Mixed-sex
5.1   [No preference]
2.2   (It depends)
0.2   (Don't Know)
0.1   (Refusal/NA)

Q414 **IF 'Single-sex' AT [SegEdGrl]**
[SingleGr]
Is this because ... **READ OUT** ...

16.7 ...you think girls do better at their school work at single sex schools,
3.9   girls are happier to be with other girls at that age,
1.1   or, for some other reason (**WRITE IN**)?
0.3   (Don't Know)

Q417 **IF 'Mixed-sex' AT [SegEdGrl]**
[MixedGrl]
Is this because ... **READ OUT** ...

2.0   ...you think girls do better at their school work at mixed sex schools,
67.5 boys and girls should mix with each other,
0.7   or, for some other reason (**WRITE IN**)?
0.2   (Don't Know)
0.3   (Refusal/NA)

VERSION A: ASK ALL

Q420 [HEdOpp]
Do you feel that opportunities for young people in Britain to go on to **higher education** - to a university or college - should be increased or reduced, or are they at about the right level now?
IF INCREASED OR REDUCED: a lot or a little?

28.2 Increased a lot
18.8 Increased a little
47.5 About right
2.6   Reduced a little
0.6   Reduced a lot
2.3   (Don't Know)
0.1   (Refusal/NA)

n=1253

Q421 [HEFees]
At present, British university students get their **teaching** fees paid by their Local Authorities. Do you think that students should ... **READ OUT** ...

%
24.0 ... pay something towards their own teaching fees,
72.7 or, should Local Authorities continue to pay the whole amount?
3.1   (Don't Know)
0.2   (Refusal/NA)

Q422 [HEGrant]
And, at present, some full-time British university students get grants to help cover their **living** costs. Getting a grant depends upon the student's circumstances and those of their family. Do you think that ... **READ OUT** ...

%
30.2 ..**all** students should get grants to help cover their living costs,
64.8 **some** students should get grants to help cover their living costs, as now,
1.5   or, that no grants should be given to help cover students' living costs?
2.0   (It depends)
1.4   (Don't Know)
0.1   (Refusal/NA)

Q423 [HELoan]
Many full-time university students are now taking out government loans to help cover their living costs. They have to start repaying these loans when they begin working. Generally speaking, do you think that ... **READ OUT** ...

%
25.6 ..students **should** be expected to take out loans to help cover their living costs,
64.3 or, students **should not** be expected to take out loans to help cover living costs?
7.7   (It depends)
2.4   (Don't Know)
0.1   (Refusal/NA)

DRUGS (VERSION A)

VERSION A: ASK ALL

Q427 [HerUsNow]
I'd like to ask you some questions about illegal drug-use in Britain. First, thinking about the drug **heroin** ... Do you think there are **more** people taking heroin in Britain now than there were 5 years ago, **less**, or about the **same** number?

%
70.8 More now
3.3 Less now
16.4 About the same number
- Other answer (**WRITE IN**)
9.3 (Don't Know)
0.2 (Refusal/NA)

Q430 [HerCrime]
CARD
And how much do you agree or disagree that ... heroin is a cause of crime and violence?

Q431 [HeroinOK]
CARD AGAIN
(How much do you agree or disagree that ...) heroin isn't nearly as damaging to users as some people think?

Q432 [HerLegAd]
CARD AGAIN
(How much do you agree or disagree that ...) if you legalise heroin many more people will become addicts?

Q433 [HerUsePr]
CARD AGAIN
(How much do you agree or disagree that ...) people should **not** be prosecuted for possessing small amounts of heroin for their own use?

Q434 [HerSelPr]
CARD AGAIN
(How much do you agree or disagree that ...) people who **sell** heroin should always be prosecuted?

	[HerCrime]	[HeroinOK]	[HerLegAd]	[HerUsePr]	[HerSelPr]
	%	%	%	%	%
Strongly agree	57.6	2.7	37.2	5.2	81.9
Agree	32.0	6.2	34.6	15.6	13.3
Neither agree nor disagree	5.5	7.3	8.1	7.5	1.7
Disagree	2.8	35.3	14.2	37.5	0.7
Strongly disagree	0.3	41.4	2.7	32.4	1.1
(Don't Know)	1.6	6.9	3.0	1.6	1.2
(Refusal/NA)	0.2	0.2	0.2	0.2	0.2

Q435 [HerLegal]
CARD
Which of these statements comes closest to your own view?
%
1.4 Taking heroin should be legal, without restrictions
10.4 Taking heroin should be legal, but it should only be available from licensed shops
86.2 Taking heroin should remain illegal
1.9 (Don't Know)
0.2 (Refusal/NA)

Q436 [CanUsNow]
Now thinking about the drug **cannabis** ...Do you think there are **more** people taking cannabis in Britain now than there were 5 years ago, **less**, or about the **same** number?
%
66.0 More
2.7 Less
22.4 About the same number
0.0 Other answer (**WRITE IN**)
8.7 (Don't Know)
0.2 (Refusal/NA)

Q439 [CanUsFut]
Do you think there will be **more**, **less**, or about the **same** number of people taking cannabis in Britain in 5 years' time compared with now?
%
66.3 More in 5 years
4.1 Less
22.3 About the same number
7.1 (Don't Know)
0.2 (Refusal/NA)

Q440 [CanYoung]
Do you think cannabis is mainly used just by young people nowadays?
%
37.2 Yes
53.7 No
9.0 (Don't Know)
0.2 (Refusal/NA)

Q441 [CanSelf]
And have you yourself **ever tried** cannabis?
%
20.5 Yes
78.1 No
1.1 (Don't Know)
0.3 (Refusal/NA)

IF 'Yes' AT [CanSelf]
Q442 [CanFreq]
Have you tried it often, occasionally, hardly ever or only once?
%
2.7 often
5.5 Occasionally
5.7 Hardly ever
6.6 Only once
0.1 Other answer (**WRITE IN**)
1.4 (Refusal/NA)

n=1253

n=1253

VERSION A: ASK ALL

Q445 [CanCrime]
CARD
How much do you agree or disagree that ... cannabis is a cause of crime and violence?

Q446 [CannabOK]
CARD AGAIN
(How much do you agree or disagree that ...) cannabis isn't nearly as damaging as some people think?

Q447 [CanLegAd]
CARD AGAIN
(How much do you agree or disagree that ...) if you legalise cannabis many more people will become addicts?

Q448 [CanUsePr]
CARD AGAIN
(How much do you agree or disagree that ...) people should not be prosecuted for possessing small amounts of cannabis for their own use?

Q449 [CanSelPr]
CARD AGAIN
(How much do you agree or disagree that ...) people who sell cannabis should always be prosecuted?

	[CanCrime]	[CannabOK]	[CanLegAd]	[CanUsePr]	[CanSelPr]
	%	%	%	%	%
Strongly agree	22.0	5.5	22.1	11.0	47.4
Agree	28.9	27.0	37.6	29.9	31.0
Neither agree nor disagree	18.4	16.6	9.6	7.3	7.8
Disagree	22.0	30.3	23.1	34.4	9.8
Strongly disagree	5.7	12.5	4.9	14.6	2.6
(Don't Know)	2.7	7.9	2.4	2.7	1.3
(Refusal/NA)	0.2	0.2	0.2	0.2	0.2

Q450 [CanLegal]
CARD
Which of these statements comes closest to your own view?
%
5.7 Taking cannabis should be legal, without restrictions
27.6 Taking cannabis should be legal, but it should only be available from licensed shops
64.3 Taking cannabis should remain illegal
2.3 (Don't Know)
0.2 (Refusal/NA)

n=1253

NORTHERN IRELAND (VERSION A)

VERSION A: ASK ALL

Q455 [PrejRC]
Now I would like to ask some questions about religious prejudice against both Catholics and Protestants in Northern Ireland. First thinking of Catholics - do you think there is a lot of prejudice against them in Northern Ireland nowadays, a little, or hardly any?

Q456 [PrejProt]
And now thinking of Protestants - do you think there is a lot of prejudice against them in Northern Ireland nowadays, a little, or hardly any?

	[PrejRC]	[PrejProt]
	%	%
A lot	41.8	34.8
A little	38.1	41.7
Hardly any	5.4	9.1
(Don't Know)	14.2	13.9
(Refusal/NA)	0.5	0.5

Q457 [SrRlPrej]
How would you describe yourself ... READ OUT ...
%
0.4 ... as very prejudiced against people of other religions,
10.7 a little prejudiced,
87.3 or, not prejudiced at all?
0.6 Other answer (WRITE IN)
0.5 (Don't Know)
0.4 (Refusal/NA)

Q460 [RIRelAgo]
What about relations between Protestants and Catholics in Northern Ireland? Would you say they are better than they were 5 years ago, worse, or about the same now as then?
IF 'IT DEPENDS', PROBE BEFORE CODING 'Other'
%
57.0 Better
2.6 Worse
32.9 About the same
0.2 Other answer (WRITE IN)
6.9 (Don't Know)
0.4 (Refusal/NA)

Q463 [RIRelFut]
And what about in 5 year's time? Do you think relations between Protestants and Catholics will be better than now, worse than now, or about the same as now?
IF 'IT DEPENDS', PROBE BEFORE CODING 'Other'
%
55.9 Better than now
2.1 Worse than now
32.6 About the same
0.9 Other answer (WRITE IN)
8.1 (Don't Know)
0.4 (Refusal/NA)

n=1253

Q466 [RelgAlwy]
Do you think that religion will **always** make a difference to the way people feel about each other in Northern Ireland?
%
84.2 Yes
10.4 No
2.1 Other answer (**WRITE IN**)
2.9 (Don't Know)
0.4 (Refusal/NA)

Q469 [OwnMxSch]
If you were deciding where to send your children to school, would you prefer a school with children of **only** your own religion, or a **mixed-religion** school?
PROBE IF NECESSARY : Say if you **did** have school-age children...
%
18.1 Own religion only
78.1 Mixed-religion school
3.4 (Don't Know)
0.4 (Refusal/NA)

Q470 [BrtIrSde]
When there is an argument between Britain and the Republic of Ireland, do you generally find yourself on the side of the British or of the Irish government?
IF 'IT DEPENDS', PROBE BEFORE CODING
%
52.2 Generally British government
8.5 Generally Irish government
17.3 It depends (**AFTER PROBE**)
17.6 (Neither)
4.1 (Don't Know)
0.4 (Refusal/NA)

Q471 [UntdIrel]
At any time in the next 20 years, do you think it is likely or unlikely that there will be a united Ireland?
PROBE: Very likely/unlikely or quite likely/unlikely?
%
9.7 Very likely
47.6 Quite likely
22.1 Quite unlikely
11.8 Very unlikely
3.1 (Even chance)
5.6 (Don't Know)
0.2 (Refusal/NA)

Q472 [GovIntNI]
CARD
Under direct rule from Britain, as now, how much do you generally trust **British governments** of **any** party to act in the best interests of Northern Ireland?
CODE ONE ONLY

Q473 [StrIntNI]
CARD AGAIN
If there was self-rule, how much do you think you would trust a **Belfast government** to act in the best interests of Northern Ireland?
CODE ONE ONLY

n=1253

Q474 [IreIntNI]
CARD AGAIN
And if there was a united Ireland, how much do you think you would generally trust an **Irish government** to act in the best interests of Northern Ireland?
CODE ONE ONLY

	[GovIntNI]	[StrIntNI]	[IreIntNI]
	%	%	%
Just about always	4.3	8.1	7.0
Most of the time	29.4	43.7	44.7
Only some of the time	46.2	27.8	30.8
Rarely	11.2	9.4	7.5
Never	3.1	2.1	1.5
(Don't Know)	5.6	8.6	8.2
(Refusal/NA)	0.3	0.3	0.4

HOUSING

n=3633

ASK ALL

Q718 [HomeType]
Now a few questions on housing.
INTERVIEWER CODE FROM OBSERVATION AND CHECK WITH RESPONDENT
Would I be right in describing this accommodation as a ...
READ OUT ONE YOU THINK APPLIES

%
21.7   ... detached house or bungalow,
36.1   ... semi-detached house or bungalow,
27.2   ... terraced house,
10.5   ... self-contained, purpose-built flat/maisonette (inc. in tenement block),
3.5   ... self-contained converted flat/maisonette,
0.6   ... room(s), not self-contained
0.0   Other answer (WRITE IN)
0.1   (Don't Know)
        (Refusal/NA)

Q722 [HomeEst]
May I just check, is your home part of a housing estate?
NOTE: MAY BE PUBLIC OR PRIVATE, BUT IT IS THE RESPONDENT'S VIEW WE WANT

%
41.6   Yes, part of estate
58.0   No
0.4   (Don't Know)
0.1   (Refusal/NA)

Q723 [Tenure1]
Does your household own or rent this accommodation?
PROBE IF NECESSARY
IF OWNS: Outright or on a mortgage?
IF RENTS: From whom?

%
26.0   OWNS: Own (leasehold/freehold) outright
42.5   OWNS: Buying (leasehold/freehold) on mortgage
17.7   RENTS: Local authority
0.4   RENTS: New Town Development Corporation
3.2   RENTS: Housing Association
0.7   RENTS: Property company
1.0   RENTS: Employer
1.2   RENTS: Other organisation
0.5   RENTS: Relative
5.6   RENTS: Other individual
0.3   RENTS: Housing Trust
0.5   Rent free, squatting, etc.
0.2   (Don't Know)
0.2   (Refusal/NA)

VERSION C: ASK ALL

n=1199

Q725 [CounTxB]
What is the council tax band of the (house/flat) ?
IF RESPONDENT IS NOT SURE: ACCEPT A GUESS IF POSSIBLE, ELSE CODE DON'T KNOW

%
15.8   Band A
15.5   Band B
16.0   Band C
14.8   Band D
6.9   Band E
3.7   Band F
1.8   Band G
0.9   Band H
24.1   (Don't Know)
0.4   (Refusal/NA)

ASK ALL

n=3633

Q726 [Move3Yrs]
Have you moved home in the last three years?

%
24.4   Yes
72.5   No
0.0   (Don't Know)
0.1   (Refusal/NA)

IF 'Yes' AT [Move3Yrs]

Q727 [MoveFar]
CARD
How far away is your present address from where you lived before? Please choose an answer from this card.

%
7.2   1 mile or less
7.3   More than 1 mile but no more than 5 miles
4.3   More than 5 miles but no more than 20 miles
2.5   More than 20 miles but no more than 100 miles
3.1   More than 100 miles
-       (Don't Know)
0.1   (Refusal/NA)

RELIGION AND ETHNIC ORIGIN

n=3633

ASK ALL
[Religion]

Q733   Do you regard yourself as belonging to any particular religion?

IF YES: Which?

CODE ONE ONLY - DO NOT PROMPT

%	
40.4	No religion
4.9	Christian - no denomination
8.9	Roman Catholic
31.9	Church of England/Anglican
3.6	Baptist
1.1	Methodist
3.4	Presbyterian/Church of Scotland
0.1	Other Christian
0.7	Hindu
0.4	Jewish
1.6	Islam/Muslim
0.4	Sikh
0.1	Buddhist
0.2	Other non-Christian
0.0	Free Presbyterian
0.0	Brethren
0.5	United Reform Church (URC)/Congregational
1.7	Other Protestant
0.0	(Don't Know)
0.1	(Refusal/NA)

IF NOT 'Refusal/NA' AT *[Religion]*
[FamRelig]

Q741   In what religion, if any, were you brought up?

PROBE IF NECESSARY: What was your family's religion?

CODE ONE ONLY - DO NOT PROMPT

%	
8.9	No religion
4.0	Christian - no denomination
12.8	Roman Catholic
54.0	Church of England/Anglican
1.6	Baptist
7.2	Methodist
5.0	Presbyterian/Church of Scotland
0.2	Other Christian
0.7	Hindu
0.5	Jewish
1.8	Islam/Muslim
0.5	Sikh
0.2	Buddhist
0.0	Other non-Christian
0.1	Free Presbyterian
0.1	Brethren
0.7	United Reform Church (URC)/Congregational
1.4	Other Protestant
0.2	(Don't Know)
0.1	(Refusal/NA)

IF RELIGION GIVEN AT EITHER *[Religion]* OR *[FamRelig]*   n=3633
[ChAttend]

Q749   Apart from such special occasions as weddings, funerals and baptisms, how often nowadays do you attend services or meetings connected with your religion?

PROBE AS NECESSARY.

%	
11.5	Once a week or more
2.3	Less often but at least once in two weeks
5.5	Less often but at least once a month
10.5	Less often but at least twice a year
6.6	Less often but at least once a year
4.1	Less often
50.7	Never or practically never
0.5	Varies too much to say
-	(Don't Know)
-	(Refusal/NA)

ASK ALL
[RaceOrig]

Q750   To which of these groups do you consider you belong?

CARD

CODE ONE ONLY

%	
1.6	**BLACK:** of African or Caribbean or other origin
1.3	**ASIAN:** of Indian origin
0.6	**ASIAN:** of Pakistani origin
0.3	**ASIAN:** of Bangladeshi origin
0.2	**ASIAN:** of Chinese origin
0.4	**ASIAN:** of other origin (WRITE IN)
90.0	**WHITE:** of British origin
3.1	**WHITE:** of Irish origin
1.8	**WHITE:** of other origin (WRITE IN)
0.5	**MIXED ORIGIN (WRITE IN)**
0.0	(Don't Know)
0.1	(Refusal/NA)

CLASSIFICATION

ASK ALL
Q763 [MarStat]
Can I just check whether at present you are ... READ OUT
...
CODE FIRST TO APPLY
%
59.4 ...married,
6.4   living as married,
7.4   separated or divorced after marrying,
8.2   widowed,
18.5 or not married?
0.0   (Don't Know)
0.0   (Refusal/NA)

Q765 [Household]
Finally, a few questions about you and your household.
Including yourself, how many people live here regularly as members of this household ?
CHECK INTERVIEWER MANUAL FOR DEFINITION OF HOUSEHOLD IF NECESSARY.
%
15.1 One person
34.3 Two people
20.6 Three people
19.9 Four people
6.8   Five people
2.3   Six people
0.5   Seven people
0.1   Eight people
0.1   Nine people
0.2   Ten people
0.1   Twelve people

HOUSEHOLD GRID: QUESTIONS [PerNo] TO [LegalR] ARE ASKED ONCE FOR EACH HOUSEHOLD MEMBER

[Name] (NOT ON DATA FILE)
FIRST PERSON IN GRID: Please type in the first name of respondent
SECOND AND SUBSEQUENT PERSONS IN GRID: Please type in the name of person number (number)
Open Question (Maximum of 10 characters)

IF SECOND AND SUBSEQUENT PERSONS IN GRID
[P2Sex-P12Sex]
PLEASE CODE SEX OF (Name)
Male
Female

IF (FIRST PERSON IN GRID AND NO AGE RECORDED AT [EChAge] OR [SChAge] OR [NFChAge]) OR IF SECOND AND SUBSEQUENT PERSONS IN GRID
[RAge], [P2Age-P12Age]
FIRST PERSON IN GRID: Now I'd like to ask you a few details about each person in your household. Starting with yourself, what was your age last birthday?
SECOND AND SUBSEQUENT PERSONS IN GRID: PLEASE ENTER AGE OF (Name)
PLEASE ENTER AGE OF (Name)
Range: 1 ... 97
Median: 44 years (refers to [RAge])
0.0   (Don't Know)
0.2   (Refusal/NA)

PLEASE ENTER RELATIONSHIP OF (Name) TO RESPONDENT
[P2Rel]-[P12Rel]
Partner/spouse/cohabitee
Son/daughter (inc. step/adopted)
Parent/ parent-in-law
Other relative
Other non-relative
(Don't Know)
(Refusal/NA)

IF FIRST PERSON OR IF PERSONS AGED 16 OR OVER AT [P2Age] etc.
[RResp], [P2Resp]-[P12Resp]
(Are you/Is he/she) legally responsible for the accommodation?
(INCLUDE JOINT/SHARED RESPONSIBILITY)
Yes
No
(Don't Know)
(Refusal/NA)

END OF HOUSEHOLD GRID

ASK ALL
Q887 [OthChld2]
Apart from any children who live here now, have you ever been responsible for bringing up any (other) children including stepchildren?
%
39.2 Yes
60.8 No
-     (Don't Know)
-     (Refusal/NA)

Q888 [RPrivEd]
Have you ever attended a fee-paying, private primary or secondary school in the United Kingdom?
NOTE: 'PRIVATE' INCLUDES INDEPENDENT PUBLIC SCHOOLS, BUT EXCLUDES DIRECT GRANT SCHOOLS, VOLUNTARY-AIDED SCHOOLS AND 'OPTED OUT' GRANT-MAINTAINED SCHOOLS (AS ALL OF THESE ARE/ WERE NOT 'FEE PAYING'). IT ALSO EXCLUDES NURSERY SCHOOLS

Q889 IF 'married' OR 'living as married' AT [MarStat]
[SPrivEd]
Has your (wife/husband/partner) ever attended a fee-paying,
private primary or secondary school in the United Kingdom?
**NOTE: 'PRIVATE' INCLUDES INDEPENDENT PUBLIC SCHOOLS, BUT
EXCLUDES DIRECT GRANT SCHOOLS, VOLUNTARY-AIDED SCHOOLS AND
'OPTED OUT' GRANT-MAINTAINED SCHOOLS (AS ALL OF THESE
ARE/WERE NOT 'FEE PAYING'). IT ALSO EXCLUDES NURSERY
SCHOOLS**

IF RESPONDENT HAS CHILDREN AGED 5 OR OVER (AS GIVEN
IN HOUSEHOLD GRID) OR ANSWERED 'Yes' AT [OthChid2]
Q890 *[ChPrivEd]*
And (have any of your children/has your child) ever
attended a fee-paying private primary or secondary school
in United Kingdom?
**NOTE: 'PRIVATE' INCLUDES INDEPENDENT PUBLIC SCHOOLS, BUT
EXCLUDES DIRECT GRANT SCHOOLS, VOLUNTARY-AIDED SCHOOLS AND
'OPTED OUT' GRANT-MAINTAINED SCHOOLS (AS ALL OF THESE
ARE/WERE NOT 'FEE PAYING'). IT ALSO EXCLUDES NURSERY
SCHOOLS**

VERSION C: IF 'Yes' AT [ChPrivEd]   n=1199
Q891 *[ChPEdNow]*
(Are any of your children/is your child) attending a
fee-paying private primary or secondary school in the
United Kingdom at present?
**INCLUDE IF ON SCHOOL HOLIDAY.
NOTE: 'PRIVATE' INCLUDES INDEPENDENT / PUBLIC SCHOOLS [not
'DIRECT GRANT', as these were/are not 'fee-paying'] BUT
EXCLUDES NURSERY SCHOOLS, VOLUNTARY-AIDED SCHOOLS AND
'OPTED OUT' GRANT-MAINTAINED SCHOOLS.**

	[RPrivEd]	[SPrivEd]	[ChPrivEd]	[ChPEdNow]
	%	%	%	%
Yes	10.7	5.7	7.2	1.1
No	89.3	60.0	56.3	4.7
(Don't Know)	-	0.1	0.0	-
(Refusal/NA)	-	0.0	-	0.0

ASK ALL   n=3633
[TEA]
Q892 How old were you when you completed your continuous
full-time education? **PROBE IF NECESSARY**
%
40.1 15 or under
26.5 16
8.7   17
13.5 18
0.4   19 or over
2.6   Still at school
0.1   Still at college or university
0.0   Other answer **(WRITE IN)**
0.0   (Don't Know)
0.1   (Refusal/NA)

73

Q895 *[SchQual]*
CARD
Have you passed any of the examinations on this card?
%
55.7 Yes
44.1 No
0.1   (Don't Know)
0.1   (Refusal/NA)

IF 'Yes' AT [SchQual]
Q896 Which ones? **PROBE: Any others?
CODE ALL THAT APPLY**
%   Multicoded (Maximum of 16 codes)
      CSE Grades 2-5   *[EdQual1]*
17.9 GCSE Grades D-G

      CSE-Grade 1
      GCE 'O'level
      GCE - Grades A-C
44.1 School certificate
      Scottish (SCE) Ordinary
      Scottish School-leaving Certificate lower grade
      SUPE Ordinary
      Northern Ireland Junior Certificate   *[EdQual2]*

      GCE 'A'level/'S'level
      Higher school certificate
19.7 Matriculation
      Scottish SCE/SLC/SUPE at Higher grade
      Northern Ireland Senior Certificate   *[EdQual3]*

1.2   Overseas school leaving exam or certificate   *[EdQual4]*

0.1   (Don't know)
0.1   (Refusal/NA)

ASK ALL
[PSchQual]
CARD
Q901 And have you passed any of the exams or got any of the
qualifications on **this** card?
%
49.6 Yes
50.2 No
0.1   (Don't Know)
0.1   (Refusal/NA)

74

n=3633

Q902   **IF 'Yes' AT [PSchQual]**
Which ones? PROBE: Any others?
CODE ALL THAT APPLY
Multicoded (Maximum of 12 codes)
%
5.9   Recognised trade apprenticeship **completed** [EdQual5]
11.0 RSA/other clerical, commercial qualification [EdQual6]
9.5   City & Guilds Certificate - Craft/Intermediate/Ordinary/ Part I [EdQual7]
5.9   City & Guilds Certificate - Advanced/Final/ Part II or Part III [EdQual8]
2.0   City & Guilds Certificate - Full technological [EdQual9]
5.5   BEC/TEC General/Ordinary National Certificate (ONC) or Diploma (OND) [EdQual10]
3.5   BEC/TEC Higher/Higher National Certificate (HNC) or Diploma (HND) [EdQual11]
3.2   Teacher training qualification [EdQual12]
3.0   Nursing qualification [EdQual13]
5.0   University or CNAA degree or diploma [EdQual14]
9.6   Other recognised academic or vocational qualification (WRITE IN) [EdQual15]
7.8   Other technical or business qualification/certificate [EdQual16]
-     (Don't know)
0.1   (Refusal/NA)

IF NOT 'in paid work' OR 'waiting to take up paid work' AT [REconAct] (Q111)
[JobChk]
Q923   Have you **ever** had a job?
%
45.0 Yes
2.8   No, never
-     (Don't Know)
0.1   (Refusal/NA)

n=3532

ASK ALL WHO HAVE EVER WORKED (IF 'in paid work' OR 'waiting to take up paid work' AT [REconAct] (Q111) OR 'Yes' AT [JobChk])
[RTitle] **(NOT ON DATA FILE)**
Q924   **IF 'in paid work' AT [REconAct]**: Now I want to ask you about your present job. What is your job? **PROBE IF NECESSARY:** What is the name or title of the job?

IF 'waiting to take up paid work' AT [REconAct]: Now I want to ask you about your future job. What is your job? **PROBE IF NECESSARY:** What is the name or title of the job?

IF EVER HAD JOB ('yes' AT [JobChk]): Now I want to ask you about your last job. What was your job? **PROBE IF NECESSARY:** What was the name or title of the job?
Open Question (Maximum of 50 characters)

Q925   [RTypeWk]   **(NOT ON DATA FILE)**
What kind of work (do/will/did) you do most of the time?
IF RELEVANT: What materials/machinery (do/will/did) you use?
Open Question (Maximum of 50 characters)

Q926   [RTrain]   **(NOT ON DATA FILE)**
What training or qualifications (are/were) needed for that job?
Open Question (Maximum of 50 characters)

n=3532

Q927   [RSuper2]
(Do/Will/Did) you directly supervise or (are you/will you be/were you) directly responsible for the work of any other people?
%
37.0 Yes
62.8 No
0.0   (Don't Know)
0.1   (Refusal/NA)

Q928   **IF 'Yes' AT [RSuper2]**
[RMany]
How many?
Range: 0 ... 9997
Median (of those supervising any): 5
0.3   (Don't Know)
0.2   (Refusal/NA)

ASK ALL WHO HAVE EVER WORKED
Q929   [RSupMan]
Can I just check, (are you/will you be/were you) ...
READ OUT ...
%
18.5 ... a manager,
14.5 a foreman or supervisor,
66.9 or not?
0.0   (Don't Know)
0.1   (Refusal/NA)

Q930   [REmployee]
Can I just check, (are you/will you be/were you) ...
READ OUT ...
%
87.0 ... an employee
12.8 or, self-employed?
0.0   (Don't Know)
0.1   (Refusal/NA)

Q931   **IF 'employee' OR 'Don't Know' AT [REmployee]**
[Premises]
(Is/Was) where you (work/will work/worked) your employer's **only** premises, or (are/were) there other premises elsewhere?
%
24.6 Employer's only premises
61.9 Employer has other premises elsewhere
0.5   (Don't Know)
0.1   (Refusal/NA)

ASK ALL WHO HAVE EVER WORKED (NOT ON DATA FILE)
Q932   [REmpMake]
What (does/did) your employer (IF SELF EMPLOYED: you) make or do at the place where you usually (work/will work/worked) (from)?
Open Question (Maximum of 50 characters)

Q933 [REmpWork]
Including yourself, how many people (are/were) employed at the place where you usually (work/will work/worked) (from)?
IF SELF-EMPLOYED: (Do/Will/Did) you have any employees?
IF YES: PROBE FOR CORRECT PRECODE

n=3532

%	
4.4	None
20.8	Under 10
15.3	10-24
21.4	25-99
21.2	100-499
15.6	500 or more
1.1	(Don't Know)
0.2	(Refusal/NA)

Q934 [RPartFul]
(Is/Was) the job ... READ OUT ...

77.0	...full-time (30+ HOURS)
22.8	or, part-time (10-29 HOURS)?
0.1	(Don't Know)
0.1	(Refusal/NA)

ASK ALL

n=3633

Q953 [UnionSA]
(May I just check) are you now a member of a trade union or staff association?
CODE FIRST TO APPLY

Q954 IF 'No' AT [UnionSA]
[TUSABver]
Have you ever been a member of a trade union or staff association?
CODE FIRST TO APPLY

	[UnionSA]	[TUSABver]
	%	%
Yes, trade union	18.4	26.3
Yes, staff association	3.4	3.1
No	78.0	48.5
(Don't Know)	0.1	0.1
(Refusal/NA)	0.1	0.2

ASK ALL WHO ARE 'married' OR 'living as married' AT [MarStat] (Q763)

n=2393

Q955 [SEconAct]
CARD
Which of these descriptions applied to what your (wife/husband/partner) was doing last week, that is the seven days ending last Sunday? PROBE: Any others?
CODE ALL THAT APPLY

Partner's economic activity:

%	
0.5	In full-time education (not paid for by employer, including on vacation)
0.2	On government training/employment programme (e.g. Employment Training, Youth Training, etc.)
57.5	In paid work (or away temporarily) for at least 10 hours in week
0.2	Waiting to take up paid work already accepted
3.7	Unemployed and registered at a benefit office
0.9	Unemployed, not registered, but actively looking for a job
0.5	Unemployed, wanting a job (of at least 10 hrs a week), but not actively looking for a job
4.0	Permanently sick or disabled
15.8	Wholly retired from work
15.5	Looking after the home
0.9	(Doing something else) (WRITE IN)
-	(Don't Know)
0.2	(Refusal/NA)

IF PARTNER IS NOT IN PAID WORK

Q959 [SLastJob]
How long ago did your (wife/husband/partner) last have a paid job of at least 10 hours a week?
GOVERNMENT PROGRAMS / SCHEMES DO NOT COUNT AT 'PAID JOBS'

%	
5.3	Within past 12 months
11.2	Over 1, up to 5 years ago
8.9	Over 5, up to 10 years ago
8.0	Over 10, up to 20 years ago
5.7	Over 20 years ago
2.1	Never had a paid job of 10+ hours a week
0.3	(Don't Know)
0.5	(Refusal/NA)

ASK ALL WHOSE PARTNER HAS EVER WORKED

n=2342

[STitle] (NOT ON DATA FILE)

Q960 IF 'in paid work' AT [SEconAct]: Now I want to ask you about your (wife's/husband's/partner's) present job. What is (her/his) job? PROBE IF NECESSARY: What is the name or title of the job?

IF 'waiting to take up paid work' AT [SEconAct]: Now I want to ask you about your (wife's/husband's/partner's) future job. What is (her/his) job? PROBE IF NECESSARY: What is the name or title of the job?

IF EVER HAD JOB ('yes' AT [SLastJob]): Now I want to ask you about your (wife's/husband's/partner's) last job. What was (her/his) job? PROBE IF NECESSARY: What was the name or title of the job?

Open Question (Maximum of 50 characters)

n=2342

Q961 *[STypeWk]* **(NOT ON DATA FILE)**
What kind of work *(do/will/did)* *(she/he)* do most of the time?
IF RELEVANT: What materials/machinery *(do/will/did)* *(she/he)* use?
Open Question (Maximum of 50 characters)

Q962 *[STrain]* **(NOT ON DATA FILE)**
What training or qualifications *(are/were)* needed for that job?
Open Question (Maximum of 50 characters)

Q963 *[SSuper2]*
(Do/Will/Did) *(she/he)* directly supervise or *(is/will/was)* *(she/he)* directly responsible for the work of any other people?
%
37.5 Yes
60.7 No
0.8 (Don't Know)
1.0 (Refusal/NA)

Q964 IF 'Yes' AT [SSuper2]
[SMany]
How many?
Range: 0 ... 9997
Median (of those who supervise any): 6
3.2 (Don't know)
1.8 (Refusal/NA)

ASK ALL WHOSE PARTNER HAS EVER WORKED
Q965 *[SSupMan]*
Can I just check, *(is/will/was)* *(she/he)* ... **READ OUT** ...
%
21.2 ...a manager,
13.5 a foreman or supervisor,
63.7 or not?
0.5 (Don't Know)
1.0 (Refusal/NA)

Q966 *[SEmploye]*
Can I just check, *(is/will/was)* *(she/he)* ... **READ OUT** ...
%
84.0 ... an employee,
14.8 or, self-employed?
0.3 (Don't Know)
1.0 (Refusal/NA)

Q967 *[SEmpMake]* **(NOT ON DATA FILE)**
What *(does/did)* the employer **(IF SELF EMPLOYED**: *(she/he))*
make or do at the place where *(she/he)* usually *(works/will work/worked)* *(from)*?
Open Question (Maximum of 50 characters)

n=2342

Q968 *[SEmpWork]*
Including *(herself/himself)*, how many people *(are/were)* employed at the place where *(she/he)* usually *(works/will work/worked)* *(from)*?
IF SELF-EMPLOYED: *(Do/Will/Did)* *(she/he)* have any employees?
IF YES: PROBE FOR CORRECT PRECODE
%
4.4 None
21.0 Under 10
13.2 10-24
21.0 25-99
18.7 100-499
15.7 500 or more
4.9 (Don't Know)
1.0 (Refusal/NA)

Q969 *[SPartFul]*
(Is/Was) the job ... **READ OUT** ...
%
78.4 full-time (30+ HOURS)
20.6 or, part-time (10-29 HOURS)?
0.2 (Don't Know)
0.9 (Refusal/NA)

ASK ALL[1]
Q988 *[TransCar]*

n=3633

Do you, or does anyone in your household, own or have the regular use of a car or a van?
IF YES', PROBE FOR WHETHER RESPONDENT, OR OTHER PERSON(S) ONLY, OR BOTH.
%
24.1 Yes, respondent only
16.1 Yes, other only
37.8 Yes, both
21.9 No
0.0 (Don't Know)
0.2 (Refusal/NA)

Q989 *[CarOwn]* **(DERIVED VARIABLE NOT ON SCREEN)**
Does respondent or respondent's household have the use of a car?
%
78.0 Yes
21.9 No
0.0 (Don't Know)
0.2 (Refusal/NA)

---

[1] On version B this question was asked as part of the Countryside, Environment and Transport section - see Q497.

n=1199

Q990 **VERSION C: ASK ALL**
[HowOfPTr]
Is there anyone in your household who uses train, underground or bus ... **READ OUT** ...
CODE FIRST THAT APPLIES
%
22.1 ...5 days a week or more,
13.4 more than once a week, but not as often as five days a week,
8.9 about once a week,
8.9 less than once a week, but at least once a month,
15.8 less often than once a month,
30.6 or does no one in your household use train, underground or bus nowadays?
0.0 (Don't Know)
0.2 (Refusal/NA)

n=2380

Q991 **VERSION B AND C: IF 'Yes, respondent only' OR 'Yes, both' AT [TransCar]**
[NCarIncV].
If for some reason you could no longer have use of a car (or a van), would you find it **really** inconvenient ...
READ OUT ...
%
39.0 ...more or less every day of your life,
12.7 several times a week,
3.3 several times a month,
4.5 only occasionally,
1.7 or - would you never **really** find it inconvenient?
0.0 (Don't Know)
0.2 (Refusal/NA)

Q992 [NCarPTr.]
Now, suppose that public transport in your area were better or less expensive. Do you think you would then use a car (or a van) as much as now, or might you use it less?
IF LESS: Would that be much less or a bit less?
%
7.9 Use it much less
15.8 Use it a bit less
35.5 Use it as much as now
0.4 (Don't Know)
0.2 (Refusal/NA)

n=3633

Q993 **ASK ALL**
[AnyBNew]
CARD
Do you (or your wife/husband/partner) receive any of the state benefits on this card at present?
%
30.6 Yes
68.8 No
0.2 (Don't Know)
0.4 (Refusal/NA)

On version B this question was asked as part of the Countryside, Environment and Transport section - see Q506.
On version B this question was asked as part of the Countryside, Environment and Transport section - see Q511.

n=3633

Q994 **IF 'Yes' AT [AnyBNew]**
[BenftFW]
Which ones? Any others?
CODE ALL THAT APPLY
Multicoded (Maximum of 12 codes)
%
2.4 Unemployment benefit [BenftN1]
12.1 Income support [BenftN2]
2.9 One-parent benefit [BenftN3]
2.0 Family credit [BenftN4]
9.9 Housing benefit (rent-rebate) [BenftN5]
6.7 Statutory sick pay/sickness benefit [BenftN6]
1.2 Invalidity benefit/Incapacity benefit [BenftN7]
3.5 Disability living allowance [BenftN8]
2.4 Widow's pension [BenftN9]
10.6 Council tax rebate [BenftN10]
1.7 Attendance allowance [BenftN11]
0.9 Severe disablement allowance [BenftN12]
0.9 Other state benefit(s) **(PLEASE SAY WHAT)** [BenftN13]
- (Don't know)
0.6 (Refusal/NA)

Q1009 **ASK ALL**
[Disab]
Do you have any long-standing health problems or disabilities which limit what you can do at work, at home or in your leisure time?
INTERVIEWER: 'LONG-STANDING' MEANS HAVE HAD PROBLEM FOR 3 YEARS OR MORE OR EXPECT PROBLEM TO LAST FOR 3 YEARS OR MORE
%
22.7 Yes
77.0 No
0.1 (Don't Know)
0.1 (Refusal/NA)

n=1199

Q1010 **VERSION C: ASK ALL**
[MainInc]
CARD
Which of these if the **main** source of income for you (and your partner) at present?
CODE ONE ONLY
%
56.7 Earnings from employment (own or spouse / partner's)
6.4 Occupational pension(s) - from previous employer(s)
15.9 State retirement or widow's pension(s)
8.3 Unemployment benefit
0.4 Income Support
4.3 Family Credit
0.8 Invalidity, sickness or disabled pension or benefit(s)
1.3 Other state benefit (**WRITE IN**)
1.7 Interest from savings or investments
1.1 Student grant
0.6 Dependent on parents/other relatives
0.4 Other main source (**WRITE IN**)
0.4 (Don't Know)
(Refusal/NA)

ASK ALL
[HHIncome]
CARD

Q1015   Which of the letters on this card represents the total income of your household from **all** sources **before tax**?
Please just tell me the letter.
NOTE: INCLUDES INCOME FROM BENEFITS, SAVINGS, ETC.

n=3633

ASK ALL IN PAID WORK (AT [REconAct] (Q111))   n=1881
[REarn]
CARD AGAIN

Q1016   Which of the letters on this card represents your **own** gross or total **earnings**, before deduction of income tax and national insurance?

	[HHIncome]	[REarn]
	%	%
Q	6.9	7.6
T	10.7	7.7
O	7.3	9.2
K	5.4	8.7
L	5.5	11.4
B	7.3	13.5
Z	7.0	8.9
M	4.1	6.0
F	5.1	5.7
J	4.9	3.6
D	3.9	2.4
H	3.2	1.3
C	2.7	1.9
G	2.9	1.1
P	2.7	1.1
N	6.6	3.3
(Don't Know)	8.7	2.2
(Refusal/NA)	5.0	4.4

ASK ALL
[OwnShare]

Q1017   Do you (or your wife/husband/partner) own any shares quoted on the Stock Exchange, including unit trusts?

%	
24.8	Yes
74.2	No
0.4	(Don't Know)
0.7	(Refusal/NA)

n=3633

ADMINISTRATION

n=3633

ASK ALL
[PhoneX]

Q1058   Is there a telephone in (your part of) this accommodation?

%	
92.5	Yes
7.4	No
0.0	(Don't Know)
0.1	(Refusal/NA)

IF 'Yes' AT [PhoneX]
[TelNum]

Q1059   Some of my interviews are checked. May I take your 'phone number for that purpose?
ADD IF NECESSARY
Your 'phone number will **not** be passed to anyone outside SCPR.
IF NUMBER GIVEN, WRITE ON THE ARF - DO NOT KEY IT IN !

%	
84.8	Number given
7.4	Number refused
0.1	(Don't Know)
0.3	(Refusal/NA)

ASK ALL
[ComeBack]

Q1060   In a year's time we may be doing a similar survey and we may wish to include you again. Would this be all right?

%	
89.2	Yes
10.2	No
0.5	(Don't Know)
0.1	(Refusal/NA)

[QFilled]

Q1061   **INTERVIEWER: THANK RESPONDENT FOR HIS OR HER HELP AND EXPLAIN ABOUT THE SELF-COMPLETION QUESTIONNAIRE. PLEASE MAKE SURE YOU GIVE THE RESPONDENT THE (GREEN/GOLD/MAUVE) QUESTIONNAIRE THEN TELL US WHETHER IT IS TO BE ...**

%	
19.5	... filled in immediately after interview in your presence,
74.8	or, left behind to be filled in later,
5.6	or, if the respondent refused.
0.1	(Don't Know)
0.0	(Refusal/NA)

[Duration]

Q1064   **THIS INTERVIEW WAS STARTED AT (START TIME) AND IT IS NOW (CURRENT TIME). PLEASE ENTER LENGTH OF INTERVIEW IN MINUTES (IF YOU HAVE HAD TO STOP AN INTERVIEW AND START AGAIN, JUST ENTER TIME SPENT INTERVIEWING)**
Range: 1 ... 150
Median:
   Version A: 60 minutes
   Version B: 56 minutes
   Version C: 60 minutes

[SelfComp]

Q1068   Status of self-completion questionnaire

%	
13.4	Not returned
86.6	Returned

COUNTRYSIDE, THE ENVIRONMENT AND TRANSPORT (VERSION B)

n=1180

VERSION B: ASK ALL
Q479   [CthtNew1]
CARD
Now a few questions about the countryside.
Which, if any, of the things on this card do you think is
the **greatest threat** to the countryside?
If you think none of them is a threat, please say so.
CODE ONE ONLY

IF ANSWER GIVEN AT [CthtNew1]
Q482   [CthtNew2]
CARD AGAIN
And which do you think is the **next greatest threat** (to the
countryside)?
CODE ONE ONLY

	[CthtNew1]	[CthtNew2]
	%	%
Litter and fly-tipping of rubbish	20.1	13.7
New housing and urban sprawl	9.7	9.8
Superstores and out-of-town shopping centres	5.3	7.3
Building new roads and motorways	13.8	14.7
Industrial development like factories, quarries and power stations	11.7	17.4
Land and air pollution, or discharges into rivers and lakes	32.7	25.0
Changes to traditional ways of farming and of using farmland	1.9	3.3
Changes to the ordinary natural appearance of the countryside, including plants and wildlife	1.5	3.5
The number of tourists and visitors in the countryside	0.9	1.8
Other answer (WRITE IN)	0.5	0.5
(None of these)	0.6	0.5
(Don't Know)	0.1	0.4
(Refusal/NA)	1.2	1.9

VERSION B: ASK ALL
Q485   [Crowded1]
CARD
Beauty spots and other popular places in the countryside
often get crowded. Suppose one of these was visited so
much that enjoying its peace and quiet was being spoiled.
Using this card, are you in favour of or against ...
cutting down or closing car parks near the site?

Q486   [Crowded2]
CARD AGAIN
(To limit the number of visitors, are you in favour of or
against)
...stopping anyone at all from visiting it at particular
times each year?

Q487   [Crowded3]
CARD AGAIN
(To limit the number of visitors, are you in favour of or
against...)
...making visitors pay and using the extra money to help
protect it?

85

Q488   [Crowded4]
CARD AGAIN
(To limit the number of visitors, are you in favour of or
against...)
... issuing free permits in advance so people will have to
plan their visits?

Q489   [Crowded5]
CARD AGAIN
(To limit the number of visitors, are you in favour of or
against...)
... cutting down on advertising and promoting it?

Q490   [Crowded6]
CARD AGAIN
(To limit the number of visitors, are you in favour of or
against...)
... advertising and promoting other popular places in the
countryside instead?

	[Crowded1]	[Crowded2]	[Crowded3]
	%	%	%
Strongly in favour	9.9	7.8	11.8
In favour	34.3	39.5	38.8
Neither in favour nor against	23.8	15.6	12.3
Against	26.1	29.5	15.6
Strongly against	4.4	6.2	3.7
(Don't Know)	1.5	1.3	1.1
(Refusal/NA)	0.1	0.1	0.1

	[Crowded4]	[Crowded5]	[Crowded6]
	%	%	%
Strongly in favour	6.2	5.3	5.3
In favour	38.8	37.3	45.5
Neither in favour nor against	17.8	27.7	29.0
Against	31.4	26.4	16.7
Strongly against	4.4	1.9	1.4
(Don't Know)	1.4	1.4	2.0
(Refusal/NA)	0.1	0.1	0.1

Q491   [TrafPrb6]
CARD
Now thinking about traffic and transport problems,
how serious a problem is congestion on motorways?

Q492   [TrafPrb7]
CARD AGAIN
(And how serious a problem is ...)
... increased traffic on country roads and lanes?

Q493   [TrafPrb8]
CARD AGAIN
(And how serious a problem is ...)
... traffic congestion at popular places in the countryside?

86

Q494 [TrfPrb9]
CARD AGAIN
(And how serious a problem is ...)
... traffic congestion in towns and cities?

Q495 [TrfPrb10]
CARD AGAIN
(And how serious a problem are ...)
... exhaust fumes from traffic in towns and cities?

Q496 [TrfPrb11]
CARD AGAIN
(And how serious a problem is ...)
... noise from traffic in towns and cities?

n=1180

	[TrfPrb6]	[TrfPrb7]	[TrfPrb8]
	%	%	%
A very serious problem	41.6	20.6	22.1
A serious problem	45.8	47.1	53.1
Not a very serious problem	9.7	27.3	20.4
Not a problem at all	0.7	1.9	1.3
(Don't Know)	2.2	3.1	3.1
(Refusal/NA)	0.1	0.1	0.1

	[TrfPrb9]	[TrfPrb10]	[TrfPrb11]
	%	%	%
A very serious problem	50.2	62.6	31.9
A serious problem	43.7	32.2	46.3
Not a very serious problem	4.7	3.8	19.0
Not a problem at all	0.4	0.3	1.5
(Don't Know)	0.9	1.0	1.2
(Refusal/NA)	0.1	0.1	0.1

Q497 **ASK ALL**
[TransCar][1]
(May I just check) ... do you, or does anyone in your
household, own or have the regular use of a car or a van ?
**IF 'YES' PROBE FOR WHETHER RESPONDENT, OR OTHER PERSON(S)
ONLY, OR BOTH**

n=3633

%
24.1 Yes, respondent only
16.1 Yes, other(s) only
37.8 Yes, both
21.9 No
0.0   (Don't Know)
0.2   (Refusal/NA)

Q498 **VERSION B: IF 'Yes, AT [TransCar]**
[NumbCars]
How many vehicles in all?

n=1180

%
43.9 One
24.8 Two
6.3   Three
2.3   Four
1.2   Five or more
-     (Don't Know)
0.1   (Refusal/NA)

---

[1] On versions A and C this question was asked as part of the Classification
section - see Q988.

87

Q499 [CompCar]
Is this vehicle (Are any of these vehicles ...) provided
by an employer or run as a business expense?

n=1180

%
58.8 No
16.4 Yes, one (of them)
2.6   Yes, two (of them)
0.6   Yes, three or more (of them)
-     (Don't Know)
0.1   (Refusal/NA)

Q500 **VERSION B: IF 'Yes, respondent only' OR 'Yes, both' AT
[TransCar]**
[MotMembR]
Do you **yourself** belong to any motoring association?
IF 'Yes' PROBE FOR WHICH
%
16.5 Automobile Association (AA)
12.0 The Royal Automobile Club (RAC)
4.8   Other motoring organisation
0.1   AA and RAC
27.9 No
0.1   (Don't Know)
0.1   (Refusal/NA)

Q503 **VERSION B: IF 'No' at [MotMembR] OR 'Yes, other(s) only'
AT [TransCar]**
[MotMemHH]
Does any member of your household belong to any motoring
association?
IF 'Yes' PROBE FOR WHICH
%
5.6   Automobile Association (AA)
3.4   The Royal Automobile Club (RAC)
1.1   Other motoring organisation (**WRITE IN**)
6.2   No
0.7   (Don't Know)
0.1   (Refusal/NA)

n=2380

Q506 **VERSION B AND C: IF 'Yes, respondent' OR 'Yes, both'
AT [TransCar]**
[NCarIncv]
If for some reason you could no longer have the use of a
car (or a van), would you find it **really** inconvenient
... **READ OUT** ..
%
39.0 ... more or less every day of your life,
12.7 several times a week,
3.3   several times a month,
4.5   only occasionally,
1.7   or - would you never **really** find it inconvenient?
0.0   (Don't Know)
0.2   (Refusal/NA)

n=1180

Q507 **VERSION B: IF EVER AT [NCarInv]**
[NeedCar1]
I am going to read out some reasons people give as to why
they **really** need a car (or a van). For each, please say
whether it applies or does not apply to you. First, you
live too far from a station or bus-stop.

---

[1] On version C this question was asked as part of the Classification
section - see Q991.

88

Q508 [NeedCar2]
Does this apply? ... Bus or train (or underground) does not run often enough.

Q509 [NeedCar3]
And does this apply? ...No convenient bus or train (or underground) route to where you need to go.

Q510 [NeedCar4]
And does this apply? .... Cost of bus or train (or underground) travel is too high.

	[NeedCar1]	[NeedCar2]	[NeedCar3]	[NeedCar4]
	%	%	%	%
Yes, applies	14.5	24.7	28.5	26.5
No, does not apply	45.2	34.7	30.9	31.2
(Don't Know)	0.0	0.9	0.3	2.0
(Refusal/NA)	0.1	0.1	0.1	0.1

Q511 [NCarPTr]
VERSION B AND C: IF EVER AT [NCarInv] n=2380
Now, suppose that public transport in your area were better or less expensive. Do you think you would then use a car (or a van) as much as now, or might you use it less?
IF 'LESS': Would that be much less or a bit less?

%
35.5 Use it as much as now
15.8 Use it a bit less
7.9 Use it much less
0.4 (Don't Know)
0.2 (Refusal/NA)

Q512 [Drive]
VERSION B: ASK ALL n=1180
May I just check, do you **drive** a car at all these days?

%
64.6 Yes
35.3 No
- (Don't Know)
0.1 (Refusal/NA)

Q513 [Travel1]
IF 'Yes' AT [Drive]
CARD
How often nowadays do you **usually** travel
... by car as a driver?

Q514 [Travel2]
VERSION B: ASK ALL
CARD AGAIN
(And how often do you **usually**)
... travel by car as a passenger?

Q516 [Travel4]
CARD AGAIN
(And how often do you **usually**)
... travel by train?

Q517 [Travel6]
CARD AGAIN
(And how often do you **usually**)
... travel by bicycle?

Q518 [Travel9]
CARD AGAIN
(And how often do you **usually**)
... go somewhere on foot at least 15 minutes' walk away?

n=1180

	[Travel1]	[Travel2]	[Travel3]
	%	%	%
Every day or nearly every day	42.7	10.3	7.1
2-5 days a week	15.1	22.9	11.0
Once a week	3.1	23.0	9.4
Less often but at least once a month	1.6	17.6	9.3
Less often than that	1.6	13.9	14.8
Never nowadays	0.5	12.1	48.3
(Don't Know)	-	-	-
(Refusal/NA)	0.1	0.1	0.1

	[Travel4]	[Travel6]	[Travel9]
	%	%	%
Every day or nearly every day	2.2	4.1	32.8
2-5 days a week	1.9	3.8	24.1
Once a week	2.2	4.3	15.9
Less often but at least once a month	11.3	3.8	7.9
Less often than that	32.6	7.0	4.5
Never nowadays	49.8	77.0	14.7
(Don't Know)	-	-	-
(Refusal/NA)	0.1	0.1	0.1

On version C this question was asked as part of the Classification section - see q992.

TASTE AND DECENCY (VERSION B)

n=1180

VERSION B: ASK ALL

Q523 [SexCine]
CARD
I am now going to ask what you think should be allowed or not allowed to be shown on television or at the cinema.
Thinking first about a frank scene in a film showing **a man and a woman character having sex.**
Using this card, please say what you feel about **a film at the cinema** which includes a scene like that?

%
18.6 Not be allowed to be shown at all
18.8 Allowed but only at special adult cinemas
47.2 Allowed at ordinary cinemas but only to people of 18 or over
12.0 Allowed but only to people of 15 or over
1.6 Allowed but only to people of 12 or over
1.0 Allowed to be shown to anyone
0.3 (Don't Know)
0.5 (Refusal/NA)

Q524 [SexRegTV]
CARD
How about the **same** scene in a film on one of the **regular television channels**, that is BBC1 and 2, ITV and (Channel 4/S4C)?
Using this card, please say what you would feel about that.

%
26.7 Not be allowed to be shown at all
19.7 Allowed but only after midnight
39.6 Allowed but only after 10 o'clock in the evening
13.3 Allowed but only after 9 o'clock in the evening
1.3 Allowed but only after 8 o'clock in the evening
0.6 Allowed to be shown at any time
0.2 (Don't Know)
0.5 (Refusal/NA)

525 [SexCabTV]
CARD
And the **same** scene in a film on a **paid satellite or cable channel**?

%
21.2 Not be allowed to be shown at all
17.0 Allowed but only on a special adult channel
13.5 Allowed but only after midnight
30.7 Allowed but only after 10 o'clock in the evening
11.1 Allowed but only after 9 o'clock in the evening
2.0 Allowed but only after 8 o'clock in the evening
2.6 Allowed to be shown at any time
1.2 (Don't Know)
0.5 (Refusal/NA)

91

n=1180

Q526 [SexVideo]
CARD
Now suppose the **same** film, including the frank scene of a man and woman character having sex, was available on a **video for sale or rent.**
Using this card, please say how widely you think the video should be available.

%
19.9 Should be banned altogether
22.4 Available only in special adult shops
45.2 In any shop but available only to people aged 18 or over
9.7 In any shop but available only to people aged 15 or over
0.9 In any shop but available only to people aged 12 or over
1.0 In any shop and available to anyone
0.5 (Don't Know)
0.5 (Refusal/NA)

Q527 [SexSee]
If you heard of a film that contained a scene like this, would you try to avoid seeing the film, or would you think quite interested to see it, or would you treat it just like any other film?

%
31.2 Try to avoid
5.0 Interested to see
62.7 Treat like any other film
0.6 (Don't Know)
0.5 (Refusal/NA)

Q528 [SexPhoto]
CARD AGAIN
Now suppose instead that a **still photograph** of the same frank sex scene appeared in an **adult magazine**. Using this card, how widely would you say the magazine should be available?

%
16.8 Should be banned altogether
31.4 Available only in special adult shops
40.7 In any shop but available only to people aged 18 or over
7.5 In any shop but available only to people aged 15 or over
0.3 In any shop but available only to people aged 12 or over
1.8 In any shop and available to anyone
1.0 (Don't Know)
0.5 (Refusal/NA)

Q529 [SexRadio]
CARD
Now imagine a frank sex scene in a **radio drama** in which you could hear a man and a woman character having sex.
Using this card, what would your opinion be?

%
24.1 Not be allowed to be broadcast at all
14.1 Allowed but only after midnight
35.8 Allowed but only after 10 o'clock in the evening
15.0 Allowed but only after 9 o'clock in the evening
4.4 Allowed but only after 8 o'clock in the evening
4.4 Allowed to be broadcast at any time
1.4 (Don't Know)
0.7 (Refusal/NA)

92

n=1180

Q530 *[SexTel]*
CARD
There are certain **recorded messages** which people can ring to hear sexual **recorded messages**. Please use this card to say how widely you think these telephone numbers should be available. Imagine a telephone number where a woman describes sexual acts with a man and uses explicit language.

%
55.8 Should be barred altogether
40.4 Available but only to adults who have chosen to have the service
2.3 Available on all private telephone lines
0.9 (Don't Know)
0.5 (Refusal/NA)

Q531 IF 'adults who have chosen the service' AT [SexTel]
[SexTelRe]
CARD
On this card are described two ways of making sure that only adults who have chosen to have the service can ring these numbers. Which of these do you think would be best?
... **READ OUT** ...
%
35.2 ...that they are available only to adults who have **applied for a special code** OR
5.0 ...that they are available on all phones **unless** the subscriber has asked for these numbers **not** to be available from their phone?
0.2 (Don't Know)
1.5 (Refusal/NA)

VERSION B: ASK ALL
Q532 *[SexAdv]*
CARD
And, using this card, please say what you feel about **adverts** for these telephone numbers?
Should be banned altogether
Allowed but only in adult magazines
Allowed in any newspaper or magazine as long as it is not too explicit
Allowed in any newspaper or magazine in any form
(Don't Know)
(Refusal/NA)
%
54.9
32.4
10.2
0.9
1.0
0.5

Q533 *[HSexCin]*
CARD AGAIN
Now I want to ask you about a **different** kind of scene that may appear in a film. This time, instead of a male and a female character, there is a frank scene of **two adult male characters** having sex.
Using this card again, what would your opinion be of a film at the **cinema** including a scene like that?
%
44.5 Not be allowed to be shown at all
24.6 Allowed but only at special adult cinemas
25.2 Allowed at ordinary cinemas but only to people of 18 or over
3.6 Allowed but only to people of 15 or over
0.6 Allowed but only to people of 12 or over
0.6 Allowed to be shown to anyone
0.7 (Don't Know)
0.5 (Refusal/NA)

n=1180

Q534 *[HSexRgTV]*
CARD AGAIN
How about the **same** scene in a film on one of the **regular television channels**, that is, BBC1 and 2, ITV and (Channel 4/S4C)? What would your opinion be?
%
54.3 Not be allowed to be shown at all
19.4 Allowed but only after midnight
18.7 Allowed but only after 10 o'clock in the evening
5.5 Allowed but only after 9 o'clock in the evening
0.5 Allowed but only after 8 o'clock in the evening
0.4 Allowed to be shown at any time
0.7 (Don't Know)
0.5 (Refusal/NA)

Q535 *[HSexCaTV]*
CARD AGAIN
And the **same** scene in a film on a **paid satellite or cable channel**?
%
46.7 Not be allowed to be shown at all
18.7 Allowed but only on a special adult channel
11.6 Allowed but only after midnight
14.9 Allowed but only after 10 o'clock in the evening
4.6 Allowed but only after 9 o'clock in the evening
0.6 Allowed but only after 8 o'clock in the evening
1.3 Allowed to be shown at any time
1.0 (Don't Know)
0.5 (Refusal/NA)

Q536 *[HSexVide]*
CARD AGAIN
Now suppose the **same** film, including the frank scene of two adult male characters having sex, was available on a **video for sale or rent**.
Using this card, please say how widely you think the video should be available.
%
41.9 Should be banned altogether
27.1 Available only in special adult shops
26.1 In any shop but available only to people aged 18 or over
3.1 In any shop but available only to people aged 15 or over
0.3 In any shop but available only to people aged 12 or over
0.2 In any shop and available to anyone
0.7 (Don't Know)
0.5 (Refusal/NA)

Q537 *[HSexSee]*
If you heard of a film that contained a scene like this, would you try to avoid seeing the film, or would you be quite interested in seeing it, or would you treat it just like any other film?
%
64.6 Try to avoid
1.4 Interested to see
32.7 Treat like any other film
0.8 (Don't Know)
0.5 (Refusal/NA)

n=1180

Q538 [HSexPhot]
CARD AGAIN
Now suppose instead that a **still photograph** of the same
frank scene appeared in an **adult magazine**. Using this
card, how widely would you say the magazine should be
available?

%
36.6 Should be banned altogether
35.4 Available only in special adult shops
23.6 In any shop but available only to people aged 18 or over
2.3   In any shop but available only to people aged 15 or over
0.3   In any shop but available only to people aged 12 or over
0.4   In any shop and available to anyone
0.9   (Don't Know)
0.5   (Refusal/NA)

Q539 [HSexRadi]
CARD AGAIN
Now imagine a frank sex scene in a **radio drama** in which
you could hear two male characters having sex.
Using this card, what would your opinion be?

%
48.4 Not be allowed to be broadcast at all
17.7 Allowed but only after midnight
20.1 Allowed but only after 10 o'clock in the evening
7.1   Allowed but only after 9 o'clock in the evening
1.9   Allowed but only after 8 o'clock in the evening
3.1   Allowed to be broadcast at any time
1.0   (Don't Know)
0.7   (Refusal/NA)

Q540 [HSexTel]
CARD AGAIN
Thinking again about the **telephone numbers** which people can
ring to hear sexual **recorded messages**. Please use this card
to say how widely you think these telephone numbers should be
available. Imagine a telephone number where a man describes
sexual acts with another man and uses explicit language.

%
60.1 Should be banned altogether
36.9 Available but only to adults who have chosen to have the
      service
1.5   Available on all private telephone lines
1.0   (Don't Know)
0.5   (Refusal/NA)

Q541 [HSexAdv]
CARD AGAIN
And, using this card, please say what you feel about **adverts**
for a telephone number like this?

%
60.4 Should be banned altogether
31.3 Allowed but only in adult magazines
6.4   Allowed in any newspaper or magazine as long as it is not
      too explicit
0.3   Allowed in any newspaper or magazine in any form
1.0   (Don't Know)
0.5   (Refusal/NA)

---

n=1180

Q542 [SexGra12]
We have been talking about films and videos in general, but
there are, of course, different types of film. Some contain
sex scenes which are part of a developing relationship
between the main characters. Others show sex scenes which
don't seem to be essential to the plot.
Think first of films in which a frank sex scene between a
man and a woman character does **not** seem to be essential to
the plot. Should they **ever**, in your view be allowed to be
seen by 12 year olds?

IF 'No' OR 'Don't Know' AT [SexGra12]
Q543 [SexGra15]
(Thinking of films in which a frank sex scene between a
man and a woman character does **not** seem to be essential to
the plot. Should they **ever**, in your view be...)
...allowed to be seen by 15 year olds?

IF 'No' OR 'Don't Know' AT [SexGra15]
Q544 [SexGra18]
(Thinking of films in which a frank sex scene between a
man and a woman character does **not** seem to be essential to
the plot. Should they **ever**, in your view be...)
...allowed to be seen by 18 year olds?

IF 'No' OR 'Don't Know' AT [SexGra18]
Q545 [SexGraAn]
(Thinking of films in which a frank sex scene between a
man and a woman character does **not** seem to be essential to
the plot. Should they **ever**, in your view be...)
..allowed to be seen by **anyone at all**?

	[SexGra12]	[SexGra15]	[SexGra18]	[SexGraAn]
	%	%	%	%
Yes	4.0	20.5	52.1	2.8
No	94.5	73.5	21.5	19.0
(Don't Know)	0.8	1.2	1.1	0.8
(Refusal/NA)	0.8	0.8	0.8	0.8

VERSION B: ASK ALL
Q546 [SexRel12]
And how about films in which a frank sex scene between a
man and a woman character **is** part of a developing
relationship between the main characters. Should they
ever, in your view, be allowed to be seen by 12 year olds?

IF 'No' OR 'Don't Know' AT [SexRel12]
Q547 [SexRel15]
(Thinking of films in which a frank sex scene between a
man and a woman character **is** part of a developing
relationship between the main characters. Should they
ever, in your view be...)
...allowed to be seen by 15 year olds?

n=1180

Q548
[SexRel18]
IF 'No' OR 'Don't Know' AT [SexRel15]
(Thinking of films in which a frank sex scene between a man and a woman character **is** part of a developing relationship between the main characters. Should they **ever**, in your view, be)
...allowed to be seen by 18 year olds?

Q549
[SexRelAn]
IF 'No' OR 'Don't Know' AT [SexRel18]
(Thinking of films in which a frank sex scene between a man and a woman character **is** part of a developing relationship between the main characters. Should they **ever**, in your view, be)
...allowed to be seen by **anyone at all**?

	[SexRel12]	[SexRel15]	[SexRel18]	[SexRelAn]
	%	%	%	%
Yes	13.1	32.7	38.4	2.2
No	85.0	52.3	14.1	11.9
(Don't Know)	1.1	1.1	1.0	0.9
(Refusal/NA)	0.8	0.8	0.8	0.8

VERSION B: ASK ALL

Q550
[SexEdV12]
Now how about **educational videos** containing a frank scene of a man and woman character having sex. Should they **ever**, in your view, be allowed to be seen by 12 year olds?

Q551
[SexEdV15]
IF 'No' OR 'Don't Know' AT [SexEdV12]
(And how about **educational videos** containing a frank scene of a man and woman character having sex. Should they **ever**, in your view,)
...be allowed to be seen by 15 year olds?

Q552
[SexEdV18]
IF 'No' OR 'Don't Know' AT [SexEdV15]
(And how about **educational videos** containing a frank scene of a man and woman character having sex. Should they **ever**, in your view, be)
... allowed to be seen by 18 year olds?

Q553
[SexEdVAn]
IF 'No' OR 'Don't Know' AT [SexEdV18]
(And how about **educational videos** containing a frank scene of a man and woman character having sex. Should they **ever**, in your view, be)
... allowed to be seen by **anyone at all**?

	[SexEdV12]	[SexEdV15]	[SexEdV18]	[SexEdVAn]
	%	%	%	%
Yes	38.9	34.0	16.7	1.0
No	58.8	25.4	8.9	7.7
(Don't Know)	1.7	1.0	0.9	1.0
(Refusal/NA)	0.6	0.7	0.7	0.7

n=1180

Q554
IF ('No' OR 'Don't Know' AT [SexGraAn] AND AT [SexRelAn] AND AT [SexEdVAn]) AND ('Should not be allowed to be shown at all' AT [SexCine] AND AT [SexRegTV] AND AT [SexCabTV] AND AT [SexVideo])
[SexNever]
Is your view that frank sex scenes on film or video should **never** be seen by anyone at all, or can you imagine circumstances in which they might be acceptable?

	%
Never be seen	98.9
Can imagine acceptable circumstances	5.6
(Don't Know)	0.5
(Refusal/NA)	0.1

Q555
IF 'can imagine acceptable circumstances' AT [SexNever]
[SexCer]
Are you able to say what those circumstances might be?
Open Question (Maximum of 80 characters)

Q556
IF ('No' OR 'Don't Know' AT [SexGraAn] AND AT [SexRelAn] AND AT [SexEdVAn]) AND ('Should not be allowed to be shown at all' AT [SexCine] AND AT [SexRegTV] AND AT [SexCabTV] AND AT [SexVideo]) AND ('Should not be allowed to be shown at all' AT [HSexCin] AND AT [HSexRgTV] AND AT [HSexCaTV] AND AT [HSexVide])
[HSexNev]
And can you imagine circumstances in which frank sex scenes on film or video between two adult men would be acceptable, or should they **never** be seen by anyone at all?

	%
Never be seen	5.9
Can imagine acceptable circumstances	0.2
(Don't Know)	0.0
(Refusal/NA)	-

Q557
IF 'can imagine acceptable circumstances' AT [HSexNev]
[HSexCer]
Are you able to say what those circumstances might be?
Open Question (Maximum of 80 characters)

Q558
VERSION B: ASK ALL
[SwearTV]
CARD
And finally on this subject, some say that sexual swearwords have no place in films or in television; others say that they are so much part of modern life that they are acceptable nowadays. Using this card, at what times, if at all, would you say, a film containing lots of **sexual swearwords** should be allowed to be shown on the regular television channels?

	%
Not be allowed to be shown at all	28.8
Allowed but only after midnight	15.2
Allowed but only after 10 o'clock in the evening	35.7
Allowed but only after 9 o'clock in the evening	15.6
Allowed but only after 8 o'clock in the evening	2.2
Allowed to be shown at any time	1.3
(Don't Know)	0.5
(Refusal/NA)	0.7

n=1180

Q559 [SwearCin]
      CARD
      And by what age groups, if any, would you say a film
      containing lots of sexual swearwords should be allowed to
      be seen in **ordinary cinemas**?
      %
23.3 Not be allowed to be shown at all
10.0 Allowed but only at special adult cinemas
42.4 Allowed at ordinary cinemas but only to people of 18 or over
19.9 Allowed but only to people of 15 or over
 2.1 Allowed but only to people of 12 or over
 0.9 Allowed to be shown to anyone
 0.6 (Don't Know)
 0.7 (Refusal/NA)

Q560 [SwearVid]
      CARD
      And how about a film on **video for sale or rent** containing
      lots of sexual swearwords?
      Using this card, please say how widely you think the video
      should be available.
      %
25.3 Should be banned altogether
13.4 Available only in special adult shops
40.3 In any shop but available only to people aged 18 or over
16.8 In any shop but available only to people aged 15 or over
 2.1 In any shop but available only to people aged 12 or over
 1.1 In any shop and available to anyone
 0.4 (Don't Know)
 0.7 (Refusal/NA)

99

ECONOMIC PROSPECTS (VERSION C)   n=1199

VERSION C: ASK ALL

Q565 [Prices]
      Now I would like to ask you about two economic problems -
      inflation and **unemployment**.
      First, **inflation**: in a year from now, do you expect prices
      generally to have gone up, to have stayed the same, or to
      have gone down?
      IF GONE UP OR GONE DOWN: By a lot or a little?

Q566 [Unemp]
      Second, **unemployment**: in a year from now, do you expect
      unemployment to have gone up, to have stayed the same, or
      to have gone down?
      IF GONE UP OR GONE DOWN: By a lot or a little?

	[Prices]	[Unemp]
	%	%
To have gone up by a lot	33.8	17.2
To have gone up by a little	54.1	24.0
To have stayed the same	9.1	37.2
To have gone down by a little	1.7	18.2
To have gone down by a lot	0.2	1.3
(Don't Know)	1.0	2.1
(Refusal/NA)	-	-

Q567 [UnempInf]
      If the government **had** to choose between keeping down
      inflation or keeping down unemployment, to which do you
      think it should give highest priority?
      %
28.7 Keeping down inflation
66.7 Keeping down unemployment
 1.4 (Both equally)
 0.8 Other answer (**WRITE IN**)
 2.3 (Don't Know)
 0.1 (Refusal/NA)

Q570 [Concern]
      Which do you think is of the most concern to **you and your
      family** ... **READ OUT** ...
      %
53.8 ... inflation,
42.8 or, unemployment?
 2.0 (Both equally)
 0.1 (Neither a threat)
 0.4 Other answer (**WRITE IN**)
 0.9 (Don't Know)
    - (Refusal/NA)

100

n=1199

Q573 [Industry]
Looking ahead over the next year, do you think Britain's
general industrial performance will improve, stay much the
same, or decline?
IF IMPROVE OR DECLINE: By a lot or a little?

```
  %
 3.5   Improve a lot
18.9   Improve a little
52.3   Stay much the same
14.3   Decline a little
 6.6   Decline a lot
 4.5   (Don't Know)
  -    (Refusal/NA)
```

Q574 [IncomGap]
Thinking of income levels generally in Britain today, would
you say that the **gap** between those with high incomes and
those with low incomes is ... **READ OUT** ...

```
  %
87.2   ... too large,
 8.4   about right,
 1.7   or, too small?
 2.6   (Don't Know)
 0.1   (Refusal/NA)
```

Q575 [TaxHi]
CARD
Generally, how would you describe **levels of taxation**?
Firstly, for those with **high** incomes? Please choose a
phrase from this card.

.Q576 [TaxMid]
CARD AGAIN
Next for those with **middle** incomes? Please choose a phrase
from this card.

Q577 [TaxLow]
CARD AGAIN
Next for those with **low** incomes? Please choose a phrase
from this card.

	[TaxHi]	[TaxMid]	[TaxLow]
	%	%	%
Much too high	4.0	3.3	23.8
Too high	10.4	24.0	48.6
About right	30.9	62.6	21.7
Too low	38.5	5.1	1.4
Much too low	12.3	0.5	0.5
(Don't Know)	3.9	4.5	4.0
(Refusal/NA)	-	-	-

Q578 [SRInc]
Among which group would you place yourself ... **READ OUT** ...

```
  %
 2.8   ... high income,
44.3   middle income,
52.4   or, low income?
 0.4   (Don't Know)
 0.1   (Refusal/NA)
```

n=1199

Q579 [HIncDiff]
CARD
Which of the phrases on this card would you say comes
closest to your feelings about your household's income
these days?

```
  %
24.4   Living comfortably on present income
51.6   Coping on present income
16.5   Finding it difficult on present income
 7.2   Finding it very difficult on present income
 0.1   Other answer (**WRITE IN**)
 0.1   (Don't Know)
 0.1   (Refusal/NA)
```

Q582 [HIncPast]
Looking back over the **last year** or so, would you say your
household's income has ... **READ OUT** ...

```
  %
50.5   ... fallen behind prices,
40.7   kept up with prices,
 7.5   or, gone up by more than prices?
 1.3   (Don't Know)
 0.0   (Refusal/NA)
```

Q583 [HIncXpct]
And looking forward to the **year ahead**, do you expect your
household income will ... **READ OUT** ...

```
  %
45.8   ... fall behind prices,
42.7   keep up with prices,
 8.7   or, go up by more than prices?
 2.6   (Don't know)
 0.0   (Refusal/NA)
```

Q584 [Prosper]
Compared with other parts of Britain over the last ten
years, would you say that (this part of Britain/Scotland/
Wales) has been getting **more** prosperous than average,
stayed about average, or been getting **less** prosperous?
IF MORE/LESS PROSPEROUS:- A lot more/less prosperous or a
little?

```
  %
 3.1   Much more prosperous than average
11.2   A little more prosperous than average
38.8   Stayed about average
26.4   A little less prosperous than average
16.3   Much less prosperous than average
 4.2   (Don't Know)
 0.1   (Refusal/NA)
```

TAXATION/PUBLIC SPENDING (VERSION C)

VERSION C: ASK ALL

Q589 [SizeTax]
CARD
About how much do you think that an extra one penny in the pound on the basic rate of income tax would cost your household?
IF RESPONDENT DOES NOT KNOW, ENCOURAGE THEM TO GIVE AN ESTIMATE
IF THEY CAN'T, CODE 'DON'T KNOW'

Q590 [SizeVAT]
CARD AGAIN
About how much do you think that a one percentage point increase in the rate of VAT (that is, from 17½ percent to 18½ percent) would cost your household?
IF RESPONDENT DOES NOT KNOW, ENCOURAGE THEM TO GIVE AN ESTIMATE
IF THEY CAN'T, CODE 'DON'T KNOW'

		[SizeTax]	[SizeVAT]
		%	%
A	Nothing	18.5	2.0
B	<£1 per week - <£50 per year	16.0	15.4
C	£1-2 per week - £50-100 per year	17.2	19.2
D	£2-3 per week - £100-£150 per year	16.8	17.3
E	>£3 per week - >£150 per year	13.5	26.9
	(Don't Know)	17.7	18.9
	(Refusal/NA)	0.3	0.3

Q591 [SpdPre1]
Now some questions about government spending and the taxes to pay for it. Suppose that if spending goes up, then taxes have to be raised to pay for it. If it goes down, taxes can be cut.

VERSION C: ASK ALL WITH ODD SERIAL NUMBERS

Q593 [SpdPre2A]
HAND OVER THE BLUE ANSWER SHEET. Here are seven areas of government spending. POINT TO THE SEVEN SPENDING AREAS.
Suppose that the government had to choose between these three options ... READ OUT ...
... increasing spending and putting up income tax rates by one penny in the pound,
... keeping spending and income tax about the same as now,
... and putting spending and taking one penny in the pound off the rate of income tax.
POINT TO THREE TAX/SPENDING OPTIONS.

Q595 [SpdPre3]
For each of these seven areas of government spending, which option do you think would be best **for the country as a whole**?
Please tick **one** box on each line. If you change your mind as you go through, just cross your old answer out. Please tell me when you are ready.

103

---

n=599

Q596 [HlhSpdC1]
Now I'd just like to make a note of your answers.
RETRIEVE BLUE ANSWER SHEET FROM RESPONDENT.
(Which of these would be best for the country as a whole?)
HEALTH:

Q597 [PolSpdC1]
(Which of these would be best for the country as a whole?)
POLICE:

Q598 [EdcSpdC1]
(Which of these would be best for the country as a whole?)
EDUCATION:

Q599 [DfcSpdC1]
(Which of these would be best for the country as a whole?)
DEFENCE:

Q600 [EnvSpdC1]
(Which of these would be best for the country as a whole?)
THE ENVIRONMENT:

Q601 [PTrSpdC1]
(Which of these would be best for the country as a whole?)
PUBLIC TRANSPORT:

Q602 [CulSpdC1]
(Which of these would be best for the country as a whole?)
CULTURE AND THE ARTS:

	[HlhSpdC1]	[PolSpdC1]	[EdcSpdC1]	[DfcSpdC1]
	%	%	%	%
Increase spending and taxes	76.3	39.5	72.0	8.8
Keep spending and taxes the same	18.3	50.2	20.7	43.9
Cut spending and taxes	2.1	6.3	3.7	42.5
(None of these)	-	0.2	-	0.7
(Don't Know)	3.0	3.4	3.3	3.8
(Refusal/NA)	0.4	0.4	0.4	0.4

	[EnvSpdC1]	[PTrSpdC1]	[CulSpdC1]
	%	%	%
Increase spending and taxes	30.6	33.6	7.3
Keep spending and taxes the same	51.5	49.4	33.5
Cut spending and taxes	13.6	13.2	54.3
(None of these)	0.4	0.2	1.1
(Don't Know)	3.6	3.2	3.5
(Refusal/NA)	0.4	0.4	0.4

n=1199

104

n=600

Q594 VERSION C: ASK ALL WITH EVEN SERIAL NUMBERS
[SpdPre2B]
HAND OVER THE PINK ANSWER SHEET. Here are seven areas of government spending. POINT TO THE SEVEN SPENDING AREAS. Suppose that the government had to choose between these three options ... READ OUT ...
... increasing spending and raising taxes for **every** adult in Britain by £35 a year.
... keeping spending and taxes about the same as now,
... or cutting spending and reducing taxes for every adult in Britain by £35 a year.
POINT TO THREE TAX/SPENDING OPTIONS

Q595 [SpdPre3]
For each of these seven areas of government spending, which option do you think would be best **for the country as a whole**?
Please tick **one** box on each line. If you change your mind as you go through, just cross your old answer out. Please tell me when you are ready.

Q603 [H1hSpdC2]
Now I'd just like to make a note of your answers.
RETRIEVE PINK ANSWER SHEET FROM RESPONDENT.
(Which of these would be best for **the country as a whole**?)
HEALTH:

Q604 [PolSpdC2]
(Which of these would be best for **the country as a whole**?)
POLICE:

Q605 [EdcSpdC2]
(Which of these would be best for **the country as a whole**?)
EDUCATION:

Q606 [DfcSpdC2]
(Which of these would be best for **the country as a whole**?)
DEFENCE:

Q607 [EnvSpdC2]
(Which of these would be best for **the country as a whole**?)
THE ENVIRONMENT:

Q608 [PTrSpdC2]
(Which of these would be best for **the country as a whole**?)
PUBLIC TRANSPORT:

Q609 [CulSpdC2]
(Which of these would be best for **the country as a whole**?)
CULTURE AND THE ARTS:

	[H1hSpdC2]	[PolSpdC2]	[EdcSpdC2]	[DfcSpdC2]
	%	%	%	%
Increase spending and taxes	66.9	39.7	66.2	9.6
Keep spending and taxes the same	24.1	51.5	25.4	44.3
Cut spending and taxes	6.6	6.6	5.9	43.3
(None of these)	0.6	0.4	0.5	0.4
(Don't Know)	1.5	1.5	1.7	2.0
(Refusal/NA)	0.3	0.3	0.3	0.4

n=599

Q610 [SpdPre4]
HAND OVER GREY ANSWER SHEET.
Now I want to ask you which options you think would be best **for you and your household**. Again suppose that, for each of the seven areas of government spending, the government had to choose between these three options.
POINT TO THE THREE TAX/SPENDING OPTIONS. Please tick **one** box per line. If you change your mind as you go through, just cross your old answer out. Please tell me when you are ready.

Q611 [H1hSpdR1]
Now I'd just like to make a note of your answers.
RETRIEVE GREY ANSWER SHEET FROM RESPONDENT.
(Which of these would be best for **you and your household**?)
HEALTH:

Q612 [PolSpdR1]
(Which of these would be best for **you and your household**?)
POLICE:

Q613 [EdcSpdR1]
(Which of these would be best for **you and your household**?)
EDUCATION:

Q614 [DfcSpdR1]
(Which of these would be best for **you and your household**?)
DEFENCE:

Q615 [EnvSpdR1]
(Which of these would be best for **you and your household**?)
THE ENVIRONMENT:

Q616 [PTrSpdR1]
(Which of these would be best for **you and your household**?)
PUBLIC TRANSPORT:

Q617 [CulSpdR1]
(Which of these would be best for **you and your household**?)
CULTURE AND THE ARTS:

	[H1hSpdR1]	[PolSpdR1]	[EdcSpdR1]	[DfcSpdR1]
	%	%	%	%
Increase spending and taxes	65.9	39.2	50.7	10.2
Keep spending and taxes the same	25.9	45.4	30.5	36.8
Cut spending and taxes	4.6	11.4	14.1	47.3
(None of these)	0.3	0.5	0.8	1.8
(Don't Know)	3.0	3.0	3.5	3.6
(Refusal/NA)	0.4	0.4	0.4	0.4

	[EnvSpdR1]	[PTrSpdR1]	[CulSpdR1]
	%	%	%
Increase spending and taxes	26.7	29.3	8.6
Keep spending and taxes the same	50.4	41.7	29.6
Cut spending and taxes	18.3	24.4	56.5
(None of these)	0.8	1.1	3.3
(Don't Know)	3.5	3.1	1.3
(Refusal/NA)	0.4	0.4	0.4

n=600

	[EnvSpdC2]	[PTrSpdC2]	[CulSpdC2]
	%	%	%
Increase spending and taxes	29.0	30.7	7.7
Keep spending and taxes the same	55.2	53.5	38.8
Cut spending and taxes	13.5	12.8	50.1
(None of these)	-	0.2	0.6
(Don't Know)	1.9	2.4	2.5
(Refusal/NA)	0.4	0.4	0.3

Q610 [SpdPre4]
HAND OVER CREAM ANSWER SHEET.
Now I want to ask you which options you think would be best for you and your household. Again suppose that, for each of the seven areas of government spending, the government had to choose between these three options.
POINT TO THE THREE TAX/SPENDING OPTIONS. Please tick one box per line. If you change your mind as you go through, just cross your old answer out. Please tell me when you are ready.

Q618 [HlhSpdR2]
Now I'd just like to make a note of your answers.
RETRIEVE CREAM ANSWER SHEET FROM RESPONDENT.
(Which of these would be best for you and your household?)
HEALTH:

Q619 [PolSpdR2]
(Which of these would be best for you and your household?)
POLICE:

Q620 [EdcSpdR2]
(Which of these would be best for you and your household?)
EDUCATION:

Q621 [DfcSpdR2]
(Which of these would be best for you and your household?)
DEFENCE:

Q622 [EnvSpdR2]
(Which of these would be best for you and your household?)
THE ENVIRONMENT:

Q623 [PTrSpdR2]
(Which of these would be best for you and your household?)
PUBLIC TRANSPORT:

Q624 [CulSpdR2]
(Which of these would be best for you and your household?)
CULTURE AND THE ARTS:

n=600

	[HlhSpdR2]	[PolSpdR2]	[EdcSpdR2]	[DfcSpdR2]
	%	%	%	%
Increase spending and taxes	62.0	38.0	52.9	7.6
Keep spending and taxes the same	28.8	49.7	31.5	39.1
Cut spending and taxes	7.3	10.4	13.1	49.6
(None of these)	0.3	0.3	0.3	1.2
(Don't Know)	1.3	1.2	1.8	2.1
(Refusal/NA)	0.3	0.4	0.4	0.4

	[EnvSpdR2]	[PTrSpdR2]	[CulSpdR2]
	%	%	%
Increase spending and taxes	28.1	25.7	8.1
Keep spending and taxes the same	50.5	45.8	34.4
Cut spending and taxes	19.0	25.3	53.7
(None of these)	0.4	0.7	0.7
(Don't Know)	1.6	2.1	2.6
(Refusal/NA)	0.4	0.4	0.4

n=1199

VERSION C: ASK ALL

Q625 [GvChTaxP]
CARD
Suppose the government did decide to increase taxes to pay for extra spending, and suppose it had just three options
... READ OUT ...
... to put up income tax for all taxpayers, by 1p in the pound to 26p
OR
... to put income tax up only for higher taxpayers, but by 5p in the pound, to 45p
OR
... to raise VAT by one percent to 18½ per cent on all taxable goods and services.

Q626 [GvChTax1]
CARD AGAIN
If these were the only options for the government, which do you think that it should choose?
%
29.6   A penny in the pound for all taxpayers
57.3   Five pence in the pound for higher taxpayers
9.4   Raise VAT by one per cent
0.8   Other answer (WRITE IN)
2.8   (Don't Know)
0.1   (Refusal/NA)

Q629 [GvChTax2]
IF ANSWER AT [GvChTax1]
CARD AGAIN
And which one do you think should be the government's second choice?
%
48.5   A penny in the pound for all taxpayers
26.8   Five pence in the pound for higher taxpayers
19.5   Raise VAT by one per cent
0.4   Other answer (WRITE IN)
1.5   (Don't Know)
3.0   (Refusal/NA)

n=1199

Q632   **VERSION C: ASK ALL**
        [FamBTax]
        CARD AGAIN
        Which one of these three would leave you and your family
        best off?

%
24.1   A penny in the pound for all taxpayers
63.8   Five pence in the pound for higher taxpayers
6.6   Raise VAT by one per cent
0.5   (Non-(income) tax payer (so does not apply to me))
0.5   Other answer (**WRITE IN**)
4.4   (Don't Know)
0.1   (Refusal/NA)

Q635   *[FamWTax]*
        CARD AGAIN
        And which one do you think would leave you and your family
        worst off?

%
19.1   A penny in the pound for all taxpayers
7.8   Five pence in the pound for higher taxpayers
68.9   Raise VAT by one per cent
0.1   Other answer (**WRITE IN**)
4.0   (Don't Know)
0.1   (Refusal/NA)

---

n=1199

CHARITABLE GIVING (VERSION C)

VERSION C: ASK ALL

Q638   *[LottPriz]*
        CARD
        As you may know, the money raised by the National Lottery
        gets spent on a number of different things. How much, if
        any, would you say goes to ....
        ... prizes for lottery winners?
        CODE FIRST THAT APPLIES

Q639   *[LottPay]*
        CARD AGAIN
        ... payment to the places that sell lottery tickets?

Q640   *[LottProf]*
        CARD AGAIN
        ... profits for the organisation that runs the lottery?

Q641   *[LottArts]*
        CARD AGAIN
        And how much, if any, of the money raised by the lottery
        goes to ...
        ... the Arts - like galleries, theatres and orchestras?

Q642   *[LottBlds]*
        CARD AGAIN
        ... historic buildings?

Q643   *[LottSprt]*
        CARD AGAIN
        ... sport?

Q644   *[LottNHS]*
        CARD AGAIN
        ... a special fund for the NHS?

Q645   *[LottMill]*
        CARD AGAIN
        (And how much, if any, of the money raised by the lottery
        goes to ...)
        ... a special fund for celebrating the year 2000?

Q646   *[LottChar]*
        CARD AGAIN
        ... charities and other 'good causes'?

Q647   *[LottBus]*
        CARD AGAIN
        ... a special fund for business and industry?

Q648   *[LottTax]*
        CARD AGAIN
        ... tax?

n=1199

	[LottPriz]	[LottPay]	[LottProf]	[LottArts]
	%	%	%	%
A great deal	22.6	3.5	42.2	10.6
Quite a bit	51.5	25.3	44.0	34.8
Not very much	22.1	56.1	7.8	43.5
None at all	0.1	2.0	0.4	2.7
(Don't Know)	3.5	12.9	5.4	8.2
(Refusal/NA)	0.3	0.2	0.2	0.2

	[LottBlds]	[LottSprt]	[LottNHS]	[LottMill]
	%	%	%	%
A great deal	5.3	3.5	0.8	2.6
Quite a bit	21.9	30.9	5.6	21.8
Not very much	55.0	49.8	32.0	29.1
None at all	5.2	5.0	46.9	23.4
(Don't Know)	12.3	10.7	14.5	23.0
(Refusal/NA)	0.3	0.2	0.3	0.2

	[LottChar]	[LottBus]	[LottTax]
	%	%	%
A great deal	30.4	0.9	9.1
Quite a bit	54.5	11.8	34.8
Not very much	4.4	33.4	18.3
None at all	6.6	35.0	18.0
(Don't Know)	0.2	18.7	19.6
(Refusal/NA)		0.2	0.2

Q649 [LottPrt]
Have you personally ever taken part in the National
Lottery, either directly or with other people?

%	
74.5	Yes, directly
10.1	Yes, with others
15.0	No
0.2	(Don't Know)
0.2	(Refusal/NA)

IF 'No' OR 'Don't know' AT [LottPrt]
Q650 [LottNo]
Why is that? Have you ...

%	
2.2	...simply not got round to it yet,
2.2	or, do you not bother **yourself** because you would gain from someone else winning,
4.1	or, do you disapprove of the National Lottery,
3.8	or, do you think it's just a waste of money?
1.7	(Both disapprove and waste of money)
1.9	Other (**WRITE IN**)
0.3	(Don't Know)
0.3	(Refusal/NA)

IF 'Yes' AT [LottPrt]
Q653 [LottFreq]
Do you take part ... **READ OUT** ...

%	
61.5	... every week if you can,
8.9	... around 2 or 3 times a month,
6.2	... around once a month,
8.1	... or less often than that?
-	(Don't Know)
0.4	(Refusal/NA)

111

---

n=1199

VERSION C: ASK ALL
Q654 [LottOtY1]
CARD
On this card are three reasons why people may take part in
the National Lottery. In general, which one do you think
most explains why people take part?

Q655 [LottOtY2]
CARD AGAIN
And, in general, which **least** explains why people take part
in the lottery?

	[LottOtY1]	[LottOtY2]
	%	%
To win the jackpot or one of the big prizes	85.0	2.5
To have some fun, without any expectation of winning a lot of money	13.0	27.5
To contribute to the good causes that the lottery supports	1.0	68.0
(Don't Know)	0.8	1.8
(Refusal/NA)	0.2	0.2

IF 'Yes' AT [LottPrt]
Q656 [LottMeY1]
CARD AGAIN
And, again looking at the reasons on this card, which one
most explains why **you** take part in the lottery?

Q657 [LottMeY2]
CARD AGAIN
And which **least** explains why **you** take part?

	[LottMeY1]	[LottMeY2]
	%	%
To win the jackpot or one of the big prizes	62.7	8.0
To have some fun, without any expectation of winning a lot of money	19.8	29.1
To contribute to the good causes that the lottery supports	2.4	46.1
(Don't Know)	0.3	1.5
(Refusal/NA)	0.4	0.4

Q658 [LottCtChr]
Some people think that buying national lottery tickets
will affect the amount people give to good causes in other
ways. In general, do you think that ... **READ OUT** ...

%	
48.1	... because people buy lottery tickets they give **less** money to good causes in other ways,
49.5	or, that buying lottery tickets makes no real difference to the amount people give to good causes?
2.2	(Don't Know)
0.2	(Refusal/NA)

112

n=1199

IF 'Yes' AT [LottPrt]
[LotMeChr]
Q659 How about you? Do you think that buying lottery tickets means ... **READ OUT** ...
%
6.3 ... you give **less** money to good causes in other ways,
78.1 or, has it made no real difference to the amount you give to good causes?
0.3 (Don't Know)
0.4 (Refusal/NA)

VERSION C: ASK ALL
[LotOtGC]
Q660 And what if **none** of the money spent on lottery tickets went to good causes? Generally speaking, do you think ... **READ OUT**
%
14.5 ... this would make **a lot** of difference to the number of tickets sold,
36.6 **some** difference,
47.1 or, **no** difference at all?
1.7 (Don't Know)
0.2 (Refusal/NA)

IF 'Yes' AT [LottPrt]
[LotMeGC]
Q661 How about you? If **none** of the money spent on lottery tickets went to good causes, do you think ... **READ OUT** ...
%
11.3 ... this would make **a lot** of difference to whether you took part,
22.9 **some** difference,
50.0 or, **no** difference at all?
0.4 (Don't Know)
0.4 (Refusal/NA)

VERSION C: ASK ALL
[HasCut1]
Q662 A lot of people are having problems nowadays in making ends meet and have to cut down on some things. Looking back over **the last year or so**, would you say that you or your household has cut down on the amount you spend on ... ... holidays or outings?

Q663 [HasCut2]
... food or clothing?

Q664 [HasCut3]
... having evenings out?

Q665 [HasCut4]
... giving to charity or other good causes?

	[HasCut1]	[HasCut2]	[HasCut3]	[HasCut4]
	%	%	%	%
Yes	57.2	41.3	51.2	27.7
No	42.0	58.1	47.8	71.5
(Don't Know)	0.5	0.4	0.8	0.6
(Refusal/NA)	0.3	0.2	0.3	0.2

n=1199

Q666 [WillCut1]
And looking forward to **the year ahead**, do you expect you will have to cut down on the amount you spend on ... ... holidays or outings?

Q667 [WillCut2]
... food or clothing?

Q668 [WillCut3]
... having evenings out?

Q669 [WillCut4]
... giving to charity or other good causes?

	[WillCut1]	[WillCut2]	[WillCut3]	[WillCut4]
	%	%	%	%
Yes	51.2	35.4	45.8	26.9
No	46.4	63.4	52.7	71.7
(Don't Know)	2.2	1.1	1.3	1.2
(Refusal/NA)	0.2	0.2	0.2	0.2

n=1199

WELFARE/SOCIAL SECURITY (VERSION C)

VERSION C: ASK ALL

Q673 [UB1Poor]
Now some questions about welfare benefits. Think of a 25-year-old unemployed woman living alone. Her only income comes from state benefits. Would you say that she ... **READ OUT** ...

Q674 [MumPoor]
What about an unemployed single mother with a young child. Their only income comes from state benefits. Would you say they ... **READ OUT** ...

Q675 [UB1On47]
Now thinking again of that 25-year-old unemployed woman living alone. After rent, her income is £47 a week. Would you say that she ... **READ OUT** ...

Q676 [MumOn78]
And thinking again about that unemployed single mother with a young child. After rent, their income is £78 a week. Would you say they ... **READ OUT** ...

	[UB1Poor]	[MumPoor]	[UB1On47]	[MumOn78]
	%	%	%	%
... has more than enough to live on,	2.1	2.7	2.0	3.6
has enough to live on,	23.4	22.2	25.2	34.8
is hard up,	52.9	50.7	53.9	45.1
or, is really poor?	12.6	18.3	16.9	14.8
(Don't Know)	8.9	5.8	1.9	1.5
(Refusal/NA)	0.2	0.3	0.2	0.2

Q677 [PenWhoSh]
CARD
Please say, from this card, who you think should be **mainly** responsible for ensuring that people have an adequate retirement pension.

%	
46.9	Mainly the government
8.9	Mainly employers
37.3	Shared equally
6.2	Some other arrangement
0.6	(Don't Know)
0.2	(Refusal/NA)

Q678 [MstUnemp]
Suppose two people working for a large firm each became unemployed through no fault of their own. One had a very high income, one had a very low income. Do you think that the very high earner should be entitled to ... **READ OUT** ... ...more unemployment benefit than the very low earner,

%	
9.4	the same amount,
72.3	less benefit,
12.8	or, no unemployment benefit at all?
0.2	(It depends)
0.3	Other answer (**WRITE IN**)
2.0	(Don't Know)
0.2	(Refusal/NA)

n=1199

Q681 [MstRetir]
Now suppose a very high earner and a very low earner in a large firm retired. Do you think the very high earner should be entitled to ... **READ OUT** ...

%	
11.3	...a bigger **state** retirement pension than the very low earner,
68.6	the same amount,
13.2	a lower **state** pension,
3.5	or no **state** pension at all?
0.9	Other answer (**WRITE IN**)
2.3	(It depends)
2.3	(Don't Know)
0.2	(Refusal/NA)

Q684 [MstChild]
Now what about child benefit. Should very high earners be entitled to ... **READ OUT** ...

%	
0.8	...more child benefit than very low earners,
45.8	the same amount.
21.2	less,
30.0	or, no child benefit at all?
0.1	Other answer (**WRITE IN**)
1.8	(Don't Know)
0.2	(Refusal/NA)

Q687 [MtUnmar1]
Imagine an unmarried couple who split up. They have a child at primary school who remains with the mother. Do you think that the father should always be made to make maintenance payments to support the child?

Q688 [MtUnmar2]
If he **does** make maintenance payments for the child, should the amount depend on his income, or not?

Q689 [MtUnmar3]
Do you think the amount of maintenance should depend on the **mother's** income, or not?

	[MtUnmar1]	[MtUnmar2]	[MtUnmar3]
	%	%	%
Yes	84.6	88.4	72.7
No	12.6	9.6	25.3
(Don't Know)	2.5	1.7	1.8
(Refusal/NA)	0.2	0.2	0.2

Q690 [MtUnmar4]
Suppose the mother now marries someone else. Should the child's natural father go on paying maintenance for the child, should he stop, or should it depend on the step-father's income?

%	
38.6	Continue
13.9	Stop
45.3	Depends
1.9	(Don't Know)
0.2	(Refusal/NA)

n=1199

EUTHANASIA (VERSION C)

VERSION C: ASK ALL
[EuPreAm]
Q698 Now I would like to ask some questions about voluntary euthanasia - that is, when someone ends the life of another person **at their request**. I will read you some circumstances in which someone might ask a **doctor** to end their life. In each case please tell me whether you think a doctor should be allowed by law to do so.

Q699 *[EuPainSh]*
CARD
First, a person with an incurable and painful illness, from which they will die - for example someone dying of cancer. Do you think that, if they ask for it, a doctor should ever be allowed by law to end their life, or not?

%
56.3 Definitely should be allowed
24.0 Probably should be allowed
5.3 Probably should **not** be allowed
11.7 Definitely should **not** be allowed
1.5 (Don't Know)
1.3 (Refusal/NA)

Q700 *[EUPainIs]*
CARD
And do you think the law allows a doctor to do this at the moment, or not?

%
1.0 Definitely allows
2.1 Probably allows
12.2 Probably does **not** allow
80.6 Definitely does **not** allow
3.0 (Don't Know)
1.0 (Refusal/NA)

Q701 *[EuRelSh]*
CARD AGAIN
And if they ask **a close relative** to end their life, should the law ever allow the close relative to do so, or not?

%
14.7 Definitely should be allowed
16.4 Probably should be allowed
15.5 Probably should **not** be allowed
49.1 Definitely should **not** be allowed
3.0 (Don't Know)
1.2 (Refusal/NA)

Q702 *[EuRelIs]*
CARD AGAIN
And do you think the law allows a close relative to do this at the moment, or not?

%
0.8 Definitely allows
0.9 Probably allows
4.8 Probably does **not** allow
89.9 Definitely does **not** allow
2.5 (Don't Know)
1.0 (Refusal/NA)

---

n=1199

Q691 *[Worseoff]*
CARD
Please look at this card and say, as far as money is concerned, what you think happens when a marriage breaks up.

%
19.1 The woman nearly always comes off worse than the man
18.0 The woman usually comes off worse
20.5 The woman and the man usually come off about the same
22.5 The man usually comes off worse
7.8 The man nearly always comes off worse than the woman
0.8 (Varies/depends)
Other answer (**WRITE IN**)
3.0 (Don't Know)
0.2 (Refusal/NA)

n=1199

Q703 *[EuNDieSh]*
CARD AGAIN
Now, how about a person with an incurable and painful illness, from which they will **not** die – for example someone with severe arthritis. Do you think that, if they ask for it, a doctor should ever be allowed by law to end their life, or not?

Q704 *[EuNPaiSh]*
CARD AGAIN
What about a person with an incurable illness from which they will die but which is **not very painful** – as might be the case for someone dying from leukaemia? Do you think that, if they ask for it, a doctor should ever be allowed by law to end their life, or not?

Q705 *[EuDepSh]*
CARD AGAIN
And now, how about a person who is **not** in much pain **nor** in danger of death, but becomes permanently and completely **dependent** on relatives for all their needs – for example someone who cannot feed, wash or go to the toilet by themselves. Do you think that, if they ask for it, a doctor should ever be allowed by law to end their life, or not?

Q706 *[EuTireSh]*
CARD AGAIN
Now think of a person who is not ill or close to death but who is **simply tired of living** and wishes to die – for example someone who is extremely lonely and no longer enjoys life. Do you think that, if they ask for it, a doctor should ever be allowed by law to end their life, or not?

Q707 *[EuLSupSh]*
CARD AGAIN
Now think about what should happen to someone who has an incurable illness which leaves them unable to make a decision about their **own** future. For instance, imagine a person in a coma on a **life support machine** who is never expected to regain consciousness. If their relatives agreed, do you think a doctor should ever be allowed by law to turn the machine off, or not?

	[EuNDieSh]	*[EuNPaiSh]*	*[EuDepSh]*	*[EuTireSh]*	*[EuLSupSh]*
	%	%	%	%	%
Definitely should be allowed	17.1	19.4	25.0	5.9	59.0
Probably should be allowed	24.4	25.0	26.1	5.7	26.8
Probably should not be allowed	18.3	19.8	15.7	14.8	2.7
Definitely should not be allowed	35.4	31.3	28.6	69.8	7.9
(Don't Know)	3.6	3.3	3.4	2.7	2.5
(Refusal/NA)	1.2	1.2	1.2	1.2	1.2

n=1199

Q708 *[EuLSupIs]*
CARD AGAIN
And do you think the law allows a doctor to do this at the moment, or not?
```
                                      %
Definitely allows                  17.6
Probably allows                    26.7
Probably does not allow            17.0
Definitely does not allow          31.7
(Don't Know)                        6.0
(Refusal/NA)                        1.0
```

Q709 *[EuComaSh]*
CARD AGAIN
And how about someone in a coma, again never expected to regain consciousness, but who is **not** on a life support machine. If their relatives agreed, do you think a doctor should ever be allowed by law to end their life, or not?
```
                                      %
Definitely should be allowed       28.8
Probably should be allowed         29.1
Probably should not be allowed     15.8
Definitely should not be allowed   21.2
(Don't Know)                        4.1
(Refusal/NA)                        1.1
```

Q710 *[LivWilPr]*
Some people make what is called a 'living will', saying what they would wish to happen if they have an incurable illness which leaves them unable to make a decision about their own future. Suppose that someone's 'living will' includes an instruction that doctors should **not** keep them alive if they have a painful illness from which they will die.

Q711 *[LivWilSh]*
CARD AGAIN
Do you think the law should allow doctors to decide to end a patient's life on the instruction of the 'living will', or not?
```
                                      %
Definitely should be allowed       46.3
Probably should be allowed         28.0
Probably should not be allowed      7.5
Definitely should not be allowed   13.4
(Don't Know)                        4.1
(Refusal/NA)                        0.8
```

Q712 *[LivWilRg]*
CARD
And do you think the law should **require** that doctors carry out the instructions of a 'living will'?
```
                                      %
Definitely should require          33.4
Probably should require            29.1
Probably should not require        13.5
Definitely should not require      18.1
(Don't Know)                        5.1
(Refusal/NA)                         0.8
```

Q713   [LivWilSf]
        Have you by chance made, or even considered making,
        such a 'living will'?
        IF YES: Have you actually made one?

n=1199

%
1.7   Yes, made one
11.8   Yes, considered making one
84.7   No
0.8   (Don't Know)
0.9   (Refusal/NA)

PENSIONS (VERSION C)[1]

VERSION C: ASK ALL WHO ARE RETIRED OR AGED 50+

Q1023   [REmp1PnC] (see also Q278)
        Do you receive a pension from any past employer?

n=475

%
34.0   Yes
65.2   No
0.1   (Don't Know)
0.7   (Refusal/NA)

VERSION C: ASK ALL WHO ARE MARRIED OR LIVING AS
MARRIED WHO ARE EITHER RETIRED THEMSELVES OR WHOSE
PARTNER IS RETIRED OR AGED 50+

Q1027   [SEmp1Pc2] (see also Q280)
        Does your (wife/husband/partner) receive a pension from
        any past employer?

n=308

%
29.4   Yes
70.3   No
-       (Don't Know)
0.3   (Refusal/NA)

VERSION C: ASK ALL WHO ARE RETIRED OR AGED 50+

Q1030   [PrPenGtc] (see also Q281)
        And do you receive a pension from any private arrangements
        you have made in the past, that is apart from the state
        pension or one arranged through an employer?

n=475

%
3.9   Yes
95.3   No
0.1   (Don't Know)
0.7   (Refusal/NA)

        IF 'Yes' AT [PrPenGtc]
Q1031   [PersPen]
        Is that from a Personal Pension?
        IF ASKED: THESE SCHEMES ARE SOMETIMES CALLED 'PERSONAL,
        PRIVATE OR PORTABLE PENSIONS'.

%
2.7   Yes
1.2   No
-       (Don't Know)
0.8   (Refusal/NA)

VERSION C: ASK ALL WHO ARE MARRIED OR LIVING AS
MARRIED WHO ARE EITHER RETIRED THEMSELVES OR WHOSE
PARTNER IS RETIRED OR AGED 50+

Q1035   [SPrPnGtC] (see also Q282)
        And does your (wife/husband/partner) receive a pension
        from any private arrangements (she/he) has made in the
        past, that is apart from the state pension or one arranged
        through an employer?

n=308

%
2.1   Yes
97.2   No
-       (Don't Know)
0.7   (Refusal/NA)

[1] This section was asked after the end of Classification.

n=308

Q1036 [SPrsPen]
Is that from a Personal Pension?
IF ASKED: THESE SCHEMES ARE SOMETIMES CALLED 'PERSONAL, PRIVATE OR PORTABLE PENSIONS'.

%
1.4   Yes
0.7   No
-     (Don't Know)
0.7   (Refusal/NA)

VERSION C: IF RETIRED AND ABOVE PENSIONABLE AGE

Q1037 [RPension]
See Q284

Q1038 [RPenInYr]
See Q285

VERSION C: ASK ALL RETIRED

Q1039 [RetirAg2]
See Q286   n=496

VERSION C: ASK ALL CURRENT EMPLOYEES BELOW RETIREMENT AGE

Q1040 [RCmpPen]
Thinking of your present job, do you currently belong to a pension or superannuation scheme run by your employer which will give you a pension when you retire?

%
52.2   Yes
47.1   No
-      (Don't Know)
0.6   (Refusal/NA)

IF 'Yes' AT [RCmpPen]

Q1041 [RCmpPCon]
Do you make any contributions to the company pension scheme at the moment, excluding any Additional Voluntary Contributions (AVCs)?

%
38.3   Yes
14.0   No
-      (Don't Know)
0.6   (Refusal/NA)

Q1042 [RAVCs]
Do you make any Additional Voluntary Contributions (AVCs)?

%
7.7   Yes
44.6   No
-      (Don't Know)
0.6   (Refusal/NA)

VERSION C: ASK ALL WHO ARE MARRIED OR LIVING AS MARRIED AND WHOSE PARTNER IS AN EMPLOYEE BELOW RETIREMENT AGE   n=370

Q1043 [SCmpPen]
Thinking of your (wife's/husband's/partner's) present job, does (she/he) currently belong to a pension or superannuation scheme run by (her/his) employer which will give (her/him) a pension when (she/he) retires?

%
58.2   Yes
36.9   No
1.3   (Don't Know)
3.6   (Refusal/NA)

n=370

IF 'Yes' AT [SCmpPen]

Q1044 [SCmpPCon]
Does (she/he) make any contributions to the company pension scheme at the moment, excluding any Additional Voluntary Contributions (AVCs)?

%
38.9   Yes
17.3   No
1.9   (Don't Know)
4.9   (Refusal/NA)

Q1045 [SAVCs]
Does (she/he) make any Additional Voluntary Contributions (AVCs)?

%
9.0   Yes
44.8   No
4.3   (Don't Know)
4.9   (Refusal/NA)

VERSION C: ASK ALL WHO ARE NOT RETIRED AND UNDER RETIREMENT AGE   n=906

Q1046 [RFutPrPn]
IF EMPLOYEE: Now I would like to ask you about Personal Pension schemes rather than employers' pension schemes. Some people arrange pensions themselves for which contributions are income tax deductible. These schemes are sometimes called "personal private or portable pensions". Do you have any such arrangements at present? IF ASKED: EXCLUDE ADDITIONAL VOLUNTARY CONTRIBUTIONS AVCs.

IF NOT EMPLOYEE: Now I would like to ask you about Personal Pension schemes which will give you a pension when you retire. Some people arrange pensions themselves for which contributions are income tax deductible. These schemes are sometimes called "personal private or portable pensions". Do you have any such arrangements at present? IF ASKED: EXCLUDE ADDITIONAL VOLUNTARY CONTRIBUTIONS AVCs.

%
23.0   Yes
76.4   No
0.2   (Don't Know)
0.4   (Refusal/NA)

IF 'Yes' AT [RFutPrPn]

Q1047 [RFutPrPC]
Do you make any contributions to your Personal Pension at the moment?

%
18.0   Yes
5.0   No
0.6   (Don't Know)
-      (Refusal/NA)

IF 'Yes' AT [RFutPrPn] AND EMPLOYEE

Q1048 [RFutPFEm]
Does your employer contribute to your Personal Pension at the moment?

%
1.4   Yes
15.9   No
0.5   (Don't Know)
-      (Refusal/NA)

n=906

VERSION C: ASK ALL WHO ARE NOT RETIRED AND UNDER RETIREMENT AGE

Q1052 [PenXpct1]
CARD
When you have retired and have stopped doing paid work, where do you think **most** of your income will come from?
INTERVIEWER: IF RESPONDENT SAYS 'SPOUSE/ PARTNER'S COMPANY PENSION', CODE AS 'A COMPANY PENSION'. SIMILARLY FOR STATE AND PERSONAL PENSIONS.

Q1055 [PenXpct2]
CARD AGAIN
And which do you think will be your **second most important** source of income?
INTERVIEWER: IF RESPONDENT SAYS 'SPOUSE/ PARTNER'S COMPANY PENSION', CODE AS 'A COMPANY PENSION'. SIMILARLY FOR STATE AND PERSONAL PENSIONS.

	[PenXpct1]	[PenXpct2]
	%	%
State retirement pension	34.8	31.5
A company pension	31.0	14.0
A personal pension	24.6	13.5
Other savings or investments	4.8	23.8
(Earnings from job/still working)	0.1	0.9
From somewhere else (WRITE IN)	0.8	1.0
(None)	-	9.5
(Don't Know)	3.3	5.3
(Refusal/NA)	0.5	0.5

---

n=591

VERSION C: ASK ALL WHO ARE MARRIED OR LIVING AS MARRIED WHOSE PARTNER IS **NOT** RETIRED AND UNDER RETIREMENT AGE

Q1049 [SFutPrPn]
IF PARTNER IS EMPLOYEE: Now I would like to ask you about **Personal Pension** schemes rather than employers' pension schemes. Some people arrange pensions themselves for which contributions are income tax deductible. These schemes are sometimes called "personal private or portable pensions". Does your (wife/husband/partner) have any such arrangements at present? IF ASKED: **EXCLUDE ADDITIONAL VOLUNTARY CONTRIBUTIONS AVCs.**

IF PARTNER IS NOT EMPLOYEE: Now I would like to ask you about **Personal Pension** schemes which will give you a pension **when you retire**. Some people arrange pensions themselves for which contributions are income tax deductible. These schemes are sometimes called "personal private or portable pensions". Does your (wife/husband/partner) have any such arrangements at present? IF ASKED: **EXCLUDE ADDITIONAL VOLUNTARY CONTRIBUTIONS AVCs.**

%	
26.2	Yes
71.9	No
0.9	(Don't Know)
1.0	(Refusal/NA)

Q1050 [SFutPrPC]
IF 'Yes' AT [SFutPrPn]
Does your (wife/husband/partner) make any contributions to/her/his) Personal Pension at the moment?

%	
20.6	Yes
5.1	No
0.5	(Don't Know)
1.9	(Refusal/NA)

Q1051 [SFutPPEm]
IF 'Yes' AT [SFutPrPn] AND PARTNER IS EMPLOYEE
Does your (wife's/husband's/partner's) employer contribute to (her/his) Personal Pension at the moment?

%	
3.6	Yes
12.9	No
1.3	(Don't Know)
2.3	(Refusal/NA)

A

Head Office: 35 NORTHAMPTON SQUARE, LONDON EC1V 0AX
Tel: 0171-250 1866 Fax: 0171-250 1524

SCPR
SOCIAL & COMMUNITY PLANNING RESEARCH

Field and DP Office: 100 KINGS ROAD, BRENTWOOD, ESSEX CM14 4LX
Tel: 01277 200600 Fax: 01277 214117

Spring 1995

P.1430

BRITISH SOCIAL ATTITUDES 1995
MAIN SAMPLE
SELF-COMPLETION QUESTIONNAIRE

OFFICE USE ONLY		INTERVIEWER TO ENTER	
6-8	Cluster number	1-5 7	Serial number
9-13	Spare	19-22 0	Sampling point
14-15 3 0	Card no.	23-26	Interviewer number
16-18	Spare		
27-31	Batch no.		
32-34	Spare		

To the selected respondent:

Thank you very much for agreeing to take part in this important study - the eleventh in this annual series. The study consists of this self-completion questionnaire, and the interview you have already completed. The results of the survey are published in a book each autumn; some of the questions are also being asked in twenty-two other countries, as part of an international survey.

Completing the questionnaire:

The questions inside cover a wide range of subjects, but each one can be answered simply by placing a tick (✓) or a number in one or more of the boxes. No special knowledge is required: we are confident that everyone will be able to take part, not just those with strong views or particular viewpoints. The questionnaire should not take very long to complete, and we hope you will find it interesting and enjoyable. Only you should fill it in, and not anyone else at your address. The answers you give will be treated as confidential and anonymous.

Returning the questionnaire:

Your interviewer will arrange with you the most convenient way of returning the questionnaire. If the interviewer has arranged to call back for it, please fill it in and keep it safely until then. If not, please complete it and post it back in the pre-paid, addressed envelope, AS SOON AS YOU POSSIBLY CAN.

THANK YOU AGAIN FOR YOUR HELP.

Social and Community Planning Research is an independent social research institute registered as a charitable trust. Its projects are funded by government departments, local authorities, universities and foundations to provide information on social issues in Britain. The British Social Attitudes survey series is funded mainly by one of the Sainsbury Family Charitable Trusts, with contributions also from other grant-giving bodies and government departments. Please contact us if you would like further information.

A - 1

n=1079

To begin, we have some questions about <u>where you live</u>: your neighbourhood or village; your town or city, your county, and so on. (By "neighbourhood" we mean the part of the town/city you live in. If you live in a village, we take this as your "neighbourhood").

A2.01 How close do you feel to ...
PLEASE TICK ONE BOX
ON EACH LINE

		Very close	Close	Not very close	Not close at all	Can't choose/ Doesn't apply to me	(NA)
[CLOSNGBH]							
a.	... your neighbourhood (or village)?	% 16.5	43.7	24.9	9.3	2.0	3.6
[CLOSTOWN]							
b.	... your town or city?	% 10.3	40.0	31.8	9.5	2.1	6.2
[CLOSCNTY]							
c.	... your county?	% 9.4	35.0	32.8	12.8	1.8	8.1
[CLOSBRTN]							
d.	... Britain?	% 21.1	41.9	19.2	8.1	1.9	7.8
[CLOSEURP]							
e.	... Europe?	% 3.2	15.9	36.1	31.7	4.4	8.7

A2.02 If you could improve your work or living conditions, how willing or unwilling would you be to ...
PLEASE TICK ONE BOX
ON EACH LINE

		Very willing	Fairly willing	Neither willing nor unwilling	Fairly unwilling	Very unwilling	Can't choose/ Doesn't apply to me	(NA)
[MOVENGBH]								
a.	... move to another neighbourhood (or village)?	% 20.8	31.7	12.8	10.7	13.7	8.1	2.2
[MOVETOWN]								
b.	... move to another town or city within this county?	% 13.1	29.7	12.7	14.8	16.9	6.9	5.9
[MOVECNTY]								
c.	... move to another county?	% 12.1	22.1	12.4	16.8	23.0	7.5	6.1
[MOVEBRTN]								
d.	... move outside Britain?	% 7.6	14.7	8.6	16.1	39.0	8.1	6.0
[MOVEEURP]								
e.	... move outside Europe?	% 6.6	12.6	8.4	12.5	43.9	9.7	6.2

A2.03 [UKUNITED]
Which of these two statements comes closer to your own view?
PLEASE TICK ONE BOX ONLY

	%
It is essential that the United Kingdom remains one nation	61.0
OR	
Parts of the United Kingdom should be allowed to become fully separate nations if they choose to	27.8
Can't choose	10.3
(NA)	0.9

OFFICE USE ONLY

A - 2

n=1079

A2.04 Some people say the following things are important for being truly British. Others say they are not important. How important do you think each of the following is?
PLEASE TICK ONE BOX
ON EACH LINE

		Very important	Fairly important	Not very important	Not important at all	Can't choose	(NA)
[PATRIOT1]							
a.	To have been born in Britain	% 47.9	27.7	14.6	6.5	1.1	2.2
[PATRIOT2]							
b.	To have British citizenship	% 51.2	32.1	9.1	4.0	1.3	2.4
[PATRIOT3]							
c.	To have lived in Britain for most of one's life	% 38.2	33.2	17.7	5.2	1.1	4.7
[PATRIOT4]							
d.	To be able to speak English	% 62.4	22.2	7.7	4.3	0.7	2.7
[PATRIOT5]							
e.	To be a Christian	% 18.5	13.5	27.3	35.1	2.3	3.4
[PATRIOT6]							
f.	To respect Britain's political institutions and laws	% 53.5	28.4	7.8	4.6	2.7	3.0
[PATRIOT7]							
g.	To feel British	% 48.7	24.8	13.4	7.6	2.3	3.1

A2.05 How much do you agree or disagree with the following statements?
PLEASE TICK ONE BOX
ON EACH LINE

		Strongly agree	Agree	Neither agree nor disagree	Disagree	Strongly disagree	Can't choose	(NA)
[NATCITZN]								
a.	I would rather be a citizen of Britain than of any other country in the world	% 40.2	29.0	20.6	4.8	1.9	1.6	2.0
[NATASHMD]								
b.	There are some things about Britain today that make me feel ashamed of Britain	% 19.3	52.9	13.2	7.6	2.5	2.1	2.3
[NATLIKE]								
c.	The world would be a better place if people from other countries were more like the British	% 8.5	19.8	39.3	21.7	5.9	2.5	2.4
[NATBEST]								
d.	Generally speaking Britain is a better country than most other countries	% 13.0	38.8	27.7	13.0	2.6	2.5	2.4
[NATSUPP]								
e.	People should support their country even if the country is in the wrong	% 6.5	16.1	18.8	42.5	12.0	1.4	2.7
[NATSPORT]								
f.	When my country does well in international sports, it makes me proud to be British	% 29.9	42.4	18.2	2.3	2.7	2.1	2.3

OFFICE USE ONLY

A - 3

n=1079

A2.06 How proud are you of Britain in each of the following?
PLEASE TICK ONE BOX ON EACH LINE

		Very proud	Somewhat proud	Not very proud	Not proud at all	Can't choose	(NA)
a.	The way democracy works *[NATPRID1]*	12.8	47.0	24.7	5.5	8.3	1.5
b.	Its political influence in the world *[NATPRID2]*	6.7	41.0	33.3	7.7	8.7	2.5
c.	Britain's economic achievements *[NATPRID3]*	5.5	32.6	40.4	10.6	7.9	3.0
d.	Its social security system *[NATPRID4]*	6.7	37.4	31.6	16.8	5.5	2.1
e.	Its scientific and technological achievements *[NATPRID5]*	26.7	52.4	8.9	2.0	7.1	2.9
f.	Its achievements in sports *[NATPRID6]*	22.8	47.5	17.3	5.2	5.3	1.9
g.	Its achievements in the arts and literature *[NATPRID7]*	21.2	47.4	14.6	3.3	10.7	2.8
h.	Britain's armed forces *[NATPRID8]*	44.3	36.8	7.1	4.4	5.4	1.9
i.	Its history *[NATPRID9]*	46.9	36.2	6.7	3.6	5.0	1.7
j.	Its fair and equal treatment of all groups in society *[NATPRID10]*	13.2	34.1	31.3	11.1	8.4	1.8

A2.07 Now we would like to ask a few questions about relations between Britain and other countries.
How much do you agree or disagree with the following statements?
PLEASE TICK ONE BOX ON EACH LINE

		Strongly agree	Agree	Neither agree nor disagree	Disagree	Strongly disagree	Can't choose	(NA)
a.	Britain should limit the import of foreign products in order to protect its national economy *[FORGREL1]*	22.0	39.8	19.7	13.2	1.2	2.5	1.6
b.	For certain problems, like environmental pollution, international bodies should have the right to enforce solutions *[FORGREL2]*	25.8	45.0	15.7	8.0	0.7	3.4	1.4
c.	British schools should make much more effort to teach foreign languages properly *[FORGREL3]*	31.4	47.8	13.6	4.0	1.2	0.7	1.2
d.	Britain should follow its own interests, even if this leads to conflicts with other nations *[FORGREL4]*	16.3	31.8	25.3	20.0	2.2	2.7	1.7
e.	Foreigners should not be allowed to buy land in Britain *[FORGREL5]*	12.8	18.4	31.1	26.0	8.0	2.4	1.3
f.	British television should give preference to British films and programmes *[FORGREL6]*	10.5	23.8	30.9	26.4	4.9	2.3	1.2

A - 4

n=1079

A2.08 Now we would like to ask a few questions about minorities in Britain.
How much do you agree or disagree with the following statements?
PLEASE TICK ONE BOX ON EACH LINE

		Strongly agree	Agree	Neither agree nor disagree	Disagree	Strongly disagree	Can't choose	(NA)
a.	*[SHARTRAD]* It is impossible for people who do not share British customs and traditions to become fully British	18.6	31.7	21.1	20.6	4.5	2.3	1.1
b.	*[ETHNCAID]* Ethnic minorities should be given government assistance to preserve their customs and traditions	1.7	13.2	23.1	38.9	18.3	3.2	1.6

A2.09 *[ETHNCVW]* Some people say that it is better for a country if different racial and ethnic groups maintain their distinct customs and traditions. Others say that it is better if these groups adapt and blend into the larger society. Which of these views comes closer to your own?
PLEASE TICK ONE BOX ONLY

	%
It is better for society if groups maintain their distinct customs and traditions	15.6
It is better for society if groups adapt and blend into the larger society	64.7
Can't choose	17.9
(NA)	1.9

A2.10 There are different opinions about immigrants from other countries living in Britain. (By "immigrants" we mean people who come to settle in Britain.)
How much do you agree or disagree with each of the following statements?
PLEASE TICK ONE BOX ON EACH LINE

		Strongly agree	Agree	Neither agree nor disagree	Disagree	Strongly disagree	Can't choose	(NA)
a.	*[IMMIGRT1]* Immigrants increase crime rates	7.3	16.7	34.1	30.6	6.6	3.1	1.6
b.	*[IMMIGRT2]* Immigrants are generally good for Britain's economy	1.3	14.7	41.6	30.6	5.2	4.4	2.2
c.	*[IMMIGRT3]* Immigrants take jobs away from people who were born in Britain	13.7	33.3	25.4	19.2	4.9	2.1	1.3
d.	*[IMMIGRT4]* Immigrants make Britain more open to new ideas and cultures	6.1	45.2	26.4	13.9	2.7	4.2	1.4

OFFICE USE ONLY

A - 5

n=1079

A2.11 [IMMNUMB]
Do you think the number of immigrants to Britain nowadays should be …
PLEASE TICK ONE BOX ONLY

	%
… increased a lot,	0.9
increased a little,	2.9
remain the same as it is,	26.9
reduced a little,	23.6
or reduced a lot?	39.2
Can't choose	5.7
(NA)	0.7

A2.12 [REFSTAY]
How much do you agree or disagree that refugees who have suffered political repression in their own country should be allowed to stay in Britain?
PLEASE TICK ONE BOX ONLY

	%
Strongly agree	8.8
Agree	31.4
Neither agree nor disagree	28.9
Disagree	16.8
Strongly disagree	7.8
Can't choose	5.7
(NA)	0.7

A2.13 [LIVECHLD]
Where did you spend most of your childhood, that is, until you turned 17?
PLEASE TICK ONE BOX ONLY

	%
In this town (city, village)	46.5
In a different town (city, village), but in this county	26.5
In a different county in Britain	22.3
Outside Britain	3.9
(NA)	0.8

A2.14 [LIVEAREA]
How long have you lived in the town (city, village), where you live now?
PLEASE FILL IN NUMBER OF YEARS OR TICK BOX IF LESS THAN ONE YEAR

Median: 22 years
(NA) 1.1%

A - 6

n=1079

A2.15 [LIVEABRD]
About how long altogether have you lived in other countries?
PLEASE TICK ONE BOX ONLY

	%
Never lived in other countries	71.4
Less than 1 year in all	5.8
1 to 4 years in all	9.9
5 years or longer	11.1
(NA)	1.8

A2.16a What language(s) do you speak at home?
PLEASE FILL IN

At home I speak …

b. What language(s) do you speak well?
PLEASE FILL IN

	Spoken at home %		Spoken well %	
English (inc. Scottish)	[LGHMENGL]	95.4	[LGWLENGL]	57.5
Welsh	[LGHMWELS]	1.6	[LGWLWELS]	1.9
Gaelic (inc. Irish)	[LGHMGAEL]	0.3	[LGWLGAEL]	0.0
French	[LGHMFREN]	0.6	[LGWLFREN]	9.3
German	[LGHMGERM]	0.0	[LGWLGERM]	2.8
Italian	[LGHMITAL]	0.1	[LGWLITAL]	1.9
Spanish	[LGHMSPAN]	0.1	[LGWLSPAN]	1.2
Portuguese		-	[LGWLPORT]	0.1
Dutch	[LGHMDUTC]	0.0	[LGWLDUTC]	0.2
Polish	[LGHMPOLI]	0.1	[LGWLPOLI]	0.1
Russian		-	[LGWLRUSS]	0.3
Greek	[LGHMGREE]	0.1	[LGWLGREE]	0.2
Turkish		-	[LGWLTURK]	0.1
Kurdish	[LGHMKURD]	0.1		-
Arabic	[LGHMARAB]	0.1	[LGWLARAB]	0.3
Hebrew		-	[LGWLHEBR]	0.1
Punjabi	[LGHMPUNJ]	0.7	[LGWLPUNJ]	0.3
Gujarati	[LGHMGUJA]	0.6	[LGWLGUJA]	0.3
Hindi	[LGHMHIND]	0.3	[LGWLHIND]	0.2
Bengali	[LGHMBENG]	0.2	[LGWLBENG]	0.1
Urdu	[LGHMURDU]	0.1	[LGWLURDU]	0.3
Japanese	[LGHMJAPA]	0.0	[LGWLJAPA]	0.1
Somalian	[LGHMSOMA]	0.2	[LGWLSOMA]	0.2
Yoruba	[LGHMYORU]	0.3		-
Madinka		-	[LGWLMADI]	0.3
Other	[LGHMOTH]	0.1	[LGWLOTH]	0.8
None	[LGHMNONE]	0.0	[LGWLNONE]	10.1
(NA)		2.9		23.9

OFFICE USE ONLY

OFFICE USE ONLY

n=1079

[CITIZEN]

A2.17a Are you a citizen of Britain?

	%
Yes	95.8
No	2.3
(NA)	1.9

b. **[CITZPAR]**
At the time of your birth, were both, one or neither of your parents citizens of Britain?
PLEASE TICK ONE BOX ONLY

	%
Both were citizens of Britain	92.2
Only father was a citizen of Britain	1.1
Only mother was a citizen of Britain	0.9
Neither parent was a citizen of Britain	4.5
(NA)	1.3

And now a few questions about the European Union (sometimes still called the European Community).

[EUKNOW]

A2.18 How much have you heard or read about the European Union?
PLEASE TICK ONE BOX ONLY

	%
A lot	20.2
Quite a bit	36.7
Not much	33.7
Nothing at all	8.1
(NA)	1.3

OFFICE USE ONLY

n=1079

[UKBENEU]

A2.19 Generally speaking, would you say that Britain benefits or does not benefit from being a member of the European Union?
PLEASE TICK ONE BOX ONLY

	%
Benefits	40.8
Does not benefit	31.6
Have never heard of the European Union	1.8
Can't choose	24.1
(NA)	1.7

[EUUNITE]

A2.20 Which of the following statements comes closer to your own view?
PLEASE TICK ONE BOX ONLY

	%
Britain should do all it can to unite fully with the European Union	27.6

OR

Britain should do all it can to protect its independence from the European Union	48.0
Can't choose	22.6
(NA)	1.8

[IMMEXCLU]

A2.21 How much do you agree or disagree with the following statement?
"Britain should take stronger measures to exclude illegal immigrants."
PLEASE TICK ONE BOX ONLY

	%
Strongly agree	46.8
Agree	28.5
Neither agree nor disagree	13.4
Disagree	5.6
Strongly disagree	0.7
Can't choose	3.7
(NA)	1.3

A - 8

n=1079

A2.22 Britain controls the numbers of people from abroad that are allowed to settle in this country. Please say, for each of the groups below, whether you think Britain should allow more settlement, less settlement, or about the same amount as now.

PLEASE TICK ONE BOX ON EACH LINE

		More settlement	Less settlement	About the same as now	(DK)	(NA)
a.	[AUSIEIMM] Australians and New Zealanders	% 10.2	24.9	61.8	0.2	2.9
b.	[ASIANIMM] Indians and Pakistanis	% 1.6	59.7	35.4	0.2	3.0
c.	[EECIMM] People from European Union countries	% 7.5	37.9	50.6	0.4	3.6
d.	[WIIMM] West Indians	% 2.7	52.8	41.2	0.2	3.1
e.	[EEUROIMM] People from Eastern Europe	% 5.4	45.2	45.9	0.2	3.2

A2.23 [RELCONTL]
Now thinking about the families (husbands, wives, children, parents) of people who have already settled in Britain, would you say in general that Britain should ....

PLEASE TICK ONE BOX ONLY

%
... be stricter in controlling the settlement of close relatives, 49.1
OR be less strict in controlling the settlement of close relatives, 7.3
OR keep the controls about the same as now? 41.5
(DK) 0.2
(NA) 1.8

A2.24 [PASCONTL]
And how much do you agree or disagree with the following statement?
"All passport controls between countries in the European Union should be removed"

PLEASE TICK ONE BOX ONLY

%
Strongly agree 7.9
Agree 14.6
Neither agree nor disagree 15.1
Disagree 31.3
Strongly disagree 25.4
Can't choose 4.1
(NA) 1.6

A - 9

n=1079

A2.25 Please tick one box for each of these statements about the European Union (EU) to show how much you agree or disagree.

PLEASE TICK ONE BOX ON EACH LINE

		Strongly agree	Agree	Neither agree nor disagree	Disagree	Strongly disagree	Can't choose	(NA)
a.	[EECBRIT1] If we stay in the European Union, Britain will lose control over decisions that affect Britain	% 22.6	31.7	18.4	15.9	2.1	6.7	2.6
b.	[EECBRIT2] The competition from other EU countries is making Britain more modern and efficient	% 2.6	32.0	31.0	19.3	3.3	8.9	2.8
c.	[EECBRIT3] Lots of good traditions will have to be given up if we stay in the EU	% 14.9	25.5	19.3	26.6	4.2	6.7	2.8

A2.26 Some say that more decisions should be made by the European Union. Others say that more decisions should be made by individual governments. Do you think decisions about taxes should mostly be made by the European Union or mostly by individual governments?

PLEASE TICK ONE BOX ON EACH LINE

		Mostly made by the EU	Mostly made by individual governments	Made by both equally	Can't choose	(NA)
a.	[ECDEC1] Decisions about taxes?	% 3.4	72.5	13.4	8.1	2.5
b.	[ECDEC2] And what about decisions about controlling pollution?	% 29.8	26.1	35.7	5.9	2.5
c.	[ECDEC3] Decisions about defence?	% 10.9	54.4	25.1	7.1	2.6
d.	[ECDEC4] Decisions about the rights of people at work?	% 20.3	48.9	21.4	6.8	2.6
e.	[ECDEC5] Decisions about immigration?	% 6.7	64.4	17.6	8.6	2.6

A2.27 [PROPREP]
How much do you agree or disagree with this statement? Britain should introduce proportional representation so that the number of MPs each party gets matches more closely the number of votes each party gets.

PLEASE TICK ONE BOX ONLY

%
Strongly agree 20.4
Agree 31.2
Neither agree nor disagree 20.8
Disagree 12.0
Strongly disagree 4.6
Can't choose 9.1
(NA) 2.0

OFFICE USE ONLY

A - 10

OFFICE USE ONLY

n=3145

A2.28 From what you know or have heard, please tick a box for each of the items below to show whether you think the National Health Service in your area is, on the whole, satisfactory or in need of improvement.

PLEASE TICK ONE BOX ON EACH LINE

		In need of a lot of improvement	In need of some improvement	Satis-factory	Very good	(DK)	(NA)
a.	GPs' appointment systems [HSAREA1]	% 12.4	30.5	43.4	11.6	0.1	2.1
b.	Amount of time GP gives to each patient [HSAREA2]	% 9.9	23.0	52.3	12.0	0.2	2.6
c.	Being able to choose which GP to see [HSAREA3]	% 8.9	20.4	52.5	14.9	0.3	3.0
d.	Quality of medical treatment by GPs [HSAREA4]	% 6.7	18.2	50.7	21.5	0.2	2.7
e.	Hospital waiting lists for non-emergency operations [HSAREA5]	% 33.0	43.1	17.7	1.2	0.7	4.3
f.	Waiting time before getting appointments with hospital consultants [HSAREA6]	% 36.7	40.9	16.9	1.6	0.6	3.4
g.	General condition of hospital buildings [HSAREA7]	% 16.5	32.6	38.9	8.2	0.4	3.4
h.	Staffing level of nurses in hospitals [HSAREA8]	% 30.0	39.3	22.4	4.5	0.7	3.1
i.	Staffing level of doctors in hospitals [HSAREA9]	% 30.3	39.8	22.5	3.3	0.8	3.3
j.	Quality of medical treatment in hospitals [HSAREA10]	% 7.1	28.1	46.6	14.4	0.5	3.3
k.	Quality of nursing care in hospitals [HSAREA11]	% 5.5	22.5	44.8	23.6	0.5	3.2
l.	Waiting areas in accident and emergency departments [HSAREA12]	% 19.7	36.4	34.4	5.2	0.6	3.7
m.	Waiting areas for out-patients in hospitals [HSAREA13]	% 15.3	35.4	39.5	5.9	0.4	3.5
n.	Waiting areas at GPs' surgeries [HSAREA14]	% 5.0	16.6	58.6	16.9	0.2	2.7
o.	Time spent waiting in out-patient departments [HSAREA15]	% 21.8	47.5	24.8	2.3	0.4	3.3
p.	Time spent waiting in accident and emergency departments before being seen by a doctor [HSAREA16]	% 30.9	41.3	20.5	2.7	0.7	3.9
q.	Time spent waiting for an ambulance after a 999 call [HSAREA17]	% 12.2	29.8	40.8	9.6	2.0	5.8

A - 11

OFFICE USE ONLY

n=3145

A2.29 In the last two years, have you or a close family member …

PLEASE TICK ONE BOX ON EACH LINE

			Yes	No	(DK)	(NA)
a.	[NHSDOC]	…visited an NHS GP?	% 93.0	3.6	-	3.4
b.	[NHSOUTP]	…been an out-patient in an NHS hospital?	% 70.1	24.3	-	5.5
c.	[NHSINP]	…been an in-patient in an NHS hospital?	% 47.1	46.3	0.0	6.6
d.	[NHSVISIT]	…visited a patient in an NHS hospital?	% 71.0	23.1	-	5.9
e.	[PRIVPAT]	…had any medical treatment as a private patient?	% 13.0	80.5	-	6.4

n=1079

A2.30 [LEGCAN] Please tick one box to show how much you agree or disagree with this statement.

"Smoking cannabis (marijuana) should be legalised"

PLEASE TICK ONE BOX ONLY

	%
Strongly agree	10.0
Just agree	20.3
Neither agree nor disagree	11.4
Just disagree	12.7
Strongly disagree	44.0
(DK)	0.1
(NA)	1.5

Now a few questions about the disease called AIDS.

A2.31 Please tick one box for each statement to show how much you agree or disagree with it.

PLEASE TICK ONE BOX ON EACH LINE

		Strongly agree	Agree	Neither agree nor disagree	Disagree	Strongly disagree	(DK)	(NA)
a.	[AIDSBLME] Most people with AIDS have only themselves to blame	% 9.1	18.0	20.7	36.2	14.6	-	1.4
b.	[AIDSWRNG] Official warnings about AIDS should say that some sexual practices are morally wrong	% 15.8	28.7	18.7	23.3	12.0	-	1.5
c.	[AIDSPUN] AIDS is a way of punishing the world for its decline in moral standards	% 4.7	9.4	20.7	36.2	27.4	0.0	1.5
d.	[AIDSSPD] People who inject themselves with illegal drugs should be given free needles to prevent the spread of AIDS	% 23.9	36.4	12.8	15.5	10.1	0.0	1.3

A - 12

A - 13

n=3145

A2.32 [PAIDJOB]
Do you have a paid job?
PLEASE TICK ONE BOX ONLY

	%	
Yes	54.9	
No	42.9	→ PLEASE GO TO A2.37
(NA)	2.2	

PLEASE ANSWER A2.33 TO A2.36 ABOUT YOUR PAID JOB

n=1796

A2.33 [PWWKPLAN]
Which of the following statements about your work is **most** true?
PLEASE TICK ONE BOX ONLY

	%
My job allows me to design or plan most of my daily work	42.5
My job allows me to design or plan parts of my daily work	28.3
My job does not really allow me to design or plan my daily work	19.8
(NA)	9.4

A2.34 [PWWKSAT]
How satisfied are you with the amount of training you get in your (main) job?
PLEASE TICK ONE BOX ONLY

	%
Very satisfied	18.4
Fairly satisfied	31.9
Neither satisfied nor dissatisfied	22.2
Fairly dissatisfied	6.9
Very dissatisfied	4.0
Can't choose	6.2
(NA)	10.4

A2.35 [PWTRNSAT]
And how satisfied are you with the opportunities for promotion in your (main) job?
PLEASE TICK ONE BOX ONLY

	%
Very satisfied	11.0
Fairly satisfied	19.0
Neither satisfied nor dissatisfied	28.1
Fairly dissatisfied	12.9
Very dissatisfied	9.3
Can't choose	9.0
(NA)	10.7

A2.36 [PWLEARN]
On the whole, would you say that in your (main) job these days you learn new skills ...
PLEASE TICK ONE BOX ONLY

	%
... almost all the time,	9.9
... a lot of the time,	20.1
... occasionally,	43.3
... or, hardly ever or never?	17.0
(NA)	9.7

EVERYONE PLEASE ANSWER THE REST OF THE QUESTIONNAIRE

A2.37 [TRAININ]
Compared with other countries that compete with us, how good do you think Britain is at training employees in new skills?
PLEASE TICK ONE BOX ONLY

	%
Better than most	14.1
Worse than most	32.9
About the same	29.9
Can't choose	21.0
(NA)	2.1

A2.38 Please tick a box for each statement to show how you feel about disabled people and work.
PLEASE TICK ONE BOX ON EACH LINE

		Strongly agree	Agree	Neither agree nor disagree	Disagree	Strongly disagree	Can't choose	(NA)
a.	[DISINTEFF] In general, people with disabilities cannot be as effective at work as people without disabilities	% 3.3	20.7	24.0	34.9	11.6	3.3	2.2
b.	[DISPREJD] The main problem faced by disabled people at work is other people's prejudice - not their own lack of ability	% 16.8	54.6	14.5	8.1	1.0	2.8	2.2
c.	[DISNOALL] Employers should not make special allowances for people with disabilities	% 2.2	10.9	16.8	51.2	13.9	2.7	2.3
d.	[DISFORCD] Employers should be forced to employ more people with disabilities, even if it leads to extra costs	% 8.4	33.2	25.3	24.1	3.4	3.6	2.0
e.	[DISNCOLL] I would not like to work with someone who was extremely disabled	% 1.8	7.6	17.9	38.5	27.0	5.0	2.3

A - 14

OFFICE USE ONLY

n=1079

A2.39 [PROTRCMX]
Some people think that better relations between Protestants and Catholics in Northern Ireland will only come about through more mixing of the two communities. Others think that better relations will only come about through more separation. Which comes closest to your views?

PLEASE TICK ONE BOX ONLY

	%
Better relations will come about through more mixing	91.7
Better relations will come about through more separation	4.4
(DK)	0.3
(NA)	3.6

A2.40 People feel closer to some groups than to others. For you personally, how close would you say you feel towards ...

PLEASE TICK ONE BOX ON EACH LINE

		Very close	Fairly close	A little close	Not very close	Not at all close	(DK)	(NA)
[CLSEBORN] a.	... people born in the same area as you?	% 10.6	39.1	22.4	16.2	8.8	0.2	2.7
[CLSECLAS] b.	... people who have the same social class background as yours?	% 10.3	47.0	24.7	10.8	4.2	0.2	2.8
[CLSERELG] c.	... people who have the same religious background as yours?	% 7.8	31.9	24.7	18.8	13.3	0.2	3.2
[CLSERACE] d.	... people of the same race as you?	% 10.2	41.6	27.0	11.0	6.4	0.2	3.6
[CLSELIVE] e.	... people who live in the same area as you do now?	% 8.0	38.0	29.8	15.9	5.2	0.2	2.8
[CLSEPOL] f.	... people who have the same political beliefs as you?	% 3.7	28.2	29.6	23.6	11.5	0.2	3.1

A2.41 [NIGOVPRF]
Here are a number of different ways in which Northern Ireland might be governed in the future. Please tick one box to show which you would most prefer.
PLEASE TICK ONE BOX ONLY

Should Northern Ireland ...

	%
... remain part of the UK without a separate parliament in Belfast,	10.7
remain part of the UK with a separate parliament in Belfast,	14.3
become part of the Irish Republic without a separate parliament in Belfast,	13.6
become part of the Irish Republic with a separate parliament in Belfast,	12.3
be governed jointly by the UK and the Irish Republic without its own parliament in Belfast,	3.2
be governed jointly by the UK and the Irish Republic with its own parliament in Belfast,	12.2
become an independent state with its own parliament, separate from both the UK and the Irish Republic?	11.0
Can't choose	19.9
(NA)	2.7

A - 15

OFFICE USE ONLY

n=1079

A2.42 [NIGOVFUT]
Now from the same list of possibilities please tick one box to show which you think Northern Ireland will in fact have in, say, ten years' time.
PLEASE TICK ONE BOX ONLY

In ten years' time Northern Ireland will ...

	%
... remain part of the UK without a separate parliament in Belfast,	16.5
remain part of the UK with a separate parliament in Belfast,	17.4
become part of the Irish Republic without a separate parliament in Belfast,	6.9
become part of the Irish Republic with a separate parliament in Belfast,	10.9
be governed jointly by the UK and the Irish Republic without its own parliament in Belfast,	5.7
be governed jointly by the UK and the Irish Republic with its own parliament in Belfast,	8.0
become an independent state with its own parliament, separate from both the UK and the Irish Republic?	6.6
Can't choose	25.2
(NA)	2.8

A2.43a [GBGOVNI]
How much say do you think a British government of any party should have in the way Northern Ireland is run? Do you think it should have ...
PLEASE TICK ONE BOX ONLY

	%
... a great deal of say,	12.8
some say,	29.2
a little say,	17.2
or - no say at all?	21.7
Can't choose	16.9
(NA)	2.1

b. [IRGOVNI]
And how much say do you think an Irish government of any party should have in the way Northern Ireland is run? Do you think it should have ...
PLEASE TICK ONE BOX ONLY

	%
... a great deal of say,	22.4
some say,	32.4
a little say,	14.9
or - no say at all?	12.1
Can't choose	16.0
(NA)	2.2

A - 16 n=1079

A2.44 From what you know or have heard, please tick one box on each line to show how well you think state secondary schools nowadays ...

PLEASE TICK ONE BOX ON EACH LINE

	Very well	Quite well	Not very well	Not at all well	(DK)	(NA)
[STATSEC1] a. ... prepare young people for work?	% 5.2	34.6	49.2	7.0	0.1	3.8
[STATSEC2] b. ... teach young people basic skills such as reading, writing and maths?	% 10.9	49.4	29.6	6.4	0.1	3.6
[STATSEC3] c. ... bring out young people's natural abilities?	% 5.4	37.0	43.5	10.0	0.0	4.1

A2.45 From what you know or have heard, please tick one box for each statement about state secondary schools now compared with 10 years ago.

PLEASE TICK ONE BOX ON EACH LINE

	Much better now than 10 years ago	A little better	About the same	A little worse	Much worse now than 10 years ago	(DK)	(NA)
[SCHLLEAV] a. On the whole, do you think school-leavers are better qualified or worse qualified nowadays than they were 10 years ago?	% 10.8	26.9	30.1	20.0	8.4	0.2	3.5
[TEACHPAY] b. Do you think teachers are better paid or worse paid nowadays than they were 10 years ago?	% 15.1	26.4	30.8	18.5	4.6	0.3	4.3
[CLASSBEH] c. And do you think classroom behaviour is better or worse nowadays than it was 10 years ago?	% 0.8	3.3	15.7	33.2	43.0	0.1	3.9
[TEACHBET] d. And do you think the standard of teaching is better or worse nowadays than it was 10 years ago?	% 3.4	14.6	38.0	27.5	12.5	0.3	3.7

A2.46 And from what you know or have heard, please tick one box for each statement about universities and colleges now compared with 10 years ago.

PLEASE TICK ONE BOX ON EACH LINE

	Much better now than 10 years ago	A little better	About the same	A little worse	Much worse now than 10 years ago	(DK)	(NA)
[UNIQUAL] a. On the whole, do you think that students leaving university are better qualified or worse qualified nowadays than they were 10 years ago?	% 8.7	25.3	48.6	10.9	2.3	0.4	3.9
[UNITEACH] b. And do you think that the standard of teaching in universities is better or worse nowadays than it was 10 years ago?	% 6.1	18.3	56.0	11.9	2.7	0.5	4.4
[UNIJOBS] c. And do you think that students leaving university have better or worse job prospects nowadays than they had 10 years ago?	% 2.3	5.9	15.9	37.9	34.2	0.1	3.7

A - 17 n=1079

A2.47 Please tick one box to show how much you agree or disagree that ....

PLEASE TICK ONE BOX ON EACH LINE

	Strongly agree	Agree	Neither agree nor disagree	Disagree	Strongly disagree	Can't choose	(NA)
[SKILLIMP] a. ... when recruiting school-leavers, employers pay too much attention to practical skills and training, and too little to exam results	% 4.1	16.9	28.3	32.9	7.7	6.8	3.2
[EXAMIMD] b. ... when choosing students, universities pay too much attention to exam results, and too little to practical skills and training	% 10.3	38.0	24.5	14.8	2.3	6.6	3.6

A2.48 Here are some things that universities might make public, so that people can see how well they are doing. In your view how important is it that they should publish details of ...

PLEASE TICK ONE BOX ON EACH LINE

	Essential	Very important	Fairly important	Not very important	Not at all important	Can't choose	(NA)
[UNIVPUB1] a. ... how many students complete their degree?	% 18.7	33.6	30.0	8.0	1.6	4.7	3.5
[UNIVPUB2] b. ... how many students get a first class degree?	% 11.8	28.0	36.2	13.6	1.6	5.0	3.6
[UNIVPUB3] c. ... how many students get a job when they finish?	% 26.3	41.5	16.3	6.1	1.3	4.7	3.8

OFFICE USE ONLY

A - 18

n=1079

A2.49 Here are some qualities that students may have developed by the time they leave university.

a. In your view which is the most important quality universities should aim to develop in their students?

b. And which is the next most important quality that universities should aim to develop?

PLEASE TICK ONE BOX ONLY IN EACH COLUMN

	[UNISHLD1] Most important %	[UNISHLD2] Next most important %
Self-confidence	11.1	12.8
How to live among people from different backgrounds	2.9	4.9
Skills and knowledge which will get them a good job	39.6	14.3
A readiness to challenge other people's ideas	3.7	6.2
An ability to speak and write clearly	2.7	10.0
Knowledge that equips people for life in general	16.9	26.6
(NA)	23.2	25.2

A2.50a And which one of these qualities do you think universities actually do develop most in their students?

b. And which next?

PLEASE TICK ONE BOX ONLY IN EACH COLUMN

	[UNIDOES1] Most developed %	[UNIDOES2] Next most developed %
Self-confidence	13.6	14.4
How to live among people from different backgrounds	7.4	11.9
Skills and knowledge which will get them a good job	27.2	12.5
A readiness to challenge other people's ideas	12.4	12.1
An ability to speak and write clearly	7.1	8.1
Knowledge that equips people for life in general	8.9	14.2
(NA)	23.4	26.8

A - 19

n=1079

A2.51 Here are some statements about illegal drugs, such as cannabis, cocaine and heroin. PLEASE TICK ONE BOX ON EACH LINE

		Strongly agree	Agree	Neither agree nor disagree	Disagree	Strongly disagree	Can't choose	(NA)
[DRUGSC1] a.	Doctors must be allowed to prescribe drugs for those who are addicted to them	3.5	27.7	17.9	26.8	15.1	4.2	4.8
[DRUGSC2] b.	Britain should aim to become a drug-free society	36.3	36.5	12.3	6.4	2.0	1.6	5.0
[DRUGSC3] c.	Adults should be free to take any drug they wish	1.0	7.8	9.9	38.3	36.0	2.0	5.0
[DRUGSC4] d.	All adults have a duty to prevent young people from using illegal drugs	46.0	36.0	5.9	3.0	3.1	1.3	4.7
[DRUGSC5] e.	The use of 'soft' drugs leads to the use of 'hard' drugs	24.1	35.2	13.2	15.4	4.5	2.3	5.2
[DRUGSC6] f.	All illegal drugs should be made legal	4.5	5.6	3.1	33.3	47.1	1.6	4.9
[DRUGSC7] g.	The best way to treat people who are addicted to drugs is to stop them from using drugs altogether	19.6	30.4	18.5	18.3	3.9	4.6	4.7
[DRUGSC8] h.	Taking illegal drugs can sometimes be beneficial	3.0	22.2	17.7	27.4	20.6	4.2	4.9
[DRUGSC9] i.	The use of illegal drugs always leads to addiction	16.1	30.7	17.8	22.1	5.5	3.3	4.6
[DRUGSC10] j.	You can never trust someone who is addicted to drugs	20.1	41.6	17.3	10.9	2.8	2.6	4.7
[DRUGSC11] k.	People who are addicted to drugs should decide for themselves whether they have treatment	4.9	29.9	15.7	30.7	11.8	2.4	4.6
[DRUGSC12] l.	Taking drugs is always morally wrong	19.4	30.9	20.0	15.7	5.6	3.3	5.1
[DRUGSC13] m.	All use of illegal drugs is misuse	20.2	37.2	14.2	16.2	4.1	3.2	5.0
[DRUGSC14] n.	We need to accept that using illegal drugs is a normal part of some people's lives	5.4	25.4	14.8	30.7	16.3	2.9	4.6
[DRUGSC15] o.	The legalisation of drugs would lead to a considerable increase in misuse	23.2	40.3	10.1	14.9	3.6	2.9	5.0
[DRUGSC16] p.	The only way to help addicts is to make them have treatment	18.5	31.8	19.7	19.0	3.3	3.2	4.5

OFFICE USE ONLY

A - 20

n=3145

A2.52 Please tick one box for each statement to show how much you agree or disagree with it.
PLEASE TICK ONE BOX ON EACH LINE

	Agree strongly	Agree	Neither agree nor disagree	Disagree	Disagree strongly	(DK)	OFFICE USE ONLY (NA)
[WELFRESP] a. The welfare state makes people nowadays less willing to look after themselves %	12.1	35.1	21.0	25.8	3.4	0.1	2.3
[WELFSTIG] b. People receiving social security are made to feel like second class citizens %	8.6	39.6	22.2	25.4	1.9	0.1	2.2
[WELFHELP] c. The welfare state encourages people to stop helping each other %	5.2	30.5	26.7	33.0	2.3	0.1	2.2
[MOREWELF] d. The government should spend more money on welfare benefits for the poor, even if it leads to higher taxes %	10.6	38.9	25.4	20.5	2.3	0.1	2.2
[UNEMPJOB] e. Around here, most unemployed people could find a job if they really wanted one %	7.6	30.4	21.6	31.4	6.7	0.1	2.2
[SOCHELP] f. Many people who get social security don't really deserve any help %	6.0	23.7	24.3	35.9	7.3	0.1	2.7
[DOLEFIDL] g. Most people on the dole are fiddling in one way or another %	8.0	24.8	27.7	30.0	7.1	0.1	2.3
[WELFFEET] h. If welfare benefits weren't so generous, people would learn to stand on their own two feet %	7.7	25.3	21.3	32.8	10.8	0.1	2.1

A2.53 Please tick one box for each statement below to show how much you agree or disagree with it.
PLEASE TICK ONE BOX ON EACH LINE

	Agree strongly	Agree	Neither agree nor disagree	Disagree	Disagree strongly	(DK)	(NA)
[REDISTRB] a. Government should redistribute income from the better-off to those who are less well off %	14.9	32.3	22.0	24.2	4.5	0.1	2.0
[BIGBUSINN] b. Big business benefits owners at the expense of workers %	15.8	45.9	20.5	13.9	1.4	0.1	2.4
[WEALTH] c. Ordinary working people do not get their fair share of the nation's wealth %	16.9	49.6	19.1	11.4	0.8	0.0	2.2
[RICHLAW] d. There is one law for the rich and one for the poor %	28.9	42.2	13.5	11.9	1.5	0.0	2.0
[INDUST4] e. Management will always try to get the better of employees if it gets the chance %	20.6	43.4	19.6	13.0	1.2	0.1	2.1

A - 21

n=3145

A2.54 Please tick one box for each statement below to show how much you agree or disagree with it.
PLEASE TICK ONE BOX ON EACH LINE

	Agree strongly	Agree	Neither agree nor disagree	Disagree	Disagree strongly	(DK)	OFFICE USE ONLY (NA)
[TRADVALS] a. Young people today don't have enough respect for traditional British values %	18.6	48.2	20.2	10.3	0.9	0.0	1.9
[STIFSENT] b. People who break the law should be given stiffer sentences %	33.4	45.6	13.7	4.9	0.5	0.0	1.8
[DEATHAPP] c. For some crimes, the death penalty is the most appropriate sentence %	33.3	32.6	9.8	12.2	9.9	0.0	2.2
[OBEY] d. Schools should teach children to obey authority %	31.2	52.0	9.7	4.1	0.8	0.0	2.0
[WRONGLAW] e. The law should always be obeyed, even if a particular law is wrong %	8.6	32.0	29.0	24.7	3.5	0.0	2.2
[CENSOR] f. Censorship of films and magazines is necessary to uphold moral standards %	19.8	44.0	16.1	13.9	4.3	0.0	1.9

A2.55a [QTIME]
To help us plan better in future, please tell us about how long it took you to complete this questionnaire.
PLEASE TICK ONE BOX ONLY

n=1079

	%
Less than 15 minutes	5.9
Between 15 and 20 minutes	24.7
Between 21 and 30 minutes	34.4
Between 31 and 45 minutes	20.6
Between 46 and 60 minutes	8.2
Over one hour	4.9
(NA)	1.4

b. And on what date did you fill in the questionnaire?

PLEASE WRITE IN [ ] DATE [0] MONTH 1995

Thank you very much for your help

Please keep the completed questionnaire for the interviewer if he or she has arranged to call for it. Otherwise, please post it as soon as possible in the pre-paid addressed envelope provided.

B

Head Office: 35 NORTHAMPTON SQUARE,
LONDON EC1V 0AX
Tel: 0171/250 1866   Fax: 0171/250 1524

Field and DP Office: 100 KINGS ROAD,
BRENTWOOD, ESSEX CM14 4LX
Tel: 01277 200600   Fax: 01277 214117

SCPR
SOCIAL & COMMUNITY PLANNING RESEARCH

Spring 1995

P.1430

BRITISH SOCIAL ATTITUDES 1995
MAIN SAMPLE
SELF-COMPLETION QUESTIONNAIRE

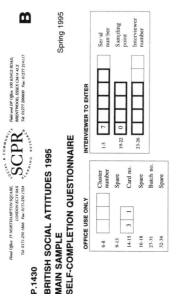

OFFICE USE ONLY

6-8		Cluster number
9-13		Spare
14-15	3	1	Card no.
16-18		Spare
27-31		Batch no.
32-34		Spare

INTERVIEWER TO ENTER

1-5	7	Serial number
19-22	0	Sampling point
23-26		Interviewer number

To the selected respondent:

Thank you very much for agreeing to take part in this important study - the eleventh in this annual series. The study consists of this self-completion questionnaire, and the interview you have already completed. The results of the survey are published in a book each autumn; some of the questions are also being asked in twenty-two other countries, as part of an international survey.

Completing the questionnaire:

The questions inside cover a wide range of subjects, but each one can be answered simply by placing a tick (✓) or a number in one or more of the boxes. No special knowledge is required: we are confident that everyone will be able to take part, not just those with strong views or particular viewpoints. The questionnaire should not take very long to complete, and we hope you will find it interesting and enjoyable. **Only you should fill it in, and not anyone else at your address.** The answers you give will be treated as confidential and anonymous.

Returning the questionnaire:

Your interviewer will arrange with you the most convenient way of returning the questionnaire. If the interviewer has arranged to call back for it, please fill it in and keep it safely until then. If not, please complete it and post it back in the pre-paid, addressed envelope, AS SOON AS YOU POSSIBLY CAN.

THANK YOU AGAIN FOR YOUR HELP.

Social and Community Planning Research is an independent social research institute registered as a charitable trust. Its projects are funded by government departments, local authorities, universities and foundations to provide information on social issues in Britain. The British Social Attitudes survey series is funded mainly by one of the Sainsbury Family Charitable Trusts, with contributions also from other grant-giving bodies and government departments. Please contact us if you would like further information.

B - 1

OFFICE USE ONLY

n=2067

In the first part of this questionnaire, we would like to ask you about your family and friends. For example, about how often you see or visit them, and when you turn to them for help and advice.

MOTHER

[MUMVIST2]
B2.01a First, your mother. How often do you see or visit her?

PLEASE TICK ONE BOX ONLY

%

She is no longer alive	41.9 → NOW PLEASE GO TO B2.02a ON PAGE 3
She lives in the same household	8.3
Daily	3.8
At least several times a week	8.2
At least once a week	11.8
At least once a fortnight	5.1
At least once a month	5.4
Several times a year	9.4
Less often	4.0
Never	1.4
(NA)	0.8

[MUMJURNY]
b. About how long would it take you to get to where your mother lives? Think of the time it usually takes door to door.

PLEASE TICK ONE BOX ONLY

%

Less than 15 minutes	15.2
Between 15 and 30 minutes	10.9
Between 30 minutes and 1 hour	5.8
Between 1 and 2 hours	4.6
Between 2 and 3 hours	3.9
Between 3 and 5 hours	3.3
Between 5 and 12 hours	2.7
Over 12 hours	2.2
(NA)	1.2

B - 2

OFFICE USE ONLY

n=2067

[MUMPHONE]
B2.01c How often do you have any contact with your mother by telephone?

PLEASE TICK ONE BOX ONLY

%

Daily	4.2
At least several times a week	11.5
At least once a week	15.6
At least once a fortnight	6.3
At least once a month	3.4
Several times a year	2.1
Less often	1.6
Never	4.1
(NA)	1.1

[MUMWRITE]
d. And how often do you have any contact with your mother by writing?

PLEASE TICK ONE BOX ONLY

%

Daily	-
At least several times a week	0.1
At least once a week	0.4
At least once a fortnight	0.7
At least once a month	1.7
Several times a year	6.5
Less often	11.2
Never	28.0
(NA)	1.1

B - 3

FATHER

n=2067   OFFICE USE ONLY

[DADVIST2]
B2.02a How often do you see or visit your father?
PLEASE TICK ONE BOX ONLY

	%	
He is no longer alive	55.2	→ NOW PLEASE GO TO B2.03a ON PAGE 5
Lives in same household	5.8	
Daily	2.3	
At least several times a week	5.7	
At least once a week	7.1	
At least once a fortnight	3.7	
At least once a month	3.9	
Several times a year	7.8	
Less often	3.5	
Never	3.6	
(NA)	1.2	

[DADJURNY]
B2.02b. About how long would it take you to get to where your father lives? Think of the time it usually takes door to door.
PLEASE TICK ONE ONE ONLY

	%
Less than 15 minutes	10.7
Between 15 and 30 minutes	7.8
Between 30 minutes and 1 hour	3.8
Between 1 and 2 hours	3.8
Between 2 and 3 hours	3.0
Between 3 and 5 hours	2.7
Between 5 and 12 hours	2.3
Over 12 hour	2.1
(NA)	2.8

[DADPHONE]
B2.02c. How often do you have any contact with your father by telephone?
PLEASE TICK ONE BOX ONLY

	%
Daily	1.3
At least several times a week	5.8
At least once a week	9.5
At least once a fortnight	4.6
At least once a month	3.9
Several times a year	3.6
Less often	6.1
Never	1.8

[DADWRITE]
d. And how often do you have any contact with your father by writing?
PLEASE TICK ONE BOX ONLY

	%
Daily	-
At least several times a week	.0
At least once a week	.1
At least once a fortnight	.3
At least once a month	.8
Several times a year	4.3
Less often	9.0
Never	22.7
(NA)	1.8

B - 4

BROTHERS AND SISTERS

n=2067   OFFICE USE ONLY

[SIBLINGS]
B2.03a How many brothers and sisters aged 18 or older do you have? (We mean brothers/sisters who are still alive, please include step-brothers/sisters, half brothers/sisters and adopted brothers/sisters).
PLEASE TICK ONE BOX ONLY

	%	
None	15.2	→ NOW PLEASE GO TO B2.04a ON PAGE 7
One	30.9	
Two	22.3	
Three	12.7	
Four	7.1	
Five or more	10.9	
(Has unknown number)	0.2	
(NA)	0.7	

The questions on this, and the next, page are about your brother/sister. If you have more than one adult brother/sister, please think about the one you have most contact with.

[BROSIS]
b. Firstly, please tick a box to show whether this person is your brother or your sister.
PLEASE TICK ONE BOX ONLY

	%
Brother	35.3
Sister	45.1
(Brother and sister)	1.8
(NA)	2.6

[SIBVISIT]
c. How often do you see or visit this brother/sister?
PLEASE TICK ONE BOX ONLY

	%	
He/she lives in the same household	3.5	→ NOW PLEASE GO TO B2.04a ON PAGE 7
Daily	3.1	
At least several times a week	7.2	
At least once a week	12.6	
At least once a fortnight	7.3	
At least once a month	9.5	
Several times a year	20.9	
Less often	15.2	
Never	3.5	
(NA)	1.9	

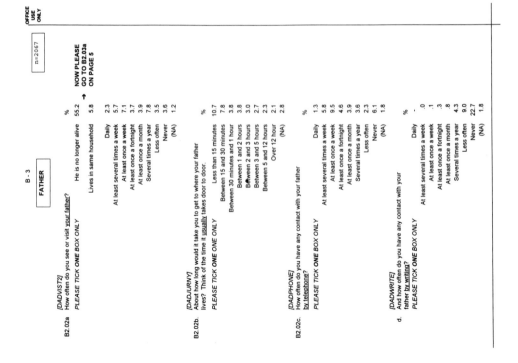

B - 5

n=2067

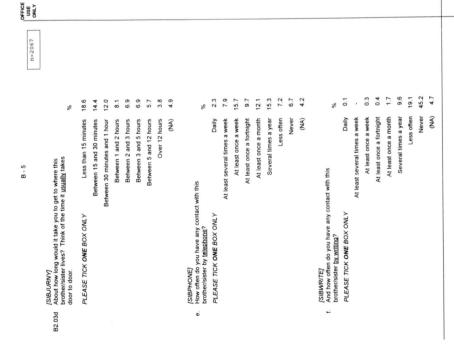

B2.03d *[SIBJURNY]*
About how long would it take you to get to where this brother/sister lives? Think of the time it *usually* takes door to door.

*PLEASE TICK **ONE** BOX ONLY*

	%
Less than 15 minutes	18.6
Between 15 and 30 minutes	14.4
Between 30 minutes and 1 hour	12.0
Between 1 and 2 hours	8.1
Between 2 and 3 hours	6.9
Between 3 and 5 hours	6.9
Between 5 and 12 hours	5.7
Over 12 hours	3.8
(NA)	4.9

e. *[SIBPHONE]*
How often do you have any contact with this brother/sister by **telephone**?

*PLEASE TICK **ONE** BOX ONLY*

	%
Daily	2.3
At least several times a week	7.9
At least once a week	15.7
At least once a fortnight	9.7
At least once a month	12.1
Several times a year	15.3
Less often	7.2
Never	6.7
(NA)	4.2

f. *[SIBWRITE]*
And how often do you have any contact with this brother/sister **by writing**?

*PLEASE TICK **ONE** BOX ONLY*

	%
Daily	0.1
At least several times a week	-
At least once a week	0.3
At least once a fortnight	0.4
At least once a month	1.7
Several times a year	9.6
Less often	19.1
Never	45.2
(NA)	4.7

B - 6

n=2067

SONS AND DAUGHTERS

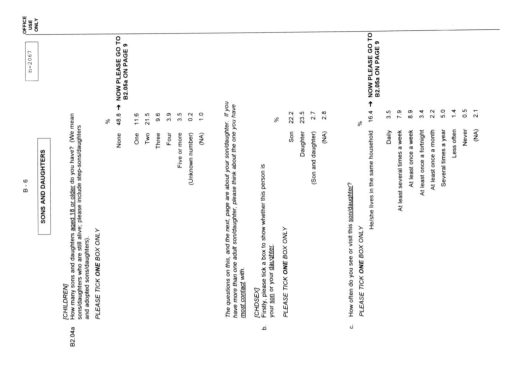

B2.04a *[CHILDREN]*
How many sons and daughters <u>aged 18 or older</u> do you have? (We mean sons/daughters who are still alive; please include step-sons/daughters and adopted sons/daughters).

*PLEASE TICK **ONE** BOX ONLY*

	%	
None	48.8	→ NOW PLEASE GO TO B2.05a ON PAGE 9
One	11.6	
Two	21.5	
Three	9.6	
Four	3.9	
Five or more	3.5	
(Unknown number)	0.2	
(NA)	1.0	

The questions on this, and the next, page are about your adult son/daughter. If you have more than one adult son/daughter, please think about the one you have most contact with.

b. *[CHDSEX]*
Firstly, please tick a box to show whether this person is your <u>son</u> or your <u>daughter</u>.

*PLEASE TICK **ONE** BOX ONLY*

	%
Son	22.2
Daughter	23.5
(Son and daughter)	2.7
(NA)	2.8

c. How often do you see or visit this <u>son/daughter</u>?

*PLEASE TICK **ONE** BOX ONLY*

	%	
He/she lives in the same household	16.4	→ NOW PLEASE GO TO B2.05a ON PAGE 9
Daily	3.5	
At least several times a week	7.9	
At least once a week	8.9	
At least once a fortnight	3.4	
At least once a month	2.2	
Several times a year	5.0	
Less often	1.4	
Never	0.5	
(NA)	2.1	

B - 7

[CHDJURNY]
B2.04d About how long would it take you to get where your son/daughter lives? Think of the time it usually takes door to door.

PLEASE TICK ONE BOX ONLY	%
Less than 15 minutes	10.5
Between 15 and 30 minutes	8.1
Between 30 minutes and 1 hour	4.6
Between 1 and 2 hours	2.8
Between 2 and 3 hours	2.0
Between 3 and 5 hours	1.7
Between 5 and 12 hours	1.2
Over 12 hours	0.5
(NA)	3.4

[CHDPHONE]
e. How often do you have any contact with this son/daughter by telephone?

PLEASE TICK ONE BOX ONLY	%
Daily	3.6
At least several times a week	9.9
At least once a week	10.4
At least once a fortnight	2.5
At least once a month	1.6
Several times a year	1.4
Less often	0.5
Never	1.7
(NA)	3.2

[CHDWRITE]
f. And how often do you have any contact with this son/daughter by writing?

PLEASE TICK ONE BOX ONLY	%
Daily	-
At least several times a week	0.1
At least once a week	0.5
At least once a fortnight	0.6
At least once a month	1.0
Several times a year	3.5
Less often	6.6
Never	18.8
(NA)	3.6

B - 8

OTHER RELATIVES

B2.05a Now think of all your other adult relatives - those still living and aged 18 or older. How many of each do you have?
(Begin with your grandparents. Please write in a number to show how many grandparents you have.
If you have none, tick 'NONE', and then go on to the next relative.)

	Median	(NA)
[GRANDPTS] Grandmother, grandfather	0	12.5
[GRANDCHN] Adult grandchildren	0	20.1
[AUNTUNCS] Aunts, uncles	3	12.4
[INLAWS] Parents-in-law and adult brothers-in-law and sisters-in-law	3	12.1
[COUSINS] Adult nieces, nephews, cousins and other relatives	8	12.1

(AN APPROXIMATE NUMBER WILL DO)

[MOSTCNTC]
b. Thinking of all these adult relatives, which one do you have most contact with?

PLEASE TICK ONE BOX ONLY	%
Grandmother	9.2
Grandfather	1.3
(Grandmother and grandfather)	0.4
Granddaughter	4.0
Grandson	1.9
(Granddaughter and grandson)	0.3
Aunt	9.7
Uncle	3.4
(Aunt and uncle)	1.1
Mother-in-law	15.8
Father-in-law	3.3
(Mother- and father-in-law)	0.7
Sister-in-law	14.2
Brother-in-law	11.0
(Sister- and brother-in-law)	0.6
Other adult female relative	7.6
Other adult male relative	3.9
(Other male and female relative)	0.6
(NA)	3.2

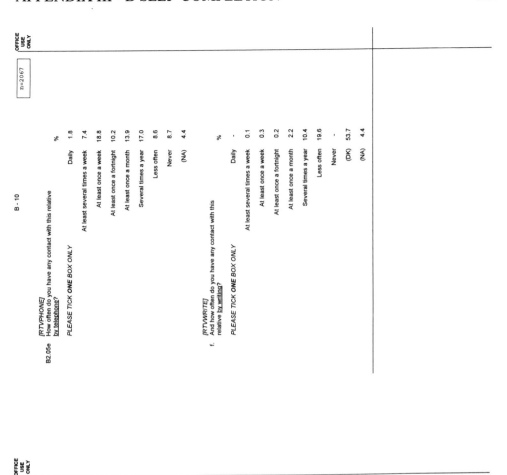

B - 10

n=2067

B2.05e *[RTVPHONE]*
How often do you have any contact with this relative by telephone?

PLEASE TICK ONE BOX ONLY

%

At least several times a week — Daily 1.8

At least once a week 7.4

At least once a fortnight 18.8

At least once a month 10.2

Several times a year 13.9

Less often 17.0

Never 8.6

(NA) 8.7

4.4

f. *[RTVWRITE]*
And how often do you have any contact with this relative by writing?

PLEASE TICK ONE BOX ONLY

%

At least several times a week — Daily -

At least once a week 0.1

At least once a fortnight 0.3

At least once a month 0.2

Several times a year 2.2

Less often 10.4

Never 19.6

(DK) -

(NA) 53.7

4.4

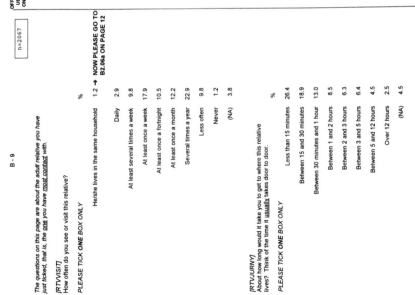

B - 9

n=2067

The questions on this page are about the adult relative you have just ticked, that is, the one you have most contact with.

B2.05c *[RTVVISIT]*
How often do you see or visit this relative?

PLEASE TICK ONE BOX ONLY

%

He/she lives in the same household 1.2 → **NOW PLEASE GO TO B2.06a ON PAGE 12**

Daily 2.9

At least several times a week 9.8

At least once a week 17.9

At least once a fortnight 10.5

At least once a month 12.2

Several times a year 22.9

Less often 9.8

Never 1.2

(NA) 3.8

d. *[RTVJURNY]*
About how long would it take you to get to where this relative lives? Think of the time it usually takes door to door.

PLEASE TICK ONE BOX ONLY

%

Less than 15 minutes 26.4

Between 15 and 30 minutes 18.9

Between 30 minutes and 1 hour 13.0

Between 1 and 2 hours 8.5

Between 2 and 3 hours 6.3

Between 3 and 5 hours 6.4

Between 5 and 12 hours 4.5

Over 12 hours 2.5

(NA) 4.5

B - 11

n=2067

FRIENDS

Thinking now of close friends - not your husband or wife or partner or family members - but people you feel fairly close to.

[PALS]
B2.06a How many close friends would you say you have?

NONE   →   NOW PLEASE GO TO B2.07 ON PAGE 14

      →   ANSWER b.- f.

Median: 4

(NA) 1.9%

[SEXPAL]
b. Now thinking of your best friend, or the friend you feel closest to. Is this friend a man or a woman?

PLEASE TICK **ONE** BOX ONLY

	%
Man	32.7
Woman	50.1
(Man and woman)	0.6
(NA)	3.0

[PALVISIT]
c. How often do you see or visit this friend?

PLEASE TICK **ONE** BOX ONLY

	%
He/she lives in the same household	1.3 → NOW PLEASE GO TO B2.07 ON PAGE 14
Daily	8.5
At least several times a week	18.3
At least once a week	22.3
At least once a fortnight	10.1
At least once a month	9.0
Several times a year	10.2
Less often	4.1
Never	0.2
(NA)	2.3

[PALJURNY]
d. About how long would it take you to get to where your friend lives? Think of the time it usually takes door to door.

PLEASE TICK **ONE** BOX ONLY

	%
Less than 15 minutes	35.8
Between 15 and 30 minutes	24.5
Between 30 minutes and 1 hour	8.5
Between 1 and 2 hours	4.7
Between 2 and 3 hours	2.7
Between 3 and 5 hours	3.6
Between 5 and 12 hours	1.3
Over 12 hours	1.2
(NA)	2.7

B - 12

n=2067

[PALPHONE]
B2.06e How often do you have any contact with this friend by telephone?

PLEASE TICK **ONE** BOX ONLY

	%
Daily	4.0
At least several times a week	13.3
At least once a week	23.8
At least once a fortnight	11.1
At least once a month	10.3
Several times a year	8.6
Less often	4.9
Never	6.2
(NA)	2.8

[PALWRITE]
f. And how often do you have any contact with this friend by writing?

PLEASE TICK **ONE** BOX ONLY

	%
Daily	0.3
At least several times a week	0.2
At least once a week	0.7
At least once a fortnight	0.7
At least once a month	1.6
Several times a year	8.3
Less often	17.4
Never	52.6
(NA)	3.3

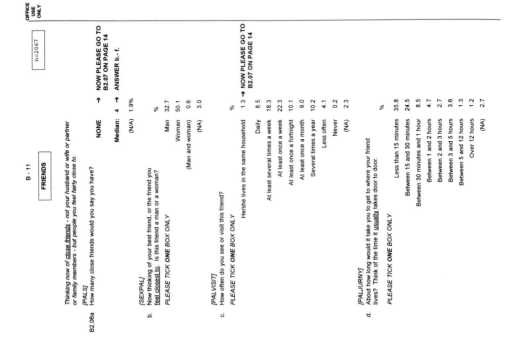

B - 13

n=2067

B2.07 Now we'd like to ask you about some problems that can happen to anyone.
First, there are some household and garden jobs you really can't do alone - for example, you may need someone to hold a ladder, or to help you move some furniture.

a. Who would you turn to first for help?

b. And who would you turn to second?

PLEASE TICK ONLY ONE AS YOUR FIRST CHOICE AND ONE AS YOUR SECOND CHOICE

	[HELPJOB1] a. FIRST CHOICE %	[HELPJOB2] b. SECOND CHOICE %
Husband/wife/partner	58.4	3.4
Mother	2.4	5.0
Father	5.2	7.4
Daughter	3.2	8.7
Son	9.3	17.8
(Daughter and son)	0.2	0.2
Sister	0.7	2.5
Brother	3.7	5.0
Other relative, including in-laws	2.5	9.9
Closest friend	5.3	10.3
Other friend	1.9	6.7
Neighbour	3.2	13.8
Someone you work with	0.4	1.1
Social service, or home help	0.5	0.4
Someone you pay to help	0.7	2.3
Other FIRST CHOICE (PLEASE WRITE IN)	0.2	-
Other SECOND CHOICE (PLEASE WRITE IN)	-	0.1
No-one	1.0	2.4
(NA)	1.3	2.9

BEFORE GOING ON TO THE NEXT QUESTION, PLEASE CHECK TO SEE THAT YOU HAVE ONLY TICKED ONE FIRST CHOICE AND ONE SECOND CHOICE

B - 14

n=2067

B2.08 Suppose you had an illness and had to stay in bed for several weeks, and needed help around the home with shopping and so on?

a. Who would you turn to first for help?

b. And who would you turn to second?

PLEASE TICK ONLY ONE AS YOUR FIRST CHOICE AND ONE AS YOUR SECOND CHOICE

	[HELPBED1] a. FIRST CHOICE %	[HELPBED2] b. SECOND CHOICE %
Husband/wife/partner	61.3	3.7
Mother	11.6	13.3
Father	0.9	4.9
(Mother and father)	0.0	0.0
Daughter	7.9	15.9
Son	3.1	11.3
(Daughter and son)	0.1	0.2
Sister	2.1	6.2
Brother	1.3	3.0
Other relative, including in-laws	1.5	10.6
Closest friend	4.5	10.3
Other friend	0.9	5.3
Neighbour	1.4	6.9
Someone you work with	0.1	0.3
Health visitor	0.2	1.0
Church, clergy or priest	0.1	0.1
Someone you pay to help	0.8	1.5
Other FIRST CHOICE (PLEASE WRITE IN)	0.3	-
Other SECOND CHOICE (PLEASE WRITE IN)	-	0.3
No-one	0.7	2.5
(NA)	1.1	2.6

BEFORE GOING ON TO THE NEXT QUESTION, PLEASE CHECK TO SEE THAT YOU HAVE ONLY TICKED ONE FIRST CHOICE AND ONE SECOND CHOICE

B - 15

n=2067

B2.09 Suppose you needed to borrow a large sum of money.

a. Who would you turn to first for help?

b. And who would you turn to second?

*PLEASE TICK ONLY ONE AS YOUR FIRST CHOICE
AND ONE AS YOUR SECOND CHOICE*

	[HELPMNY1] a. FIRST CHOICE %	[HELPMNY2] b. SECOND CHOICE %
Husband/wife/partner	21.1	2.6
Mother	9.5	9.5
Father	10.2	9.4
Daughter	2.3	3.5
Son	4.1	4.4
(Daughter and son)	0.1	0.2
Sister	2.0	3.7
Brother	2.3	3.9
(Sister and brother)	0.1	0.1
Other relative, including in-laws	3.4	11.6
Closest friend	2.0	4.6
Other friend	0.3	1.6
Neighbour	0.1	0.2
Someone you work with	0.2	0.1
Bank, Building Society or other financial institution	32.2	18.4
Employer	0.2	2.3
Government or social services	1.0	2.5
Other FIRST CHOICE (PLEASE WRITE IN)	0.1	-
Other SECOND CHOICE (PLEASE WRITE IN)	-	0.2
No-one	7.0	15.8
(DK)	0.1	0.1
(NA)	1.9	5.3

*BEFORE GOING ON TO THE NEXT QUESTION, PLEASE CHECK TO SEE THAT
YOU HAVE ONLY TICKED ONE FIRST CHOICE AND ONE SECOND CHOICE*

OFFICE USE ONLY

B - 16

n=2067

B2.10 Suppose you were very upset about a problem with your husband,
wife or partner, and haven't been able to sort it out with them.
Even if you are not married or have no partner, what would
you do if you were?

a. Who would you turn to first for help?

b. And who would you turn to second?

*PLEASE TICK ONLY ONE AS YOUR FIRST CHOICE
AND ONE AS YOUR SECOND CHOICE*

	[HELPPRB1] a. FIRST CHOICE %	[HELPPRB2] b. SECOND CHOICE %
Husband/wife/partner	9.4	0.6
Mother	12.9	8.9
Father	2.1	3.6
(Mother and father)	0.1	0.1
Daughter	10.9	5.7
Son	5.7	6.1
(Daughter and son)	0.3	0.3
Sister	8.3	9.1
Brother	3.2	3.7
(Sister and brother)	0.1	0.1
Other relative, including in-laws	3.6	8.9
Closest friend	26.3	16.5
Other friend	1.0	9.0
Neighbour	0.2	0.8
Someone you work with	0.7	1.8
Church, clergy or priest	1.6	2.2
Family doctor (GP)	1.8	3.3
Psychologist, psychiatrist, marriage guidance or other professional counsellor	1.5	3.4
Other FIRST CHOICE (PLEASE WRITE IN)	0.1	-
Other SECOND CHOICE (PLEASE WRITE IN)	-	0.1
No-one	7.6	11.1
(DK)	0.1	0.1
(NA)	2.5	4.6

*BEFORE GOING ON TO THE NEXT QUESTION, PLEASE CHECK TO SEE THAT
YOU HAVE ONLY TICKED ONE FIRST CHOICE AND ONE SECOND CHOICE*

OFFICE USE ONLY

B - 17

n=2067

B2.11 Now suppose you felt just a bit down or depressed, and you wanted to talk about it.

a. Who would you turn to first for help?

b. And who would you turn to second?

PLEASE TICK ONLY ONE AS YOUR FIRST CHOICE AND ONE AS YOUR SECOND CHOICE

	[HELPDPR1] a. FIRST CHOICE %	[HELPDDPR2] b. SECOND CHOICE %
Husband/wife/partner	47.1	3.3
Mother	7.2	11.8
Father	0.8	2.2
(Mother and father)	0.1	0.1
Daughter	4.9	8.8
Son	1.9	5.7
(Daughter and son)	0.2	0.2
Sister	4.8	8.2
Brother	1.6	3.3
Other relative, including in-laws	1.2	4.9
Closest friend	19.3	20.9
Other friend	1.1	7.9
Neighbour	0.2	1.1
Someone you work with	0.5	2.2
Church, clergy or priest	0.6	1.5
Family doctor (GP)	2.9	5.8
Psychologist, psychiatrist, marriage guidance or other professional counsellor	0.6	1.4
Other FIRST CHOICE (PLEASE WRITE IN)	0.2	-
Other SECOND CHOICE (PLEASE WRITE IN)	-	-
No-one	3.0	6.9
(DK)	0.1	0.1
(NA)	1.8	3.9

BEFORE GOING ON TO THE NEXT QUESTION, PLEASE CHECK TO SEE THAT YOU HAVE ONLY TICKED ONE FIRST CHOICE AND ONE SECOND CHOICE

OFFICE USE ONLY

B - 18

n=2067

And now some questions about things you may have done for other people.

[PROVCARE]

B2.12a Firstly, in the past five years have you yourself provided regular help or care for an adult relative, friend, neighbour or colleague because of pregnancy, an illness, disability or other problem?

PLEASE TICK ONE BOX ONLY

%

Yes 41.6 → ANSWER b.

No 56.2 → NOW PLEASE GO TO B2.13

(NA) 2.2

[CAREWHO]

b. Please tick a box to show who you provided with regular care because of pregnancy, an illness, disability or other problem.
If you have provided regular help or care more than once, please tell us about the most recent time.

PLEASE TICK ONE BOX ONLY

	%		%
Husband/wife/partner	8.3	Grandmother	0.9
Mother	9.6	Grandfather	0.2
Father	2.4	Grandmother-in-law	-
(Mother and father)	0.1	Grandfather-in-law	-
Mother-in-law	2.4	Aunt	0.7
Father-in-law	0.6	Uncle	0.2
Daughter	2.5	(Aunt and uncle)	0.1
Son	0.7	Other female relative	0.4
(Daughter and son)	0.3	Other male relative	0.3
Daughter-in-law	0.2	(Other male and female relative)	0.1
Son-in-law	-	Closest friend	2.8
Sister	1.8	Other friend	1.7
Brother	0.6	Neighbour	2.1
(Sister and brother)	0.1	Someone you work with	0.2
Sister-in-law	0.6	Other person	1.5
Brother-in-law	0.5	(NA)	2.3

OFFICE USE ONLY

B - 19

n=2067

[RECCARE]

B2.13a And in the past five years have you received regular help or care from an adult relative, friend, neighbour or colleague because of pregnancy, an illness, disability or other problem?

PLEASE TICK ONE BOX ONLY

	%	
Yes	21.6	→ ANSWER b.
No	76.8	→ NOW PLEASE GO TO B2.14
(NA)	1.6	

[CAREFRM]

b. Please tick a box to show from whom you received regular care because of pregnancy, an illness, disability or other problem.

If you have received regular help or care more than once, please tell us about the most recent time.

PLEASE TICK ONE BOX ONLY

	%		%
Husband/wife/partner	10.6	Grandmother	0.1
Mother	2.9	Grandfather	-
Father	0.2	Grandmother-in-law	-
(Mother and father)	0.2	Grandfather-in-law	-
Mother-in-law	0.3	Aunt	0.3
Father-in-law	-	Uncle	-
Daughter	1.9	Other female relative	0.0
Son	0.9	Other male relative	0.1
(Daughter and son)	0.1	(Other male and female relative)	0.0
Daughter-in-law	0.1	Closest friend	1.5
Son-in-law	-	Other friend	0.1
Sister	0.6	Neighbour	0.4
Brother	0.1	Someone you work with	0.1
Sister-in-law	0.1	Other person	0.8
Brother-in-law	-	(NA)	1.9

B - 20

n=2067

[LENDMONY]

B2.14a Have you in the past five years helped out an adult relative, friend, neighbour or colleague with a loan or gift of money of £100 or more, to help with some special emergency or problem?

PLEASE TICK ONE BOX ONLY

	%	
Yes	31.3	→ ANSWER b.
No	66.7	→ NOW PLEASE GO TO B2.15
(NA)	2.0	

[MONEYWHO]

b. Please tick a box to show who you helped out with a loan or gift of money of £100 or more, for some special emergency or problem.

If you have helped out someone more than once, please tell us about the most recent time.

PLEASE TICK ONE BOX ONLY

	%		%
Husband/wife/partner	2.3	Grandmother	-
Mother	1.9	Grandfather	-
Father	0.7	Grandmother-in-law	-
Mother-in-law	0.5	Grandfather-in-law	-
Father-in-law	0.3	Aunt	0.1
Daughter	5.4	Uncle	0.0
Son	6.1	Other female relative	0.7
(Daughter and son)	0.3	Other male relative	0.7
Daughter-in-law	0.1	Closest friend	2.4
Son-in-law	0.3	Other friend	2.9
Sister	1.6	Neighbour	0.1
Brother	1.8	Someone you work with	0.4
Sister-in-law	1.1	Other person	0.4
Brother-in-law	1.0	(NA)	2.2

B - 21

n=2067   OFFICE USE ONLY

B2.15a [BORWMONY]
And in the past five years have you personally received a loan or gift of money of £100 or more from an adult relative, friend, neighbour of colleague to help with some special emergency or problem?
PLEASE DO NOT INCLUDE MONEY LEFT TO YOU IN A WILL

%
Yes 30.5 → ANSWER b.
No 67.9 → NOW PLEASE GO TO B2.16
(NA) 1.7

b. [MONEYFRM]
Please tick a box to show from whom you received a loan or gift of money of £100 or more, for some special emergency or problem.
If you have received such a loan or gift more than once, please tell us about the most recent time.

PLEASE TICK ONE BOX ONLY

	%		%
Husband/wife/partner	1.4	Grandmother	0.8
Mother	8.1	Grandfather	0.3
Father	7.1	(Grandmother and grandfather)	0.0
(Mother and father)	0.3	Grandmother-in-law	0.1
Mother-in-law	2.3	Grandfather-in-law	-
Father-in-law	1.5	Aunt	0.4
(Mother- and father-in-law)	0.1	Uncle	0.3
Daughter	0.3	Other female relative	0.2
Son	0.9	Other male relative	0.1
Daughter-in-law	-	Closest friend	1.5
Son-in-law	0.1	Other friend	0.6
Sister	0.9	Neighbour	0.1
Brother	1.1	Someone you work with	0.1
Sister-in-law	0.4	Other person	1.1
Brother-in-law	0.2	(NA)	1.8

B - 22

n=2067   OFFICE USE ONLY

B2.16 How much do you agree or disagree with each of these statements?
PLEASE TICK ONE BOX ON EACH LINE

	Strongly agree	Agree	Neither agree nor disagree	Disagree	Strongly disagree	Can't choose	(NA)
[INTOUCH1] a. People should keep in touch with relatives like aunts, uncles and cousins even if they don't have much in common	10.9	43.6	30.8	10.4	1.4	1.5	1.3
[KIDSGO] b. Once children have left home, they should no longer expect help from their parents	2.0	9.8	13.3	47.5	24.5	1.1	1.7
[FAMHELP] c. People should always turn to their family before asking the state for help	13.4	34.8	19.4	23.1	5.5	1.6	2.2
[FRIENDS1] d. On the whole, my friends are more important to me than members of my family	2.0	5.4	12.3	47.1	29.1	2.1	2.0
[INTOUCH2] e. People should keep in touch with close family members even if they don't have much in common	15.3	54.4	17.6	7.8	1.8	1.1	2.0
[BLAMEFAM] f. People are too quick to blame the family for social problems	6.0	33.0	25.8	23.3	4.6	4.3	3.0
[ALLRELAT] g. I try to stay in touch with all my relatives, not just my close family	7.7	37.9	21.9	22.9	4.5	2.8	2.2
[FRIENDS2] h. I'd rather spend time with my friends than with my family	2.5	10.3	23.3	40.0	18.5	3.1	2.3

(Percentages; % indicated on each line)

B2.17 [MISSMOST]
Apart from people who live in your household, who would you miss most if you could no longer have any contact?

PLEASE TICK ONE BOX ONLY

%
A family member not living in my household 64.7
A member of my spouse/partner's family not living in my household 4.6
A childhood friend 4.5
Another friend 9.6
Someone else 1.8
Can't choose 12.8
(NA) 2.0

Note: Questions B2.18 - B2.26 are the same as questions A2.28 -A2.29 and A2.32 - A2.38 of version A of the questionnaire.

B - 25

n=1032

And now some questions about the environment.

B2.27 How much do you agree or disagree with each of these statements?

PLEASE TICK ONE BOX ON EACH LINE

	Strongly agree	Agree	Neither agree nor disagree	Disagree	Strongly disagree	Can't choose	(NA)
[ENVIRDIF] a. It is just too difficult for some-one like me to do much about the environment	% 5.1	24.1	20.4	36.6	7.9	2.9	2.9
[ENVIRRGT] b. I do what is right for the environment, even when it costs more money or takes more time	% 4.2	42.4	29.5	13.9	1.2	5.8	3.1

B - 26

n=1032

OFFICE USE ONLY

[PROTENVP]

B2.28 If you had to choose, which one of the following would be closest to your views?

PLEASE TICK ONE BOX ONLY

%

Government should let <u>ordinary people</u> decide for themselves how to protect the environment, even if it means they don't always do the right thing 25.9

OR

Government should pass laws to make <u>ordinary people</u> protect the environment, even if it interferes with people's rights to make their own decisions 47.5

Can't choose 24.3

(NA) 2.3

[PROTENVB]

B2.29 And which one of the following would be closest to your views?

PLEASE TICK ONE BOX ONLY

%

Government should let <u>businesses</u> decide for themselves how to protect the environment, even if it means they don't always do the right thing 8.5

OR

Government should pass laws to make <u>businesses</u> protect the environment, even if it interferes with business' rights to make their own decisions 75.0

Can't choose 14.4

(NA) 2.1

[SHORTOIL]

B2.30 How true do you think the following statement is? "Within the next twenty years or so, shortages of oil and gas will be one of the most serious problems for Britain."

PLEASE TICK ONE BOX ONLY

%

Definitely true 11.9

Probably true 43.4

Probably not true 25.4

Definitely not true 5.1

Can't choose 12.2

(NA) 1.9

[RISETEMP]

B2.31 And how true do you think the following statement is? "Within the next twenty years or so, a rise in the world's temperature caused by the 'greenhouse effect' will be one of the most serious problems for Britain."

PLEASE TICK ONE BOX ONLY

%

Definitely true 15.3

Probably true 46.1

Probably not true 22.8

Definitely not true 3.6

Can't choose 10.2

(NA) 2.0

B - 27

n=1032

B2.32 *[TRAFNOIS]*
How true do you think the following statement is?
"Within the next twenty years or so, traffic noise will be one of the most serious problems for Britain."
PLEASE TICK ONE BOX ONLY

	%
Definitely true	20.3
Probably true	42.8
Probably not true	27.1
Definitely not true	3.9
Can't choose	4.5
(NA)	1.5

B2.33 *[TRAFLONG]*
How true do you think the following statement is?
"Within the next twenty years or so, traffic congestion will be one of the most serious problems for Britain."
PLEASE TICK ONE BOX ONLY

	%
Definitely true	41.6
Probably true	44.6
Probably not true	8.2
Definitely not true	1.1
Can't choose	2.9
(NA)	1.6

B2.34 *[DAMAGE]*
Which one of these two statements comes <u>closest</u> to your own views?
PLEASE TICK ONE BOX ONLY

	%
Industry should be prevented from causing damage to the countryside, even if this sometimes leads to higher prices	91.8
OR	
Industry should keep prices down, even if this sometimes causes damage to the countryside	6.0
(DK)	0.2
(NA)	2.0

B2.35 *[CTRYJOBS]*
And which one of these two statements comes <u>closest</u> to your own views?
PLEASE TICK ONE BOX ONLY

	%
The countryside should be protected from development, even if this sometimes leads to fewer new jobs	68.7
OR	
New jobs should be created, even if this sometimes causes damage to the countryside	28.0
(DK)	0.7
(NA)	2.5

B - 28

n=1032

B2.36 Please tick <u>one</u> box for <u>each</u> statement below to show how much you agree or disagree with it.
PLEASE TICK ONE BOX ON EACH LINE

	Strongly agree	Agree	Neither agree nor disagree	Disagree	Strongly disagree	(DK)	(NA)
a. *[GOVENVIR]* The government should do more to protect the environment, even if it leads to higher taxes	% 14.3	46.4	24.9	10.8	0.8	0.1	2.8
b. *[INDENVIR]* Industry should do more to protect the environment, even if it leads to lower profits and fewer jobs	% 13.2	47.7	24.0	10.9	0.3	0.1	3.9
c. *[PLENVIR]* Ordinary people should do more to protect the environment, even if it means paying higher prices	% 11.1	55.4	22.2	7.4	0.8	0.1	3.1
d. *[CARALLOW]* People should be allowed to use their cars as much as they like, even if it causes damage to the environment	% 2.6	14.8	28.9	39.7	10.8	0.1	3.1

B2.37 *[RESPRES]*
Would you describe the place where you live as ...
PLEASE TICK ONE BOX ONLY

	%
... a big city,	9.3
the suburbs or outskirts of a big city,	22.7
a small city or town,	44.7
a country village,	18.7
or, a farm or home in the country?	3.0
(NA)	1.7

B - 29a

B2.39 Here are some things that might be done about Britain's traffic problems. Please tick one box for each to say how strongly you would be in favour of or against it.

n=1032

PLEASE TICK ONE BOX ON EACH LINE

		Strongly agree	Agree	Neither agree nor disagree	Disagree	Strongly disagree	Can't choose	(NA)
a.	[TOLLDRIV] Drivers charged tolls on all motorways	% 3.2	19.0	15.6	36.4	19.6	3.1	3.1
b.	[VEHPERM] Only vehicles with permits for essential business allowed in city centres in working hours	% 8.9	40.5	12.8	22.9	8.6	2.9	3.4
c.	[MOTCHAR] Motorists charged for driving in city centres in working hours	% 3.5	21.6	14.6	39.6	14.1	3.1	3.5
d.	[PARKCHAR] Much higher parking charges in towns and cities	% 2.9	13.7	11.0	46.3	20.7	2.1	3.3
e.	[SHOPMOVE] Shops and offices encouraged to move out of town and city centres	% 3.0	17.7	17.1	40.4	14.8	3.4	3.6
f.	[COMPCARS] Banning company cars except where they are essential for employees in their work	% 11.6	37.8	19.3	18.4	6.6	3.1	3.2
g.	[PEDESTR] Many more streets in cities and towns reserved for pedestrians only	% 15.2	52.5	16.1	8.9	2.0	2.0	3.2

OFFICE USE ONLY

B - 29

B2.38 Please tick one box for each of these statements below to show how much you agree or disagree with it.

n=1032

PLEASE TICK ONE BOX ON EACH LINE

		Strongly agree	Agree	Neither agree nor disagree	Disagree	Strongly disagree	Can't choose	(NA)
a.	[RAILSHUT] Local rail services that do not pay for themselves should be closed down	% 2.0	11.5	16.9	46.0	16.1	4.6	2.9
b.	[BUSPRIOR] Buses should be given more priority in towns and cities, even if this makes things more difficult for car drivers	% 14.0	46.5	16.2	15.2	2.8	2.0	3.4
c.	[CARCNTRY] A visitor to the countryside these days really needs a car to get around	% 10.2	60.8	9.3	13.5	1.6	1.5	3.1
d.	[CAREASY] Car drivers still are given too easy a time in Britain's towns and cities	% 4.7	24.4	26.2	32.6	4.3	4.4	3.4
e.	[BUSSHUT] Local bus services that do not pay for themselves should be closed down	% 2.3	9.8	16.0	48.9	16.8	3.1	3.0
f.	[IMPTRP] Britain should do more to improve its public transport system even if its road system suffers	% 20.7	37.5	19.2	13.8	2.0	3.6	3.1
g.	[CYCPEDPR] Cyclists and pedestrians should be given more priority in towns and cities even if this makes things more difficult for other road users	% 18.6	45.7	15.9	12.7	2.0	2.6	2.6

OFFICE USE ONLY

B - 30

n=1032

B2.40 Please tick one box on each line to show whether you would like to see more or less government spending on each of these.

Remember that if you say "more", everyone's taxes may have to go up to pay for it.

PLEASE TICK ONE BOX ON EACH LINE

		Spend much more	Spend more	Spend the same as now	Spend less	Spend much less	Can't choose	(NA)
a.	*[TRPSPND1]* Improving local bus services	% 12.1	39.3	36.8	2.8	0.7	4.9	3.4
b.	*[TRPSPND2]* Building more roads	% 3.7	16.7	36.2	23.4	9.6	6.1	4.2
c.	*[TRPSPND3]* Improving local rail services	% 15.2	39.7	30.8	4.6	1.1	4.8	3.9
d.	*[TRPSPND4]* Improving and widening the roads we already have	% 7.0	30.4	36.2	12.4	5.3	4.6	4.1
e.	*[TRPSPND5]* Improving long distance rail services	% 15.1	31.2	38.9	3.9	1.1	6.1	3.6
f.	*[TRPSPND6]* Improving facilities for cyclists and pedestrians	% 19.7	43.3	25.7	4.2	0.8	3.1	3.1

OFFICE USE ONLY

B2.41 *[PORNO1]* Which of these statements comes closest to your views on the availability of pornographic - that is, sexually explicit - magazines and films?
PLEASE TICK ONE BOX ONLY

%

They should be banned altogether 28.0

They should be available in special adult shops but not displayed to the public 41.6

They should be available in special adult shops with public display permitted 9.6

They should be available in any shop for sale to adults only 17.3

They should be available in any shop for sale to anyone 0.2

(DK) 0.2

(NA) 3.2

B2.42 *[VIOLENCE]* Which of these statements comes closest to your views on the availability of magazines and films that contain very violent scenes and actions?
PLEASE TICK ONE BOX ONLY

%

They should be banned altogether 35.6

They should be available in special adult shops but not displayed to the public 31.0

They should be available in special adult shops with public display permitted 7.7

They should be available in any shop for sale to adults only 21.7

They should be available in any shop for sale to anyone 0.8

(DK) 0.2

(NA) 3.2

B - 31

n=1032

B2.43 Please tick one box to show how much you agree or disagree with each of the following statements.

PLEASE TICK ONE BOX ON EACH LINE

		Strongly agree	Agree	Neither agree nor disagree	Disagree	Strongly disagree	Can't choose	(NA)
a.	*[NOCENSOR]* People over the age of 16 are old enough to decide for themselves what they want to see and read	% 6.8	41.5	16.5	26.0	4.8	2.1	2.4
b.	*[PORNCRIM]* The easy availability of pornography will lead to more sex crimes	% 17.2	36.5	19.9	18.3	4.0	2.0	2.1
c.	*[VIOLTV]* We should be more worried about the amount of violence on TV than the amount of sex on TV	% 16.6	45.4	20.6	9.3	1.8	4.0	2.4
d.	*[ADALLSEE]* Adults should be allowed to see whatever films they like even if some people think the films violent or pornographic	% 12.9	42.0	17.2	16.6	5.9	3.0	2.3

OFFICE USE ONLY

Note : Questions B2.44 - B2.46 are the same as questions A2.52 - A2.54 of version A of the questionnaire

B - 33

n=1032

[QTIME]
B2.47 To help us plan better in future, please tell us about
how long it took you to complete this questionnaire.

*PLEASE TICK **ONE** BOX ONLY*

	%
Less than 15 minutes	6.4
Between 15 and 20 minutes	28.8
Between 21 and 30 minutes	32.4
Between 31 and 45 minutes	19.9
Between 46 and 60 minutes	6.3
Over one hour	4.8
(NA)	1.5

b. And on what date did you fill in the questionnaire?

PLEASE WRITE IN   [ ][ ] [0][ ] 1995
                   DATE   MONTH

Thank you very much for your help

Please keep the completed questionnaire for the interviewer if he or
she has arranged to call for it. Otherwise, please post it as soon as
possible in the pre-paid addressed envelope provided.

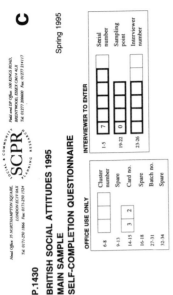

C

Head Office: 35 NORTHAMPTON SQUARE,
LONDON EC1V 0AX
Tel: 0171-250 1866   Fax: 0171-250 1524

SCPR

Field and DP Office: 100 KINGS ROAD,
BRENTWOOD, ESSEX CM14 4LX
Tel: 01277 200600   Fax: 01277 214117

Spring 1995

P.1430

BRITISH SOCIAL ATTITUDES 1995
MAIN SAMPLE
SELF-COMPLETION QUESTIONNAIRE

OFFICE USE ONLY		
6-8		Cluster number
9-13		Spare
14-15	3 2	Card no.
16-18		Spare
27-31		Batch no.
32-34		Spare

INTERVIEWER TO ENTER		
1-5	7	Serial number
19-22	0	Sampling point
23-26		Interviewer number

To the selected respondent:

Thank you very much for agreeing to take part in this important study - the eleventh in this annual series. The study consists of this self-completion questionnaire, and the interview you have already completed. The results of the survey are published in a book each autumn; some of the questions are also being asked in twenty-two other countries, as part of an international survey.

Completing the questionnaire:

The questions inside cover a wide range of subjects, but each one can be answered simply by placing a tick (✓) or a number in one or more of the boxes. No special knowledge is required: we are confident that everyone will be able to take part, not just those with strong views or particular viewpoints. The questionnaire should not take very long to complete, and we hope you will find it interesting and enjoyable. Only you should fill it in, and not anyone else at your address. The answers you give will be treated as confidential and anonymous.

Returning the questionnaire:

Your interviewer will arrange with you the most convenient way of returning the questionnaire. If the interviewer has arranged to call back for it, please fill it in and keep it safely until then. If not, please complete it and post it back in the pre-paid, addressed envelope, AS SOON AS YOU POSSIBLY CAN.

THANK YOU AGAIN FOR YOUR HELP.

Social and Community Planning Research is an independent social research institute registered as a charitable trust. Its projects are funded by government departments, local authorities, universities and foundations to provide information on social issues in Britain. The British Social Attitudes survey series is funded mainly by one of the Sainsbury Family Charitable Trusts, with contributions also from other grant-giving bodies and government departments. Please contact us if you would like further information.

C - 26

Note: Questions C2.01 to C2.17 are the same as questions B2.01 to B2.17 of version B of the questionnaire. Questions C2.18 to C2.19 are the same as questions A2.28 to A2.29 of version A of the questionnaire. Questions C2.20 to C2.26 are the same as questions A2.32 to A2.38 of version A of the questionnaire.

n=1035

C2.27 Listed below are various areas of government spending. Please show whether you would like to see more or less government spending in each area.

If you want more spending, this is likely to mean that you will have to pay more taxes. If you want less spending, this is likely to make it possible to cut taxes.

PLEASE TICK ONE BOX ON EACH LINE

		Spend much more	Spend more	Spend the same as now	Spend less	Spend much less	Can't choose	(NA)
a.	[NEWSPND1] Benefits for unemployed people	6.3	27.2	43.8	13.0	3.6	3.1	2.9
b.	[NEWSPND2] Benefits for disabled people who cannot work	12.8	49.7	30.6	1.5	0.2	2.6	2.6
c.	[NEWSPND3] Benefits for parents who work on very low incomes	10.2	54.5	27.4	2.0	0.4	2.3	3.2
d.	[NEWSPND4] Benefits for single parents	5.4	30.3	41.9	12.5	3.9	3.0	3.1
e.	[NEWSPND5] Benefits for retired people	18.9	50.6	24.8	1.9	0.3	1.3	2.3

(All rows preceded by %)

C - 27

n=1035

C2.28 Here are some things that charities can do. If you had to choose a charity on this list to support ...

a. ... which charity would be your first choice?
b. ... which charity would be your second choice?
c. ... which charity would be your third choice?

PLEASE TICK ONE BOX ONLY AS YOUR FIRST CHOICE, ONE BOX ONLY AS YOUR SECOND CHOICE AND ONE BOX ONLY AS YOUR THIRD CHOICE

	[CHARSUP1] First choice %	[CHARSUP2] Second choice %	[CHARSUP3] Third choice %	(NA)
A charity that prevented cruelty to animals in Britain	9.0	8.7	11.7	3.8
A charity for homeless people in Britain	13.5	23.3	16.8	2.8
A charity helping AIDS sufferers worldwide	1.9	4.0	4.8	4.4
A charity for British children in need	43.4	15.5	8.0	2.9
A charity that gave food aid to starving people in poor countries	7.0	10.3	14.0	3.8
A charity that protected rare animals throughout the world	1.7	4.8	7.1	4.0
A charity for British people dying of AIDS	1.9	6.1	9.3	3.9
A charity for children in need throughout the world	16.0	20.0	19.6	2.9
(NA)	5.5	7.2	8.7	

C2.29 Here are some things on which money is spent. For each one, please tell me where you think the money should come from.

PLEASE TICK ONE BOX ON EACH LINE

		Entirely from government	Mainly from government	Shared equally	Mainly from charities	Entirely from charities	(Can't choose)	(NA)
a.	[ANIMALGB] Helping prevent cruelty to animals in Britain	3.4	8.0	34.4	31.4	14.6	4.3	3.8
b.	[HOUSESGB] Housing for homeless people in Britain	32.9	45.2	14.1	1.9	1.1	2.1	2.8
c.	[AIDSWW] Helping AIDS sufferers worldwide	5.0	13.7	31.9	21.1	13.0	11.0	4.4
d.	[KIDSGB] Helping British children in need	28.1	37.1	26.7	3.4	1.2	0.6	2.9
e.	[FOODWW] Giving food aid to starving people in poor countries	6.5	11.9	36.4	23.3	13.4	4.6	3.8
f.	[ANIMALWW] Protecting rare animals throughout the world	4.0	5.3	26.8	32.0	20.2	7.7	4.0
g.	[AIDSGB] Helping British AIDS sufferers	11.6	26.6	30.6	13.1	6.8	7.4	3.9
h.	[KIDSWW] Helping children in need throughout the world	6.8	11.5	41.0	24.5	10.0	3.4	2.9

(All rows preceded by %)

C - 29

OFFICE USE ONLY

n=1035

C2.32 Please say how much you agree or disagree that ...

PLEASE TICK ONE BOX ON EACH LINE

	Strongly agree	Agree	Neither agree nor disagree	Disagree	Strongly disagree	Can't choose	(NA)
[SMARMUM1] a. ... unmarried mothers who find it hard to cope have only themselves to blame	% 11.3	20.3	24.3	24.5	12.7	3.5	3.3
[SMARMUM2] b. ... unmarried mothers get too little sympathy from society	% 4.4	22.1	30.9	25.2	8.4	3.9	5.2

C2.33 Are you in favour of or against the death penalty for ...

PLEASE TICK ONE BOX ON EACH LINE

	In favour	Against	(DK)	(NA)
	%	%	%	%
a. ... murder in the course of a terrorist act? *[CAPPUN1]*	67.0	26.5	0.2	6.4
b. ... murder of a police officer? *[CAPPUN2]*	65.0	28.4	0.2	6.4
c. ... other murders? *[CAPPUN3]*	59.4	35.2	0.5	4.9

C2.34 How much do you agree or disagree with each of these statements?

PLEASE TICK ONE BOX ON EACH LINE

	Strongly agree	Agree	Neither agree nor disagree	Disagree	Strongly disagree	Can't choose	(NA)
[SCIEBELF] a. We believe too often in science, and not enough in feelings and faith	% 7.9	32.4	33.7	14.4	1.9	6.7	3.1
[SCIEHARM] b. Overall, modern science does more harm than good	% 3.0	14.1	27.9	38.7	6.9	5.9	3.5
[CHANGBAD] c. Any change humans cause in nature - no matter how scientific - is likely to make things worse	% 5.6	27.3	27.9	24.5	3.5	7.8	3.5
[DOCSPOWR] d. Advances in medical science will give doctors too much power to decide when to end people's lives	% 4.3	16.3	23.3	40.3	7.3	5.8	2.8

C - 28

OFFICE USE ONLY

n=1035

C2.30a [SINGMUM1]
Thinking about a single mother with a child under school age.
Which one of these statements comes closest to your own view?

PLEASE TICK ONE BOX ONLY

	%
She has a special duty to go out to work to support her child	16.1
She has a special duty to stay at home to look after her child	22.6
She should do as she chooses, like everyone else	50.5
Can't choose	8.5
(NA)	2.4

b. [SINGMUM2]
Suppose this single mother did get a part-time job.
How much do you agree or disagree that the government should provide money to help with child-care?

PLEASE TICK ONE BOX ONLY

	%
Strongly agree	26.6
Agree	45.0
Neither agree nor disagree	15.1
Disagree	5.3
Strongly disagree	1.8
Can't choose	4.2
(NA)	2.1

C2.31a [SMUMSCH1]
And what about when the child reaches school age?
Which one of these statements comes closest to your view about what the single mother should do?

PLEASE TICK ONE BOX ONLY

	%
She has a special duty to go out to work to support her child	42.2
She has a special duty to stay at home to look after her child	5.4
She should do as she chooses, like everyone else	45.0
Can't choose	5.1
(NA)	2.4

b. [SMUMSCH2]
Suppose this single mother did go out to work. How much do you agree or disagree that the government should provide money to help with child-care outside school?

PLEASE TICK ONE BOX ONLY

	%
Strongly agree	17.9
Agree	39.1
Neither agree nor disagree	22.0
Disagree	12.3
Strongly disagree	1.6
Can't choose	5.0
(NA)	2.1

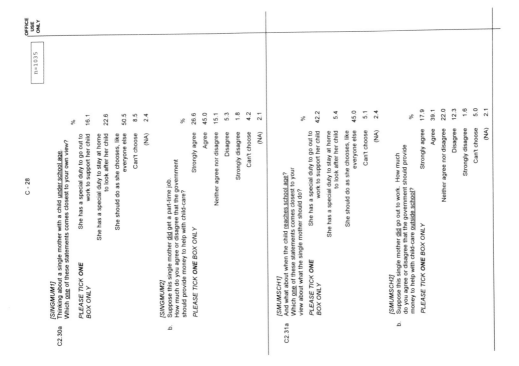

C - 30

n=1035

C2.35 Here are a number of circumstances in which a woman might consider an abortion. Please say whether or not you think the law should allow an abortion in each case.
PLEASE TICK ONE BOX ON EACH LINE

			Should abortion be allowed by law?			
			Yes	No	(DK)	(NA)
a.	[ABORT1]	The woman decides on her own she does not wish to have the child %	59.9	35.4	0.4	4.4
b.	[ABORT2]	The couple agree they do not wish to have the child %	61.6	32.7	0.3	5.4
c.	[ABORT3]	The woman is not married and does not wish to marry the man %	55.1	39.5	0.4	5.1
d.	[ABORT4]	The couple cannot afford any more children %	58.8	35.2	0.3	5.7
e.	[ABORT5]	There is a strong chance of a defect in the baby %	82.2	12.5	0.5	4.8
f.	[ABORT6]	The woman's health is seriously endangered by the pregnancy %	89.6	5.7	0.2	4.5
g.	[ABORT7]	The woman became pregnant as a result of rape %	87.5	7.6	0.4	4.5

C2.36 Please tick one box to show how much you agree or disagree with each of these statements.
PLEASE TICK ONE BOX ON EACH LINE

		Strongly agree	Agree	Neither agree nor disagree	Disagree	Strongly disagree	Can't choose	(NA)
	[BEARPAIN]							
a.	We all have a duty to accept whatever pain and suffering life may bring %	5.1	29.1	18.4	32.6	9.1	2.7	3.0
	[ENJOYLIF]							
b.	Life is not really worth living unless you can enjoy it to the full %	4.5	16.0	17.8	48.2	8.7	1.9	2.8
	[CONTROL]							
c.	Need to feel in control of my life and not have other people take decisions for me %	16.4	59.4	13.2	6.7	0.5	1.1	2.7
	[SUICIDE]							
d.	Suicide is never justified no matter how bad things are %	17.7	30.2	18.4	19.6	6.5	5.1	2.5

C2.37 [GODBELF1]
Please tick one box below to show which statement comes closest to expressing what you believe about God.
PLEASE TICK ONE BOX ONLY

	%
I don't believe in God	10.6
I don't know whether there is a God and I don't believe there is any way to find out	15.4
I don't believe in a personal God, but I do believe in a Higher Power of some kind	11.8
I find myself believing in God some of the time, but not at others	11.7
While I have doubts, I feel that I do believe in God	22.6
I know God really exists and I have no doubts about it	21.3
Can't choose	4.5
(NA)	2.0

C - 31

n=1035

C2.38 People in Britain often talk about the differences between the North and the South.

[NORSTH1]
a. How about employment prospects generally - are they ...
PLEASE TICK ONE BOX ONLY

	%
... better in the North,	6.4
better in the South,	58.4
or - is there no real difference?	32.1
(DK)	0.7
(NA)	2.4

[NORSTH2]
b. How about people wanting to set up their own businesses - are there ...
PLEASE TICK ONE BOX ONLY

	%
... more opportunities in the North,	8.2
more opportunities in the South,	41.0
or - is there no real difference?	47.1
(DK)	1.1
(NA)	2.6

[NORSTH3]
c. How about young people buying their first home - do they have ...
PLEASE TICK ONE BOX ONLY

	%
... a better chance in the North,	42.7
a better chance in the South,	14.1
or - is there no real difference?	40.1
(DK)	0.6
(NA)	2.4

[NORSTH4]
d. How about standards of education - are they ...
PLEASE TICK ONE BOX ONLY

	%
... better in the North,	9.1
better in the South,	21.1
or - is there no real difference?	66.5
(DK)	1.0
(NA)	2.3

[NORSTH5]
e. And how about the National Health Service - is it ...
PLEASE TICK ONE BOX ONLY

	%
... better in the North,	7.2
better in the South,	11.7
or - is there no real difference?	77.4
(DK)	1.5
(NA)	2.2

Note: Questions C2.39 to C2.41 are the same as questions A2.52 to A2.54 of Version A of the questionnaire

C - 33

n=1035

OFFICE
USE
ONLY

[QTIME]

C2.42   To help us plan better in future, please tell us about how long it took you to complete this questionnaire.

PLEASE TICK **ONE** BOX ONLY

%

Less than 15 minutes   7.8

Between 15 and 20 minutes   23.9

Between 21 and 30 minutes   32.7

Between 31 and 45 minutes   20.5

Between 46 and 60 minutes   7.7

Over one hour   5.3

(NA)   2.0

b.   And on what date did you fill in the questionnaire?

PLEASE WRITE IN [   ] [0] 1995

DATE   MONTH

Thank you very much for your help

Please keep the completed questionnaire for the interviewer if he or she has arranged to call for it. Otherwise, please post it <u>as soon as</u> <u>possible</u> in the pre-paid addressed envelope provided.

Subject index

on the radio 21, 25-28, 43
on video 22, 25-28, 31-32, 43
  see also: Censorship, in media;
    Swearing, sexual
  see also 19-44 *passim*
Social class, definition of 208
Socio-economic group, definition of 208
Standard occupational classification
  (SOC), definition of 207
Swearing, sexual 23, 31-32, 34-41, 44

T

Tabulations 221
Taxation,
  and socio-demographic characteristics
    188-189
  flat rate 198, 190-191, 192-193, 195
  individuals' levels of 187-188
  progressive 188, 190-191, 192-193
  see also 185-202 *passim*
Technical details of the survey 203-219
Telephone services: *see* Sex, media
  portrayal of
Television: *see* Sex, media portrayal of

U

Unemployment,
  experience of 83-84

level of 73
  see also: Employment
Unionists in Northern Ireland: *see*
  Northern Ireland, unionists
United Kingdom, and national identity
  142, 144-147
  see also 141-160 *passim*

V

Value histories 162, 178
Video: *see* Sex, media portrayal of
Video Recordings Acts 1984 and 1994 22
Violence,
  and drugs 98-100, 109-110
  in media 20, 21, 23, 25, 42

W

Wales, and national identity 142,
  144-147, 155
Watershed, nine o'clock television 21,
  24, 26-28, 31-32, 43
Weighting 205
Welfare state, demands facing 185-186
Welfarism scale 211

X

Xenophobia 146-147, 157-158